Heritage and Prophecy

Nikolai Frederik Severin Grundtvig
1783 – 1872

Heritage and Prophecy

Grundtvig and the English-Speaking World

Edited by A.M. Allchin, D. Jasper, J.H. Schjørring, and K. Stevenson

The Canterbury Press Norwich

Copyright: Aarhus University Press, Denmark, 1994
Figures and endpaper map by Inga Friis
Printed by the Alden Press, Oxford
Produced on permanent paper conforming to ANSI standard Z39.48-1984.
ISBN 1 85311 085 X

Published with the financial support of the Aarhus University
Research Foundation.

Published in the United Kingdom by
THE CANTERBURY PRESS NORWICH
St. Mary's Works
St. Mary's Plain
Norwich, Norfolk NR3 3BH

Rear cover: High Street, Oxford, on a letter from Grundtvig to his wife,
dated July 30, 1843.

Frontispiece: Portrait of Grundtvig by C.A. Jensen, 1831. Oil on canvas, 23 x 18
cm. Ny Carlsberg Glyptothek, Copenhagen.

Acknowledgements

The publication of this book results from an interdisciplinary dialogue between scholars from Denmark, England and the United States of America, organized by the Centre for Grundtvig Studies in Aarhus. The dialogue included two residential meetings, one at Sandbjerg, Denmark in April 1990, the second in Durham in April the following year.

The editors are deeply grateful to the Danish Research Council for the Humanities, Tipsmidlerne/Undervisningsministeriet, Carlsen-Langes Legat-stiftelse, G.E.C. Gads Fond, Kirkeligt Samfund and the Aarhus University Research Foundation for generous support.

Susanne Gregersen, formerly Secretary of the Centre for Grundtvig Studies in Aarhus, bore a heavy responsibility both for organizing the conferences and in carrying forward the detailed editorial work for the volume. The editors express their special gratitude to her for all the care she has taken in bringing the book to its completion; and also to the present secretary of the Centre, Kim Arne Pedersen, for preparing the index.

Contents

Abbreviations and Frequently Quoted Books

Dannevirke. Et Tids-Skrift af N.F.S. Grundtvig, I-IV. Copenhagen 1816-19, reprint 1983.

Den Danske Salmebog (Danish Hymnal Book). [DDS]

A Grundtvig Anthology. Selected from the Writings of N.F.S. Grundtvig, ed. and tr. by N.L. Jensen and E. Broadbridge, Cambridge 1984.

N.F.S. Grundtvigs Breve til hans Hustru under Englandsrejserne 1829-1831, edited by Stener Grundtvig, Copenhagen 1920.

Grundtvigs Erindringer og Erindringer om Grundtvig. Ed. by H. Høirup and S. Johansen, Copenhagen 1948.

Grundtvigs Sang-Værk til den danske kirke, I-V, reprinted Copenhagen 1982. (Grundtvig's Song Work). [GSV]

Grundtvigs prædikener 1822-26 og 1832-39, bd.I-XII, Copenhagen 1983-1986 (Grundtvig's sermons).

N.F.S. Grundtvig, *Mands Minde* 1788-1838. Foredrag over det sidste halve Aarhundredes Historie. Edited by Svend Grundtvig, Copenhagen 1877. (Within Living Memory).

N.F.S. Grundtvig, *Selected Writings*. Edited and with an introduction by Johannes Knudsen, Philadelphia 1976.

N.F.S. Grundtvig, *Tradition and Renewal*. Grundtvig's Vision of Man and People, Education and the Church, in relation to World Issues Today. Edited by Christian Thodberg and Anders Pontoppidan Thyssen. Copenhagen 1983.

N.F.S. Grundtvig, *What constitutes authentic Christianity?* translated by Ernest D. Nielsen, Philadelphia 1985.

N.F.S. Grundtvig, *Udvalgte Skrifter* I-X, edited by H. Begtrup, Copenhagen 1904-1909. [US]

N.F.S. Grundtvig, *Værker i udvalg*, I-X, edited by G. Christensen og H. Koch, Copenhagen 1940-1949.

Preface

This book has been produced through the initiative of the Centre for Grundtvig Studies in the University of Aarhus. It contains some of the results of the growing collaboration between scholars in Denmark and scholars in Britain and beyond, in the study of a man whose life and work are still very little known outside his own country, but which within that country continue after more than a century to have a remarkable influence on many aspects of life.

As the subtitle of the book suggests, it centres on the theme of the relations between Grundtvig, England and the English-speaking world. It begins with a brief presentation of the visits Grundtvig made to England in the summer of 1829, 1830, 1831 and 1843. It then looks at his lifelong interest in the literature and history of Anglo-Saxon England, the primary cause of his English journeys (Noack, Bradley). This topic proves to have wider ramifications than one might have expected. Grundtvig both as a poet and as a scholar discovered a special attraction in the early middle ages, and he acquired a masterly knowledge of the sources.

But Grundtvig was in no way only a man of the past. His life was marked by the dominant currents of thought and feeling of his own time. Thus there follow studies which look at him in the context of European romanticism and begin to explore possible parallels between his thought and that of Coleridge (Balling, Lundgreen-Nielsen, Jasper). This subject leads directly to a consideration of Grundtvig's work as a hymn-writer (Watson, Thodberg, Stevenson). Without question he was one of the outstanding hymn-writers of the Christian tradition. Throughout his long life preaching and hymn-writing went hand in hand. For him the Church was a community which found its identity above all in the acts of worship in which its life is renewed through direct contact with its origins.

The three essays which consider Grundtvig's work in this field bring us to a group of three theological studies which discuss his understanding of the relation of tradition to modernity as it developed in the 1820's and 30's (Jørgensen, Wainwright, Schjørring). Grundtvig discovered his own way of confronting the problems raised by the historical nature of Christianity, problems which have weighed heavily on all the churches in the 19th and 20th centuries. Here is a point where making allowance for the differences between his time and ours he seems to have things to say which are still of importance.

It should not be thought that Grundtvig's deep commitment to the

Church's inner life of faith and worship involved him in any withdrawal from the life of society as a whole. Quite the reverse is true. As he grew older he became more and more involved in the national political and cultural life of his people (Rerup, Wåhlin). During this time his distinct educational ideas began to work themselves out in practice and they have continued to do so ever since. This is the one area in which his influence has to some extent spread internationally, notably in the third world (Bugge, Henningsen, Hansen).

The title of this book, *Heritage and Prophecy*, points to two contrasting dimensions in Grundtvig's life. Both are vital to any understanding of this complex, gifted and volcanic man. The study of his work which this book undertakes moves from the poetry of the Anglo-Saxons to the growth of new forms of education in contemporary Africa. Grundtvig was a man who more than most believed that past, present and future belong together, and that we shall not be able to move freely into the future unless we have the lines of communication open to the past.

Deeply involved in the study of remote areas of the Judaeo-Christian tradition and our early European past he was nonetheless involved in the common life and struggle of the people to whom he belonged. For him the past is never something inert or inaccessible. In his hands it proves itself to be a living heritage, a source of prophetic insight and of incentive for action now and in the future.

Grundtvig and England.
An Introduction

By A.M. Allchin

It is the intention of the essays in this book to introduce readers in the English-speaking world to the life and thought of a great nineteenth century European. In general Denmark is known internationally on account of two of her major nineteenth century writers, Søren Kierkegaard and Hans Christian Andersen. It is paradoxical that the third great literary figure of this period, N.F.S. Grundtvig is virtually unknown outside his own country. Within Denmark, Grundtvig would be universally recognized as the greatest single influence on the development of Danish society and culture in the last hundred years. In a way which can scarcely be paralleled elsewhere in western Europe, this nineteenth-century churchman is still a living influence in the day to day life of the country to which he belongs.

The figure who is presented in these pages is then being introduced in the first place as a major figure, interesting in his own right, without whose presence our understanding of nineteenth century Europe is seriously incomplete. But he is also being presented as a writer whose work, at least in some of its aspects, proves itself surprisingly relevant to the needs of our own late twentieth century. Grundtvig was a man deeply concerned with the heritage of the past, the heritage which comes to us within the Judaeo-Christian tradition and within the whole history of Europe. But this interest in the past is never antiquarian. He is always concerned for the present and the future. His certainty that God had acted in the past made him always on the lookout for signs of divine action now and in the future.

None of the writers in this volume will of course suggest that we can find in the works of a nineteenth century scholar, poet and preacher ready-made answers to our present predicaments. Grundtvig is of his own time and place and needs to be understood in that context. But all, in varying ways and in varying degrees, would want to suggest that there are still things of importance to be found in Grundtvig's ideas. The Danish contributors do this out of their common experience that in Denmark the presence of Grundtvig is still felt in many ways as a living force. The contributors from outside Denmark come with a growing sense that Grundtvig is a figure who needs to be seen in an international perspective if he is to be seen in his true proportions. Those who write about him from a distance may at least in this respect have an advantage over those who see him from close to.

A glance at the contents of this book will at once show the variety of Grundtvig's interests. But although his life and work was remarkably many-sided, it has a strong inner consistency, and for its full significance to be seen needs to be taken as a whole. Grundtvig was a man who lived a very long life, who had an unquenchable supply of energy and who never ceased to explore new ways of thought. He combined different roles to a degree which is rare in the modern world. He was on any showing a considerable poet, some Danish critics would maintain their greatest poet. He has a strong claim to be counted amongst the very greatest hymn writers in the whole history of Christian worship. He was also a remarkable scholar, as a historian, as a student of literature and as an interpreter of Norse mythology. In some fields he was a pioneer, by his Anglo-Saxon studies for instance providing stimulus to his English contemporaries to make progress in the editing of Old English poetry. He was a man who took an active part in the public life of his country over the course of almost seventy years, often involved in controversy, frequently misunderstood and in the earlier part of his life frequently isolated. Only in his latter years did he come to be accepted, even by his opponents, as a kind of national institution. Political, social and in particular educational topics all came within his frame of interest. Indeed in the last years of his life his educational ideas were beginning to exercise a transforming influence in many areas of Danish life. But at the centre of all these activities was his work as a preacher. Ordained priest in 1811, his relations with the established Church were often difficult. But although there were times when he had no congregation in which to minister for most of the last sixty years of his life he preached every Sunday. In his own lifetime only a small selection of these sermons were published. In recent years fourteen volumes have been produced. There are at least another thirty to come. The publication of these sermons has perhaps more than anything else helped us to see the outline of Grundtvig's life in a true perspective.

Grundtvig's presentation of the Christian faith was, as we shall see, very much his own, yet it was also highly traditional. It picks up aspects of the Christian faith which at times have been almost lost to sight in western Christendom. The material world, the living world of plants and animals, for instance, is vividly present in it. We must be prepared for surprises.

Forty years ago in the years after the second world war Martin A. Hansen, a distinguished Danish novelist, critic and historian of culture, wrote that whereas Kant and Kierkegaard followed on naturally from Luther in the development of Protestantism, in Grundtvig one is aware of something new coming into being, the beginning of a new period in the

history of the West. For Hansen this difference pivots on the distinction between individual and person.

The path of personality is just as strictly defined in Grundtvig as in Kierkegaard. But
in Grundtvig one has a stronger feeling that this path is quite different from that of
individualism – is in fact its opposite. In Grundtvig the personal cannot develop
without immediately being transmitted and united with the personal in others.
Grundtvig has the effect of an originator after the three others, Luther, Kant and
Kierkegaard. The last is the Protestant consummator. Grundtvig belongs to the
future, he transcends Protestantism and in him a culture seems in embryo.

Grundtvig sees everything in terms of persons and that means persons in
relationship. He has an original vision of man in society and of the
interplay of freedom and responsibility. As Hans Henningsen puts it in this
volume,

Grundtvig was incapable of thinking individualistically. Reality everywhere consists
of relationships. Freedom must therefore always rest on reciprocity.

It is particularly interesting that this point should be made by this
particular writer. As Principal of Askov Folk High School, Henningsen is
constantly involved in the practical application and adaptation of Grundtvig's educational ideas in the late twentieth-century situation. It is in these
terms that he sees their present relevance. At a time when most of the
public expressions of Marxist communism have collapsed and when the
Capitalist world is aware of increasing inner bankruptcy, there is a suggestion here of a middle way between the individualism of the one and the
corporatism of the other which may prove to be attractive. But if persons
need to be seen in relationship with one another, so too do nations. To
reconcile respect for national identity with the growing demands of international community is another of the urgent problems of our day.
     Here too Grundtvig may have things to say. For better or for worse it
is clear that in many parts of the world the sense of national identity has
proved to be more powerful and resilient than many had imagined it to be
a generation ago. The eighteenth century vision of a common universal and
in the end uniform humanity has come up against the apparently ineradicable need of human beings to have a sense of themselves as belonging
to a particular local historically fashioned society. In face of the threat of
the trend towards uniformity posed by the great international languages,
and in particular by the menace of a bland and empty Anglo-American
culture, this obstinate diversity of language communities, this sense of the
incalculable value contained within particular traditions has suddenly made

itself felt, particularly in Eastern Europe, and sometimes in highly destructive and irrational ways. Grundtvig was in one sense a passionate nationalist. For a variety of reasons, nineteenth century Denmark felt its very existence threatened by its great southern neighbour. The word *Folkelig* is one of the most important in his vocabulary. It is also one of the most difficult to translate, speaking as it does of nation and people and all that is involved in a long and shared history. But for Grundtvig, as Henningsen points out, reality everywhere consists of relations, and while Grundtvig had three attempts at writing a universal history of mankind, he never wrote a history of Denmark alone. He was the most resolutely international of nationalists. There is between nations as between persons an inherent need for encounter and exchange.

But in the case of a man who, whatever the breadth and diversity of his social and political interests, had at the heart of his life the celebration of the Christian mystery, theological terms must necessarily play an essential part in our understanding. At the heart of the Christian vision of things is an understanding of God which involves persons and relationships. Grundtvig's view of Christianity is ineradicably trinitarian, and at least in essentials it aims to be non-sectarian. Certainly Grundtvig stands within the Lutheran tradition of the Church of his land but he illuminates and develops that tradition in surprising ways. For those whose vision of the Reformation is formed rather by Geneva than Wittenberg, he seems, to say the least of it, a very Catholic kind of Protestant. His theology is incarnational through and through. The sacraments hold a central place in his understanding of Christian faith and worship. In his hymns and sermons he works out a truly liturgical theology of a highly original yet highly traditional kind. His ample and unanxious meditation on the role of Mary in the incarnation, for instance, or his magnificent presentation of the presence of the risen Christ, the conqueror of death at the heart of the church's worship – these are things so familiar to Danish Christians as to be taken for granted. To those who come from outside they have surprising resonances, showing at times both in his sermons and his hymns an unexpected likeness to the tradition of Eastern Orthodoxy. His ecumenical significance in terms of the recovery of a more unified and integrated vision of the Christian tradition as a whole demands much further exploration than it has at present received. In this area in particular it seems appropriate to speak of his work in terms both of heritage and of prophecy. To make a preliminary study of all these areas is the primary purpose of this book which, in the whole field of Grundtvig's activities and interests, focusses particularly on his longstanding interest in England and the visits which he made to that country in the years between 1829 and 1843.

Grundtvig was born in 1783. He was the youngest son of elderly parents. His father was already almost fifty at this time of his birth. He grew to maturity in the years of the French revolution, and having passed through an adolescent phase of Voltairean cynicism, he came under the full influence of European romanticism. This came to him partly through the experience of falling in love with the lady of the manor of the family where he was a tutor, partly through the influence of the lectures on literature given in Copenhagen by his cousin Henrik Steffens in 1802-3, a crucial moment in the development of romanticism in Denmark. But Grundtvig, though greatly influenced by romantic ideas, was never to become a romantic pure and simple. There were eighteenth century ideals, particularly those of popular enlightenment, which he never altogether abandoned. His romantic idealism came into conflict with the realism, pessimism even, of his Lutheran background. His own temperament tended to be manic-depressive. If there were periods of great elation there were also times of great darkness. He underwent a first and rather violent religious crisis in 1811 and emerged from it with the surprising and courageous decision to return to the village in which he had grown up and to act as his father's curate so that the old man might be able to pass his last years in the vicarage where he had lived so long.

It was a startling decision, leaving a promising if contentious life as a writer and publicist in Copenhagen for the quiet of a country village, where everyone had known him as a boy. It rooted him in the life of the people and of the church of Denmark in a way which influenced his whole subsequent development. Grundtvig was in many ways a very different person from his younger contemporary John Keble; he was a more complex, tempestuous, troubled character. But in this acceptance of pastoral office in place of a life of public academic activity, in this sense of indebtedness and respect to a father who in his case, as in Keble's, was a man without any of his son's brilliance or ability, they have something fundamental in common. Grundtvig is not a peasant. He lived much the greater part of his life in Copenhagen. But he has something of the peasant and the countryman ineradicably in him. In the opening of Grundtvig's Christmas sermon of 1822 the preacher describes how in the old days country people would indulge a kind of rivalry as to who could shout "Happy Christmas" loudest. This unaffected joy had resounded in Grundtvig's heart as a child; it never ceased to resound. And now he hears the greeting coming from previous generations of believers who shout "Happy Christmas" to us through the Christmas hymns and carols which we have inherited from them. There is a living tradition of celebration and praise at the heart of the Church's life and at the heart of the life of each Christian. This affirmation of human life through the gift of divine life runs like a connecting thread through all the changes of Grundtvig's development.

This early period of pastoral activity did not last long, and from 1815 until 1821 Grundtvig retired from active ministry in the Church and devoted himself to writing and study. He burrowed deep into the past becoming, as he says, "a bookworm" attempting to digest the dusty unexplored riches of history. From this period come his translations of the medieval Danish chronicles and much of his work on Norse mythology. Also from this period come some of his most interesting essays on the nature of poetry and the place of the imagination in the apprehension of religious truth. It does not seem that he knew the writings of Coleridge, but there are evident parallels here to which David Jasper points in his essay. Grundtvig's view is always at once poetic and historical. The individual discovers himself as part of a tradition even when he may be most aware of his isolation. He knows himself not as an analytical intellect alone, but as a thinking, feeling, acting person in relationship with others, his contemporaries and his predecessors.

If Grundtvig in the romantic era writes much about the spirit and what is spiritual, he always insists that bodily and spiritual go together and are not to be separated from one another, still less put in opposition to one another. There is here as elsewhere reciprocity and interaction. The realm of the symbol becomes vitally important. It is in the realm of the symbolic that feeling and thinking, inner and outer are best able to come together. As Lundgreen-Nielsen remarks in his essay, "unlike allegory, that intellectual tool of the Enlightenment, symbols are not to be understood fully, they should be felt, experienced, relived". At the end of this period in 1824, Grundtvig produced one of the greatest and most enigmatic of his poems, *New Year's Morning*. It was a poem which had come out of his deepest experience, in which he laboured to express a vision which he felt was not for Denmark alone, but for all the people of the North. In it, as Lundgreen-Nielsen observes, he "offered himself as a symbol of the rebirth of Christian Denmark, of the God-given role of the Danish people in history". Because this poem has never been translated, let alone interpreted and presented to a non-Danish audience, it is difficult for us to seize its full significance. On the basis of his studies in the theological poetry of the European tradition, in particular of Dante and Milton, Jakob Balling is able to place it in something like an adequate perspective, to see how the poet hints at an analogy between himself "in his capacity as delver into the past, as translator and historia" and the Christ who goes down into death and rises triumphantly. "The re-awakening of the historical sense, the sense of a living community with the past, the discovery of the gold under the black earth", all these things point to a resurrection from the dead.

These are large claims for any human being to make for himself! But they can be paralleled in our own time by poets and writers of other small nations who have found themselves called to embody the continuity and vitality of their people, the possibilities of resurrection inherent in national languages and traditions which are threatened with extinction. The presence for a time of a playwright in the presidential palace in Prague, the emergence of a scholar who had studied the musical traditions of his people, as president of Lithuania, suggests that in totally unexpected ways the past contains resources for the present which we have not allowed for. Nearer home, anyone who knows the life and work of Saunders Lewis cannot fail to be aware of how he in Wales felt called to delve into the past as translator and historian and to re-awaken the historical sense, the sense of a living community with the past, of his own people and nation. In his study of this poem Balling points to the apparent isolation of the "I" of the poem, the problematic nature of his relationship "with the brothers and fellows he wishes to serve".

The relatedness which Grundtvig seeks is not easily won in a world as pluralist and fragmented as that of post-Napoleonic Europe, let alone that of the late twentieth-century. But there is one figure in Grundtvig's childhood who appears in *New Year's Morning* and who seems to stand as a symbol of continuity with the faith and experience of his people. This is Malene, the old crippled maidservant, who had lived her whole life in the vicarage at Udby – she was an orphan as well as disabled – and who had looked after Grundtvig as a child. We are given a picture of the old peasant woman, whom Grundtvig does not hesitate to call his "teacher in speech", sitting with her book in her lap singing the old hymns of the Church. It is a very vividly imagined portrait. Grundtvig sees the old woman with the eyes of a child, and he sees in her the shrewdness, the longing and the lore which he attributes to his people. It is a striking tribute from a writer of European stature to an old serving woman who in her youth had had to live on the charity of the parish.

If 1824 sees one of the high points in Grundtvig's poetic production, the following year sees the most explosive and in some ways the most significant of his theological essays, *The Church's Retort*. Stirred into violent indignation by an academic work produced by one of the professors at the University of Copenhagen, H.N. Clausen, all Grundtvig's historical, poetic intuitions fused together into one. Suddenly things become plain to him. The Church is not founded on the Bible. It is a great historical fact, there

before all our explanations or theories about it. Its life is rooted in Christ
and the Spirit and it exists especially where Christ is present in the sacraments of baptism and eucharist, sacraments which he has given to his
people. Where the sacraments are celebrated, where the apostolic faith is
professed, where Christ's words are spoken in the midst of his people,
especially where the greeting of the resurrection "Peace be with you"
resounds, there the Church is gathered in the power of the Spirit. Suddenly
Grundtvig has an ecumenical, all-embracing vision of this one unshakable
Church of Christ. Is it not time, he asks, for all who truly wish to be
Christians to join together in one choir, to reach out their hands to one
another over the font and to exchange the kiss of peace before the altar,
sharing together in the one bread and the one cup, leaving aside all that
divides them, finding themselves united in faith and love? "The multidimensional understanding of Christianity" involved in this vision is
carefully analysed and examined in Theodor Jørgensen's essay.

If Grundtvig found himself carried away by inspiration in the
composition of his poems he no less found himself carried away in
moments like that which produced *The Church's Retort*. Indeed his polemic
against Clausen became so violent that the latter initiated a libel action
against him, which he won. Grundtvig not only had to pay a substantial
fine, but his books were subject to censorship for a number of years to
come. The heat of the controversy was unfortunate for it somewhat disguised the importance of what Grundtvig was saying. Here were insights
into the nature of the Church's life and tradition and of the place of the
Bible within it which are still of relevance today. Grundtvig certainly does
not resolve the problems posed to all the churches by the contrast between
tradition and modernity, and the sense which the modern world has of
being cut off from its own past. But as both Wainwright and Schjørring
suggest he has things of importance to say on these issues, particularly in
pointing us to the eucharist as the focal point in which the church
rediscovers its life and mission through becoming again and again
contemporary with its origins. It may be that Grundtvig's gifts as a poet
give him insights here not usually open to the theologian, for the poet too
is concerned with the way in which visions and meanings may cross the
barriers created by the centuries. It seems possible that Grundtvig's views
may prove particularly important in places where Lutherans are living in
close contact with other Christian traditions, Roman Catholic and Anglican
for instance, and involved in dialogue with them. It is significant in this
regard that St. John's University at Collegeville, MN is one of the few
places in the English speaking world where the ecumenical potential of
Grundtvig's theology begins to be discovered.

In this contact it is important to recognize how all-important for

Grundtvig is the first of the two sacraments of the Gospel, baptism. For him as for the contemporary ecumenical movement, baptism is the foundation sacrament which unites all Christians in a common fellowship. Writing in 1845, at the time of Newman's conversion, Grundtvig says that if the nineteenth century is in any sense a time for enlightenment, then both from the side of Rome and Reformation

> we must discover and see ever more clearly that on both sides we have done each other an injustice, shamed our common Lord, and in so doing wounded ourselves in many ways

by failing to recognize the vital significance of what unites the two parties to the great schism in the western church. What this sacrament of baptism means to Grundtvig, and how fundamental it was to the whole of his understanding of Christian life, we see very clearly in Christian Thodberg's article in this book. It is an essay which shows not only the close interrelationship of Grundtvig's hymns with his preaching but the rootedness of both in the actual liturgy of the Danish church in which he participated Sunday by Sunday.

The year 1825 marks one of the major turning points in Grundtvig's life; it is not the only one of such moments nor necessarily the most important, but it is certainly one which had a good deal to do with the development of his interest in England. In view of the response to *The Church's Retort*, Grundtvig again retired from active ministry and found himself as a freelance writer and scholar. In 1828 King Frederik VI gave him a research grant to go to England to work on the Anglo-Saxon manuscripts. So in each of the following Summers, 1829, 1830 and 1831, Grundtvig went across the North Sea and became involved in an intensive period of the study of Old English literature. His interest in Anglo-Saxon went back to his time as a student and continued throughout his life. He finally brought out his own edition of Beowulf in 1861 and was talking animatedly about the significance of Old English poetry a few days before his death in 1872. Nowhere perhaps is Grundtvig's poetic-historical nature more vividly exemplified that in his Anglo-Saxon interests. There can be no doubt about the seriousness and accuracy of his linguistic and textual work. It still wins the admiration of scholars today. But to his scientific concern for accuracy he wedded a poet's intuitive grasp of meter, rhyme and metaphor. His approach to Anglo-Saxon literature had both strands in it and from this point of view was not altogether unlike that of J.R.R. Tolkien. Indeed an eminent Anglo-Saxon scholar once remarked that of the few people in the modern world who have written successful verse in Anglo-Saxon, one was Grundtvig and the other Tolkien.

But Grundtvig's delight in Anglo-Saxon literature was not only literary and linguistic. His discovery of Anglo-Saxon England contributed another strand to his vision of the Church and his grasp of the heritage of Christian worship. For him the history of Anglo-Saxon Christianity and especially of the Church in Northumbria in the time of Bede formed a crucial episode in the development of Catholic Christendom. It was the moment when the centre of the Christian world moved north and west, up from the Mediterranean where it had its origin into the northwest of Europe where much of its future lay. The subsequent Anglo-Saxon missions to Germany and Scandinavia had of course outstanding importance for him. They pointed towards developments which for him would reach a climax in the life and teaching of Luther and in the growth of the Churches of the North which were influenced by his vision.

But Grundtvig was not only convinced of the historical importance of Anglo-Saxon Christianity. He found in its religious poetry themes and motifs which responded to some of his own deepest religious convictions. In particular the emphasis on Christ's descent into Hell, his triumph over death through death, echoed one of the deepest themes of his whole life. "Mein Gegenstand ist Leben und Tod (my subject is life and death)", as he once said to a visiting German professor who had asked him his attitude toward dialectic philosophy. So it is that Grundtvig made a significant number of translations from the Christian poetry of Anglo-Saxon England, with the result that congregations in Denmark can and do sing at Easter and Ascension his free but faithful renderings of Anglo-Saxon verses which are virtually unknown in the English-speaking world.

Grundtvig's first three visits to England were made before the beginning of the Oxford Movement. In the decade following 1833 Grundtvig became aware of the developments taking place in Oxford and felt considerable interest in them. One of his students came and stayed for a while with Pusey at Christ Church. But this desire for contact was in the end to lead to disappointment. When in 1843 on his last visit to England Grundtvig finally came into contact with the leaders of the movement, he found Newman already almost decided to go to Rome and Pusey embroiled in the controversy which followed on the condemnation of his University Sermon on the eucharist. Grundtvig was already a man sixty years old, set in his ways. The differences between him and the men at Oxford whom he met, many of them much younger than himself, hardened into irreconcilable disagreement. They were perhaps too close to one another to perceive, as we can now, how many things they had in common. As Jens Holger Schjørring remarks, here is another task for the future.

But strangely enough the deepest and most important influence on Grundtvig of the first three English journeys was in a totally different dimension and was altogether unexpected. Denmark before 1848 was still an absolute monarchy. Grundtvig himself, as we have seen, could be put under censorship. At the beginning of the century a writer could suffer lifelong banishment for criticising the government. In the 1820's there were still cases of Baptist parents having their children forcibly taken away in order that the legal requirement of Baptism could be fulfilled. Denmark was a small country and although in general its legislation was interpreted with moderation and some liberality, it was still in principle highly autocratic and closed in on itself. In the first part of the nineteenth century it lost its control of Norway. The years following the Napoleonic Wars, in which Denmark was the last European country to be allied with France, were a time of prolonged economic crisis. Only gradually did the situation change and the beneficial results of the great land reforms of the late 1780's declare themselves. But by the middle of the century it was clear that the large class of peasant farmers had become the backbone of Danish society. It was this social group which particularly responded to Grundtvig's teaching, profiting from the new freedoms granted after 1848.

In his visits to England Grundtvig found himself in the midst of a society becoming daily more liberal, full of activity, full of new projects, caught up in the rapid development of industrialisation and in contact with the whole world. All this enthralled him. He felt that he had lived for too long amongst books and theories. As Hans Henningsen remarks,

in England Grundtvig made one of his most important discoveries, namely the discovery of the present. Admittedly he still insisted that history is the source above all for the enlightenment of man, but his attention to history now turned to the present and also to the future, to the possibilities and tasks that lay ahead. Grundtvig had become conscious of himself as a modern man.

Here is another turning point in Grundtvig's life. From this time onwards he becomes more open to the world and more involved in public life. He welcomed the establishment of the Consultative Assemblies in 1836-7, and in 1849 took part in the Constitutional Assembly which began the transformation of Denmark into a parliamentary democracy in which the king had strictly limited functions. He saw much more clearly the necessity for freedom for the development of civil society, and was more ready to allow for the value of conflict and competition. But as we have seen for him the freedom of the individual always implies the freedom of the other. "Freedom must always rest on reciprocity".

He also saw that his old idea of a wholly Christian society simply did not correspond with the facts of nineteenth century life. He recognised the need to distinguish more clearly between the Church and the School, between faith and reason, between what is Christian and what is human; more and more he recognised the proper autonomy of the latter. From this time there dates one of his most famous sayings, "First human, then Christian", a formula which some have interpreted as implying a radical change in his whole attitude to life. Others have seen it in less disruptive terms, maintaining that Grundtvig's constant stress on the ideas of interaction and reciprocity prevented him from making any radical disjunction between the two spheres, human and divine. In his mind there was always an interplay between them. The affirmation of the joy of human life through the gift of divine life, expressed so powerfully in his hymns and sermons for the great feasts of the Christian year was now expressed less directly but no less powerfully in a more practical sense of the happiness to be found in a simple, active, human life on earth, when that life is seen as always open to receive the unexpected gifts of the Spirit. One thing is ineradicable in the popular memory of Grundtvig. He was a joyful man.

It was in this period that he began to work out his ideas for a Folk High School, a centre for adult education which was to be a school for life, in which students and teachers would live together and in which there would be no exam system and no pressure to acquire professional qualifications. This educational ideal in his mind involved a community of life in which there would be a living interaction between teacher and taught, between young and old. All had something to give, all had something to learn. Singing, discussion, shared activities were all an important part in the life of a Folk High School of the nineteenth century and in different ways still are today. And from the very beginning in the 1850's young women began to attend the school as well as men.

There were doubtless many sources for the Folk High School idea in Grundtvig's mind. One element is to be found in England. For while the schools are emphatically not Oxford or Cambridge colleges, there can be no doubt that the two weeks Grundtvig spent at Trinity College, Cambridge, in the summer of 1831 were a highpoint in his visits to England. There he saw an academic community in which teachers and learners shared a common life and set their intellectual work within that context. Writing a few years later to William Whewell, the Master of Trinity, Grundtvig says,

Many a time in the years already past, I have delighted and evermore shall delight in thinking me back again into the solemn and yet cheerful abode of study and kindness where for the first time I learned duly to appreciate the spirit and institutions of Old England.

There is something particularly delightful in the conjunction of solemn and cheerful, study and kindness; head and heart need not be at war with one another. Time and eternity need not be opposed. The solemnity with which we approach ultimate questions needs to be tempered at times with the humour and irony with which we enter into the gifts and events of everyday.

It is at this stage in his life that we can see most clearly that Grundtvig was a man of ideas rather than a man of organising or administrative ability, for the actual founding of the first Folk High Schools was done by others. Often in practice things worked out rather differently from the way which Grundtvig had planned. But there can be no question about the success of the movement nor of the fact that Grundtvig himself and the ideas which he expressed remained central in its growth. Not only did the movement give a new sense of purpose and confidence to large parts of the Danish farming community. It was one of the factors which sustained the Danish people in the conflict with Germany over the duchies of Slesvig and Holstein, and helped them to recover from the devastating defeat which took place in 1864 when large parts of southern Jutland were lost.

In his article, Vagn Wåhlin shows yet again the profound coherence which unites the different aspects of Grundtvig's life and writing. It is the same man who is at work when he deals with national, political and economic affairs as when he deals with questions of history or literature or religion. Grundtvig's view of national life and identity is at once historic and poetic. He sees the nation as a historical reality built up slowly through the centuries. To appreciate its life and character we have need of poetry as well as prose. The imagination must move as well as the intellect. If we are to understand Grundtvig here we have to tackle head on the problems raised by the translation of the words *Folk* and *Folkelig*. Folk means both nation and people. Rather, it means nation understood as people. In Grundtvig's usage, this is an entity with a shared language, a shared experience of history, a shared loyalty to a particular set of places. To be a member of a Folk means to assume some share in the responsibility of its common life. To take part actively, in however small a way, in building up a nation's life, contributing to its shared attitudes and assumptions, its shared understanding of what it is to be human in failure as well as in success.

This concept of *Folk* and *Folkelighed* does not exclude the dimension of political and economic institutions. Normally, of course, it presupposes them, and such things will be truly Folkelig when they respond to needs and potentials of the people. But in this perspective the institutional element does not take first place. What comes first is the shared commitment and the shared responsibility. In this sense it is possible to speak of a Folk even when there are no independent political institutions.

This way of understanding how nations develop through history is one which comes rather easily to someone like Grundtvig in a small nation deeply united by language and culture. The situation is very different in Great Britain, for instance, where unity is more in shared institutions, than in shared language or shared historic memory. The situation is different again in a country like the U.S.A. where the nation is still in process of formation, where every generation has, as it were, to make America afresh. Clearly nations are of many kinds and have many different possibilities and dangers. This is an area where Grundtvig's thought is particularly linked to his own time and place; it is usually considered to be altogether impenetrable by foreigners. Perhaps for this very reason it is worth our while trying to penetrate it. It can help us to approach some of the more intractable and unexpected phenomena of our decade.

It would be easy for someone coming to the subject for the first time to suppose that there was a radical disjunction between the Grundtvig of the 1820's, so involved with poetry, with history and theology and the Grundtvig of the 50's and 60's who has become so involved in all kinds of political, social and educational movements. Indeed the way in which the study of Grundtvig has developed over the last 45 years can sometimes reinforce this impression. Grundtvig's work has never ceased to be studied in Denmark in the 120 years since his death, but undoubtedly the study of his life has been pursued more systematically and thoroughly since 1947 when the *Grundtvig Selskab* (Grundtvig Society) was founded. This society has acted as a focal point for those interested in deepening understanding in Grundtvig and his work. But it is striking that the Grundtvig who has been the subject of theses and monographs and innumerable shorter articles is for the most part the thinker, the poet, the historian, the theologian of the first fifty years. Comparatively less has been done on the last forty years when a distinct party of "Grundtvigians" was beginning to form itself around the old man and to carry his ideas out into the life of the people. But while the "scholar's Grundtvig" is for the most part that of the earlier part of his life, the popular image of Grundtvig which has remained in people's minds is that of the grand old man, the founder of the Folk High Schools, the champion of the rights of the peasants and small farmers.

But once again this amazingly many-sided man continues to perplex and amaze us. The elements of continuity in his life are at least as strong as the elements of change. He never stopped writing poetry. At the time of his second marriage in 1851, when he was 69, he produced some of the most perfect of all his lyrics. Later in that decade, there was a further outburst of hymnwriting, culminating in 1856. But the greatest period of all in his production of hymns had been earlier, in 1837, when he set out on the publication of his *Sang-Værk til den Danske Kirke*, a collection of hymns in which by translating from Greek, Latin, Anglo-Saxon, German and modern English he hoped to make a new experience of the catholicity of the Church available to ordinary members of ordinary congregations in Denmark. Here was a practical working out of the ideas put forward in the *The Church's Retort*. In the course of his work on the hymns one particular incident sparked off a new set of ideas and visions. Early in 1837 he took out from the Royal Library in Copenhagen a Greek liturgical book in order to translate hymns from the Byzantine offices. In Eastern Christian hymnody as in Anglo-Saxon poetry he found themes which were particularly congenial. Christian Thodberg, who has studied both the hymns and the sermons of this period with attention, does not hesitate to refer to this time as "the Greek awakening". Here again, as in the later decades, the hymns illuminate the sermons, and the sermons the hymns. There is a whole mass of material here which would repay further study.

Many would say, however, that it is in the field of education that the contemporary relevance of Grundtvig's ideas is exemplified most practically. Above all, in the way in which some of his ideas have proved unexpectedly useful in countries of the Third World. This particular aspect of his influence is dealt with in the final essay of this book. A notable example is the work of Dr. Kachi Ozumba in Nigeria. It is striking that Dr Ozumba was already deeply involved in educational work before he became aware of Grundtvig's particular insights. He felt at once that they had a direct application to the educational problems of a modern African country and he has since then tried to put them into practice. He is not alone among educationalists in Asia and Africa in holding this view.

But it is not only in the Third World that Grundtvig's name is beginning to be better known. We have already noticed that in the United States there are signs of interest in Grundtvig not only in the area of education. One such sign is the publication by an American sociologist in 1991 of a major study of contemporary Danish society and the influence of the Folk High Schools within it, *The Land of the Living*. Its author Steven Borish, who has lived for a time in Denmark and who has a practical as well as a theoretical knowledge of the Folk High Schools, is in no doubt as to the all-pervasive influence of Grundtvig, sometimes recognised sometimes not, in late twentieth century Denmark. He sees clearly the dangers to Denmark of a process which he summarizes with the term "Germanisation/Thatcherisation/Americanisation", but he believes that there still exist the inner resources to combat this tendency. The belief that human beings are more important than money or machines is tenaciously rooted in Danish society.

It is not within the scope of a volume of this kind to offer firm or definitive conclusions. Its purpose is rather to open up avenues of exploration, to indicate promising lines for future investigation. In a radio broadcast given in 1980 in the years before the celebration of the bicentenary of Grundtvig's birth Poul Borum, a distinguished Danish poet and critic and author of a remarkable study of Grundtvig as a writer, commented on him like this:

It is strange to think that Denmark's greatest contributors to world literature, Grundtvig, Hans Christian Andersen and Kierkegaard were all active in Copenhagen in the 1840's producing works that lie outside the three main genres – drama, the novel, poetry – that are dominant in the European literature of the time. Grundtvig wrote hymns, Andersen fairytales and Kierkegaard philosophical writings which often approach intellectual novels and the poetry of ideas – in the great wide world Kierkegaard is known and respected as a philosopher not as a poet, Andersen is "merely" a writer of children's stories, and Grundtvig is unknown.

Yet Grundtvig is not really known within Denmark either. We read Andersen as children and take him with us through life; some of us discover Kierkegaard and plunge into him from a giddy height; but Grundtvig is so enormous and formidable and mysterious and remote, and seems to be reserved as it were to two strange races called "Grundtvigians" and "Grundtvig-scholars". Even so there is of course a Grundtvig for the people; many of us have been connected with the Folk High Schools he inspired, and we are all influenced indirectly in our upbringing by his educational ideas. Then there are the hymns which we have all met at Church and at school and cannot help remembering bits of, bits that turn up at the most impossible moments.

For foreigners who are likely to feel daunted by the many sides of Grundtvig's thought and activity and by the massive quantity of work that has been done on it in Denmark, it is comforting to know that also to his compatriots he can seem enormous and formidable, mysterious and remote. It is perhaps in the collaboration of those who see him from close to, and those who see him from afar that we shall get a clearer and more coherent picture of this man who in his own time touched the life of his nation at so many points and whose ideas have never ceased to be fruitful and influential in the years that have followed.

Grundtvig's Relationship to England

By Anders Pontoppidan Thyssen and A. M. Allchin

Grundtvig's view of England varied a great deal through the years. His first more detailed discussion is to be found in *The World Chronicle* which he published in 1812 (about 450 pages) and this was critical to say the least. It concludes:

In every manner England resembles a whited sepulchre, shining without, but within full of uncleanness and dead men's bones. There is no protestant country in which the externals of the cult of the Deity are held in so high esteem...[1]

this, however, is only as an outward custom based on the fact that worship is part of the official constitution.

Whilst therefore self-interest, luxury and the lust of the flesh are rampant ... the poor imagine that they will be able to save their souls by the repetition of the Church's set prayers and by giving tithes ... Of all things spiritual as of the faith itself, there remains but a lifeless shadow.[2]

There is almost nothing worth mentioning being written; poets sing the praises of wool and sugar beet, and history has almost lost its voice.

The death of the spirit is to be seen most clearly in that the majority of the most excellent brains busy themselves with mechanics, for here the body has totally swallowed the spirit and appears to move by its own power... daily humanity becomes more and more a mere thought-machine, wound up by instincts and desires and hastening thoughtlessly to the edge of the grave. Soon this will be the lot of England...[3]

These harsh words were not only occasioned by the war being waged at that time between England and Denmark. The book contains judgements almost as hard on the development of other countries. It was above all

---

1. N.F.S. Grundtvig, "Kort Begreb af Verdens Krønike i Sammenhæng" (1812) in *US* vol 2. p. 345.
2. ibid.
3. ibid., p.346.

Grundtvig's way of throwing down the gauntlet to the rationalism and the eagerness for earthly bliss of the eighteenth century.

Only a few years earlier, however, Grundtvig had publicly confessed to having the same outlook himself, intoxicated with the hope of "being able to stand as a free rational being on the firm earth". But shortly afterwards he had felt a chill at the sight of "the naked skeleton standing before us without strength or marrow". The change had begun in 1805 with a personal crisis and at the same time coming under the influence of German romantic poetry and philosophy. In this way poetry became for Grundtvig more than one of the arts, rather it was a new view of life, pointing to a deeper meaning beyond everything earthly, and he himself became one of Denmark's greatest poets. Romantic philosophy also made a great impression on him, especially Schelling's attempt to find an all-embracing meaning in life, but it was not long before he came to have reservations about this approach.

Instead he buried himself in the past, first and foremost in the old Nordic myths and sagas. For Grundtvig these cast light on human existence in a different way by telling of gods and heroes and of great struggles between good and evil powers. But it was precisely in this that Grundtvig found their message: human life in the world is to be understood as a continuous struggle. In addition, he understood the myths as a whole, as a grand historical drama extending from the beginning of time to the final all-embracing battle after which life is again renewed by a higher controlling power. (The main work was *Nordic Mythology*, 1808). *The World Chronicle* of 1812 also understood the history of the world as a consecutive drama in which the life of action throws light on human destiny. Human actions arise at bottom out of the view which human beings have of the relationship between God and the world, the visible and the invisible; belief in a spiritual power is the fundamental driving force of history. But during his work on this book Grundtvig had returned to the old Lutheran faith he had known in his own home. Therefore biblical and church history became the leitmotiv for the course of history and the basis for his clash with the increasing disbelief of more recent times.

The World Chronicle was a challenge to his contemporaries, and criticism of it was harsh. This became the main reason why Grundtvig was not finally installed as a priest until 1821 although he had received his degree in theology in 1803. But despite straitened circumstances, and without a regular income, he continued the same cultural conflict, at the outset through polemical treatises, later more irenically in essays of a philosophical nature, historical pieces and translations of old Nordic chronicles.

The polemic dealt in particular with Schelling's speculative philosophy which in Grundtvig's view led to pantheism. Both here and in relation to rationalist metaphysics Grundtvig looked for support to John Locke's experiential philosophy. Grundtvig maintained along with Locke that rational knowledge is dependent on experience gained through sense perception and imagination. Both in Locke and Grundtvig knowledge aims at God but not immediately; it must build on the evidence of himself that God has given through experience, "since we have sense, perception, and reason". "This plain historical method" of Locke's apparently corresponded with Grundtvig's own stress on historical experience as the only source for understanding life and is directed against all atemporal philosophical systems. But in Grundtvig there is the question of a deeper understanding of human destiny and the goal of history, inspired particularly by the biblical-christian idea of creation and salvation history. In addition, sense experience and imagination take on for Grundtvig a significance of their own as sources for a poetic-figurative apprehension of truth, which seeks traces of the Creator in the created world.

Grundtvig's increasing knowledge of English literature is evident in particular in the new and larger *World Chronicle* which he published in 1817. Its tendency is the same as the first, but the presentation is more detailed and informative and the judgments are milder, as is clear in the motto of the work: "What truth is, time must show". There are about 100 pages on England mentioning numerous great names in church life, philosophy and literature, sometimes critically, sometimes in a more or less commendatory way, with most understanding for the dissenters and only a little for the Anglican Church. As a whole, the picture is full of contradictions, but in Grundtvig's own words:

In no country is the bible more fiercely attacked, more lukewarmly defended, while services in church look much as they did in Elizabeth's days and large sums are expended yearly on the dissemination of the Bible... No people calls so loudly for its good old days nor so anxiously preserves inherited customs, but there can hardly be a people which so readily lets go of the language and spiritual tone of its fathers, and indeed takes so little trouble to know them.[4]

But during the same years a profound change in Grundtvig's relationship to England was in preparation as a result of his old Nordic studies. His translations were exceedingly demanding both philologically and historically, but in Grundtvig's opinion they were necessary to bring the ancient history of Denmark, Norway and Iceland to life. Their first focus was Saxo's history of Denmark in Latin and Snorre's chronicle of Norway extant

---

4. N.F.S. Grundtvig, *Udsigt over Verdens-Krøniken* (Copenhagen, 1817), p.612.

in Icelandic. Towards 1820 these were supplemented by the Anglo-Saxon poem *Beowulf*. This immense poetic fantasy had for a long time absorbed Grundtvig, and it now became for him an important testimony to the wide-ranging interconnections in old Nordic literature. The poem certainly was Anglo-Saxon, but its hero was in the service of the Danish king, and his struggle with dangerous monsters symbolised for Grundtvig the fighting spirit of the Nordic countries, and the struggle between life and death which characterizes history as a whole.

Reflections of this kind found expression soon afterwards in a manuscript of Grundtvig's on "the history of poesy" from the year 1822, which has recently been published. It is a sketch for a survey of the main streams of the cultural history of humanity, and here the old Nordic and Anglo-Saxon culture is emphasized as a single culminating achievement. Nordic poetry flowered not least with the Anglo-Saxons, and on such a grand scale, says Grundtvig, that if one only knew it from the Anglo-Saxon poems, it would have to be accorded greater significance in the history of poetic art than either the *Iliad* or the *Odyssey*. In addition Grundtvig praises Shakespeare whom he had always appreciated. Here he is mentioned as a new climax in the history of poetry. Undoubtedly, he says, Shakespeare's work had almost been forgotten, even in England, but, he adds significantly, it can and must be continued!

Seen in this light, it is understandable that Grundtvig felt an urge to resume his study of old English writings when he was obliged to resign his office as a priest in 1826. Following a grant from the king he undertook three journeys to England, in 1829, 1830 and 1831, each time with a view to manuscript studies during the summer months. These began with a *Beowulf* manuscript in the British Museum, but he found many other Anglo-Saxon manuscripts both in the British Museum, the cathedral library at Exeter, the university library in Oxford and college libraries in Cambridge, so many that in 1830 he was able to reach an agreement with a publisher on the production of no less than 10 volumes.

At the outset, Grundtvig had difficulty in making personal contacts in England. His style undoubtedly made a strange impression. He himself noticed, as he writes, that "in England loud speech is not approved except in church, nor loud laughter except in parliament". So Grundtvig himself certainly spoke loudly! Neither did he conceal his critical view of many things, especially the lack of appreciation on the part of the English for their own past. From a lady with whom he had a good deal of conversation in Exeter he received a friendly letter in August 1830, but she writes that she feels obliged first and foremost to ask if Grundtvig "still views the English as the most vain and uncivilised people on the face of the earth"! Her sister adds that Danes are capable of cheering up the tedium of the

English – to some extent – "even if they (the Danes) cannot bring life to their stony character"!

But it was the stay in Exeter in August 1830 which became a turning point. Grundtvig had a very kind reception both by the cathedral clergy and by several families in the town and the surrounding district. Also in London he gradually came to know a great many people, and on his visit in 1831 he experienced a new climax during a two-week stay at Trinity College, Cambridge. From here he wrote to his wife: never have I

had such good days in England, as here where I have made contact with a little circle of knowledgeable, friendly, Christian-thinking clergy and professors whom I visit, when I am not poring over manuscripts.[5]

The great publishing plan was something Grundtvig had to give up as the publishers preferred English editors. But the three journeys changed his view of England decisively. This already found expression in his prospectus, which the publisher issued before his third journey. This takes up again the historical perspective, suggested in the previously mentioned manuscript of 1822, but formulated much more forcefully. The main idea – briefly expressed – is that when the European culture of the old world was destroyed in the fall of the western Roman empire, both education and Christianity obtained a new centre with the Anglo-Saxons in England. The Anglo-Saxon writings are therefore fundamental to the understanding of the later and more recent history of culture, indeed they are among "the most valuable documents and reports we have for the universal history of the human race".

Grundtvig's new view of England, however, did not evolve more fully until his new book, *Nordic Mythology*, which he published in 1832. In this England is incorporated without hesitation into the old Nordic culture, which in Grundtvig's opinion should now be resurrected. It was, he wrote, "the Nordic spirit in alliance with Christianity which, through the Nordic migrants on the island, created the world of our folklore." The "migrants" from England converted Germany and the Nordic countries and founded a literature in their mother tongue which underwent subsequent development, in which the English Bible and Shakespeare are high water marks. The "spirit of struggle" of the migrants has manifested itself throughout the history of England; at the current time Grundtvig especially fixed his attention on the free circumstances of Church and citizen and of "the strong

5. *N.F.S. Grundtvigs Breve til hans Hustru under Englandsrejserne 1829-1831* (published by Stener Grundtvig, Copenhagen 1920, p. 145).

drive to enterprise for great ends" with respect both for what is hereditary and for experience, and with an unshakeable belief in providence.

The introduction to *Nordic Mythology*, taken as a whole, was an enthusiastic program for a Nordic-christian cultural renewal to which all the Nordic peoples would contribute, including the descendants of the Anglo-Saxons. In this way Grundtvig took up the cultural struggle of his youth in a new way. The basis for this struggle was now found in his dominant standpoint that the rationalist view of life of the enlightenment had arisen as the consequence of the classical education given in the grammar schools and universities, which at bottom was alien to the Nordic peoples. The rationalist view of life involved the denial of the deep and mysterious aspects of human life; only what was clear and the tangible could be acknowledged. Human beings were hereby reduced to animal status wanting only to dominate and change the world according to their own abstract inventions. This must necessarily lead to bloody revolutions and wars.

Over against all this stood the biblical-historical view of humanity according to which a human being is not an unchangeable ape, but "an incomparable, wonderful creation, in whom divine powers will make themselves known, develop, and hold their own through thousands of generations". This view of humanity had found some receptive hearts among the old Nordic peoples who had long felt themselves related to the gods and who looked on history as a constant struggle for life and renewal, not in opposition to but inspired by the spiritual values of their predecessors.

The strong emphasis of the book on the "Nordic spirit" must be understood in this context. The "spirit" of Nordic peoples is not an abstract concept but a vigorous term for the dynamic power, which is the special mark of human beings as historical beings. It is given to human nature at the creation of the world and, despite the fall, preserved as the driving force of life, expressing itself in the living word of mouth and in the deeds of heroes, in faithfulness and in readiness to make sacrifices for the common good. This concept of spirit at once broad and yet specific is the basis for Grundtvig's now almost unconditional enthusiasm for England – both the old Anglo-Saxons and the England he had himself experienced.

This is especially apparent in some lectures Grundtvig gave in 1838 (published as *Within Living Memory* 1877). Here he draws attention to precisely those aspects of life in English society, from which he had earlier distanced himself.

His immediate impression of England had been of an immense rush of activity, and he suspected there was a good deal of despair behind the rush. He also had a certain horror of the English "mechanical spirit" which made human beings a side issue. But here too he was obliged to conclude from the results there was the presence of a driving human spirit. When he saw

that boldness with which the Englishman sets his hand to everything, that sureness with which he immediately discovers the heart of the matter... and that perseverance with which he attacks all difficulties and in general overcomes them,[6]

he felt himself to be on the territory of the Nordic fighting spirit and was filled with hopes of co-operation between England and the Nordic peoples.

It must also be mentioned that his journeys to England in all probability contributed to the crystallisation of Grundtvig's thoughts on education which have since been important in many countries. He published a series of writings on this theme in the 1830s and 1840s with proposals for a more experimental form of school for the older youth, the basis of the so-called Folk High Schools. The inspiration from England is at all events clear in a paper from 1839, which recommends an internordic university with reference to the English college system. Here he expressly draws attention to the interdisciplinary fellowship between researchers in different fields which he had experienced in Cambridge.

Grundtvig's first three visits to England had primarily a literary and historical aim, to make first-hand contact with the Anglo-Saxon manuscripts preserved in English archives. Paradoxically, but in a way typical for Grundtvig, the most evident influence of the visits on his subsequent development was on his attitude to the contemporary world, outside the church, outside the realm of scholarship. In England, Grundtvig got a taste of a society in which a growing liberalism was opening up all kinds of new avenues of exploration, political, geographical, intellectual. He suddenly realized how enclosed the Danish society of his time still was, and how much his own life had been shut away in the field of the history of ideas. But he also had a further desire to get to know more about the Church of England. In many places, especially in later life, Grundtvig could be highly critical of Anglicanism. It seems important to notice that at least for a time he had great hopes for his meeting with the Church of England. Perhaps the sharpness of his later criticism is the result of his sense of disappointment.

As has already been remarked, on his first visit in 1829, Grundtvig had at the start real difficulties with the English language. He found it difficult to understand people on the streets and they found it difficult to under-

---

6. N.F.S. Grundtvig, *Mands Minde* (Within Living Memory, lectures 1838, published by Svend Grundtvig, Copenhagen 1877, p. 443f.).

stand him. Even his knowledge of written English was uncertain at this period. This becomes very clear from the three surviving drafts of a letter to the Archbishop of Canterbury, William Howley, which he wrote during that first summer. He had come with a letter of introduction from Bishop Münter and a book to present to the Archbishop. But evidently it was only in 1830 that he actually made personal contact with Howley, who then proved welcoming and helpful in giving Grundtvig contacts in Exeter and Canterbury. In one of the 1829 drafts, Grundtvig seeks to explain his position to the Archbishop and the reason for his visit.

Allow me therefore to assure Your Grace that though I have resigned my office in the contradictory Church of Denmark, still however during a literary career of more than twenty years, I take my only pride in being a servant in the house upon the rock everlasting, and that therefore the parchments, valuable as the[y] are indeed to the history of mankind, should never have prevailed upon me to cross the sea, if not from the history of the holy catholick church, I had learned to reverence the Church of England and to long for better information about her establishment and institutions than it out of England is to be got [*sic*].[7]

In another draft he is even more explicit in speaking of his "reverence to the Episcopal Church of England, which assiduous study of the Church History in spite of many prejudices had enforced upon him."[8]

Why was Grundtvig so interested in the Church of England? Undoubtedly one reason was its episcopal ministry with its uninterrupted succession of bishops. The "matchless discovery" of 1825 had given Grundtvig a wholly new vision of the Church of Christ as a great, living, historical fact. A living church built upon the apostolic confession of faith and the two sacraments of the gospel which had come from the Lord himself. Not unnaturally he asked himself what was the place of the ministry in this church? How far did it have a role in maintaining its life and teaching? Questions such as these would have been underlined for him by the evident importance which Irenaeus gave to the episcopal succession in the second-century church. Grundtvig was faced with a quandary here. The church to which he belonged was episcopal in its structure. The bishops still occupied the pre-Reformation sees and presided over the pre-Reformation dioceses. But at the decisive moment of the break with Rome the first evangelical bishops had been ordained, not as in England (and also in Sweden), by already existing bishops, but by a German theologian, a friend and collaborator of Martin Luther, Johannes Bugenhagen, and Bugenhagen

---

7.   Grundtvig-Arkiv 446.3.d. at the Royal Library, Copenhagen.
8.   Grundtvig-Arkiv 446.3.b.II.

was a priest and not a bishop. Was this break in the chain of episcopal ordinations to be understood as an irregularity, or did it in fact make the whole subsequent Danish episcopate null and void? Grundtvig was clearly not in a position to take the second option. But at least for a time after 1825 he seems to have been ready to acknowledge that the Danish situation was irregular and to look towards England with a certain wistful admiration and even a certain expectation of help.

Grundtvig's first three visits to England took place of course before the beginning of the Oxford Movement, that movement which had at its heart a vision of the church as a great given historical fact in many ways so similar to Grundtvig's own matchless discovery. One can only speculate as to what might have happened had he chanced to make contact in 1829 or 1830 with some intelligent and open-minded pre-Tractarian high churchman. But his initial contacts in London were almost all in a circle of people whose political convictions were radical and whose religion was of the Unitarian persuasion. Grundtvig found little of interest theologically in this group, though he recognized their respect for liberty of conscience and their openness to other points of view. When finally in 1831 he visited Cambridge and came into contact with Anglican scholars and theologians of real weight, men such as Connop Thirlwall, Augustus Hare, and W.H. Whewell, the questions they would have discussed related more to developments in German theology, than to matters of church order or the theology of the sacraments. His time at Cambridge was certainly a high point for him. He found stimulating and sympathetic conversation at Trinity high table. Even there, however, there was not the real meeting of minds for which he had hoped.

In saying this, one is not merely speculative. We have evidence of Grundtvig's more strictly theological hopes for his first visits to England in another, later letter which also exists among his papers in two drafts. This is a letter written to E.B. Pusey probably in 1836 as a consequence of a visit made to Oxford by a young Danish theologian, F. Hammerich. The opening of the letter is so powerfully Grundtvigian that it deserves to be quoted at some length.

Dear sir,
Nearly for thirty years I have been cutting my way thro' the Protestant wilderness in order to find "a city to dwell in" and though the Lord wonderfully has strengthened me like "an iron pillar and brasen walls against the whole land", yet I was very sorry for it that from nowhere else I heard the trumpet sound for the primitive, true, Catholick church, the mother of us all, and even by my visits to England [1829-31] where it was most likely, that his "servants should take pleasure in her stones and favour the dust thereof," in this respect I was disappointed. But at last I heard you

were awakened from a long and deep slumber, and tho' the reports were vague, yet I begged my friend Mr. Hammerich, who had been favored with your acquaintance to tell you what was going on with us, and from your answer to him I see, you look with interest also upon this small corner of "the great Palace..."

But Grundtvig being Grundtvig will not avoid the major problem which he sees looming between them, and very soon he comes to it.

But here I stumbled upon the great question between you and us, whether you believe you may have "brethren in the Lord" or not, where there has been no un-interrupted succession of Bishops, for I don't speak of those who despise the Episcopal order and succession, never the case in Denmark, where the Superinten-dents always have been named and consecrated Bishops, only not with due respect to the uninterrupted succession. No doubt, that we ought to desire the consecration with you, but the question is whether or not you would recognize not only our Baptism, but also our ordination of Presbyters as valid, tho' our first Ordinators after the Reformation have only been Presbyters, not Bishops themselves. I am quite sure you ought to do so, for the Lord has blessed my own ordination to such a degree, that I might as well slighten my Baptism as my Ordination, and could do neither without the most barefaced ingratitude and still I doubt, whether your extravagant notions of Episcopacy would allow you to recognize me as a Presbyter.[9]

During the 1830s Grundtvig's knowledge of what was going on in England and his interest in it was greatly increased by the presence in Denmark from 1833-39 of a young Irish clergyman, Nugent Wade (1809-1890), who in these years was the Anglican chaplain in Helsingør. Wade is revealed in his letters and diaries as an intelligent, sympathetic person greatly inter-ested in what was going on in Oxford, though not able to follow it all the way, and at the same time profoundly impressed by his meetings with Grundtvig. Between the younger and the older man a real friendship grew up. Wade's diaries give us one of the very few pictures of Grundtvig as seen by someone from a world very different from his own. From the very beginning they got on well. Already in 1834 he notes,

... had a most delightful and useful interview with Pastor Gruntvig: he is decidedly a man of genius and of a first-rate order. I don't know that I ever met with so comprehensive a mind. He seems to sweep the whole world history at a glance and philosophize upon it and that soundly and with *one* scope God and his dealing with man for his Redemption.[10]

9. Grundtvig-Arkiv 446.6.a.
10. Helge Toldberg, "Nugent Wade i Helsingør", *Grundtvig-Studier* (1948), p. 48.

Two years later after many fascinating hours spent with the great man he was still as enthusiastic:

Was repaid for my journey by a long evening Intellectual feast with Gruntvig – on a great variety of subjects – Irish manuscripts – Northern languages – History of the very Northern nations, particularly of Iceland from its Earliest settlement by the Norwegian petty kings in I think the ninth century – then Philosophy its relative bearing on religion – and then my just touching on the Law as contrasted with the Gospel – when we had to break up it being late...[11]

This friendship with Wade was to be of great significance for Grundtvig's fourth and final visit to England. Not only did Wade continue to supply him with books and periodicals which kept him in touch with the development of affairs at Oxford, he also offered to accommodate him in London whenever he should be able to visit England again. On his return from Denmark Wade had been appointed to the newly established parish of St Paul's Finsbury by Bishop Blomfield despite the Bishop's "avowed prejudice against preferring Irishmen". When finally in 1843 Grundtvig was able to come to England with his son Svend, Wade accommodated them in his home and accompanied them on their journeys both to Oxford and to Edinburgh.

In these years between 1839 and 1843 the Oxford Movement was approaching its first major crisis. It was beginning to become clear that Newman himself no longer felt secure in his Anglican position. Could it be that he and at least some of those who were influenced by him could find their way into the church of Rome? To contemporaries the prospect seemed almost unthinkable. No such movement had taken place since the Reformation. It is difficult at this length of time to realize the depth of feeling involved. It was partly to avert this impending disaster that Grundtvig came on his last visit to England, to see whether or not he could convince the Oxford leaders to find another way for understanding the catholicity of the church, a way which he believed could lead to a genuine interaction of Catholic and Evangelical.

As was perhaps inevitable, Grundtvig's visit was from this point of view a total failure. He came to Oxford in July 1843. It was a time when Pusey was ill and overshadowed by the controversy on his sermon on the Eucharist. The two men met on one or two occasions, but though their conversation was friendly it seems to have been only superficial. With Newman Grundtvig seems to have been getting further. After a first

11. ibid., p. 53.

meeting in which Newman had been notably reserved there was a second and much more fruitful conversation, but this was interrupted by a well-meaning but unintelligent clergyman of evangelical convictions and aristocratic connections. Newman slipped away and did not return. Even if circumstances had been different, it is difficult to think that the outcome could have been other than it was. Grundtvig was now a man of sixty, set in his ways, firmly established in his views and himself aware that he was less adaptable than he had been. Pusey and Newman, though fifteen years junior to him, were also firmly established in their theological convictions and both must have had a sense that they were coming to a parting of the ways. The theological freshness and creativity of the movement, so evident in 1836 or 1837, had passed.

As it was, Grundtvig was left to have conversations with younger men. The one occasion on which he tells us he lost his temper was not with a young Tractarian but with an evangelical! Of his exchanges with the younger members of the Oxford school we have only a couple of letters from William Palmer of Magdalen. They reveal the absolute intransigence of Palmer on the subject of ordination but also the fact that he had been deeply moved by his meetings with Grundtvig.

What I said with respect to yourself was *not* that you were or were not a member of the visible Church, nor that you were or were not a servant or "minister" of Christ working among your fellow men for good and it may be in a high degree an instrument of grace to them – but *this* is what I *did* and *do* say, that you cannot (in my judgment) be recognized as a "Clerk", a "Presbyter", a "Priest", a "Sacerdos", or "Ιερευς" in the Ecclesiastic and Canonical sense of these words. I cannot make things to be other than they are by my own opinion about them – otherwise I hope I should have charity enough to make all people in the world whom I now think to be wrong in position to be right...

It is evident from the letter that Grundtvig had written with some warmth and Palmer feels the older man has been unfair to him, but he speaks of Grundtvig's generosity and kindness. There is corresponding warmth in his letter in reply, certainly no coldness or indifference.

... Believe me to be always with great respect and affection for all the zeal which you show for all you know or think to be Catholic, and sympathy for you in all the difficulty and reproach which you must encounter from heretical Protestantism insofar as you diverge from or are opposed to its spirit...[12]

12. Grundtvig-Arkiv 448.18.b.

Grundtvig for his part felt rebuffed. It would be interesting to have his side of the correspondence. Later he was to reflect bitterly on what seemed to him the arrogance of the high churchmen.

Newman was received into the Roman Catholic church on October 9, 1845. Two weeks later Pusey published an open letter to a friend in one of the Anglican periodicals of the time in which he spoke of Newman's departure with great sadness but absolutely no bitterness. Perplexing though his friend's move was to him, he could not believe Newman had gone against God's will. So it was that he was able to see the possibility of great good in Newman's conversion. It could be, he believed, an event which opened up the possibility of contact and even reconciliation between Canterbury and Rome.

Newman's conversion was of course reported across Europe and just as it drew from Pusey a remarkably eirenic and ecumenical reaction, so perhaps surprisingly it did from Grundtvig. In an article published in *Dansk Kirketidende* at the end of November he comments on the events in Oxford and compares them to reports of German Catholic theologians who were being strongly influenced by Reformation ideas and attracted towards them.

If we consider the so-called reformation, or the great division of the sixteenth century from a Christian vantage-point, then we see straightaway that insofar as the two parties kept the old Catholic faith and baptism, the divorce was not basically churchly but national, civil, and cultural. Thus it was blindness on both sides when the papists anathematized us as heretics and we condemned them as the army of antichrist. Only then because human life goes as a whole, so that no principle part of it can be changed without it having a recognizable influence on life as a whole, and because on both sides, with blind hatred we have made a point of laying as little weight as possible on what we had in common with one another, only then has the divorce between Rome and us had a powerful influence on the churchly relation between us, and given birth to the absurd assertion that the two circles of the Christian society, which confessed the same faith, baptized with the same baptism, and worshipped the same Jesus Christ as God, were really opposed to one another. If this really is a time of enlightenment we are living in, then it cannot but be that, serious and God-fearing people on both sides must discover and see constantly more clearly, that we have both done each other an injustice, shamed our common Lord, and in doing so wounded ourselves in many ways, so that a certain tendency on the Roman side towards us and on our side towards Rome is not only to be expected, but is amongst the best signs of the time for the holy universal church to which we on both sides belong.

If we now consider the great point of controversy between Rome and us, it is not just a matter of the relationship between church and scripture, between spiritual and worldly, between the language of Rome and the vernacular, but rather it is the all-inclusive relationship between what is common and particular, what is fixed and changing, the visible and invisible, and while we can dispute much on who has been the most one-sided, it is only too clear that the so-called Roman church has become almost fossilized and the Protestant church has blown away, so that the conflict is now up in the air as between the wind and an old ruin.[13]

The details of Grundtvig's attempts to make contact with the Oxford Movement, often frustrating and disappointing to him, are here put into an altogether larger and more inclusive perspective. Perhaps it is in such a perspective that we need to see these baffled attempts at contact today.

13. *Dansk Kirketidende*, vol. 8 (Nov 23rd 1845), p. 113.

Grundtvig and Anglo-Saxon Poetry

By Bent Noack

The subject Grundtvig and England has many aspects, as may be seen by looking at the contents of this volume. But, whatever English enterprise, educational system, and political life may have influenced Grundtvig and inspired him, it should not be forgotten that it was Anglo-Saxon literature which brought him to England. Of course he knew English history after the Old English period, but the Norman conquest could not alter his opinion: "Anglo-Saxon" is an honorific name and "Norman" almost the opposite. It is no great surprise to find Martin Luther appointed an Anglo-Saxon honoris causa.[1]

The first and most important piece of Anglo-Saxon literature to arouse Grundtvig's interest was the poem *Beowulf*, and it was as an historian that he got interested in it. "The history of my country has always been my hobby", he wrote in his diary as early as December 31, 1804, when he was 21, and he mentions that it was his friend P.N. Skovgaard who induced him to study Icelandic. Grundtvig belonged to the generation which rediscovered Nordic Antiquity and the Middle Ages, a rediscovery characteristic of romanticism: after ages of oblivion the ancient history and traditions of the people must be brought back into the light of day! In Danish literature, the first attempts had already been made in the last decades of the 18th century, but the turning point was Henrik Steffens' lectures in the winter of 1802-3 and Adam Oehlenschlaeger's poem *The Gold Horns*. But even before Oehlenschlaeger wrote his famous poem and Steffens gave his inspiring lectures, the 18 years old Grundtvig had already in 1801 written a series of verses on subjects from Norse mythology.

During the following years Nordic studies were his principal interest and he published a couple of papers on this theme before, in 1808, he wrote his epoch-making work on *Norse Mythology* (*Nordens Mytologi*). In this book he expressed the need for an edition of *Beowulf*.[2] By then he was 25, and he

---

1. *Nordisk Tidsskrift for Teologi* (1842), p. 117.
2. "It is only about the Volsungs and the Niflungs (Gjukungs) that we possess Nordic poems strictly speaking, but both these and, especially, the Skjoldungs and the Skilfings will no doubt appear in a splendid new light when Mr. Thorkelin (and may it be soon) erects a luminous monument to himself with an edition of the Anglo-Saxon poem he is working on." *US*, vol. I (1904), pp. 326-27, note.

returned time and again to Anglo-Saxon literature, especially to *Beowulf*, and finished his work on it in 1865, when he was 82.

The longed-for edition was published in 1815, G.J. Thorkelin's transcript of the destroyed MS Cotton Vitellius A xv.[3] This edition gave a starting point to Grundtvig's work, not only on its contents, but also on its texts. No sooner had it been published before Grundtvig, in the same year, wrote a review of it and criticized Thorkelin for some of his readings and transcriptions. Grundtvig's review included a translation of his own of the first section of *Beowulf* into Danish. When Thorkelin published a rejoinder and rejected some of Grundtvig's criticisms, Grundtvig printed a smaller part of the Anglo-Saxon text of the poem, together with his own translation and a rendering in prose. In his poetic reproduction of the original in Danish, he already exhibits an essential feature in his work as a translator: he uses far more lines than the Anglo-Saxon original, not because he was not able to reproduce the verses more exactly and briefly, but because he was convinced that it was necessary to transform the verses considerably if he wanted to render the Anglo-Saxon according to the Danish language and poetic style of his own time.

His criticism of Thorkelin was supplemented in a paper of 1817, *On the Beowulf Heroic Song, being the Anglo-Saxon Poem edited by J.G. Thorkelin Esq. in 1815*,[4] and a few years later he published *Pieces of the Skjoldung Poem, or Beowulf*.[5]

Meantime he had learned Anglo-Saxon. For years he had studied Icelandic, and already during his preliminary studies, before writing his *Norse Mythology* in 1808, he became aware of the relationship between many Nordic and Anglo-Saxon words. When Thorkelin's book appeared, he took up Anglo-Saxon which, for some time, he studied with the famous philologist Rasmus Rask, who published an Anglo-Saxon grammar in 1817. The two of them planned an extensive cooperation, as Grundtvig tells in his above mentioned *Pieces*:

For some time to come, the new edition which is so sorely needed, will not be carried out, but when Professor Rask is back from his journey, I think we shall be able to carry out our plan.

However, when Rask returned in 1823, after a stay in Sweden and a long journey in the Orient, Grundtvig had taken holy orders and become a parish minister. For some years he had other things to do, and it was not

---

3.   *De Danorum rebus gestis seculo III. et IV. Poema Danicum, dialecto Anglo-Saxonica.*
4.   *Om Bjovulfs Drape, eller det af Hr. Etatsraad Thorkelin 1815 udgivne angelsachsiske Digt.*
5.   *Stykker af Skjoldung-Kvadet eller Bjovulfs Minde.*

until his journeys to England in 1829, 1830, and 1831 that he was able to continue – or resume – his work on Anglo-Saxon literature.

And again it was *Beowulf* he proposed to work on. In 1826, he had resigned as a minister of the Danish church. When, a couple of years later, he was received in audience by the King and was asked what he was doing and how he was going to spend his time, he answered that he had nothing special in mind, unless the King would be gracious enough to grant him a sum to go to England and study the Anglo-Saxon manuscripts that were so important for the oldest history of our country.

So in three succeeding years, he went to England for several months, searching libraries, museums, and the universities for Anglo-Saxon manuscripts. He was not impressed by the knowledge which the British had of the treasures they possessed nor by their interest in them, and he even, somewhat haughtily, expressed his wish to teach them to appreciate Anglo-Saxon literature and their own Anglo-Saxon past. In his lectures of 1838, *Mands Minde* (*Within Living Memory*),[6] Grundtvig said:

My principal object was to get in touch with the Englishman and win him over to things Anglo-Saxon and thereby to the North. The prospect was despairing, for the praise of Old England which is on the lips of all, does not apply to the Old English in History's sense but, on the contrary, to the New England after the Glorious Revolution of 1689. Even the most meticulous historians of the Island rarely went further back than to the Norman Conquest of 1066; at any rate they dispensed with the Anglo-Saxon and Danish epochs as horrible barbarisms which, unfortunately, both too early and for too long had interrupted ancient Rome's mild and beneficial influence under Domitian and Nero.

Through his letters to his wife and some Danish friends we are fairly well informed about his travels in England, the places he visited and the persons he met and whose help he received during his stays. In 1830 he made an agreement with the publishers Black and Young about an edition of Anglo-Saxon poems[7] and in 1831 he had a *Prospectus* printed with the wording:

Bibliotheca Anglo-Saxonica. Prospectus and Proposals for the Publication of the Anglo-Saxon Manuscripts illustrative of the poetry and literature of our language, most of which has never yet been printed. Edited by the Rev. N.F.S. Grundtvig of Copenhagen, London 1831, 16 pp.[8]

---

6. N.F.S. Grundtvig, *Af Mands Minde, 1788-1838*, ed. Svend Grundtvig (1877).
7. Letter to his wife of September 17, 1830. His letters to his wife during his journeys to England have been edited by his grandchildren: *N.F.S. Grundtvigs Breve til hans Hustru under Englandsrejserne 1829-1831. Udgivne af deres Børnebørn* (1920).
8. The text of the *Prospectus* according to the Letters, p. 197, n. 132.

As for editing, the *Prospectus* was the whole achievement of Grundtvig's. It was Benjamin Thorpe who took over. But Grundtvig's work on the Anglo-Saxon manuscripts did not stop. In 1841 he wrote an article about *Beowulf*, and in 1861 he made his own edition of it, an edition which he even accompanied with a poem of his own, written in the Anglo-Saxon language. There is another famous piece of Anglo-Saxon poetry which he managed to publish: *The Phenix, An Anglo-Saxon Poem, edited for the first time, with Introduction, a Danish Translation, and an Echo.*[9]

It is an impressive work that Grundtvig has done on Anglo-Saxon poetry. First he had to study the language and master it, or rather the languages, for although he was well read in old English, he had to learn most of his modern English after he came to England. Then came the search for the manuscripts, which took much time and many miles; his letters show how much this sometimes delayed him. Finally he had to read the manuscripts and transcribe them. The reading and editing took all his philological knowledge and skill, and his intuition as well. All of these abilities he had shown already in his criticism of Thorkelin. Modern editions and books on Anglo-Saxon literature give him due credit for his work. Some of his readings, emendations, and conjectures are still considered correct, as may be seen, e.g., in the Wyatt and Chambers edition of *Beowulf.*[10] It is true, as has often been pointed out, that for him as an historian, a theologian, and a hymnwriter, philology was only a necessary tool, but none the less one is impressed by his work in the field of philology.

It was the historian Grundtvig whom the King sent to England. But the outcome of his English visits was not limited to history and editions of texts. Also as a clergyman and hymnwriter Grundtvig availed himself of the access he gained to the manuscripts and the studies they demanded. During his second visit to England in 1830, he became aware that there was an old manuscript in Exeter, the one now called the Exeter Book, and he went to Exeter and read the manuscript before it was transferred to London, where Grundtvig had originally asked for it. By that time it had become almost forgotten in the learned world of Britain, although it had

---

9. *Phenix-Fuglen, et angelsachsisk Kvad, førstegang udgivet med Indledning, Fordanskning og Efterklang* (Copenhagen, 1840)
10. *Beowulf with the Finnsburg Fragment*, ed. by A.J. Wyatt, rev. by R.W. Chambers (Cambridge, (1914) 1968), p xx.: "He made many conjectures which, on a more careful examination, were actually found to be the readings of the MS. Such success naturally aroused confidence in his conjectural restorations."

been described by Wanley as early as 1705. Many years later, Grundtvig wrote in one of his longer poems, remembering his journeys to England:

> The British Museum
> went so far as to scold us,
> because an old scroll,
> full of Anglo-Saxon songs
> · and now buried in Exeter,
> had not been transcribed
> for seven hundred years.[11]

But in 1830 it was in fact otherwise than his later memory of it: he soon learned that English students were also interested in the Exeter manuscript, and after Grundtvig had read and transcribed it, Robert Chambers transcribed it in 1831-32, when it had been transferred to London. The only philological work Grundtvig did on the Exeter Book was his edition of *Phoenix*.

But in another field and in other respects his acquaintance with this manuscript turned out to be no less important for him and for his work as a poet and hymnwriter than *Beowulf*. And for his church and his people it opened up a view which had till now been unknown, and it was to have a great influence upon Danish theology and church life.

In 1835, a few years after his third journey to England, Grundtvig went to work on his hymns which eventually, after his death, were published in five volumes comprising more than 1500 hymns and songs. The first of these volumes, published by himself in 1836-37, he called *Sang-Værk til den danske Kirke*.[12] In this collection he not only wrote hymns of his own, but translated and rewrote hymns from all parts of the world. Therefore, a few words must be said to show the place and importance of Anglo-Saxon poetry in particular for his historical and theological outlook as a whole.

We have presented Grundtvig as an historian. But his work as an historian cannot be described as purely historical. In his view, it was never history for history's sake in the sense of *l'art pour l'art*. History was for him essentially God's leading of mankind through the ages and through all the developments and revolutions the world had experienced and still was to experience till the final fulfilment. A purely positivistic approach to history he detested and ridiculed as a relic of the age of Enlightenment.

11. My translation.
12. To convey Grundtvig's intention, *Sangværk* should not be taken as *Hymn Work* in the sense of a poet's work or works, but rather as an equivalent to *hymn organ*, to match the organ as an instrument of praise.

In the first volume of his *Sang-Værk* there is a double structure. The first part, consisting of 146 hymns, deals with the Church, the Sunday service, baptism and holy communion. The second part follows the ecclesiastical year and contains hymns for Advent, Christmas, Lent, Easter, Ascension, and Whitsun. But within these sections he proceeds according to an historical outlook he had conceived already in his youth and which, many years later, he was to display at full length in a long poem called *Christenhedens Syvstjerne* (*The Pleiades of Christendom*): he structured the whole history of the Church according to the seven letters in *Revelation* chapters 2-3, each letter being meant for and representing, as a prophecy, a national church or congregation: the Hebrew, the Greek, the Latin (Roman), the English, the German, and the Nordic, with the seventh still to be materialized in future history. Of the seven, with one of them still to come, the "English" is the middle one, and also the one to mark the turning point in the history of the Christian Church. From the initial height the Church declines through Greek and Latin Christianity, but rises again with the "English", i.e., the Anglo-Saxon Church, the rise continuing through the German Church (Luther) and the Nordic Church. Grundtvig maintains the continuity of the Anglo-Saxon and the later English Church (which for him does not mean the same as the Anglican Church). It is the English Church in this sense which Grundtvig addresses with his lines in *The Pleiades of Christendom*: "You are the bridge spanning from the East and the South to the North."

So, in his collections of hymns, Grundtvig translated, successively, items from the Old Testament Psalter (and some of the Prophets), ancient Greek hymns, mediaeval Latin, and English hymns. His intimate knowledge of the Exeter Book induced him to begin his "English" sections, not with translations of Watts and Wesley and other modern hymnwriters, but with renderings from Anglo-Saxon. Two of his re-written Anglo-Saxon hymns are still sung and are among the most used of his hymns.

A few examples might be useful to show how Grundtvig used his sources. To make sure that readers specially interested in the matter can give the examples a closer examination, the numbers of the hymns in the first volume of the *Sang-Værk* are given in brackets. An English translation in prose of parts of Grundtvig's verses may serve as a help towards appreciating his working method.

The first hymn to be noticed (No. 124) is in the "Church section" and begins with "Higher than houses and rocks / King of the heavenly abodes!" In a footnote Grundtvig says: "From the Anglo-Saxon Messiade in the Exeter Book". I think it could be proved that this and other notes are not put at random and that "re-written", "imitated", "free translation", and "from" mark degrees of loyalty and literalness in regard to the original. In this case the original is No. I of the first part of *Christ*, which is generally called *Advent Lyrics*. But, as in his first attempt at rendering a piece of *Beowulf*, the rendering is expanded to ten stanzas of seven lines, using other parts of the *Advent Lyrics* also. The first lines of *Christ*, I. 2-3, "Ðu cart se weallstan / þe ða wyrhtan iu / wiðwurpon to weorce", that is in Campbell's translation:[13] "You are the wall-stone which the workmen of old rejected from the work", are rendered:

> Thou art yourself the precious stone
> which, in days of old,
> to their brain's mischief,
> the masters dared to reject.

A Christmas hymn (No. 158) is according to the footnote "from" the Exeter Book, but this one too is a longer rendering of pieces corresponding to the *Antiphons* VIII and IX. In the Exeter Book the opening lines (214-15) run: "Eala þu soða/ond þu sibsuma / ealra cyninga cyning / Crist ælmihtig", that is "O true and pacific / king of all kings / Almighty Christ" and in Grundtvig's hymn:

> Truthful and peacemaking[14]
> Saviour, deity's offspring,
> King of all kings.

Lines 219-23 go on with: "There is not now any man under the skies, any clever-thinking man so deeply wise that he may to mortals say, explain aright how the Guardian of the Heavens at the beginning took you as his noble Son", and Grundtvig has:

> How in the heavenly kingdom
> secretly begot Thee
> the everlasting Father,
> man of clay cannot fathom.

Also in the rest of his 14 stanzas he follows the original, e.g., in his stanza 7, where he uses the imagery of the Golden Gate[15] which, just as in the Anglo-Saxon, is also applied to the Virgin Mary as the gate through which Christ made his way to the world.

---

13. Jackson J. Campbell, *The Advent Lyrics of the Exeter Book* (Princeton, 1959).
14. Grundtvig renders *sibsuma*, "peace-making", *Fredegod*, using the name of one of the kings in legendary history.
15. Ezech. 44:1-2.

Of three succeeding numbers (243-45), the first has the footnote "According to the Anglo-Saxon in Cædmon". It describes the *descensio ad inferos*. Grundtvig regarded the descent as a most important part of the Creed. He had, of course, known it since he was a child, the Creed being part of the baptismal liturgy. But he had also experienced the general neglect of the Creed in Christian theology and liturgy and, especially, he had seen how the descent was considered a mere relic without any meaning or purpose. In another of his hymns he addresses it as "Thou element of the Creed, so curiously abhorred." He knew the importance of the descent for the Church fathers, and he was happy to find that it was dealt with at length in the *Junius* MS. So he wrote a long song in a style and a language comparable to those of the early ballads, where he faithfully rendered many of the expressions of the original, e.g., that the prisoners in Hell propped themselves on their arms and leaned on their hands. His last line is characteristic: "Therefore, on earth it is a matter of salvation, that the Son of God visited Hell."

The second is a hymn on the Ascension, "from the Anglo-Saxon Messiade in the Exeter Book". Even in details, this follows its source, and it is not an exaggeration to call it a regular translation. Through this hymn, which is sung in practically all churches on Ascension Day, Danish congregations have a real access to Old English poetry and Christianity.

The last one is never used and could not be found in any Danish hymnbook, but it shows Grundtvig's dependence on his reading of Anglo-Saxon poetry. In fact, he had the Exeter Book lying on his desk when he wrote these numbers of his *Sang-Værk*. After writing the previous hymn on the ascension, he went straight on with the next stanzas of the Exeter Book and wrote a hymn on "The Six Leaps of the Lord", from Heaven to the womb of the Virgin, from there to the manger, from life to the cross, the fifth down to Hell, and the sixth when he ascended to Heaven. This motif is known from the homilies of the primitive and mediaeval Church, among others from Gregory's 29th Homily, which is probably the source of the Anglo-Saxon poem. Grundtvig has used this motif only a few pages before, rewriting a mediaeval Latin hymn. But apparently he wanted to make not only the Latin, but also the Anglo-Saxon voice heard in what he elsewhere called "the full chorus of the Christian Church".

Grundtvig would not have spent so much time and energy on Anglo-Saxon literature unless he had considered it extremely important. It appealed to him in an extraordinary manner and gave him ideas and angles of approach which he had always cherished, but which were confirmed and manifested through his Anglo-Saxon studies.

What appealed to him first was the language itself which, although not

Nordic but Saxon and related to the Saxon dialect in Germany, he felt to be not only contemporary with Old Norse but also akin to it. As a poet he was impressed by the poetic form, which is the same as in Old Norse. He loved, and he used abundantly, the poetic terms that are characteristic of Anglo-Saxon poetry. The adjectives it uses to an almost Homeric extent are faithfully reproduced, and one of his best known expressions, "hvalernes veje", "the roads of the whales", is from *Beowulf* 1,10 *"hron-rad"*.

For the historian Grundtvig, the English national congregation – meaning primarily the Anglo-Saxon congregation – gives coherence and continuity to history, to Danish and Nordic history and to Church history as well. He had profound historical knowledge and understanding, and a keen eye for the currents and trends in both universal history and ecclesiastical history, "the journey of the Christian community", as he called it. His starting point was in the connections, hostile and friendly, between Britain and the Northern countries in the times of the Vikings. But he had also a profound understanding of the links between Antiquity and English Christianity and theology, and he appreciated more than most people the ways in which Latin and Greek church life and theology had influenced England. He saw clearly that it was at the time of the Anglo-Saxons that Britain inherited this legacy and began to minister it to others.

The ways this influence made itself manifest were important. Of course, the study of the Greek and Latin Church fathers and the actual use of their writings in sermons and prayers and hymns played a part which must not be overlooked. But, to Grundtvig, what is essential is that it has also come in the shape of the Anglo-Saxon narrative poems. Here, he found real biblical history told to the people, in the people's own language, with love and skill, with dramatic impact and sympathetic understanding, "understanding of the heart", as he liked to say. Anglo-Saxon poetry was written down in monasteries and schools, not in the cottages of peasants and fishermen, but it is not told as learned people would tell the stories, it is told in the imagery ordinary people used.

In spite of the distance in time and circumstance, Grundtvig could recognize the rural milieu of Southern Zealand where he was born, and of central Jutland where he went to school as a youngster. In language and diction, in imagery and outlook, he found a happy integration and combination of every day life with Christian faith and life. He saw that these mediaeval poems had achieved what he aimed at, transplanting biblical history into one's own times and surroundings. Just as he himself has Jesus go, not in the desert, but "in the pathless heath", and his St. Peter of Luke 5 is almost a fisherman from the Northern countries some 150 years ago. In his hymns, he moves Christmas from Palestine A.D. 1 to Denmark A.D. 1824. He heartily agrees with the Anglo-Saxons, when they sing of sea and navigation, of boats and fishing and warfare, and when they make the British weather, with fog and rain and wind and cold and dark winter, the climate and home of mankind as a whole. The Gospel is absorbed in the life of the people as Grundtvig would have it in his own time and in his own country, so that "the sound of our songs may make people hop barefeet in the streets", as he wrote.

As for the Christian Anglo-Saxon poems, Grundtvig felt at home in them, because they contained and expressed the essence of the Gospel, all the belief which the Enlightenment of his youth had tried to abandon.

Above all, he found the Gospel of Christ and belief in him expressed in words and conceptions that were in accord with the New Testament and the Fathers. Christ is God's Son, and he is God. This christology, and its implications for soteriology and anthropology, is the core of Christianity and of its theology. This is not to say that he did not find it everywhere in what he regarded as "Christianity of old", but it is remarkable how he appreciated his findings in Anglo-Saxon poetry, be it in *Beowulf* or the *Christ-poem*. It is true that Anglo-Saxon christology, to use dogmatic terms, is not what a logician would call consistent. There may be traces of Christ's subordination to God, as when Christ is the One who gives less splendour than God. But that could not disturb Grundtvig, and after all it is what the Fourth Gospel, his favourite gospel, says in 14:28, "The Father is greater than I". But the same gospel says, 10:30, "My Father and I are one". In Grundtvig's hymns it is often hard to tell whether he speaks of God or of Christ when he says "the Lord", and that is not due to a lack of ability to express himself unmistakably: the same thing can be found in the Old English poems; only when the narrative itself demands it, are God and Christ held apart. In the story of Creation God is called "Our Saviour", as is also the case in the New Testament, and both He and Christ are "the faithful King". As Eve says to Christ, when he has descended into Hell: "You were born by one of my daughters, You are God, the eternal Creator of all creation." He is "the Creator of mankind, God's own Son who created the world", a very pointed rendering of John 1:3.

Christ's glorious deed as manifest in his death and resurrection is pre-eminently viewed as redemption through battle and victory. His expiatory sacrifice is not wholly absent from the Anglo-Saxon poems, nor from Grundtvig's theology and soteriology. But it plays a minor part as compared with the redemption Christ won in his battle against all the destructive forces, and in the victory he won by his descent into Hell, his resurrection and ascension. These are conceptions dating from the very first centuries of the Church, and they were known to Grundtvig from his studies in Irenaeus and in the ancient Greek hymns which he also used in 1835-37. But it was a great satisfaction to find them so strongly maintained by the Anglo-Saxons, the kinsmen of his own forefathers.

"The First New-European Literature": N.F.S. Grundtvig's Reception of Anglo-Saxon Literature

S.A.J. Bradley

The general outline of Grundtvig's encounter with Anglo-Saxon culture and its more obvious consequences are now fairly well-charted. An indicator of the considerable breadth and of the chronological incidence of his interest in Anglo-Saxon literary records in particular is the corpus of his transcribed and annotated materials gathered in the Grundtvig Arkiv in the Royal Library, Copenhagen.[1] Anglo-Saxon texts featured there include excerpts from the Exeter Book (Exeter Cathedral Library MS 3501), the *Beowulf* Codex (London British Library MS Cotton Vitellius A xv), the Vercelli Book (Vercelli, Biblioteca Capitolare CXVII) and the Junius Codex (the so-called "Cædmon" Manuscript, Oxford, Bodleian Library MS Junius 11), *The Finnesburh Fragment, Waldhere, The Battle of Maldon, Judgement Day, Salomon and Saturn, The Letter of Alexander, Apollonius of Tyre, The Gospel of Nicodemus, Maxims*, extracts from Bede and Alcuin, *De xii Abusis*, Alfred's letter to his bishops prefacing *The Pastoral Care*, Alfred's translation of Boethius' *Consolation of Philosophy, The Anglo-Saxon Chronicle*, Ælfric's translations from the Old Testament and his prefatory letters, Ælfric's Grammar, Ælfrician homilies, psalms from the Vespasian Psalter and historical extracts relating to Boniface and other Anglo-Saxon missionaries. Scholars whose lexical work, editorial readings, emendations, conjectures and interpretations Grundtvig annotated and often countered with his own judgements in documents surviving in the Arkiv include Junius, Rawlinson, Hickes, Wanley, Hearne, Warton, Thorkelin, Rask, Lye, Ingram, Conybeare, Price, Thorpe, Kemble, Grein, Grimm, Wright, Halliwell, Stephens, Leo and Etmüller.

To be fair to English scholars, one must not overbid the initial originality or vision of Grundtvig's assessment of Anglo-Saxon literary culture or of the publication proposals in his Prospectus, *Bibliotheca Anglo-*

---

1. Høirup, H. and H. Topsøe-Jensen (eds.), *Registrant over N.F.S. Grundtvigs Papirer: Udgivet af Grundtvig Selskabet af 8. September 1947 og Det Danske Sprog- og Litteraturselskab, 30 volumes* (Copenhagen, 1957-64).

Saxonica.[2] There can be no doubt that whether he sufficiently acknowledged it or not – "it was a bit much of a certain man to declare that the
publication of an Anglo-Saxon Library was *his* big idea, which I had casu-
ally snapped up and now wanted to ruin him by carrying out"[3] – he was
indebted to the prior work of John Conybeare, sometime Professor of
Poetry in Christ Church Oxford. In 1813 Conybeare communicated a series
of papers to the Society of Antiquaries, published in *Archaeologia*, which
included transcriptions, translations and studies in versification, of poetry
from the Exeter Book. Conybeare was in turn indebted to the recent work
of Sharon Turner[4] – who, incidentally, regarded himself as the first scholar
properly to note *Beowulf* as well as to the earlier work of Wanley, Hickes
and Junius; and he could well have owed something to the attention drawn
to the significance of Anglo-Saxon literature by James Ingram in his
inaugural lecture as Rawlinsonian Professor of Anglo-Saxon in Oxford in
1807. In 1826 Conybeare published his *Illustrations of Anglo-Saxon Poetry* in
fulfilment of a Subscription Prospectus proposing a publication of "reliques
of Anglo-Saxon" intended to raise money for a school in Bath Easton where
he was vicar. The *Illustrations* contained among other things the *Archaeologia*
articles, a critique of Thorkelin's edition of *Beowulf*, his own analysis
(sometimes rather erroneous) of the story, a metrical version of the poem
with passages of the original, notes and variant readings (giving no
indication that he knew of Grundtvig's already published work on *Beowulf*),
and specimens from the Exeter Book, including *The Phoenix* and *The Ruin*.
In a "Catalogue of Extant Relics" (pp. lxxvi-lxxxvi) he expressed regret at
the neglect shown by English scholars towards Anglo-Saxon antiquities,
and he proposed, in continuation of what he had already partly fulfilled, a
series of publications to make good the want: an edition of *Beowulf* to be
undertaken by Richard Price, an edition and translation of Alfred's Boethius, an edition of the Cædmonian Paraphrases by himself, and an edition
of the Exeter Book. He did not know of the existence of the Vercelli Book.
All this was in print and surely known to Grundtvig before the publication

2.   Grundtvig, N.F.S., *Bibliotheca Anglo-Saxonica. Prospectus and Proposals of a subscription
     for the publication of the most valuable Anglo-Saxon manuscripts illustrative of the early
     poetry and literature of our Language, most of which have never yet been printed* (London,
     1830).
3.   Grundtvig, N.F.S., *Phenix-Fuglen. Et angelsachsisk Kvad. Førstegang udgivet med
     Indledning, Fordanskning og Efterklang* (Copenhagen, 1840); Introduction partly
     translated in Johansen, S. and Høirup, H. (eds.), *Grundtvigs Erindringer og Erin-
     dringer om Grundtvig* (Copenhagen, 1948), p. 75; my translation here and throughout
     unless otherwise specified.
4.   Turner, S., *The History of the Manners, Landed Property, Government, Laws, Poetry,
     Literature, Religion and Language of the Anglo-Saxons* (London, 1805).

of his prospectus *Bibliotheca Anglo-Saxonica* in 1830 with its strikingly similar polemic and proposals, including a similarly framed commendation of Richard Price.

What Grundtvig eventually came to make of his encounter is a different matter. Apart from a considerable quantity of more or less popular and polemical critical discussion of text, content and interpretation,[5] he produced an edition of *Beowulf*,[6] an edition of *The Phoenix*,[7] a Danish translation of *Beowulf* with copious apparatus,[8] translated excerpts from *Beowulf* in *Nyeste Skilderier af Kjøbenhavn* (1815), a pastiche poem based partly upon Anglo-Saxon poetry,[9] and free renderings of a small amount of Anglo-Saxon poetry in the form of Danish hymns – most notably *I Kveld blev der banket paa Helvedes Port* [Yestereve came a knock on the portals of Hell][10] which was inspired by lines from *Christ and Satan* in the "Cædmon" manuscript, and *Kommer, Sjæle dyrekiøbte* [O come, you souls so dearly purchased] (1837) which is freely based upon lines in Cynewulf's poem, *Christ II (The Ascension)* in the Exeter Book. These comprise the most direct and explicit responses and have been well documented; and here he has earned his reputation, if belatedly, for – in Professor Eric Stanley's evaluation of his work on *Beowulf*[11] – "astonishing brilliance". But there is probably embedded in his writings a wealth of recall – direct reference, reminiscence and half-unconscious echo – particularly of this poetry of the early Church, which Grundtvig scholars have far from exhausted. "All the time, images are flashing into Grundtvig's hymns that build bridges to the early Church and the Eastern Church".[12] In translating them, says Professor Bent Noack,[13] "a certain biblical and liturgical flavour in style and word-choice is in my opinion reasonable, if regard is to be given to the poems' background and

5. Particularly of *Beowulf*; notably in his periodicals *Danne-Virke*, 1816-19, and in Grundtvig, N.F.S., *Brage og Idun* (Copenhagen, 1841).
6. Grundtvig, N.F.S., *Beowulfes Beorh* (Copenhagen, 1861).
7. *Phenix-Fuglen*, (Copenhagen, 1840).
8. Grundtvig, N.F.S., *Bjowulfs Drape. Et Gothisk Helte-Digt fra forrige Aar-Tusinde af Angel-Saxisk paa Danske Riim* (Copenhagen, 1820).
9. Grundtvig, N.F.S., "Ragna-Roke" in *Danne-Virke III* (Copenhagen, 1817), pp. 301ff.
10. No. 243 in Grundtvig, N.F.S., *Sangværk til den Danske Kirke* (Copenhagen, 1836-37); Friis, O., Damon, S.F. and Hillyer, R.S. (trs.), *A Book of Danish Verse* (New York, 1922), p. 57.
11. Stanley, E.G., "The scholarly recovery of the significance of Anglo-Saxon records in prose and verse: a new bibliography" in *Anglo-Saxon England* 9, (1981), p. 246.
12. Thomsen, N., "Grundtvig in the Mirror of the Early Church" in Thodberg, C. and Thyssen, A.P. (ed.), and Broadbridge, E. (tr.), *N.F.S. Grundtvig: Tradition and Renewal* (Copenhagen, 1983), pp. 197-198.
13. Noack, B., *Helvedstorm og Himmelfart* (Copenhagen, 1983).

origin"; and judiciously he notes that "Grundtvig's word-choice and mode of expression, especially in the 1830's, is flavoured by this poetry and, not to be forgotten, its and his premises deriving from the early Church".

It is clear that two broad (and inseparable) questions need to be asked of Grundtvig as a creative thinker and writer engaging in the study of an ancient literature: what did he find when he encountered Anglo-Saxon literature and culture, which may have given him some sense of discovering – within northern antiquity – an almost providential affirmation of views he had been formulating in a particularly difficult period of his early life, when several of the greater absolutes seemed to him, in terms of his own life and destiny, to be in a state of flux; and what then did he take away from the encounter, to be used as a source of affirmation, inspiration, supplementation and illustration in the working-out and frequent reappraisals of his philosophies, his life and his destiny onwards into his mature years to the very end of his life?

Back home in Denmark in 1838 Grundtvig could confide to his Danish audience the view that England was a prodigal son and Denmark the venerable father praying for his return and rediscovery of his true life-of-the-heart which resided of course in the ancient Northern culture: his main aim in his visits to England, he said "was to get into contact with the Englishman and win him for the Anglo-Saxon and so for Scandinavia".[14] The Grundtvig who complains about nineteenth-century German cultural imperialism claiming northern (including Anglo-Saxon) languages and culture as "Germanic" can reveal something similarly proprietary in his own attitude towards the Anglo-Saxon literature he had discovered.[15] But though he may characterize Anglo-Saxon poetry as the product of "those tough warriors who crushed Rome and created a new world of nations",[16] his subsequent larger reading of *Beowulf* and his response to other Anglo-Saxon poetry makes the imperialist-militaristic polemic of some other nineteenth and early twentieth-century German and English-speaking commentators appear small-minded. A false impression of "Norse" chauvinism or at least parochialism is conveyed by modern scholars and translators of Grundtvig, when they translate, or accept the translation of, his "Nordisk"

14. Grundtvig, N.F.S., *Mands Minde* [Within Living Memory] (1838), excerpt translated in Jensen, N.L. (ed. and tr.) and Broadbridge, E. (tr.), *A Grundtvig Anthology: Selections from the Writings of N.F.S. Grundtvig (1783-1872)* (Cambridge, 1984)., pp. 118, 121. (Grundtvig 1838a).

15. ibid., pp. 99-101. See also passim Stanley, E.G., *The Search for Anglo-Saxon Paganism* (Cambridge, 1975) and Haarder, A., *Beowulf: The Appeal of a Poem* (Aarhus, 1975).

16. Grundtvig, N.F.S., *Nordens Mythologi* (Copenhagen, 1808), tr. in Jensen and Broadbridge, pp. 33-62.

as "Norse" – as, for instance, when he claims Beowulf as a "Nordiske Helt [N. hero]" and when he declares the poem "ægte Nordisk af Aand, saavelsom af Indhold og Bygningskonst" [pure N. in spirit, in its content just as in its compositional art].[17] Thus, for example, a notion unintelligible to Anglo-Saxonists ensues when Grundtvig's translators have him say: "especially the old Norse literature in Anglo-Saxon and Icelandic must be published".[18] Whereas common modern English literary usage signifies by "Norse" that which belongs specifically to Scandinavia and could not be taken to embrace English, Grundtvig routinely uses "Nordisk" as the adjective derived from "Norden", "the North" – a region and a cultural entity within which he specifically does include Anglo-Saxon culture. "Nordisk", then, suggests "northern", even, one might claim, north-European. Couched though it was in the imagery of northern myth and legend, polarized though it was about Denmark and England, Grundtvig's long-sustained vision was of a new European order, which would realize the ancient poets' intuitions of an age of universal peace and innocent happiness.

So in the semi-cryptic visionary poem in Danish and Anglo-Saxon prefacing his edition of *Beowulfes Beorh* (1861) the poet prays for the reunion of the legendary eponymous brothers Dan and Angul in a new Golden Age of the North:

Give Gud, at Anglers Æt,/ Nu for Norden fremmed,/ Mindes maatte Videslet,/ Mindes Vane-Hjemmet,/ Bryde af den Grændels-Haand/ I det Puddervælske,/ Som uddrev med Anglers Aand/ Hjerte-Ordet 'elske'!
[God grant that the Anglo-Saxons' descendants, now alienated from the North, might remember the wide plain, might remember the home of the gods, and wrest off that Grendel's hand in the double Dutch which drove out, along with the spirit of the Anglo-Saxons, the heart-word, 'to love'!] (p. xi).

And may "Dan og Angul midt paa hav /Trykke Broder-Hænder" [Dan and Angul in mid-ocean shake their brother-hands] (p. xi). Thus legend history of the Danish Saxo Grammaticus will have come full circle with the reunion of Dan and Angul, and the Golden Age of Norse myth will be fulfilled. The golden chess-pieces of the gods – or rather, he says, the "gamle, gyldne Ord" [ancient, golden words] of the old poems – will be rediscovered, and at last "Leges Tavl, som Nornen vil,/ Under grønne Linde,/ Voves alt paa Lykke-Spil,/ Hvori alle vinde" [Chess is played, as wills the Norn, under the green linden; all is dared in game of chance, wherein all are winners]

---

17. *Bjowulfs Drape*, p. L; Grundtvig, *Beowulfes Beorh*, p. xxiv.
18. Jensen and Broadbridge, p. 55.

(p. xiii). In other departments of his public life, of course, Grundtvig pursued these poetically couched visions through debate and action within contemporary institutions and systems – economic, commercial, political, ecclesiastical – where the northern nations had, as he saw it, common interests and things to teach each other.

It was indeed Grundtvig's bold assertion that this literature of the Anglo-Saxons was nothing less than "den første nyeuropæiske Literatur" [the first new-European literature].[19] For him, the concept of a new Europe with the literature of the Anglo-Saxons as its first self-expression, had a special meaning – though he had discovered that it was a concept the leading English antiquaries neither themselves perceived nor esteemed when he put it to them.[20] For him, *Beowulf*, for example, was a work which marked a new departure of great significance in his personal world-historical view. The poet, he found, had generated out of the individual incidents or circumstances of his plot materials ("Begivenheder") intimations of universal truth ("Bedrift"): "therefore the stories about Grendel and about the Dragon stand as the poem's chief content, as a continuation of the struggle of the devil and of the ancient giants against God"; in it the poet had gambled on gathering "heathen" episodic materials into "a kind of relationship to Christian Truth"[21] *Beowulf* was "the earliest known attempt, in any vernacular dialect of modern Europe, to produce an epic poem" and "as the first attempt in [Northern] Christendom to raise secular history to epic, it deserves our special attention".[22] Along with the wider corpus of Anglo-Saxon literature, the poem represented the self-articulation of a Christian society providentially appointed to transport the purer tradition of the Church from Rome to the North.[23] In Grundtvig's world-historical view the North's history up to and essentially including his own time was that new future which lay ahead of these new circumstances; it was a future in which he himself now presently lived, and which would lead onwards into the future lying ahead of his own times. In so far as that future could and ought to be shaped by human endeavour and choice, Grundtvig believed

19. *Phenix-Fuglen* in Johansen and Høirup, p. 75.
20. ibid., p. 73; and Toldberg, H., "Grundtvig og de engelske Antikvarer" in *Orbis Litterarum*, vol. 5, fasc. 34 (1947).
21. Grundtvig, N.F.S., *Danne-Virke* II (Copenhagen, 1817), p. 278.
22. ibid., p. 277.
23. See for example Grundtvig, N.F.S., *Haandbog i Verdens-Historien. Efter de bedste Kilder. Et Forsøg af N.F.S. Grundtvig* (Copenhagen, 1833-43), vol. II; Malone, K., "Grundtvig's Philosophy of History" in *Journal of the History of Ideas*, vol. 1 (1940), pp. 281-298; and Toldberg, H., "Grundtvig belyst af en moderne anglist" in *Grundtvig-Studier* (1948), pp. 98-102.

that the ideal model for it could be projected in part at least from patterns already discernible in the past. The intellectual stimulation of his encounter with Anglo-Saxon as a "new-European" literature was, then, very considerable – even if his Europe has a distinctly northerly focus.

These Grundtvigian aspects of Anglo-Saxon cultural studies gained little international attention during his lifetime; nor indeed did Grundtvig go out of his way to win reciprocal compliments. He could be sweepingly dismissive of such "spiritless and lifeless learning" as that of the Roman-Italian tradition;[24] and heavily sarcastic when speaking of German philosophy and scholarship. As for his English rivals, he neatly cuts them down to size whilst about his main business of damning Grein with faint praise: Grein's 1857 edition of *Beowulf*, he says, was superior to both Kemble's (1833) and Thorpe's (1855), but it lacked "intimate acquaintance with the spirit and the language of the High North" and showed

sufficient misunderstanding of the content of the poem that I, as an old friend and one knowledgeable of both, have been able to give a new edition of that very same heroic poem an obvious advantage.[25]

Today, a modern consensus proves to agree with – some would say has caught up with – Grundtvig, in so far as Anglo-Saxon poetry, and particularly *Beowulf*, is no longer perceived as the trailing tail of a Teutonic heathen antiquity whose context is best found in Tacitus' *Germania*, but as an early literature of the pan-European Christian middle ages with all the ramifications and realignments and aspects of new beginnings with centuries of subsequent currency that this implies.[26]

Grundtvig's disposition towards Anglo-Saxon studies was certainly in part that of the objective scholar. Emendations he proposed to Thorkelin's text of *Beowulf* hold their permanent place in modern editions, and he identified (in Hygelac) the only likely historical figure in the poem, to mention but two out of many qualifications. But also, far more extensively and consequentially, it was an interactive and creative response, which was facilitated by what the modern Anglo-Saxonist observes as a striking fact: that Grundtvig, by virtue of the special mix of his education, interests, priestly calling and so on, was peculiarly close, at least in broad terms, to

24. *Nordens Mythologi* 1808; Jensen and Broadbridge, p. 41.
25. *Beowulfes Beorh*, p. xxii.
26. Kiernan, K.S. (ed.), *Beowulf and the Beowulf Manuscript* (New Brunswick, 1981); Chase, C., (ed.), *The Dating of Beowulf* (Toronto, 1981); Bradley, S.A.J., "Tyranny and the Concept of Law: An Anglo-Saxon Poet's View" in *Sewanee Medieval Studies* vol. 5 (1990), pp. 130-142; Malone, K., "Grundtvig as Beowulf Critic" in *Review of English Studies* vol. 17, no. 66 (1941), pp. 129-38, particularly p. 135.

the spiritual sensibilities and the intellectual dispositions of the early medieval world of the Anglo-Saxons so that, as his scholarly friend Hammerich said, "right from the start he was at home in their writings".[27]

The *prima facie* case for considering the likelihood of some sort of symbiotic relationship with Anglo-Saxon literature within Grundtvig's own creative writing is fairly plain. "Conspicuous in his style," writes Niels Lyhne Jensen, "is the use of antitheses such as life and death, summer and winter, night and day, which are all pregnant with connotations lent to them by Grundtvig's symbolic universe".[28] The same scholar goes on to note Grundtvig's characteristic "frequent references to phenomena of light and radiance" and he continues:

Grundtvig's predominantly substantival language is made even more compact by his predilection for compound nouns. He also writes with a keen sense of the root meanings of words, and he is an irrepressible punner.[29]

If this is true of Grundtvig, then Grundtvig found style, themes and lexical usage that were highly amenable and congenial to him when he encountered Anglo-Saxon literature. The typical Anglo-Saxon poet's perception of the world and its issues is fundamentally and distinctively antithetical. Consider, for example, a couple of passages from the *Christ* poems of the Exeter Book transcribed by Grundtvig while he was studying the codex in Exeter in 1830. First, a description of the bliss of heaven from *Christ III (The Judgement)*, lines 1649-60:

> Ðær is engla song, eadigra blis,
> þær is seo dyre dryhtnes onsien
> eallum þæm gesælgum sunnan leohtra.
> Ðær is leofra lufu, lif butan endedeaðe,
> glæd gumena weorud, gioguð butan ylde,
> heofonduguða þrym, hælu butan sare,
> ryhtfremmendum ræst butan gewinne,
> domeadigra dæg butan þeostrum,
> beorht blædes full, blis butan sorgum,
> frið freondum bitweon forð butan æfestum,
> gesælgum on swegle, sib butan niþe
> halgum on gemonge.[30]

27. Hammerich, F. *Et Levnetsløb*, II (1882), quoted in Johansen and Høirup, p. 262.
28. Jensen and Broadbridge, p. 25.
29. ibid., p. 25.
30. Krapp, G.P. and Dobbie, E.V.K. (eds.), *The Exeter Book, The Anglo-Saxon Poetic Records: A Collective Edition*, vol. 3 (New York, 1936), p. 49.

[There is angels' song, bliss of the blessed; there is the Lord's precious face, to all those happy beings more radiant than the sun. There is the love of dear ones, life without end-death, a glad multitude of men, youth without age, the majesty of the heaven-hosts, health without sickness, for right-doers rest without toil, for the renown-blest day without darkness, radiant, replete with splendour, bliss without sorrows, peace without rivalries thenceforth between friends happy in heaven, and love without hostility among the holy.]

Second, the ending of Fitt VII of the *Christ* cycle, lines 586-99 of *Christ II* (*The Ascension*):

> Hwæt, we nu gehyrdan hu þæt hælubearn
> þurh his hidercyme hals eft forgeaf,
> gefreode ond gefreoþade folc under wolcnum,
> mære meotudes sunu, þæt nu monna gehwylc
> cwic þendan her wunað, geceosan mot
> swa helle hienþu swa heofones mærþu,
> swa þæt leohte leoht swa ða laþan niht,
> swa þrymmes þræce swa þystra wræce,
> swa mid dryhten dream swa mid deoflum hream,
> swa wite mid wraþum swa wuldor mid arum,
> swa lif swa deað, swa him leofre bið
> to gefremmanne, þenden flæsc ond gæst
> wuniað in worulde. Wuldor þæs age
> þrynysse þrym, þonc butan ende![31]

[So now we have heard how the Salvation-child by his hither-coming gave back health and freed and defended folk below the heavens, illustrious Ordainer's son, so that every living person now while dwelling here might choose as well hell's abjection as heaven's splendour, as well that radiant radiance as the loathsome night, as well the throng of the heavenly host as the exile of darkness, as well joy with the Lord as lamentation with the devils, as well torment among furious foes as glory with the angels, as well life as death, according as one prefers to do while body and soul dwell in the world. For this may the Majesty of the Trinity have glory and thanks without end.]

Such distinctively substantival passages with their typical compound nouns interested Grundtvig enough for him to underline many such words in his transcription of the Exeter Book, as for example in Grundtvig Arkiv, Fasc. 316, 8, fol. 144v, where, in the "sea-faring" epilogue to *Christ II* discussed below, *sund-hengestum* [ocean-horses, ships] is on two occasions underlined.

---

31. ibid., p. 19.

These passages also well illustrate the early English poets' celebration of radiance as an attribute of God and of good – just as the poet of *Beowulf* sees it, symbolically and antithetically set off against the darkness of evil. As for alertness to the root-meanings of words, that too is a typical characteristic of Anglo-Saxon poets; they, however, deserve a better label than "punner" – they are habitual riddlers, who know the compressed power of calculated ambivalence of meaning, and the unique capacity of enigmatic statement to engage the creative intellect of the audience. Their sophisticated skills are displayed of course in the riddles of the Exeter Book; however they also play a crucial part in creating the density of meaning of such "enigmatic" lyric and elegiac poetry as *The Dream of the Rood, The Wanderer, The Seafarer, The Wife's Lament* and *The Husband's Message*.

For Grundtvig, Christian poetry was itself potentially a vehicle of divine inspiration, at least when its composition was the fruit of the poet's endeavour to apprehend and articulate the truth of the Creator, source of all creativity. Then the words of poesy were charged with the power of "Ordet" [the Word] – which was itself the creative fiat.

His distinctive and complex philosophy of "Ordet" Grundtvig began in earnest to formulate during his second visit to England in 1830, but it had been in gestation for some years. In an early discussion of the ending of *Beowulf* he says:

We glimpse the funeral pyre burning, the burial-mound rising over the hero's ashes and antiquity's gold, and the bard with tear-filled eyes moving his lips in a lamentation upon the hero, but that is virtually all, for it is as though the smoke enveloped the figures and weeping choked the word.[32]

Here his imagistic language is founded upon the literal level of the narrative. At this level, "Ordet" is the speech or song of Beowulf's mourners which weeping overpowers. But Grundtvig's application of it in his own discourse is metaphorical. By it, he suggests an analogy between this closing scene of the narrative and our latter-day viewpoint upon the poem itself as a monument of antiquity: like an ancient golden harp plucked from the pyre, with strings burst and tuning-pegs melted, *Beowulf* cannot articulate for us the full and original tone and meaning of its "Ord". "Ordet", then, is not only Grundtvig's word for voices within the poem's narrative, it is his word for the voice of the poem itself. This voice, notwithstanding its imperfections, succeeds for Grundtvig in communicating a decorum, an inward fervency, and an underlying religious tone.[33] It also

32. *Danne-Virke* II, pp. 270-71.
33. *Bjowulfs Drape*, Indledning, p. LII.

articulates a philosophical view of the human condition which transcends
the materials of plot: the world is the battleground between light and dark,
good and evil, God and the Power of Darkness [hin Mørkets Magt], Truth
and Falsehood [Løgnen, the Lie]; Grendel's attack on Heorot is a metaphor
of the assault made by the Lie upon the realm of Truth; the dragon's
annexation of the treasure hoard is a metaphor of the Lie's annexation of
Truth's lawful property; Grendel symbolizes the Lie's prevalence in time;
the dragon symbolizes the Lie embedded in nature – the fallen nature of
the world and of man; the hero's death represents the necessary truth that
the Lie can be finally destroyed in nature only at the cost of a man's earthly
life.[34] This reading he incorporates in his impressive Preface to *Bjowulfs
Drape*, where he says

I find in fact that Beowulf is depicted with a deep poetic insight and vitally
projected as humankind's northern hero who, finally at the cost of his own life,
disarms the Power of darkness and by his strength saves the dying life of the people.[35]

"Ordet" is all this; and it is, as his discussions of Cædmon and Anglo-
Saxon religious poetry more widely show, the word for the voice of
"proper" [egentlig] poesy as a whole, speaking for and to its parent culture.
But Grundtvig, as he pioneeringly grapples with his comprehensive
interpretation of *Beowulf* in 1817, conceptualizes a still greater continuum of
connections than this. "Ordet" relates also to the life of the spirit and its
expression, not merely in this poem, not only in all poesy, but in the whole
record of human affairs that comprises history:

The Word is, as Scripture teaches, and as we can now understand, the highest and
the deepest expression of Life's revelation, and the whole of history must be
perceived as the Word's struggle for victory.[36]

"Ordet" is indeed Christ, in the terminological usage derived from John's
Gospel; and the record of the Word's incarnate life on earth, Grundtvig
says, is the only true Epic that may be elicited from History:

The life of Christ on earth, the Word's pilgrimage in the flesh ... is an event which
not only mirrors but comprises truth's struggle and its victory, and seems, when

---

34. *Danne-Virke* II, p. 279.
35. *Bjowulfs Drape*, Indledning pp. L-LI.
36. *Danne-Virke* II, p. 273; Haarder 1975, pp. 68ff.

spiritually perceived, necessarily to result in the sole true epic which it is possible to create in history.[37]

"Ordet", then, is Truth [Sandhed], absolute, and in all its reflexes; and it is the proper calling of the poet of *Beowulf*, as of all great poets, to portray the world as the arena for the "Kamp mellem Sandhed og Løgn" [battle between Truth and Falsehood],[38] and to articulate, and indeed guide, humankind's yearnings towards that which is true, that which is of the spirit, and that which is beyond the temporal and the sensory.

Grundtvig's perception of a grand conformity between the experiencing of poetry and the experiencing of religion is well summed up by Helge Grell:

Nor is his problem the way in which the eternal and the spiritual are knowable within the temporal-sensory condition in this world. For him it is possible to see them perfectly clearly through poetry which, in dreaming and in yearning, causes humankind to turn towards the eternal and the spiritual as its proper dwelling-place, where its life can fully unfold in truth and freedom. It happens too through such philosophy as addresses that dilemma of humankind which consists in the fact that it does not manage to realize that life which in poetry it certainly intuits, but instead turns towards the temporal-sensory as its self-willed goal. And finally, the eternal and the spiritual are knowable not least in religion which according to Grundtvig's understanding comprehends in a single unity the poetic as well as the philosophical modes of knowing the eternal and the spiritual.[39]

Grundtvig thus argues an integral connection between the articulate voice of universal truth he finds in ancient poetry of England and Scandinavia, and that concept of "det levende Ord" ["the living Word"] he developed as a central conviction in his definition of the congregation of God's people, and of the sacramental heart of Christian living, and in his proposals for the proper education of the people.[40]

It was with such theorizing already substantially formulated in published articles that Grundtvig came to esteem *Beowulf* for its underlying religious tone [dets religiøse grundtone].[41] His esteem was not without reserve, however. The poem fell short of perfection, he thought; indeed there was a sense in which, for Grundtvig, the poem could never have been

---

37. ibid., p. 275.
38. ibid., p. 278.
39. Grell, H., *Skaberordet og Billedordet: Studier over Grundtvigs Teologi om Ordet* (Copenhagen, 1980), p. 16.
40. Grundtvig, N.F.S., *Skolen for Livet* (Copenhagen, 1838).
41. *Phenix-Fuglen*, Indledning, p. LII.

perfect. He had already, in 1817, chided the poet (and in fact *all* English poets) for a lack of "Smag" [taste, decorum] in the ordering of the two chief episodes and the various digressive allusions to other stories than that of the main plot. The poem, he says,

> is a spiritual – but artistically not quite ordered – whole; the eye saw aright but the hand was in error; in short, one perceives here, as in Shakespeare and indeed in all English poesy, an aspiration structurally to devise colossal works of art, which can never succeed without what the Angles and English have ever lacked, that is: Taste.[42]

In his judgement upon the structural form of the poem Grundtvig, speaking in this instance with the voice of nineteenth-century classicism, anticipates the complaints of early twentieth-century English critics such as Ker and Chambers. In his insistence, nonetheless, that the two great episodes shadow forth aspects of the same perceived truth and that this truth corresponds with philosophically tenable interpretations of the real human condition,[43] he anticipates J.R.R. Tolkien's great accomplishment, which was to extend to *Beowulf* studies the twentieth-century break with classicism and to clear a way for others to discern more clearly the poem's organizational principles and to reveal their narratorial, aesthetic, and corresponding psychological and philosophical integrity.

It was also a special problem for Grundtvig that the poem mixed fable with history: "For when fable and history are mixed together in the way they are here then inner unity is lost".[44] Because of this shortcoming Grundtvig was never quite able, almost despite himself, to accord the poem the accolade of the label "Epos" [epic]. He was inhibited not solely by nineteenth-century criteria of decorum here, but by a more idiosyncratic philosophy of history. History furnished only one true "Epos" – "The life of Christ on earth, the Word's pilgrimage in the flesh" which "not only mirrors but comprises Truth's struggle and its victory". This distinctive viewpoint, usually diagnosed as the legacy of Grundtvig's engagement with Lutheran doctrine, rationalism and romanticism,[45] has also a certain striking conformity with a medieval and patristic view of what comprises history, with which Bede and his Anglo-Saxon successors could have felt at

---

42. *Danne-Virke* II, p. 271; Haarder, A., "Et gammelt indlæg i en ny debat: Grundtvigs vurdering af Beowulf som kunstværk", in *Grundtvig-Studier* (1965), p. 22; and Haarder 1975 (see note 15), particularly pp. 68 ff.
43. *Danne-Virke* II, p. 279.
44. *Bjowulfs Drape*, Indledning, p. LI.
45. Aarnes, S.Aa. "Omkring Grundtvigs historieskrivning-status og fremtidsperspektiver", in *Grundtvig-Studier* (1965).

home. Certainly it was what gave Grundtvig such excitement in his
encounter with the story and poetry of Cædmon and with the Anglo-Saxon
world view in general: but it separated him from the prevailing consensus
of his age in Denmark and contributed to the antiquarian establishment's
wariness of him as a scholar in England.[46] However, Grundtvig's readiness to find typical truth even amid an absence of verifiable fact enabled
him to assert that:

the poem's definite historical worth lies in the historical vision it articulates; and
here it would make no great difference if the names and doings of the personae had
absolutely no other location in history.[47]

Subsequently Grundtvig was able to propose the identification of Hygelac,
Beowulf's maternal uncle, with Chocilaicus, a figure mentioned by Gregory
of Tours.[48] This remains in fact the only grounding in historical record,
flimsy as it is, found for the poem; nevertheless, the poem now had some
firmer grounding in historic record, and this greatly enhanced its status
within Grundtvig's world-historical thesis, so that he was able to say,
reviewing the work of international editors and translators of *Beowulf* in
1841:

This historical yield is now both so great and so certain that henceforth *Beowulf*,
alongside the *Edda*, must always be placed in the forefront of research in Northern
antiquity and it is in this regard an inestimable treasure.[49]

His perception of the poem as a serious and universal statement about the
human condition, consistent with a Christian philosophy of history if not in
any explicit way a Christian-polemical work, accords in broad terms with
the critical consensus established since Tolkien's lecture to the British

---

46. Toldberg 1947, p. 310.
47. *Danne-Virke* II, p. 280.
48. Høirup and Topsøe-Jensen, vol. xv, fasc. 328, 9-11: historical extracts relating to
    Anglo-Saxon literature copied by Grundtvig from Bouquet's text of Gregory of
    Tours' History of the Franks. The identification is ostentatiously attributed to
    Heinrich Leo [Leo 1839] by Frederik Schaldemose, who derides Grundtvig, without
    naming him, for his attacks on the work of Thorkelin, see Schaldemose, F. (ed.), *Beo-
    Wulf og Scopes Widsið. To angelsaxiske Digte med Oversættelse og oplysende
    Bemærkninger* (Copenhagen, 1847), p. 157. For an account of the rivalry between
    Copenhagen and Kiel which led to an attempt to discredit Grundtvig's title to the
    discovery, see Cooley, F., "Contemporary Reaction to the Identification of Hygelac"
    in Kirby, T.A. and Woolf, H.B. (eds.), *Philologica: The Malone Anniversary Studies*
    (Baltimore, 1949).
49. *Brage og Idun*, vol. 4, pt. 2, p. 510.

Academy in 1936.[50] The differences of both principle and detail between Grundtvig's reading and Tolkien's are considerable, and have perhaps been over-enthusiastically minimized, but in Grundtvig's theories of "Ordet", of universal history, of the nature of epic, we may see what led him to perceive unities in the poem which others until Tolkien missed. We may also see, of course, what may account for others discounting Grundtvig's work over the latter half of the nineteenth century and the first part of the twentieth.

Grundtvig's Christian inspirational reading of ancient Germanic poetry, with its bearing upon his own self-perception as a poet and poet-translator, was a view that increasingly defined his independence from the Romantics whose poetry had once absorbed him and from a Romantic critique of poetry, as well as from much nineteenth-century pagan-affecting German scholarship and its English derivatives alike.

So Flemming Lundgreen-Nielsen while acknowledging that "romantic ideas, patterns and concepts are to be found in ... Grundtvig's writing, right up until his death in 1872" also stresses Grundtvig's rejection of some of the favourite ideas of the romantics such as that of the artist as creator or the primacy placed upon the originality of the artist and the projection of the idiosyncratic self.[51] Thus for Grundtvig the Anglo-Saxon poet Cædmon was, like his own and king David's harp, an "instrument for the holy spirit of the Bible".[52] It was there, and not in any independent imaginative resource of his own, that Cædmon discovered those "exalted images" [Billeder høie] which inform what Grundtvig calls "Billedsprog", image-language. As Helge Grell has observed:

Grundtvig differentiates ... between the imaginative faculty's reception of an imagised vision and its rendering of this vision in image-language; and in the latter connection the poet distinguishes himself from the visionary and the prophet, whose rendering of the imagised vision does not need to be worked out in "poetic artifice". But regardless of whether a person is visionary, prophet or neither of the two, the representations of the imaginative faculty must be embodied in words in order to become comprehensible. And the language which must be taken into usage in order to facilitate imagised comprehension is image-language, the special character of which consists, for Grundtvig, in its managing to speak of spiritual things through images drawn from the world of the temporal-sensory.[53]

50. Tolkien, J.R.R., "Beowulf, the Monsters and the Critics", *Proceedings of the British Academy* vol. 22 (1936), pp. 245-95.
51. Lundgreen-Nielsen, F., "Grundtvig and Romanticism" in Thodberg and Thyssen, pp. 33 and 38-39.
52. *Ragna-Roke*, p. 301ff.
53. Grell, pp. 50-51.

Thus Cædmon images forth Truth as did the inspired poetry of the Psal-mist, concerning the relationship of the Creator and his creatures.[54] The utterances of a poet who had thus inclined his ear to "Ordet" were for Grundtvig "proper poetry" [egentlig poesi] as opposed to "artificial poetry" [kunstpoesi].[55] Conspicuously, he weaves into Cædmon's speech the opening lines of both *Genesis* (Us is riht micel ðæt we rodora weard,/ wereda wuldorcining wordum herigen) and *Beowulf* (Hwæt we Gardena in geardagum/ Þeodcyninga þrym gefrunon):

Jeg drømde, jeg drømde,	*I dreamed, I dreamed*
Kong David jeg saae,	*King David I saw,*
Han gav mig i Hænde	*He gave into my hand*
Sin Harpe saa prud,	*his harp so fair,*
Strængene gyldne	*the golden strings*
Slog jeg med Vælde,	*I struck with might:*
End vel i Midgard	*in Middle-earth still*
Mindes mit Kvad.	*my song is recalled.*
Jeg bøied mit Øre	*I bent my ear*
Til Bogen hin gamle,	*to the ancient book:*
Dens Tale fik Tone,	*its speech received tone*
Og Tungen fik Røst,	*and its tongue received voice.*
Billeder høie	*Pictures sublime*
Blikket opdaget,	*my eye discovered:*
Venlig jeg skiænked	*I cheerfully paid*
Skriften mit Pund.	*to the writing my due.*
Us is riht micel	*"Great duty is ours*
Dhæt ve rodera-veard	*that we heaven's Keeper,*
Vereda vuldor-cining	*Glory-King of hosts,*
Vordum herigen!	*should praise with words".*
Toner som disse	*Tones such as these*
Tør jeg vel haabe,	*I dare well hope*
Sank ei i Tidens	*sank never in time's*
Skummende Bølger.	*foam-bearing waves.*
Jeg Øre og laande	*An ear too I lent*
Til Oldtidens Sagn,	*to antiquity's myth:*
I Krands jeg dem fletted,	*I wove them in garlands,*
Med Konst jeg dem bandt	*I bound them with art*

54. *Ragna-Roke*, pp. 340-42.
55. Grell, pp. 48-51, particularly p. 49.

Hvæt ve gar-dena	*"Lo! we of the Spear-Danes*
In gear-dægum,	*in long-gone days,*
Theod-cyninga	*of the kings of the people,*
Thrym gefrunon	*the glory heard tell".*
Saa jeg paa Harpen	*Thus I to the harp*
Hævede Sandsagn,	*raised up myth that was true,*
Adled til Epos	*ennobled to epic*
Oldtidens Digt,	*the past age's poesy,*
Stridige Stykker	*fragments in strife*
Snild jeg forbandt:	*deft I forged into one:*
Yndig blev Sandhed,	*truth grew to be lovely*
Og Æmter sansynligt.	*and legend seemed true.*

The spirit of Luther responds, acknowledging that:

Da ydmyg dit Øre du bøied	*In humility bent you your ear*
hen Til Ordet, som Engle ophøied,	*to the Word, which angels exalted,*
Som høit over Stjernerne svæver,	*which over the stars on high hovers,*
Som Aander nedstyrter og hæver.	*as spirits swoop low and ascend.*

This estimation of the creative process and its product is not so far (*mutatis mutandis*) from Bede's, in his account of the miracle of Cædmon by which the traditional vernacular and secular *ars poetica* of the English was rehabilitated into Christian usage, in the stable at Whitby.[56] For Bede too this was "proper poetry". Nor is Grundtvig's estimation far from the Anglo-Saxon poet Cynewulf's account of his own experiencing of the poetic creative process. Though Cynewulf's epilogue to *Elene* allows room for the self-projection of the individual poet as the inspired bard in the midst of his experiencing, it makes explicit declaration of an Anglo-Saxon belief that insight into Truth and poetic creativity spring both alike from a gift of "flawless grace" from God, given to the end that divine redemptive wisdom may be relayed through the poet to all humankind.[57] In Cynewulf as in Cædmon, Grundtvig could find an exemplary and historical model of

---

56. Sherley-Price, L. (tr.), *A History of the English Church and People* (Harmondsworth, 1968), book 4, chapter 24. Various extracts from the Alfredian Bede occur among papers in the Grundtvig Arkiv, apparently gathered as preparatory material for a universal history.
57. *Elene*, 1236-51; Krapp, G.P. (ed.), *The Vercelli Book, Anglo-Saxon Poetic Records*, vol. II (New York, 1932), p. 100; Bradley, S.A.J. (tr.), *Anglo-Saxon Poetry. An anthology of Old English poems in prose translation with introduction and headnotes* (London, 1982), p. 195.

that creative relationship between God-Creator and creature-poet about which he developed much of his earlier philosophy of the word and particularly of image-language. For in his evaluation of the Anglo-Saxons as the people providentially appointed to inherit the Gospel from decaying imperial Rome and to become the founders of a new Christianity, carrying it abroad into the North through Boniface and the other English missionaries, the Anglo-Saxon mother-tongue had its symbolic and crucial place. As Grundtvig characteristically saw it, the Anglo-Saxon instinct to articulate the faith in the vernacular language of the northern world, according English exalted status alongside the Latin of the Mediterranean world, was precisely that genius which gave the Word access to work in and through the thinking-habits and the character of the community of the Anglo-Saxon people. In this it was an example to Danish and to every national mother-tongue, that the mother-tongue alone could deliver to its people, and express for its people, the fullest vitality of the living Word.

Grundtvig's philosophical and theological positions naturally underwent considerable evolution over his long life. His earlier conviction had been that there was an efficacious truth resident in ancient writings which, properly delivered to the modern world, could help restore the whole Northern world (with its poles in Denmark and England) to its providentially appointed pre-eminence. But nearly a decade on from the first of his three England-visits which furnished him with so much intellectual fodder, this had yielded to the far profounder implications of his "discovery" of the truth of "det levende Ord" [the living Word] – though he still publicly proclaimed England "the natural Protector of the Northern spirit".[58]

As a further token exploration of what Grundtvig may have found in Anglo-Saxon literature that was peculiarly and immediately congenial to him by virtue of what he brought to it, I turn to his prose compositions, or rather, the prose-poems he developed within his sermon style; here, "the amazing sermon for the 1st Sunday in Advent 1812":

> But is it right
> that you will let the enemy live in the house
> that I have built
> and have even repurchased,
> not with silver or gold
> but with my holy and precious blood.
> Is this the thanks I am to have,
> I who, being in the form of God

---

58. *Mands Minde*, (Within Living Memory), lecture for November 16th; tr. in Jensen and Broadbridge, p. 119, as "*Norse* spirit").

> humbled myself
> and took upon me the form of a servant
> and became obedient unto death,
> even the death on the cross.[59]

upon which Christian Thodberg accurately observes:

The whole sermon is reminiscent of the Roman Church's *improperia* in the Good Friday Liturgy, in which Christ reproachfully holds out His arms to His people. Such consistent use of the first-person in a sermon in the style of a prose-poem is quite unique and extremely convincing evidence of Grundtvig's self-awareness. It is after all Grundtvig himself who says "I" from the pulpit![60]

Compare the Anglo-Saxon poem *Christ III* in the Exeter Book:

I took on your pain so that you might enjoy my kingdom, happy and blessed, and with my death I bought you lasting life, so that you might thereafter dwell in light ... My body, which harmed no one, lay buried in earth, hidden down in the tomb, so that you might be bright above in the skies, ranking among the angels ... Why did you forgo that lustrous life that for love I faithfully purchased with my body? ... Why did you grow so witless that you knew no gratitude to the Ruler for your redemption? ... Why did you of your own free will ... pollute the lodging-place, the cherished house I hallowed within you? ... Why do you more grievously hang me on the cross of your hands than I hung before? for indeed this seems to me more painful ... [61]

The Anglo-Saxon poem, like Grundtvig's sermon, is strikingly reminiscent of the *improperia*, the liturgical meditation upon Christ's reproaches from the cross; as does much other Anglo-Saxon poetry, it stands in a relationship with the liturgy of the Anglo-Saxon Church, and is in fact a remarkable anticipation of later medieval penitential poetry and drama founded upon this theme. The poem, like the sermon, exploits the potency of the I-voice – which has a particular, complex aspect of *mimesis* in circumstances of *oral* delivery (such as Anglo-Saxon poetry shared with homily and sermon) where the speaker assumes the identity of the I-voice. Indeed, the I-voice is a device highly distinctive of Anglo-Saxon poetry, and its usage there furnishes an exemplary model of the diverse control of audience reception of the poetic discourse attainable through the device. As

---

59. Thodberg, C., "Grundtvig the Preacher: The Poet in the Pulpit" in Thodberg and Thyssen, pp. 123-159.
60. ibid., p. 129.
61. *Christ III*, 1460-88; Krapp and Dobbie, pp. 43-44; Bradley 1982, p. 243.

for the rhetorical mode of prose-poetry itself, this again is a distinctive commonplace in Anglo-Saxon literature – for example, in homilies and sermons such as those by Ælfric and Wulfstan, in certain annals of the Anglo-Saxon Chronicles such as the celebration of the Battle of Brunanburh in the annal for 937, in meditational elaborations upon such liturgical items as the Creed, the Lord's Prayer and the Gloria in the Exeter Book, and in English renderings of the psalms. It was in fact part of Grundtvig's Prospectus proposals in 1830 that the Anglo-Saxon homilies should be represented there, in the eighth, ninth and tenth volumes, and to that end he had looked at the contents of London British Library MS Cotton Faustina A ix, a collection of mainly Ælfrician homilies. He wrote:

I am no great admirer of printed sermons, yet I have felt a high degree of interest in looking into this mirror of Anglo-Saxon divinity, not only because Anglo-Saxon preachers were the great instructors of the new Christian world, but also because these homilies are almost the only original performances in Anglo-Saxon prose.[62]

Grundtvig was already well advanced in his own original development of his prose-poems before he made his main encounter with Anglo-Saxon literature, so there is no question, at any rate initially, of influence of Anglo-Saxon models upon his sermon style. I draw attention to the affinities here rather in order to illustrate the measure of fellow-feeling Grundtvig must have experienced in exploring the work of the Anglo-Saxon word-smiths not only on account of their kinship in that northern culture he so highly esteemed but also because they so clearly represented in their themes the assimilation of the earliest catholic Christianity into the northern vernacular; and because their rhetorical forms affirmed his own place in an ancient literary tradition fundamentally and essentially true to the genius of northern languages and northern cultures.

Given the strong sense of quite personal affirmations he was entitled to take from this newly discovered treasury, it would not be surprising to find him, at a practical level, absorbing much of this literature into the very fabric of his own future literary discourses; and it is easier to see, on a more philosophical plane, how he might come to discern a providential aspect in affirmations he found between Anglo-Saxon culture and his own life and times, and so to crystallize his notions of the crucial Anglo-Saxon position in a Christian universal history.

Grundtvig's poetic sensibilities, then, already conditioned by his long study of Icelandic poetry, stood to be deeply confirmed by his encounter

62. *Bibliotheca Anglo-Saxonica. Prospectus*, p. 13.

with the Anglo-Saxon – which shared important distinctive rhetorical features whilst being expressive of a markedly different culture. The full extent of his ultimate indebtedness to this literature, of his remarkable powers of recall and synthesis of it, still remains to be established. Many of the seeming echoes of Anglo-Saxon texts will no doubt prove in the end to belong to that great stock of common symbols and formulae which are the general inheritance of the western literary – and indeed liturgical – tradition. Others will be opportunistic references, to a degree revealing, but slight, as where in one of his reminiscences he speaks of finding "the indifference of the age as stiff-necked as Grendel's Mother, the troll-wife in *Beowulf*.[63] But many will surely prove to witness to Grundtvig's recall of images and idiom from Anglo-Saxon which so deeply impressed his literary, intellectual and spiritual sensibilities in his earlier years, and which he renewed at intervals throughout his life – of which possibility I venture the following exploration.

In the elegiac poem written in his last year of life, *Gammel nok nu er jeg blevet* [Old enough now am I grown], are a metaphor and a collocation of ideas immediately familiar to Anglo-Saxonists:

Gammel nok nu er jeg blevet	*Old enough now am I grown*
mellem vuggen min og grav,	*betwixt my cradle and my grave;*
nu jeg staar ved falderebet	*Now by gunnel-rope I stand,*
ved det store, vilde hav,	*beside the ocean vast and wild*
hvor magneten er Gudsordet,	*where the magnet is God's word*
og Guds aand staar selv ved roret.	*and God's own spirit stands and steers.*
Stormene er frygtelige,	*Fear-instilling are the storms,*
stille staar her mandevid,	*silenced here stands mortal wit;*
nærmest er de dødes rige,	*nearest landfall is the dead's realm,*
nemt det er at stævne did.	*easy it were to steer that way.*
Men o ve for uglesangen!	*But ah! ill-omened is the owl's song:*
Bundløs der er undergangen!	*bottomless the destruction there.*
Vel, paa jordisk vis at regne	*True, to measure earthly-wise,*
langt af led er paradis,	*a long way off lies paradise,*
er os nært dog allevegne,	*yet on all sides it is near us,*
hvor hos ordet er Guds pris,	*where, in the word, is praise of God:*
saa for sjæle-færge-stavnen	*thus before the soul-ship's prow*
brat sig aabner himmel-havnen.	*straight Heaven's haven opens wide.*

63. Grundtvig, N.F.S., "Kirke-Speil eller Udsigt over den christne Menigheds Levnetsløb" (1871) in Johansen and Høirup, p. 103.

Of this poem, Flemming Lundgreen-Nielsen has written:

Even in Grundtvig's last poem from 1872 the romantic features of his imagery and combinations of images form largely unevangelical myth. The recognition "old enough I have become" (*Gammel nok jeg nu er blevet*) is an echo of Norna-Gest's last words in *Olaf Tryggvason's Saga*. The voyage across the stormy sea to destruction or the safe haven, here to the kingdom of the dead or Paradise, is well-known as an aria metaphor in the 18th century. *The Owl's Song* in the kingdom of the dead may be Minerva's, that is human reason's, helplessness, but in Ewald's heroic ballad opera *The Fishermen* (1799) the owl's song with its howling u-vowel expresses exactly in music the danger of shipwreck and destruction. *Soul-Ferry-Prow* is Grundtvig's positive adaptation of Charon's boat. Not until the two final stanzas, where the haven of heaven opens before him, does the poet turn to Christian expressions.[64]

The situation of the poet here – that of a real, old, tired and sometimes troubled man projecting himself once more through the dramatic I-persona of a poem as a way of turning his personal condition and self-analysis into something of universal applicability – compels an Anglo-Saxonist to think of Cynewulf's projection of himself as soul-troubled poet in his epilogue to *Elene*.[65] Here, potentially, was indeed a great revelation to Grundtvig, among the many which the Exeter Book held in store for him. His earlier notion of the venerable ancient Northern bard, founded upon the pagan poets of the Eddic and skaldic traditions of medieval Iceland, had been substantially modified, more fully integrated with Grundtvig's Christian world-historical overview – and in this sense, brought nearer to identity with himself – by his encounter with the English poet of *Beowulf*. But here in Cynewulf was waiting to be discovered an ancient, hitherto hidden, model of the new northern Christian bard, an heir to Cædmon, who found in his poetic narration of Christian legend-truth the divine illumination of his own spiritual darkness in the present world; and who made of his own spiritual troubles the stuff of poetry for the enlightenment of others.

Imagery of the sea as a symbol of this worldly existence through which the corporeally-housed soul must navigate its perilous way is a medieval commonplace in scriptural exegesis, homily and hymn. It has scriptural origins: Ælfric, for example, spells out the metaphor in his sermon for Mid-Lent Sunday[66] on *John 6:9-21* (the sermon refers to the narrative of Christ walking upon the stormy Sea of Galilee to the disciples' imperilled ship)

---

64. Lundgreen-Nielsen, p. 42.
65. Elene, 1236-51; Krapp 1932, p. 100; Bradley 1982, p. 195.
66. Catholic Homilies, series I, xii. The homilies were later edited by Grundtvig's rival Benjamin Thorpe: Thorpe, B. (ed.), *The Sermones Catholici or Homilies of Ælfric*, 2 vols. (London, 1844-46).

and Boniface, Bede, Alcuin and others can all be found using it. The metaphor draws much of its force from further association with Noah's Flood, where the ark prefigures the Church. The poems *Genesis* and *Exodus* in Oxford Bodleian Junius 11 both to varying extents exploit the metaphor, and in this sense it was used by Grundtvig himself in a sermon of 1848 where he envisages the Church and the Danish nation as two ships. The nation, troubled not only by enemies without but by a failure to look for true guidance into its own warm, Godward-seeking heart, is like a ship in distress. But by providential means it has ever kept close course with the great ship of the Church and so it may be hoped that the Lord "that saves his own great ship also saves the little Danish one which for a thousand years has sailed alongside enjoying the calm sea He has created!".[67]

But the collocation of motifs in Grundtvig's lyric is particularly power-fully reminiscent of a similar collocation in a group of Anglo-Saxon sea-faring poems which includes *The Wanderer, The Seafarer, Resignation* (or *The Exile's Prayer*) and the Epilogue to Cynewulf's poem *Christ II (The Ascension)*, all in the Exeter Book,[68] and in the great narrative of the apostle Andrew's sea-crossing to Mermedonia in *Andreas* in the Vercelli Book.[69] In *Andreas* the hired helmsman who safely pilots the ship through a tempest at sea, proves to be Christ himself, disguised. Amidst the tempest he recalls with Andrew the stilling of the tempest on the Sea of Galilee and says:

It often chances that we are scudding over the seaway on a voyage in our ocean steeds ... when a storm comes on ... The ocean-flood's turbulence cannot suddenly impede any man against the consent of the ordaining Lord: he reserves to himself power over life, he who binds the waters and rebukes and checks the brown waves. He must of right have control over men, who with his own hands raised heaven on high and established it ... and filled it with glory ... Therefore the plain truth is manifest, that you are the excellent thane of the King dwelling in majesty, because the sea ... at once acknowledged ... that you possessed the grace of the Holy Spirit ... the menace, the broad-breasted wave, was stilled, and the waters subsided when they understood that God, who by his strong powers founded heaven's splendour, had lapped you about with his safekeeping.[70]

Peril is forgotten as the helmsman tests Andrew's faith by questioning him about the teachings of Jesus, "how he revealed by his words a multitude of wonders" (812). The apostle's recall of the word – the Word incarnate (744-

---

67. Cited in Thyssen, A.P., "Grundtvig's Ideas on the Church and the People 1848-72" in Thodberg and Thyssen 1983, p. 360.
68. Krapp and Dobbie; Bradley 1982.
69. Krapp 1932; Bradley 1982.
70. ibid., 511-536.

60), and the word of Christ's preaching – is abundant and articulate: "Thus all day long Andrew eloquently praised the teaching of the Holy One until suddenly sleep overwhelmed him on the whale-ridden ocean, at the side of the heaven-King" (818-21). Finally, when he awakes safely ashore, Andrew understands:

that you, the Glory of kings, were not far away on the ocean road when I embarked aboard ship, although I could not recognize you on the voyage ... now afterwards I know who was ferrying me across the waters in the wooden ship. He is the Holy Ghost, the Comforter of mankind. Help and mercy are ready there at the hands of that glorious Being, and the power to prevail is granted to everyone who looks to him[71]

Compare Grundtvig's distillation of such ideas into the dense suggestiveness of lyrical statement:

... nu jeg staar ved falderebet/ ved det store, vilde hav, hvor magneten er Gudsordet, /og Guds aand staar selv ved roret./ Stormene er frygtelige, /stille staar her mandevid ... /Vel, paa jordisk vis at regne/ langt af led er paradis, /er os nært dog allevegne, /hvor hos ordet er Guds pris, /saa for sjæle-færge-stavnen /brat sig aabner himmel-havnen.

In *The Wanderer*, a troubled mind affords the weary-minded wayfarer no help against the force of his fortune upon the ocean paths (15-16), nor in *The Seafarer* does the storm-lashed pilgrim have thinking-space left for anything but the hostile seascape and the surging of the waves (44-46): mortal wit stands silenced there too – and so yields place to the passionate and instinctive yearnings of the heart towards its Lord and its true home.

In the Epilogue to *Christ II*, a long poem upon the Ascension, Cynewulf says of this worldly existence:

Nu is þon gelicost swa we on laguflode
ofer cald wæter ceolum liðan
geond sidne sæ, sundhengestum,
flodwudu fergen. Is þæt frecne stream
yða ofermæta þe we her on lacað
geond þas wacan woruld, windge holmas
ofer deop gelad. Wæs se drohtað strong
ærþon we to londe geliden hæfdon
ofer hreone hrycg. Þa us help bicwom,
þæt us to hælo hyþe gelædde,

71. ibid., 898-909; Bradley 1982, pp. 124-25, 1334.

godes gæstsunu, ond us giefe sealde
þæt we oncnawan magun ofer ceoles bord
hwær we sælan sceolon sundhengestas,
ealde yðmearas, ancrum fæste.
Utan us to þære hyðe hyht staþelian,
ða us gerymde rodera waldend,
halge on heahþu, þa he on heofonum astag.[72]

[Now it is very much like this, as though upon the water-flood we were sailing in
keels across the chill water, navigating flood-timbers, ocean-steeds over the wide sea
The perilous tide is beyond measure in its waves on which we toss here through this
frail world, windy the waters across the deep seaway. Dire would have been our
plight before we had sailed to a landfall over its rough ridge. Then help came to us
which led us to safety in haven – God's Spirit-Son – and granted us grace that we
might know where we should secure our ocean-steeds, our old wave-horses, fast
with anchors, over the ship's side. Let us found our hope upon that haven which the
ruler of the skies, the holy one in the heights, opened up for us when he ascended
into heaven].

Again, the Anglo-Saxon may read like a great poetic gloss upon Grundtvig's terser lyric statement that " ... saa for sjæle-færge-stavnen /brat sig
aabner himmel-havnen".

Finally, in *Resignation* is to be found what is, in its sentiment, evolution
of thought, and imagery, virtually an Anglo-Saxon alternative poetic
conception of Grundtvig's moving contemplation of mortality:

Forstond þu mec ond gestyr him, þonne storm cyme
minum gæste ongegn; geoca þonne,
mihtig dryhten, minre sawle,
gefreoþa hyre ond gefeorma hy, fæder moncynnes,
hædre gehogode, hæl, ece god,
meotod meahtum swiþ. Min is nu þa
sefa synnum fah, ond ic ymb sawle eom
feam siþum forht, þeah þu me fela sealde
arna on þisse eorþan. Þe sie ealles þonc
meorda ond miltsa, þara þu me sealdest.
No ðæs earninga ænige wæron mid;
hwæþre ic me ealles þæs ellen wylle
habban ond hlyhhan ond me hyhtan to,
frætwian mec on ferðweg ond fundian
sylf to þam siþe þe ic asettan sceal,

72. *Christ II*, 850-66; Krapp and Dobbie, pp. 26-27.

gæst gearwian, ond me þæt eal for gode þolian
bliþe mode, nu ic gebunden eom
fæste in minum ferþe.[73]

[Stand by me and when the storm closes in upon my spirit, steer it; then, mighty
Lord, succour my soul, preserve it and sustain it, Father of mankind, and save it as
being intended for celestial light, eternal God, ordainer strong in might; for now my
spirit is stained with sins and I am sometimes afraid for my soul, though you have
granted me many mercies in this world. Thanks be to you for all the bounties and
favours which you have granted me. Not any of them were through my merit; but
from all this I will take courage to myself and rejoice and rest my hope in and array
myself for the spirit-road and address myself to that journey which I needs must
travel and make ready my soul and suffer all this for God in cheerful mood, now
that I am firmly chastened in my spirit].

This then is the material through which the spiritual imagination and the
creative insight of Grundtvig was singularly well-prepared to roam as he
read and reread the poetry of the Anglo-Saxons. Has he forgotten it all by
1872, substituting for it classical allusion and reference to operas and arias
of the previous century: or has it been nurtured over a lifetime, to surface
with a self-recommending aptness in the last poem he wrote? There is
surely much here still to be searched out – a seam of Grundtvigian creative
response to Anglo-Saxon poetry hitherto little broached.

Grundtvig's was a mind in some respects anomalous, idiosyncratic in its
own nineteenth-century context, yet at home – and not wholly fortuitously
so – in the early medieval world of Christian literature. He believed in the
power of poetry to "conjure up an image of the indivisible word [Christ],
whose metaphor the word originally is".[74] He "lived" this poetic encounter and, in a sense by no means fanciful, experienced Anglo-Saxon poetry
as it was composed to be experienced – as a religious experience which
would truly feed the religious and spiritual life. If such subjective enthusiasm, such personalization of scholarship, was distasteful to the English antiquarian establishment, he was nonetheless one of the most dynamic respon-
dents of any time to Anglo-Saxon culture viewed in historical retrospect, a
remarkable phenomenon in nineteenth-century European culture, drawing
upon a genuine insight into the Anglo-Saxon literary mentality. And in the
course of this complex symbiotic relationship with the records of antiquity,
a fair share of the insights Grundtvig delivered maintain their absolute

73. *Resignation*, 59-76; Krapp and Dobbie, p. 217.
74. Cited Thodberg, p. 125, from Grundtvig Arkiv, Fasc. 72 [ca. 1813] on sermons as a
    genre.

value to the generations of Anglo-Saxonists who follow after him. He was a substantial contributor to Anglo-Saxon scholarship: and yet not primarily a scholar adding objectively to the store of knowledge and understanding, but rather a seeker after truth, who saw ancient poetry not as a matter of dead antiquity but as a manifestation of the living word which was the same living word as lay upon his own lips, who followed what seemed to him trails of revelation towards his own living creed, to be lived out in shaping his own world to conform with the models of truth which he found abiding from ancient times. The truth, however clad in cherished forms of northern antiquity, however widely and diversely tracked beyond the confines of literary form into the realms of education, politics, international affairs or any of the other great issues that preoccupied him over his long life, was a Christian truth of long ancestry in the annals of European culture. And in so far as the historical and spiritual heritage of this truth is not only common to European peoples since divided by politics and religion, but even extends its community from West to East, it comprises an important focus for the ideal of a new order which could far outstretch the boundaries of the North.

The course of Anglo-Saxon studies in the nineteenth and early twentieth centuries would surely have gone differently if Grundtvig had been able to command greater international attention for his work and insights. Not all of his ideas proved to have a lengthy life; others have only relatively recently come into their own, albeit modified into contemporary terminology and categories. One of the impediments was, ironically, that very Danish language of which he was so zealous a proponent, because in it was embodied the essence of that ancient and modern, domestic and international, secular and spiritual Danishness he celebrated and trusted, and to which he committed his life's work. As many have observed, he does not easily translate, either as poet or as prose-writer. And there have been few like Thorpe, who would trouble themselves to seek out the Danes and Danish in their homeland, to learn what they had to say. In the context of late-twentieth-century Europeanism the problem has presented itself even more acutely and with a relevance touching more peoples than the Danes alone; though it fell to the Danes in the year of Europe to utter the democratic No – Denmark rejected the Maastricht Treaty by referendum in 1992 – which historically registered, whatever its ultimate practical efficacy, a sentiment expressed by Grundtvig on behalf of any individual nation-state concerned for its identity within a wider family and working partnership of nation-states: "My first wish is that we should have the courage to be ourselves and show ourselves for what we are".

The lecture cited here, in which Grundtvig is speaking of his visit to England, is worth quoting more fully as an example of the way in which

Grundtvig's cultural-historical convictions, founded at least in part upon his encounter with the ancient and modern Anglo-Saxons, fed directly into Danish political and economic contexts:

It was a trip I shall never forget. Whether or not as a result I have been stricken with what is known as "Anglo-mania" ... I shall endeavour to show you that one does not necessarily have to be mad to have an unquestionably historical preference (among all the great powers) for England ... To be honest I prefer the small nations, and incomparably most of all our little Fatherland. But to confess to such an unquestionably historical partiality towards one's own is also something that the Danish people need to learn from the Englishman, who would unhesitatingly assure us, soberly and seriously, that even if England could not survive unless the rest of the world perished, he would still vote for old England ... You see, gentlemen, in every nation this must be the way of thinking and self-reliance of the citizens that will make them lead any life worth talking about; and it is a lamentable state of affairs when, as is still the custom with us, we cherish that basic principle at heart, but for fear of the Latins, the Germans and the moralists, we dare not stand up for it, we hide our unquestionable partiality towards our Fatherland, our mother tongue, and all that belongs to them as though it were a crime, and we waste our energy on an inevitably stiff, torpid and unsuccessful copy of something foreign that we do not love but often actually hate. However, I point this out only in order to draw your attention to the fact that I have in no way gone so mad on England that I would prefer England to Denmark, or wish my Fatherland to be in any way anglicized, but that my first wish is that we should have the courage to be ourselves and show ourselves for what we are, and then to realize that of all the great powers England is the one, both spiritually and temporally, to whom we wish all the good fortune that can be consistent with the freedom of Greece and Scandinavia, and the one which we must compete with to the best of our ability by removing all the bounds that impede or encumber our living industry, and above all by considering what is useful and to our lasting honour.[75]

Inevitably subject to the stigmatisms of his age and yet in various respects a visionary speaking for an awareness of cultural-historical foundations in the forging of peaceable supranational alliances among the European nation-states, Grundtvig deserves to remain accessible to those concerned with the diverse cultural roots of the new Europe.

75. *Mands Minde*, (Within Living Memory), Jensen and Broadbridge, pp. 104-105.

Grundtvig, Dante, Milton, and the Problem of European Continuity

By Jakob L. Balling

In this essay I propose to take a look – from one rather limited angle, it must be admitted – at the question of Grundtvig's place in European tradition.

Grundtvig was the quintessential Dane, so that it might be said that any questions pertaining to his relation to European tradition are of purely secondary interest.

At a first glance, this objection seems not entirely unfounded. Grundtvig certainly is difficult to imagine as anything other than Danish. Not only is his best poetry virtually untranslateable (that, incidentally, constitutes one of my more painful problems in what follows, since my approach to Grundtvig and European tradition is largely through his poetry). Not only that, but there indubitably is more than a streak of cultural chauvinism in his thinking and writing and, more seriously for my present purpose, a distinct aversion towards some of the main commonplaces of classical humanism. Educational key-words of Grundtvig's like "The Black School", "The School for Death" etc. are, to say the least, pointers in that direction, and they must be understood in a religious and political as well as in a cultural sense and context. Grundtvig's aggressively Protestant denunciation of "the lies of Popes and the dreams of monks" reinforces and is reinforced by his ultra-Danish or ultra-Nordic loathing of things German and – beyond that – things French, Italian, in a word: Latin. A good case could indeed be made for interpreting Grundtvig's infatuation with things English as one aspect of this attitude!

All the same, this picture is altogether too simplistic. Without dwelling on the rather endearing trait that the fierce anti-Latinist was in fact an accomplished Latinist, it must, in the first place, be remembered that the reaction against classical humanism and against its image of man is itself a vital element in European tradition at least from the latter half of the eighteenth century onwards. The same goes for cultural nationalism – which is, as a matter of fact, a thoroughly international phenomenon!

Secondly, and more importantly, Grundtvig's struggle against the Latin strain in European tradition is, in a very real sense, also a struggle *for* other strains in the same tradition, namely the pre-philosophic Greek one and, above all, the Judaeo-Christian one which, in Grundtvig's view, had been damaged by its alliance with Rome and everything Rome stood for, and which the Nordic peoples were called to set free and to let shine in its ancient glory.

Both these considerations help us understand an important fact about Grundtvig. He was no admirer of the European humanist tradition as commonly understood and practised by the learned establishment, but he was no anti-European either. He was a Danish European with some clear ideas of what to accept and what to reject in a broadly defined common heritage. And for my present purposes it is important to add that it wasn't a matter of clear ideas entirely. There are elements in Grundtvig's "Europeanism" which depended more on unconscious or half-conscious than on fully conscious reception.

In what follows, I propose to develop some of the implications of these loosely formulated points insofar as they can be elucidated by a look at some themes and treatments in Grundtvig's poetical work. These are themes which he has in common with the classic "theological" poets, Dante and Milton – both of them, incidentally, faithful followers of Vergil (whom Grundtvig detested) and genuine exponents of mainstream European humanism.

My point of departure lies in some conclusions I drew from my studies in Dante and Milton in their capacity as "theological" poets, that is to say, as poets who set themselves the task of formulating a rationally coherent view of the Christian message in all its dimensions, but doing it in the poetic mode, as poets, using the tools of their craft, the metaphorical interplay of meanings, the epic narrative, and the dramatic confrontation.[1] But before I try to set out these conclusions with a view to using them in my reading of Grundtvig, I have to interpose a word or two on the meaning implied when I connect Grundtvig with Dante and Milton.

Grundtvig does not seem to have possessed any intimate knowledge of the two earlier poets. He must have known Milton somewhat better than he knew Dante; there are excerpts from *Paradise Lost* in the Grundtvig Archives and a short critique of the poem in an article on *Beowulf* from 1817. But none of this contains proof of any deeper interest or understanding.

This means that the narrower concept of tradition, which presupposes a demonstrable genetic link, an "influence" from one poet on another, is inapplicable to our present purposes. If we use the term "tradition" and say that Grundtvig "stands" in the tradition of the great theological poets, the term must be more broadly and loosely defined. But the justification for

---

1.   Jakob Balling, *Poeterne som Kirkelærere* (Copenhagen, 1983).

such an expression can of course only be assessed in the light of what follows.

Now, briefly and summarily presented, my conclusions from Dante and Milton look like this:

In the first place: In *Paradise Lost* as well as in the *Divina Commedia* the speaker's voice is a prophetic voice. Its utterances are divinely authorised, the bearer of the voice is sent to pronounce judgment, to promise salvation, to teach the way of the world, and of God.

Secondly: This task entails an obligation to make clear what – in Goethe's words – "holds the world together". To put it another way, the obligation to make clear the shape of history and of the cosmos. In both the great poems the whole of history is presented in a series of narratives, long or episodic, as well as in a series of dramatically shaped confrontations and conflicts. In both poems the course of history is interpreted by means of a guiding principle which – to put it briefly – could be described as the Augustinian concept of love and of order. This same principle holds good for the cosmic order set forth – in widely different ways – by the two prophetic voices.

Thirdly: In accordance with the prophetic dignity of the poet's voice and with the task of universal interpreter entrusted to him, both poems assume the shape of what I venture to call a modernized Scripture. By this concept, which, incidentally, can be seen hinted at in Dante's *Epistle xiii* to Can Grande della Scala, I try to express not only the combination just mentioned (the combination of prophetic inspiration and universal exposition and interpretation) but also the calculated effort which is common to both poets of supplementing the "old" Scripture by putting in what it omits, by straightening out and rationalizing its lines of thought, by commenting on it, and by prolonging its course of narrative down to the poet's own time.

Fourthly: One of the things which constitute the calculated novelty of the "modernized Scripture" is the way in which the historical and the cosmic strands in the exposition are mutually interwoven. The combination, the "poetic universe", is worked out as a vast network of narrative, of metaphorical associations, and of dramatic confrontations, whereby one realm of experience (history) is seen to "comment upon" and deepen the understanding of the other (the cosmic order) and *vice versa*. Most importantly, however, the ultimate point of these interrelated structures is to be found in the fact that the meaning and the "drift" of both realms are concentrated in one person's experience. Both "orders" as well as their combination, their mutual commentary, are mirrored and internalized in Dante's pilgrim and Milton's Adam respectively.

Finally: From the "modernized Scripture", organized as a "poetic universe", springs an inherent appeal. The appeal is not an outwardly-added "moral" but that which by means of metaphor, narrative action, and dramatic confrontation is, as it were, spoken by the order of things to persons in lack of order, the protagonists, the poet, and the reader.

Taken as a whole, these fundamental common characteristics can be said to coincide in one common intention, that of giving expression to the Christian postulates concerning order – the creation, the breakdown, and the restoration of order. But although this common intention is pursued by means of analogous patterns of thought, there are highly significant differences between the ways in which the poets use the common patterns. That becomes clear, above all, in the difference between the Dantesque and the Miltonic interplay of cosmos and history. Milton's asymmetric conglomerate of worlds corresponds to his clash of personal wills, forcefully acting in conflict; and this complex is tellingly different from Dante's interplay of cosmic symmetry with a historical action conceived in monistic terms.

I would like to let these conclusions serve as a point of departure for a further consideration of Grundtvig. In what follows, I shall take a look at some characteristic instances of the way in which themes and patterns closely resembling Dante's and Milton's appear, function, and are transformed under the hands of Grundtvig in his poem from 1824, *Nyaars-Morgen* ("New Year's Morning").[2] This longish work (it consists of 312 eleven-line stanzas) occupies a central place in Grundtvig's development as a poet. It constitutes one of the series of crucial break-throughs or turning points so typical of his life and thought. Grundtvig was not one of nature's once-born sons, cruising serenely through life, calmly unfolding his essence through a straight line of unambiguously interrelated experiences. The terms that come to mind are, rather, sudden conversions, abrupt discoveries, thunderbolts from heaven, pitch-black nights and glorious mornings.

Now, such a morning is celebrated in *Nyaars-Morgen*. The poet finds himself suddenly standing in the light of day after a long and laborious night beset with worries and uncertain gropings after truth and community with fellow-men. Now he sees clearly everything he needs to see, and joyfully acknowledges a duty to proclaim his vision to "brothers in the North".

Three things have to be noted about this general character of the poem. The vision is a vision of national brotherhood in past, present, and future.

---

2. "Nyaars-Morgen" in N.F.S. Grundtvig's *Udvalgte Skrifter*, ed. Holger Begtrup, vol. 4 (Copenhagen, 1906), pp. 238-343.

It is a vision of living community with the people's past. And it is a vision of personal destiny, realized through a series of discoveries of religion, history, and community, made in the course of the poet's life until now and pointing the way to a prophetic duty.

All these aspects of the poem's general structure and trend stand in an interesting relation, formally and materially, to fundamental structures and trends in the great theological epics. That can be shown by way of a closer reading of two central passages to which I shall return in a moment, but also in numerous details scattered throughout the work. One such detail could very justifiably be called common to all poetry, but it certainly is an important feature in Dante and Milton, and above all, it constitutes an essential vehicle for their incorporation of history, sacred and profane, into the action of the moment. I refer to the "sign character" of things and events, their "polysemia" or multiple meaning. Things and events are real and unambiguous enough in themselves and in immediate encounter, but "in" them, "behind" them, "beneath" them a world of collateral meanings are hidden, until revealed by the poet-prophet's word as in a deeper sense determining their nature. When Milton uses the leaf-covered brooks of present-day Vallombrosa as well as the Exodus events by the Red Sea in his description of the fallen angels, lying prostrate in the hellish lake, one of the effects of this composite picture lies in the stimulation of the reader's awareness of the depths beneath everyday things, the numinous presence in them of history, of the divine counsel for the course of human events. Precisely this is what Grundtvig does when, speaking of the native landscape, he says:

Er Øen i Vove, / Med Fjorden fra Hav, / Med maigrønne Skove, / og Fædrenes Grav, / For Eder ei Andet, / End Støv-Øiet seer: / En Tue paa Vandet / Af Kalk og af Leer, / Ei Tegn paa det Kjære, / I Barmen vi bære: / Bøg-Holmen i Fædrenes Blod; / Da sang jeg forgjæves ...

("This island in the sea, this fiord, these may-green woods with the graves of ancestors – if that is nothing to you except what meets the mortal eye, if it is only a hillock on the water, of chalk and of clay, if it is not a sign of dear things in our bosoms: an island of beech-trees in the blood of the fathers, then I have sung in vain ...").[3]

What is indicated in a sketchy form in details like this one is, as I suggested a moment ago, unfolded and developed in two long sequences, centrally placed in the poem. They merit a closer look, because they bring

---

3.   Stanzas 261-262.

us considerably closer to specifically Dantesque and Miltonic concerns and formulations.

The first passage constitutes what we may call the Hadding episode.[4] Looking back at his struggle to revivify national history and make it meaningful to his fellow countrymen, the poet gives expression to his experience by means of a modified retelling in the first person singular of the ancient tale – transmitted around the year 1200 by Saxo Grammaticus in his *Gesta Danorum* – of King Hadding's descent to the underworld (We may note here the analogy to Dante's use of the Sixth *Aeneid*!). The poet has met a woman with fresh flowers at her bosom in spite of the season being midwinter. She has led him down under the earth, where he has seen the ancient Danish heroes; where the woman has shown him the wall that divides the land of the dead from that of the living; and where she has given him the sign of the crossing of the wall: she takes a cock, wrings its neck, throws its head over the wall – and the cock crows on the other side. It becomes clear that the woman is our mother, Denmark herself, and that the subterranean experience must lead the poet to an appeal to his countrymen. Descent, passing over the wall from death to life, reascent into the light, all this is seen as the experience that makes a true community with fellow men possible; and the bearer of the experience, the prophetic voice of the poet, is the chosen instrument of proclamation and appeal to fellows and brethren. Such is, in summary, the story and its implications, taken in itself. But in order to be understood in its full significance, it must be read in concert with a number of other passages in which the ideas of descent, of passing through death to life, of reascent, of darkness and light, night and morning, doubt and certainty, fear and confidence are employed in ever-varying contexts. It is eminently characteristic that not only are these pairings of notions and words, these dual concepts, used both of the cock which the poet sees, and of the poet in his capacity as delver into the past and as translator and historian, and of Christ, the dead and risen Lord, but the uses are allowed to interpenetrate each other. The poet calls himself the cock whose head is cut off but who crows all the same, and the reawakening of the historical sense, the sense of a living community with the past, the discovery of the gold under the black earth, is likened to the resurrection of Christ.

When, in addition to this whole network of interconnected meanings, it is remembered that past experiences of discovery or awakening must be seen in the light of the present great morning, it becomes amply clear that the Hadding episode is a key passage, perhaps in a way the central myth

4.   Stanzas 111-139, 144, 159-160, 167-168.

of the poem. Its utterances are endowed with interpretative power for the message of the poem as a whole.

It may safely be said that all this reminds the Dante-reader of something. What goes on in the Hadding episode is to a large extent the same thing as what happens in the *Comedy* of Dante. There – as here – we witness the protagonist-poet's struggle for identity, for making sense of his life, past and present, to himself and to others. There – as well as here – this struggle takes the shape of a movement, with a mentor, down behind and beneath the world as it looks on the surface and in the fleeting moment; down to a confrontation with and an appropriation and internalization of history; and a corresponding movement across and upwards to life and light. No less important, the outcome of the struggle is shown to be of importance to the people through the prophetic appeal that springs from the experience and finds expression in words of judgment and of promise from the mouth of the poet. Lastly, here – as well as there – these movements stand, as it were, in a relationship of interpenetration with the history of Christ Himself, through death to life.

I now turn to a consideration of my other "key episode", that of "The Mermaid of the North".[5]

The poet lets it shine through that this woman is identical with the one in the Hadding episode. But now it is her history we are being told. She is, we hear, a female descendant of Noah, who from her place of origin in the east has ventured out on the long voyage to the northern seas. There, she has made herself a new home on the green islands which are our home too. In point of fact, she is Denmark, our mother herself, whose longing for the land of the living has driven her out on the journey and who knows that her island is destined to last until the Lord shall come and open the way.

Looking at this somewhat strange, but in Danish very impressive sequence of stanzas, the first thing we may note is that here again dimensions of depth in ordinary landscapes are subtly indicated. That connects the passage with other passages, for instance the Hadding episode.

But apart from that, the reflection that is given poetic expression here is not the same as the one we met in the previous text. There the centre, so to speak, was occupied by the suffering and acting poet's "I" – by him and by what came to him and happened to him, and through him to the people, by means of the visions he received in the depths of the earth, in the abyss of history, and brought back to the light of day. Here, something outside him is in focus, namely Denmark and the meaning of Denmark in a great, divinely ordained whole.

5. Stanzas 238-258, 311.

The poetic device Grundtvig makes use of in order to clarify this meaning and this coherent whole reminds us strikingly of something we know from the two classic poets, namely the prolonging and filling out of sacred history. When Dante and Milton give their kerygmatic narrative the shape of what I have tentatively called a reformulated or modernized Scripture, one of the means they use is precisely this prolonging the action of the "old" Bible and the filling out of its lacunae. That, to take an example, is what happens when Dante, in the last canto of the *Inferno*, lets Vergil tell what nobody has told before of the fall of Satan. We are given to understand that when the rebellious angel hit our earth in the middle of the southern hemisphere and bored his way down to the centre, there to lead his frozen existence, the earth-masses that he pressed up in the process were used by the Creator in the infinite inventiveness of His love in order to form the mountain of Paradise for the first human couple, and later on, when man had fallen and the great redemptive events had taken place, used again by Him for the purification of sinful souls. As I said, when Dante lets Vergil tell this story and so gives poetic expression to a theological reflection on the coherence of God's creative and redemptive action in history and nature, then he uses the same device as we have just seen used by Grundtvig. The same thing happens when Milton in Book Eleven of *Paradise Lost* lets Michael the Archangel narrate the vicissitudes of the Garden during and after the Flood:

...Then shall this Mount / of Paradise by might of Waves be moovd / Out of his place, pushd by the horned floud, / With all his verdure spoil'd, and Trees adrift / Down the great River to the op'ning Gulf, / And there take root an Iland salt and bare, / the haunt of Seales and Orcs, and Sea-mews clang

– and in this way lets him convey a reflection on true worship:

To teach thee that God attributes to place / No sanctitie, if none be thither brought / By Men who there frequent, or therein dwell.

That is precisely how the poet of *Nyaars-Morgen* works when he tells his tale of the Mermaid as Noah's "daughter" who leaves her home in the east, flies westwards and northwards and finds her new home on Zealand. That, evidently, is a way of making it clear that Denmark and Danish history have a meaning that connects them with sacred history and makes them a part of it. Behind the woods and the waves, the chalk and the clay of Denmark lies an abyss of divine counsel, the counsel which in the "old" Bible has governed the movement from Noah to Israel and which in the "new" one – the one that the poet has been inspired to write – governs the movement from Noah to Denmark – "Historiens Palæstina", "the Palestine of history", as Grundtvig rather quaintly but not senselessly calls it in his preface to the poem.

Within this framework of "biblical reformulation" the poet gives poetic expression to several further reflections. I will briefly mention two. One of them we know from the Hadding episode: the connection between Danishness and Christian salvation. The other concerns the nexus between, on one side, the complex of sacred history and Danish history and, on the other side, the doctrine of First and Last Things. This trait finds its incomparably finest expression outside the Mermaid episode, although in explicit relationship with it, namely in the four last stanzas of the entire poem. Here the poet makes clearer than anywhere else what is in the last resort meant by the words "New Year's Morning" in the title. That it is morning now for the poet after his long night – that is a matter of experience for the poet and the people who become themselves in the course of the poem. But this experience, according to the implied message of the last four stanzas, is incomplete if it does not encompass the complementary knowledge that, in a sense, night and winter is there yet, that they will become denser and colder, and that the contemporary word and concept "morning" can only be said and thought in its deepest significance because, after the worst and last of all winter nights, a great morning will dawn, without any subsequent night. That, we are told – and here we discern an immensely apposite reference to the story of the Mermaid – is "what stood before your eyes when you saw the Ark floating by the roots of the beech-trees". The consciousness that the poet and his people have of themselves as historical beings is a consciousness of First and Last Things. Winter will come (and this great winter is emblematically signified by an everyday thing: the sleighs that every Northerner knows) but the singing, and the blessing it conveys, will not cease. The last lines of the poem run like this:

Mens Markerne bølge / Med staaende Korn, / Mens Fuglene følge / Det gamle Skov-Horn, / Mens Krøniken rækkes / og tækkes de Smaa, / Om Dagen end stækkes, / Og Slæderne gaae, / Syng lavt over Skoven, / Syng høit over Voven: / Guds Fred over Folket i Nord!!

In rather painful English prose:

While the fields are waving with standing corn; while the birds follow the old wood-horn; while the chronicle is given to the small ones and gives them joy; even if day grows shorter; even if the sleighs shall run; sing lowly over the wood; sing highly over the wave: the peace of God be with the people of the North!

I find that the last stanzas are one of the places where we come close to an insight into the opportunities inherent in "poetic theology" as compared to those which ordinary theological discourse offers.

Be that as it may, the foregoing observations will, I hope, have shown that the Grundtvig we meet in *Nyaars-Morgen* may not unmeaningfully be said to "stand" in the tradition of Dante and Milton. This confirms a preconception of mine, namely that when speaking of literary works from within one and the same civilizational context, one is entitled to give the concept of tradition a wider definition than the one which operates with genetic links in the strict sense. We are usefully reminded of the fact that when an inmate of Old Europe like Grundtvig – and he certainly was that, beside other things – takes it upon himself to render account of his innermost being, defined as a result of a series of historical experiences, then the outcome of his self-examination is likely to resemble the accounts rendered by people like Dante and Milton.

Nevertheless, when all that is said and done, it remains to be noted that Grundtvig "stands" in the tradition in his own way, fashioned by his own genius and the mood and circumstances of his time.

That is what can be meant by speaking of "modernity" as well as "tradition" in connection with our poem. Here as always, modernity presupposes tradition; modernity is defined by tradition. But tradition conversely presupposes modernity, in the sense that reception of something that is handed down is unthinkable without the transforming pressures that spring from a situation open to the future: pressures of an individual, a social or a cultural nature. Any other reception would be a reception of a dead tradition, as it is called – I do not think that is a meaningful term at all!

That is by the way. What concerns us here is the question of Grundtvig's *way* of "standing" in the tradition, as an individual and as some sort of member of the Romantic movement.

It is of course a question that cannot be treated in anything like completeness here. But I may be allowed some tentative remarks of a preliminary nature:

Coming from the study of Dante and of Milton I am struck by four things in *Nyaars-Morgen*.

In the first place: the ambiguous and dreamlike quality of the whole. This could only be demonstrated by lengthy analyses of individual texts; for my present purposes I only need to state it as a general impression. Where the classic theological poets are difficult in a clear and clean-cut manner, Grundtvig is difficult in manner as well as in substance. What he has to say cannot apparently be said in clear and well-ordered sequences of words and ideas, even if – as is generally the case – the individual words and ideas are bathed in freshness, clarity and light. What he means – and that includes the meanings I have tried to work out in the foregoing parts of this essay – must be wrested from a context that does not encourage the reader to draw unambiguous conclusions. I mention this impression in the first place because this is something that distinctly connects Grundtvig with his time and with his fellow-Romantics, but chiefly because it is an important fact to remember when considering each of the other three characteristics on my summary list.

The first of these has to do with the kind of history to which the poem and its "I" relate. As I have tried to show, there is a community of structure and of function in the three histories, Dante's, Milton's, and Grundtvig's, insofar as they are histories of pristine purity, of fall, and of restoration; insofar as images of descent etc. recur in them; and insofar as they are seen as vitally necessary for the acquisition of identity, of self-knowledge, and of courage. But much more than is the case in the great predecessors, Grundtvig's history is a national history. Not only is "profane" world-history conspicuous by its absence, but sacred history itself is much less in evidence than could be expected, considering the distinctly Christian character of the poet's attitude towards life and the place that Christian insights occupy in the poem as a whole (this, incidentally, is of course something to which a complete treatment of the work would have to pay much more attention than I have done).

This trait must, I believe, have a great deal to do with a common feature in post-Reformation and specifically Romantic culture: a tendency towards dissolution of traditional ideas about universal history as a common heritage of thinking men; and, perhaps, an incipient tendency towards attributing some kind of salvific quality to national history. In Grundtvig's case a special emphasis must perhaps be laid on his hostile attitude towards Classical culture as commonly understood. There indubitably is an immense distance between Dante and Grundtvig on this count, but certainly also between Grundtvig and Milton, although the classicism of the latter is outwardly much less conspicuous than that of Dante. This movement "from" Dante "via" Milton "to" Grundtvig must be kept in mind when we go on to my two final points.

The third point concerns the relation to the cosmic order, or rather, the absence of such a relation in our poem. This certainly is the dog that did not bark in the night before New Year's morning, or for that matter on that morning itself, and that is a circumstance of prime significance for assessing the "modernity" of the poem. If anything mattered in the *Commedia* and in *Paradise Lost*, this relation did. Notwithstanding the differences to which I alluded earlier regarding the structure of the cosmos, the protagonists in both poems define themselves and their history in relation to a coherent cosmic order. Their acquisition of an identity pleasing to God is understood as a grateful insertion into and conformation with that order, and their loss of such a status is likewise understood as a contribution to the breaking down or the pulling askew of cosmic order. The history which they encounter and internalize is interpreted by means of the cosmic order, and *vice versa*. Not so in *Nyaars-Morgen*. This is a poem without an image of the world. It most certainly is not a poem without sharply sensed and precisely communicated things and landscapes, but their mutual coherence *as* things and landscapes is something that does not interest it at all. The contrast to Dante is indeed the sharpest imaginable. With very few – very calculated – exceptions, exact questions as to place and time and movement and relation are questions that are happily welcomed and carefully answered in the *Comedy*, in spite of, or perhaps because of the fact that Dante fully as much as Grundtvig wanted to give expression to interior experiences, processes in the soul. Dante, evidently, needed the external coherence, the concrete "thus-and-not-otherwise"ness of the world in order to talk of the soul at all. Not so in Grundtvig's poem, where such questions are largely meaningless. Why? Well, that is one of the big questions. It does not allow of one single answer, in view of the trivial but crucial fact that people are different and don't absolutely need the movement of history to provide them with different concerns. But one of the possible answers surely must be sought in the movement of history, in the sense that in the course of the interval between Dante and Grundtvig something demonstrably has happened to many people's experience of what the world looks like and what, if anything, holds it together. This goes for the period between Milton and Grundtvig also, in spite of the significant fact that – as mentioned before – Milton differs from Dante by the asymmetrical character of his world and the brooding presence in it of a Chaos unknown to Dante.

My fourth and final point is this: The relationship between the "I" of the poem and the brothers and fellows whom he wishes to serve by his experiences and insights is, to say the least, problematic, or rather, unredeemed and unfulfilled. Few things impressed me more when I came to *Nyaars-Morgen* from the two earlier poems than the loneliness of its protagonist. The things that make this impression less than downright freezing are – beside and beyond the splendour of Grundtvig's verses in general – the enthusiasm and joy of the lonely discoverer of hidden things himself, and perhaps most of all the warmth and the freshness of the non-human environment of water and of cornfields, of green beech-trees and cliffs of chalk, the haunting loveliness of the landscapes "Med blommede Enge / Til Sangfugle-Senge, / Med Bælte, med Kridt og med Rav" ("With blooming meadows, beds for singing-birds, with belts, with chalk, and with amber") – the beauty of things, the things of beauty which represent, as it were, the poet's innermost and ultimate acceptance of himself and of his world, his confidence that it can be lived in and lived with.

Nevertheless, none of this affects the truth of the fact that the human environment is absent in any other than a purely symbolic or emblematic sense. Less solemnly expressed: it is rather an anaemic affair on the whole. Correspondingly, in sharp contradistinction to what is the case with the protagonists of Milton's and above all of Dante's poem, the "I" of *Nyaars-Morgen* is not a person who enters a human environment and undergoes changes, thereby becoming "another" person. What we find here is rather a – I take the expression from Rousseau deliberately – *promeneur solitaire*, a lonely wanderer in the landscape, natural and historical. In this connection, it may be found significant that the dream that hovers before the seer's eye, the dream of a national community, nourished by an internalized past, hardly ever becomes concrete in clear images. It is also significant that the much praised community is something that perhaps will have to be abandoned by voluntary exile if the people fail to appreciate what the poet-prophet lays before them. The possibility that he himself could be a failure is alien to him, as it most definitely is not to the protagonists of Dante and of Milton. At all events, the dream remains a dream; the all-encompassing fraternal community remains an unrealized object of movingly expressed longing.

On the basis of these observations I am inclined, here as above, to regard our poem as one witness of important developments in European life from the time of Dante to that of Grundtvig. What is already perceptibly present in *Paradise Lost* where, as is well known, the idea of the Christian individual's lonely imitation of that other Unique One, Christ, and of the "Paradise within" that he gains in the process, plays so significant a part, even though it is quite effectively counterbalanced by other ideas – that is palpably and insistently there in *Nyaars-Morgen*, a poem that in this respect at least there is every reason to call a Romantic one.

My concluding remarks must be of a sketchy nature, as have been many of my previous ones. I have, I believe, made a case for the need for further study with a view to a fuller assessment of "tradition" and "modernity" in *Nyaars-Morgen* and of what can be learnt from the poem concerning the question of European continuity. That, in itself, constitutes an apology for my sketchiness. But of course it does not excuse me from trying some sort of preliminary conclusion at all. It goes like this:

What I myself have learnt from this incomplete and by that very fact biased reading of a truly remarkable poem are three mutually connected things.

In the first place: Grundtvig was, in 1824, a man of his time. The things that he took over, consciously or not, from great predecessors were by him put into a mould the elements of which were contributed by his fellow Romantics as well as by his own idiosyncratic genius; and they underwent highly significant changes in the process.

But, secondly: Grundtvig was, in 1824, also a man of the Old Europe of Dante and of Milton. Quite a few of his conscious and unconscious presuppositions resembled theirs; in important respects he drew his breath like one of them.

Thirdly: This last consideration is worth stressing even more than the first one, because it helps bring into focus something that is often neglected: the vitality of the tradition of the Old Europe, stretching from, roughly, the eleventh century to the turn of the nineteenth. A case can be made for treating those centuries as one coherent unit of civilizational and cultural history, eminently dynamic, but without fissions in depth comparable to the ones we have been witnessing since the Industrial Revolution. The material for establishing such a model and for the assessment of its limits can and must be taken from all parts of the landscape of civilization – one of the faults of the predominant model is precisely to be found in the failure to draw on all parts of the landscape – but one small ingredient can, I believe, be gained from the consideration of the ambiguous and tortuous interplay of tradition and modernity in *Nyaars-Morgen* – and in Grundtvig's work as a whole. At all events, even though an approach from this angle certainly is not the only one possible or desirable, it seems to me to be worth pursuing further than has been possible here.

Grundtvig's Poetics

By Flemming Lundgreen-Nielsen

Grundtvig and the Literary Institution

Even viewed from abroad, I belong to the renowned writers of Denmark, and whether this opinion be justified or not I leave to posterity to judge without any worries that they can ever ignore me in the literary history of Denmark.

This is how Grundtvig defines his position in Danish literary life in a private letter to a fellow parson in 1825, a time when he had voluntarily withdrawn himself from modern literature and its established institutions: the Royal Theatre in Copenhagen and the Copenhagen circle of critics exercising their craft in pamphlets, newspapers and periodicals. He no longer claimed to be part of the world of "belles-lettres", no longer participated in the literary feuds that were frequent in his day, from now on he produced very few reviews and none with a strictly aesthetic point of departure or goal, and he did not follow the development of Danish literature closely any more. The self-appointed custodians of literature treated him accordingly: if he was considered as a writer at all on a level with the rest, he was evaluated or condemned as "Grundtvig", a legend in his own lifetime, no longer connected with the changing fashions of poetics in Scandinavian and Danish Romanticism. Nevertheless Grundtvig still insisted on being counted among the figures of Danish national literature. Although he never wrote either a coherent presentation of his poetics or an exclusive history of literature, he thought a great deal about the essence, form and effects of poetry – especially in his formative period 1800-1820.

Grundtvig's literary career

Grundtvig started out as a schoolboy, student and young theology graduate (1798-1805) in the then current fashion of Neo-Classicism and the Enlightenment. He supported the intellectualism of the late 18th century, politically he was a radical, religiously close to being an atheist. In general he favoured tolerance and personal liberty, his heroes being Voltaire, the satirists Ludvig Holberg (1684-1754) and P.A. Heiberg (1758-1841) as well as the provocative versifier T.C. Bruun (1750-1834).

An unrequited passion for the mother of a boy he tutored at the manor of Egeløkke on the island of Langeland drove the lonely Grundtvig into elaborate reflections on the meaning of existence. These matured him into a position where he was able to remember and for the first time really understand the lectures on the main ideas of Romanticism given by his cousin Henrik Steffens (1773-1845) in Copenhagen in 1802-03. For some years Grundtvig was to adhere very strongly to the German brands both of universal and national Romanticism (1805-10).

After a religious crisis which was accompanied by a serious fit of insanity, Grundtvig made the Bible and the creeds of orthodox Lutheranism his sole doctrinal base, trying to christianize his Romantic concepts of poetry, as he put his literary activities at the service of God. In particular he emphasized the historical dimensions of Christianity. Rather unsuccessfully, he endeavoured to confine his own poetry to a dry and ascetic style, but he soon discovered that his accustomed imagery came through anyway (1811-15). In 1814-15 he decided once again to take up the features of Romanticism, but this time under the full control of his Christian faith. In 1824 he published a comprehensive and ambiguous visionary poem called *New Year's Morning*, where he turned his own personality and life into a symbol of Denmark's fate in antiquity, the present time and the future. For the remaining part of his literary career until his death in September 1872, at the age of nearly 89, Grundtvig was only remotely influenced by contemporary literary fashions. Admittedly his writings show traces of a budding, yet harmoniously conceived realism, combined with features of cozy middle-class Biedermeier culture, moments of sharpened idealism, and a certain openness to social issues. But he did not accommodate himself fundamentally to changes in the artistic and cultural climate. Technically, his literary means of expression usually went against the stream: he retrieved the rhyming chronicles of the Middle Ages, reintroduced the didactic verse-epics of the Renaissance and the 17th-18th century and wrote popular songs with an uncomplicated phrasing. He kept up with his contemporaries mainly through his national songs and ballads which relied heavily on Danish historical tradition. On the other hand he detested the favourite literary genres of the 19th century – clever or thrilling short stories, sentimental tragedies and psychological novels. He also, somewhat disinterestedly, rejected any philosophy of pure materialism along with political theories of the class-struggle, and he associated trade unions with national anarchy.

In Grundtvig's thinking, a writer, even though a private person, had *to serve and to serve* God, the church, the king, the country, the people, and so avoid becoming self-contained or self-complimentary in the style of a misconceived Romanticism. Such an attitude appears early in his career, when he fervently strives to outdo Adam Oehlenschläger (1779-1850), the prime young lion of Scandinavian romanticists, because he thinks his own message more pure and more necessary than the superficially pleasant, but actually vain sensuality of his competitor. In a newspaper feud (1809) about an unimportant matter, Grundtvig solemnly declared that any undeserved praise or blame of a writer and his works, any delivery of literary abortions constitute a crime that any competent person simply must protest against; – he himself at any rate is willing to adapt such a stance. This procedure of course, did not win him many friends, particularly since his victims were to some extent justified in not thinking too highly of Grundtvig's own poetic attempts so far.

After 1815 Grundtvig promised only to take part in literary feuds (these in a society, which lacked means for the expression of public opinion on political matters, served as a way of say) from a farcical point of view. He added in 1817 that he would do so exclusively in rhyming epistles, a dying genre from the previous century. It was indeed a limited programme, but fortunately he did more than that. A big newspaper feud among twelve admirers of Oehlenschläger and the fading poet and critic Jens Baggesen (1764-1826) in the autumn of 1818 brought him into the arena. The issue at stake concerned Oehlenschläger's supposed declining quality as a poet versus Baggesen's supposed envy of his better gifted rival. Grundtvig earned the merit of elevating the discussion above personal accusations. He also took the occasion to suggest the introduction of a special court of literature. He wanted to institute a watch to be manned by writers in their 30's and 60's, so that in the case of literary rows a younger member was to make an objective report of the proceedings, and a counsel of older members would then be assigned to give a verdict for the guidance of the public. In this way Grundtvig hoped to keep the affairs of literature, art and culture out of the common law courts of the absolute state, thus preserving the freedom of the individual writer. The background to this proposal was a couple of cases of sentences to lifelong banishment from the kingdom, imposed on radical writers in Grundtvig's early youth (1799-1800). As Grundtvig himself in 1826 became subject to imposed lifelong censorship on account of a work which was condemned as a slanderous attack on a professor of theology, but which by Grundtvig was considered to be no more than an academic discussion, his suggestion of 1818 seems quite sensible. His plan was never published, but even as late as 1831 Grundtvig wanted to formalize the world of literature. He maintained in a pamphlet that the right to publish one's thoughts in print should be limited to a certain number of writers over 40 years old. However, a system of licences would allow for exceptions to be made for truly gifted younger persons, if for instance a new Shakespeare appeared! This plan was not realized either. The liberal constitution of 1849 rendered these kinds of measure superfluous.

Another institutional step promoted by Grundtvig was more lucky, though by no means a success: an attempt to educate and awaken the Danes through offering them valuable reading material. From 1815 to 1822 he translated the historian Saxo's Latin chronicle *Gesta Danorum* (The Deeds of the Danes, finished ca 1220) and *Heimskringla*, the Old Norse chronicle of the Norwegian kings by Snorri Sturluson (a few years later) into common Danish or rather the colloquial language of South Zealand. The style, although bearing little resemblance to the respective original versions, exhibited considerable narrative qualities, but was coolly received by the academic critics and remained undiscovered by readers until late in the century. Most important of all: Grundtvig set up an editorial society for the appropriate distribution of the books, an early form of book club whose members paid fees of a voluntary amount, but who were to enjoy the privilege of reduced prices according to their means. Grundtvig made an express point of eliminating commercial booksellers. Unfortunately his revolutionary concept did not work, for though the subscription procedure through local parsons and other public servants was fairly successful, the inflation of the post-Napoleonic years and the European crisis in agriculture slowed down the sale to a virtual stop, when the printing of all six volumes was finally completed (in the summer of 1823). People simply did not have the money. In 1834 the books were donated to the Danish public elementary schools, only a few hundred of the 2000 subscription copies of each title having been distributed as Grundtvig planned. This failure may be part of the background for Grundtvig's later preference for oral delivery.

Three summer study tours to England (1829-31) opened Grundtvig's eyes to the contrast between vibrant British society and sleepy Danish society as it was under the absolute monarchy of Frederik VI. Grundtvig realized the need for the awakening of the whole Danish people and soon coined the phrase "First a man – then a Christian" (1837), reversing his former attitude about conversion. Grundtvig consequently started a long campaign for the erection of a national Folk High School in Denmark to counterbalance the dominant Latin-oriented University of Copenhagen. Growing demands from the academics and upper middle-class citizens for active participation in political affairs were reluctantly met by the old king through the introduction of advisory provincial assemblies (which met from 1835 onwards). At this time education of the non-academic portion of the population seemed more vital than ever. Grundtvig was encouraged, when reading the minutes of the Roskilde provincial assembly, by the evident common sense of the peasant representatives. He now considered the peasants who – like women! – were unspoiled by a knowledge of the Latin language and German philosophy the true core of the people. Grundtvig therefore changed his general educational objective: refraining from the conquest of the rather limited cultured circles of Copenhagen he concentrated increasingly on the peasantry. Here he was really pointing to the future, since the farmers made up more than 80 % of Denmark's population, yet had not been given much attention culturally or politically by the government. Grundtvig wrote seven booklets (1836-47) on the issue of a Danish Folk High School where everybody would be trained to voice their own opinion.

Grundtvig's new "folke-lige" (a rather rare Danish synonynom for "national", interpreted by him as: of the people; like the people) ideas were not just theories set out in writing. In two consecutive phases he finally managed to break through the barrier separating him personally from the people. The first phase was marked by the public lectures on European history 1788-1838 that Grundtvig gave in Copenhagen in 1838 to celebrate the fiftieth anniversary of the abolition of peasants' adscription in June 20, 1788. Up until then, Grundtvig had been a highly controversial character in Danish culture. Gradually, he had acquired a faithful following, but he certainly also had firm opponents and critics in the Copenhagen establishment, a class which up till then in the course of Danish history had always had the casting vote on shifts in religious, political or artistic trends. Grundtvig's lectures won over the younger generation of Copenhageners both because of the nature of his cause and because of his charismatic personality.

The second phase followed next year, when a prominent group of participants asked Grundtvig to set up a discussion club, where the common citizen could learn about his country and the problems of society in the light of the political changes being heralded in Europe. After some experiments, a club was established in May 1839, with Grundtvig as chairman until 1843. The idea of the club, *Danske Samfund* (The Danish Society), was not to deliver long tedious one-way lectures, but to promote lively discussions preceded by short introductions. At best 100-150 participants gathered for the weekly session on Tuesday evenings. This was in a real sense the very first beginning of practical Folk High School work in Denmark – five and a half year before the first regular Folk High School at Rødding in Northern Slesvig was opened on November 7, 1844.

Grundtvig's 1838-lectures were published posthumously by his son Svend in the book *Within Living Memory* (1877); the majority of his contributions to the discussion club are preserved as unprinted manuscripts in the Grundtvig archive in Denmark's Royal Library. Grundtvig's success in presenting his material orally led him to value the living word more than ever before, though in a theological context from 1825 onwards he had been working hard to prove the superiority of the spoken words over written statements. He had also observed in British public life how the spoken word had a positive effect on the general mood of society. In 1842 Grundtvig even stressed that Christ himself had never been a writer of books, but had relied entirely on oral delivery. This incidentally served to estrange Grundtvig further from the literary sphere of his own day, since in the 19th century the emphasis was increasingly shifting from public and private recitation of poetry or fiction to silent individual reading. On the other hand, Grundtvig in this way unwillingly paved the way for the new secular public rhetoric that would be particularly needed for a democratic Denmark after the signing of the constitution in 1849. And in spite of his harsh assaults on the allegedly dead books, Grundtvig certainly through his own and his disciples' efforts opened up the realm of literature to the peasant class.

When the struggle between the Danish and German language in Slesvig sharpened in the 1840's, Grundtvig came to understand that there can be no such thing as a human being *in abstract*: ever since the Tower of Babel every person belongs to a particular people and can have only one vernacular. His ideas of the Danish national character started to grow, and in his defence of the Danish language he step by step substituted German for Latin as the arch enemy. For a Dane, the living word could only really be Danish. National language, poetry and literature were truly nation-building factors to be cherished and promoted in every way. In 1847 Grundtvig supplemented the formula of 1837 so as to read like this: "First a Dane, then a man, finally a Christian".

Grundtvig's ideas of poetry and literature

Grundtvig's aesthetic ideas are astonishingly unchanged through the various phases of his life as sketched above. His thoughts on poetry seem to bridge the gaps left by his religious, psychological and pedagogical break-throughs. But quite often he throws them out as minor parts of major presentations of other issues. Accordingly, to a large extent chronology may be disregarded when trying to piece together Grundtvig's poetics.

First of all it is a striking feature in Grundtvig that he takes poetry so seriously. He not only sees the poet as a responsible educator of the people along 18th century lines, but in the spirit of Romanticism he also sees him as a link with the divine.

The Romantic concept of *originality* is introduced already in 1804. From Addison's *The Spectator* (No. 160, 1711, Danish translation 1743) Grundtvig borrows the dichotomy of Genius of Nature versus Talent of Art. He shows growing sympathy for natural geniuses like Homer and Shakespeare, but feels that as yet culture cannot do without intellectual schooling and some rules as exemplified in Vergil and Milton. Grundtvig agrees with Addison's imagery, and so acquiesces in the thought that a wild landscape in a warm climate, and a well-kept park both have tangible advantages. Having launched himself at first in a Neo-Classical emulation of great predecessors he does not now totally disregard training and deliberate development in favour of passive "natural" growth. Today Grundtvig's practice in combining these alternative views seems more fortunate than a truly Romantic attitude such as that of Oehlenschläger, where everything is expected to spring from inner resources, since these are often exhausted in a short space of time, thus leading to a feeling of emptiness or monotonous repetitions. Unparalleled as Grundtvig's visionary power was (and is), it would have been less convincing had he not managed to connect it with external realities. In a fruitful manner he harmonizes the poetics of the 18th and the 19th century – even though his all too frequent attacks on the age of Enlightenment made from a religious point of view tend to cloud the picture.

Grundtvig always suspected pure fiction. His mind was filled with *history*. Most of his writings rely on historical facts as well as subjectively presented interpretations. In 1804 he wanted to combine the advantages of the historical account and the novel, i.e., the reality of historical facts combined with thrilling composition and flowery style. In this way the writer would evade the boredom of too many historical details as well as the improbable fantasy of cheap fiction. Grundtvig formulated this programme in relation to some short stories that he wished to write in continuation of the ancient Icelandic sagas and recent historical tales by Voltaire and P.F. Suhm (1728-1798). He never published any text in this vein, yet somehow a modified version of the programme lies behind his six comprehensive volumes of world history (1812, 1814, 1817, 1833, 1836, 1843-56-69).

In his diary entries of September 1805, Grundtvig conducts an elaborate discussion with himself and with his cousin Henrik Steffens (the latter being present in Grundtvig's personal notes from the lectures of 1802-03 and in his copy of the printed book from 1803, purchased on November 18, 1804). The question is *the essence of poetry*. Grundtvig raises the question of what really constitutes poetry. In a few words he dismisses the mundane, formal and rhetorical definitions of poetry, and concludes in agreement with Steffens that poetry is everything which bears an imprint of eternity, and it requires an innate inner capacity to find the reflection of eternity in all material, earthly phenomena – in short, the higher meaning of things only appears to the chosen persons. A few months before, in the same diary Grundtvig had introduced a useful terminological distinction between art and poetry. Art consists of the various types of form and matter of the crafts, and falls into randomly divided subjects. Poetry crosses the boundaries of these subjects by orienting itself towards a higher existence in eternity. He thus transfers the terms to Steffens' philosophy.

However, Grundtvig in 1805 is not entirely taken in by the Romantic favourite idea of the "called ones" – those rare few evoked by Oehlenschläger in his programmatic poem *Guldhornene* (The Golden Horns), 1802. Grundtvig has objections. How do you express a poetic totality in earthly form, e.g., language? You can never have a perfect assimilation of the inner experience and the material medium. It is a further problem for Grundtvig that life on earth striving towards the higher sphere of eternity will have to carry with it a painful discrepancy between dull everyday life and the higher, but intangible existence. This, he thinks, is the reason why so many Romantic poets suffer from a certain sickliness, as Klopstock and Wieland did, remaining "half healthy, half sick individuals". To get round the problem by conjuring up an illusory worldly harmony, as Goethe and Schiller did, seems equally false to Grundtvig. He ends the lengthy diary-entry by suggesting a practical compromise: degrees of poetry that are lower and less perfect than the absolute should also be recognized as valid instances of the spirit's striving to arrive at the essence of poetry. It is characteristic of Grundtvig that he takes the poet's practical position into consideration rather than turning his back on the frail world in order to plumb his own inner depths. In spite of Grundtvig's much advertized sudden break-throughs, his conversion here to the main principles of poetry in Romantic philosophy actually occurs rationally, because it is developed gradually and logically over three whole days. It is not achieved through an uncontrolled bursting of some emotional dam.

In a published article in 1807 Grundtvig emphasizes the relation between poetry and *scholarship* ("Videnskabelighed"). Just as poetry in its direction upwards encompasses everything on earth, true scholarship must be based upon a religious mentality, a feeling of the glory of life after death. In practical terms, Grundtvig urges the scholar always to have an overall view of his topic, along with a careful examination of small details. This piece of advice Grundtvig himself largely adhered to, whereas unfortunately many of his pupils in and outside vicarages and Folk High Schools instead stuck to bold and – to put it politely – airy visions, which were passed off as results of "Grundtvig's synthetic method". This is a pity, for Grundtvig was a very learned man and generally thought of himself as a true realist. But his realism went beyond mere positivistic materialism.

In another printed essay from that good year, 1807, but prepared in draft in 1806, Grundtvig discusses the experimental renewal of ancient Greek tragedy in Schiller's play *The Bride from Messina* (1801). Does Schiller actually offer his reader *the ultimate pleasure of art*? Grundtvig credits Schiller with the idealistic direction his drama takes, but regrets that Schiller, as stated already in his preface, has engaged himself in an artificial man-made harmonization of the eternal and the temporal. This means little to a modern reader, Grundtvig states, and instead he points to heroes like Schiller's Karl Moor (*The Robbers*), Don Carlos and Joan of Arc, the optimal pattern being Shakespeare's Hamlet. These characters were all fighting against worldly evils during a miserable existence on earth, having experienced enough glimpses of the eternal to assure them of the hope of a better, more meaningful existence after death, and this is what their readers must do today. The unharmonious and incomplete element in their characters stems from the fact that their lives are not perfectly rounded off – here Grundtvig notices flaws in the art of the playwright. But this is the never failing signal for the existence in them of "a profusion of poetry", a longing for eternity. And that is exactly where the modern reader can invest his feelings and be carried away in joy and tears. Schiller's Sicilian characters in *The Bride from Messina* on the other hand, in imitation of the ancient style of tragedy are not moved even by their own predicament: they submit calmly to the vicissitudes of life in their firm belief in a superhuman and impersonal fate. The Neo-Classical idea of Schiller concerning the supreme balance in the reader's soul when faced with such monumental objectivity was clearly derived from Immanuel Kant's notion of disinterested pleasure.

Grundtvig denounces this aesthetic theory as not true for a modern mind. He offers quite a different idea: only the unconditioned and absolute involvement in the poetic endeavour can free man from his detested earthly existence, even though this may only be allowed to occur in flashes. In his printed essay, Grundtvig thus shares with other Romantics the high estimation of poetry as a path to the eternal. In a deleted passage from his private notes he further clarified his philosophy: the reconciliation of the classical Schiller – and his friend Goethe – to earthly life is an obvious illusion, in fact identical with St. Paul's category called man's service of vanity. The poetic understanding of life, on the other hand, corresponds to the description in St. Paul of the sighing of the creature longing for the glorious liberty of the children of God (cf. Romans 8:19-23). In other words, by rejecting Neo-Classical attitudes Grundtvig moves from self-centred modern humanism to a subject greater than any single person: Christianity. Therefore he is able to give an unharmonious, imperfect literary work of poetry priority over the most perfect piece of art.

In the following years Grundtvig treated the various literary genres from Aristotle until the moment of writing in the light of a basic Christian attitude. A *drama* to him falls into three main elements: plot or story, matter or characters, style or presentation (cf. Aristotle's *Poetics*, chapter 6). Of these he considers the first the most important, because it will always have to include a religious understanding of the course of historical events. On the other hand an *epic* often limits itself to hero-worship or mere dry historical facts and seldom allows for a synthesis. A chronicle play with its artificially concentrated composition and selective dramatic highlights may be effective, but a self-invented genre, *dramatized history*, will be more truthful, Grundtvig suggests, through the solid historical information which it renders in the form of entertaining fictional conversations. He himself wrote two experimental volumes of the kind dealing with the decline of paganism in Scandinavia (1809-11). As to *hymns and spiritual songs*, Grundtvig prefers attachment to men and deeds based on biblical and world history to trite didactic lessons on the doctrine, rendered in verse form.

Grundtvig's religious and psychological crisis in December 1810 sharpened his conception of the relation between Christianity and poetry. At first he sincerely felt that he ought to give up composing poetry altogether, but soon great examples of loyal Christian poetry came to his attention and modified his decision. In particular the church hymns of Thomas Kingo (1634-1703), the confessional religious poems of Johannes Ewald (1743-81), and a lyrical collection, *Newest Poems*, 1810, by the Norwegian clergyman Jonas Rein (1760-1821) helped to change his mind. He was also spurred on by the thought that St. Paul in his speech on the Areopagus in Athens had justified even pagan poetry as a true relic of the image of God which was lost at the Fall (cf. Acts 17:28). A poet may, knowingly or not, be God's mouth-piece, God's spokesman, God's forerunner.

How do you become *a true poet* in terms of Romanticism and Christianity? The notion of poetic genius in Romanticism was partly derived from the Old Testament prophets, partly from figures such as Homer, Milton and Ossian. Now Grundtvig in his own way returns to the desert-roaming seers of antiquity. A retrospective collection of lyrical poetry on his own life, *Saga*, published in December 1811, carries a motto from the prophet Ezekiel (33:32):

And, lo, thou art unto them as a very lovely song of one that hath a pleasant voice, and can play well on an instrument, for they hear thy words, but they do them not.

In the foreword of the book, where the motto is given a commentary, Grundtvig even continues the quotation: "And when this cometh to pass, (lo, it will come,) then shall they know that a prophet hath been among them" (33:33). And in a draft for the foreword, Grundtvig worked more on his Christian definition of a poet. He gives an empirical account of two types of poets. One is the passive poet who makes himself an unresisting tool of his own imagination and its impulses – presumably the Romantic. The other is the active poet who strictly controls his imagination in order to obtain a particular goal – presumably the moralizing, didactic, rule-conscious Neo-Classicist. Alongside these, Grundtvig proposes a third type which he labels *the deponent poet*, punning on the linguistic term denoting a combination of passive form and active meaning. The deponent poet observes the flight of his imagination intellectually in order to ascertain its direction, before he gives himself up to it. Since in 1811 Grundtvig had already for years been defining true poetry by its aim for eternity, it is not surprising that his manuscript concludes by stating that deponent poets must be "religious or Christian".

Grundtvig's poetics reach a climax in his depiction of the poet, *the "scald"*, as he calls him by the use of an Old Norse word. In his *World Chronicle* from 1814, Grundtvig finds the "scalds" to be closest of all men to the Jewish prophets in inspiration and enthusiasm. This, he writes, is a mental state which signifies neither inactivity nor lack of life. To the contrary the "scald" feels life to be more intense and warm than ever. He feels life and work to be merged miraculously. He gets visions from what he sees and he sings about what he envisions. Afterthought and reflection alone are rejected as a suitable medium through which to gain impressions and express oneself.

Exclusive as this may seem, Grundtvig later becomes willing to grant such a feeling to other people than gifted poets. In his first pamphlet about a central Danish Folk High School he confers the qualities and attitudes of the "scald" on the common citizen he hopes to attract. The key-word is still enthusiasm, when the participant in a High School programme acquires knowledge of "the mood" that shapes his life, of "the eye" through which he conceives of its events and important moments, and of "the tone" in which he expresses his experiences (1836).

The true "scald" does not plan everything that may be contained in his work. Grundtvig sees *obscurity* almost as a guarantee of poetic quality. Vivacity and melodious form produce pleasure even when reading the most obscure poem. They are accordingly a token that the "scald" was granted a beautiful vision, even though he was incapable of making it clear to himself or the reader. When a "scald" strives to render the truth in a poem, the connection between the external and the internal that is always there often reveals itself without the "scald's" knowledge. Grundtvig in fact launches a philosophy of language which is also applicable to his own practice when making translations. The mere use of certain words carries the meaning, even where it has been forgotten or lost – words recreate the original idea and mood. So, when words are recorded in the corporal (i.e., concrete) meaning, a spiritual meaning follows naturally, a meaning that nobody should look down upon.

The "scald's" art to Grundtvig is therefore identifiable with order, clarity, firmness and coherence in the endeavour to render Truth. It should never be defined as something exclusively beautiful, artistic or contrived. In fact, Grundtvig finds it necessary *to warn against beauty* in poetry (1817). The Fall and Original Sin that followed cause a poet to reflect the spirit of Truth (God) as well as the spirit of Lie in his inner mirror. Fine poetic imagery can always be suspected of lieing or seducing. Apparently visionary poetry sometimes only features empty jingles or, worse, gilded sensuality – "savoury sausages" in Grundtvig's frank way of speaking. Since the spiritual and the corporal have to coincide in the human heart, the surface will look superficially the same, no matter whether the underlying experience is truly spiritual or not. Grundtvig can only appeal to the reader's innate sense of genuine spirituality to discard all parasitic art.

In the same vein *inspiration* in 1813 is understood biblically as "God's breath in his chosen ones" rather than in a pagan or Romantic secular sense. Modern self-reliant poets are compared to a renowned Italian daredevil who the previous year had perished with his dirigible balloon.

It is further Grundtvig's conviction that no human being can create anything from nothing – that is God's privilege. *Invention* and *imagination* are unthinkable qualities without belief in God. Any stylization or idealization of something invisible, or any description of elements that cannot be perceived through the five senses, must be referred to an invisible sphere that is created by an invisible but nonetheless very real creator (1814).

Finally, the problem of *individualism* is important in Grundtvig's poetics. Since the classical ideals were abolished and the popular collective types of (mainly oral) literature from the Middle Ages were replaced by the printed words and so had died or were living on underground, the idea of individual composition and the idea of originality had prevailed in European literature. Grundtvig is very conscious of this and certainly recognizes the need to curb his own independent personality when writing something that is to be more than personal confession. Hence his preference for genres of "the people" such as proverbs, medieval ballads ("folkeviser") and the anonymous *Rhyming Chronicle of Denmark* (printed 1495). To his mind, modern writers of church hymns unfortunately have much less feeling for essential common values than the old hymn writers, and much more predilection for an individualistic point of view. They gain far too much personal pleasure from their own products (1834). Such modern expectations of artistic individualism, independence and originality are seen by Grundtvig as detrimental to the general acceptance, validity and use of poetry, for Grundtvig was himself most of the time absorbed in collective categories such as people, society, nation, congregation and the common good.

Other prominent features of 19th century poetics that are unacceptable to Grundtvig include *the deification of poetry and art, the total relativism* which allows the artist to erase the difference between good and evil (as e.g., Schelling and Kierkegaard's demonic aesthetic characters did), and *the possibility of self-redemption* through Neo-Humanistic and Romantic self-analysis. Grundtvig looked down upon psychology as a superficial and ignorant discipline.

As a theorist in poetics Grundtvig seems to move in a stable world of thought-forms. However, he never managed to work out his various ideas into a clear, categorical system. His problem probably was that when he tried to do so, his deep-rooted and often admitted sense of history, time and again made him lapse into historical surveys, from which he produced spirited visions for future development.

Grundtvig's practical application of his poetics

Grundtvig in his poetics acknowledges neither the so-called total creative freedom of the modern poet nor the image of the poet as a mere mouth-piece of higher powers, in Romanticism often described as an Æolian harp sounding its strings in an invisible but effective breeze. In his idea of the deponent poet, Grundtvig seeks a balance between these extremes. Certainly his own numerous and frequently very lengthy manuscripts, often corrected time and again, bear sufficient witness to the way he checked the direction of his inner visions before giving way to them. His goal in this was definitely not the refined polishing of details. Once he trusted the direction of his impulses, he poured out his material in almost infinite quantities. However he did not mind when he himself or some of his admirers would later cut the products down to an appropriate size in order to ensure their better presentation. The visions were to be used and put to work in practical life – in national ballads and hymns, and in rousing epics. Least of all did Grundtvig want to set up monuments to his own poetic capabilities. Though asked a couple of times to edit his collected works he never did so, whereas most major poets of the age were flattered to consent to such public demand (e.g., Oehlenschläger, Ingemann, J.L. Heiberg, Hans Christian Andersen). Grundtvig had absolutely no desire to be embalmed in the majestic self-sufficient pyramid of literary history.

Nor should it be overlooked that Grundtvig, as he aged, increasingly wrote a kind of poetry that differed from the aesthetic doctrines of Romanticism. From around 1830 he learned to use less complicated metrical forms and less strained symbolism. In this way he echoed the popular ballads, didactic verse writings of the 18th century, and abstract spiritual songs and hymns which were put together in a simple style. In a style that was artlessly smooth Grundtvig successfully merged every-day idioms with proverbial expressions of a faintly old-fashioned hue, and this gave his verses a particular charming ring that is just as easy to recognize as it is difficult to define. His songs and poems belonging to this category were often commissioned at short notice by younger friends and admirers for special occasions. That to Grundtvig could evidently also spell inspiration in itself. His works in this genre hardly require explanation or background poetics: clarity is both their medium and their goal.

Seen from the normal standards of literary art, Grundtvig was gifted with a fabulous ability to rhyme. He usually expressed himself better and faster in verse than in prose. The point of departure for his poetry in many cases would be a particular personal mood overwhelming him with emotions that were so intense that he saw no other way out of them than to slip into poetical action with pen and paper. The purpose of such poetry is not to describe, but to move, to speak from his own heart to another heart. This he states in an early song about the naval hero Willemoes (1810), which probably indirectly quoted Goethe's Faust teaching his assistant Wagner a natural rhetoric. Poetry is made up of spiritual activities of the heart – that part of the human body which Grundtvig's anthropology considers to be closest to the divine.

Grundtvig was often accused of obscurity. His general attitude was that everything living has to be imperfect and uncertain, whereas dead objects may be measured and precisely defined. It was on the basis of this philosophy he answered, when even his friend and fellow-poet Ingemann complained – and justifiably so – of obscurities in his great poem *New Year's Morning*. Grundtvig wrote back to him on December 4, 1824:

God has given me a poetico-historical eye by means of which I, in the light of the Lord, survey the huge chaos formed by human activities in all their more or less erring directions. I see a miraculous coherence in everything, but at best I can only present it in an obscure manner, and my readers only dimly see what is clear to me, and accordingly they only perceive darkness where I am able to see something. It is unreasonable to require from me that this should be otherwise; it is also unreasonable that my readers demand me to express something more clearly than I am able to see it, or want me to be silent about the great and wonderful things which I do see, because they are what they necessarily have to be: obscure ... With relative ease I master a good many traditional poetic forms and can use them to convey my views and my thoughts; but in that case I am not enthused. As soon as I *am* enthused, all the forms I have learned go to pieces, and then I take fragments from all of them and thereby through hieroglyphs signify what I cannot at all express, if I take them in their own right. Later, when the vision gradually has become clearer, I may be able to explain myself in a vivid, half joking manner, and thus in a way be my own commentator; but that is another matter and naturally only goes for the least and nearest of what I have envisioned: that on which I may (so to speak) lay my hands. It follows that either I have to forget my poetical tongue altogether, or I have to speak as obscurely, ruggedly and often jarringly as my tongue usually does. Since the first possibility would to me at least be tantamount to the loss of my life, it is merely up to me to be patient: i.e., patiently to listen to the criticism that my verses are formless, meaningless, tasteless etc., even to accept that poetical and friendly readers shake their heads – to accept all this without getting angry or discouraged, for in both cases I lose out, most surely in the latter case, for there I lose my enthusiasm.

In a way Grundtvig's symbols and images thus serve to demonstrate the inadequacy of words – though he considered literary art to be the most spiritual of all. The inner vision and the mind which reflects and transforms it are both richer and more ambiguous than any language allows for. It is the use of *symbolism* which is a hallmark of being human. In a speech delivered in *Danske Samfund* on October 12, 1841, called *What is Man?*, rejecting current theories about man's relation to monkeys or rats Grundtvig answers as follows: Man is created in the image of God, man communicates through the faculty of speech, and man perceives the world in symbols – whereas animals have no idea whatsoever of the visible being a sign of something invisible.

Grundtvig's rich symbolism is perhaps his greatest contribution to Danish lyrical poetry. Let one example illustrate this. If Grundtvig in a poem compares the Danish national spirit to *Signe*, a pagan princess mentioned in Book VII of Saxo's medieval Chronicle, in the movement of history this woman stands first of all for love and loyalty unto death. She is also naturally associated with Saxo, the most patriotic historian of the Danish Middle Ages, and with a certain type of landscape, such as the archetypically Danish woods and streams of her mid-Zealand home, Ringsted, which, incidentally, later became the burial ground for some of the prominent Danish medieval kings and queens. Since her lover was a Norwegian prince called Hagbard, she also evokes a tender recollection of the Union between Denmark and Norway and their centuries-old close friendship. In Grundtvig's understanding she further incorporates the idea that women have deeper emotions ("Hierte", heart) than men, and through her voluntary death after the hanging of her lover she demonstrates that a longing for an after-life exists even in the pre-Christian periods of Danish history. Philologically her name resembles the Danish word "(vel)signe" meaning to bless. Finally it could be relevant too that in 1815 Signe had been revived in one of Oehlenschläger's better tragedies. Very likely it would be possible to add still more connotations. You simply have to possess an ear for all the notes which Grundtvig plays; by touching a very few keys on his poetical instrument he is able to launch a whole symphony.

In fact, already in his first and most traditional period as a writer Grundtvig offered *himself as a symbol* of the rebirth of Christian Denmark and of the God-given role of the Danish people in history (*The Daffodil*, 1817; *New Year's Morning*, 1824). At his death in 1872 he had become and was widely accepted as such a symbol. Even a century later there is still considerable energy in Grundtvig's name, as (for example) the Danes learned during the 1972 campaign for or against membership of the EEC, and as they are still learning daily whenever Grundtvig is included in contemporary discussion.

Unlike allegory, that intellectual tool of the Enlightenment, symbols are not to be understood fully, not to be exhausted. They should be felt, experienced, relived. And they are in no sense a roundabout way for the reader; they are the best existing short cuts available. In Grundtvig's mind no purely human manifestation of life compares to poetry.

N.F.S. Grundtvig, S.T. Coleridge: The Hymnwriter and the Poet

By David Jasper

Both Grundtvig and Coleridge lived into an old age which granted them the status of the sage. In 1872, Edmund Gosse graphically described the ninety-year old Grundtvig:

For a man of ninety, he could not be called infirm: his gestures were rapid and his step steady. But the attention was riveted on his appearance of excessive age. He looked like a troll from some cave in Norway; he might have been centuries old.

From the vast orb of his bald head, very long strings of silky hair fell over his shoulders and mingled with a long and loose white beard. His eyes flamed under very beetling brows, and they were the only part of his face that seemed alive, for he spoke without moving his lips. His features were still shapely, but colourless and dry, and as the draught from an open door caught them, the silken hairs were blown across his face like a thin curtain. While he perambulated the church with these stiff gestures and ventriloquist murmurings, his disciples fell on their knees behind him, stroking the skirts of his robe, touching the heels of his shoes. Finally, he ascended the pulpit and began to preach; in his dead voice he warned us to beware of false spirits, and to try every spirit whether it be of God. He laboured extremely with his speech, becoming slower and huskier, with longer pauses between the words like a clock that is running down. He looked supernatural, but hardly Christian.[1]

Almost half a century earlier, Thomas Carlyle had described Coleridge, the "Sage of Highgate", in *The Life of John Sterling* (1851):

I have seen many curiosities; not the least of them I reckon Coleridge, the Kantean metaphysician and quondam Lake poet. I will tell you all about our interview when we met. Figure a fat, flabby, incurvated personage, at once short, rotund, and relaxed, with a watery mouth, a snuffy nose, a pair of strange brown, timid, yet earnest-looking eyes, a high tapering brow, and a great bush of grey hair, and you have some faint idea of Coleridge. He is a kind good soul, full of religion and affection and poetry and animal magnetism. His cardinal sin is that he wants *will*. He has no resolution. He shrinks from pain or labor in any of its shapes. His very

---

1. Edmund Gosse, *Two Visits to Denmark* (1911).

attitude bespeaks this. He never straightens his knee-joints. He stoops with fat, ill-shapen shoulders, and in walking he does not tread, but shovel and slide. My father would call it "skluiffing." He is always busied to keep, by strong and frequent inhalations, the water of his mouth from overflowing, and his eyes have a look of anxious impotence. He would do with all his heart, but he knows he dares not. The conversation of the man is much as I anticipated – a forest of thoughts, some true, many false, more part dubious, all of them ingenious in some degree. But there is no method in his talk: he wanders like a man sailing among many currents, whithersoever his lazy mind directs him; and, what is more unpleasant, he preaches, or rather soliloquizes. He cannot speak, he can only tal-k (so he names it). Hence I found him unprofitable, even tedious; but we parted very good friends, I promising to go back some evening – a promise which I fully intend to keep. I sent him a copy of "Meister", about which we had some friendly talk. I reckon him a man of great and useless genius: a strange, not at all a great man.

The comparison is illuminating. Grundtvig a prophetic figure, almost Godlike beyond the Christian. Coleridge, the embodiment of his own mazy thoughts, philosophizing and endlessly talking even beyond the edge of comprehension. Both seem barely within the world which, in their different ways, they so profoundly affect. They have become, in a way, worlds in themselves.

Coleridge has been the object of my study for many years. Grundtvig has taken a place in my reading only very lately and then, of necessity, through translations and English commentaries. Although some extraordinary similarities as well as profound differences between the two men have struck me, I remain distrustful of my impressions of Grundtvig. What I offer, therefore, is a series of reflections on Coleridge as one of the major intellectual, theological, and poetic figures in and beyond English Romanticism, and compare them with a reading of one of Grundtvig's hymns, thinking of both men as at once, and interconnectedly, religious and poetic.

Perhaps most obviously, both men had an almost unparalleled range of intellectual and theological interests; both were, in Coleridge's term "library cormorants", yet equally they never lost sight of the practical necessities of existence. For Coleridge, such practical necessities could not be separated from an intense absorption in epistemology and theories of knowledge ("I reverence Immanuel Kant with my whole heart and soul", he once wrote), which, in turn, arose out of the underlying theological implications of both his poetic and his speculative activities. Richard Holmes, in his brilliant new biography of the young Coleridge, has recently indicated how the early "conversation" poems continually move beyond a young poet's natural interest in the problem of personal "authenticity" to questions of whether life – or literature – can have real meaning without some form of Divine continuity or assurance within the structure of reality. Does language itself ultimately depend on the notion of Divine articulation within the universe? From whence does its power arise?[2]

I cannot imagine Coleridge experiencing anything like the spiritual breakthrough after crisis that Grundtvig seems to have achieved in 1810. While Grundtvig in 1811 begins to search for new poetic assurance in the Bible and the history of the Church, Coleridge (never a historian in any sense, and metaphysician to the core) continues to live reflexively within the visions of romanticism. I doubt if Coleridge could have written a hymn if he tried, given the public, communal and metrical demands of hymnody.[3]

On the other hand, like Grundtvig, Coleridge, at least as a young man, was a remarkable preacher. The sermons which Grundtvig preached between 1811-1813 in Udby must have been very different from Coleridge's Dissenting and Unitarian sermons of the 1790's, yet their effect may have been in the end not dissimilar. Classical in structure, profoundly biblical in their language and poetry, Grundtvig's sermons, it seems to me, are passionately and morally practical in their exhortation to his contemporaries. Coleridge, also, with all the radical fervour of youth, never strays far from biblical language and imagery in sermons "precociously peppered with Politics", as he himself put it.[4] For, Coleridge never fell into the position of imagining that an uncritical Christianity or religious orthodoxy would guarantee right belief or behaviour. The truth, closely pursued and poetically realized, was what above all mattered to him; as he crisply put it in the late work *Aids to Reflection* (1828):

He, who begins by loving Christianity better than Truth, will proceed by loving his own Sect or Church better than Christianity, and end in loving himself better than all.

Christianity must efficiently *work* in the world; hence Coleridge's deep moral and political concerns. Hence also, as in Grundtvig's thought, his careful reflections on the relationship and distinctions between church and state and the role of education in the religious life of the nation all seen within the greater formal realm of poetry and universal questions. Like Grundtvig, Coleridge was acutely aware of the need to distinguish between temporal and eternal truth, and the nature of moral and political action considered obliquely within this distinction.

2. Richard Holmes, *Coleridge. Early Visions* (London, 1989), p. 320. See also, George Steiner, *Real Presences* (London, 1989).
3. See, C. Thodberg & A.P. Thyssen (eds.), *Tradition and Renewal*, p. 29.
4. Holmes, p. 108 and *Letters*.

Unlike Grundtvig, however, Coleridge never actively engaged in political life. Nor was he an ordained minister of any church. He was, however, a brilliant journalist, continuing in his occasional political essays and leaders a sensitivity to contemporary issues with an uncanny sense of the relationship between the immediate and universals. As he put it in a letter written in June 1817 to the Prime Minister, Lord Liverpool, always "the whole is prior to the parts".[5] National health depended upon not simply the immediate exercise of political practicalities and negotiations, but a broadly based "dynamic philosophy", a speculative philosophy. I sense that in both Coleridge and Grundtvig, in different ways, a reaction against eighteenth century rationalism, and the influence of Romanticism engendered in both men a lasting quality of active combination, the "esemplastic" ability to draw together into unity vastly disparate elements in a multiplicity of immediate concerns. There is a remarkable similarity within the Romantic tradition between the ambivalent poetics of Coleridge's great poem *Kubla Khan* and Grundtvig's Christian definition of the poet in the draft of the Foreword to his collection of poetry *Saga* (1811).[6] Coleridge's poetic mind hovers between activity and passivity, between perception as creative and receptive, energetic and participatory.[7] Grundtvig describes the types of the passive and active poet, and between them a third type which he calls the "deponent" as a union of a passive form and active meaning. Such a poet scrutinizes and shapes his imagination with intellectual, shaping energy, before submitting to its processes and flights. For both men, to perceive poetically is both to create and to submit.

What I wish to establish initially, therefore, is a series of similarities between these two very different sages, and proceed now to focus specifically upon them as poets as a way of suggesting a fundamental unity within the Christian tradition and, equally, a profound theological distinction which makes of one a great Romantic poet and the other a great hymnwriter. Coleridge in his later years, in his *Letters*, *Notebooks* and particularly the posthumously published *Confessions of an Inquiring Spirit* (1840) presents an increasing sense of the genius of Calvin "in his best works",[8] as he in an intense privacy "[groans] under a deep sense of infirmity and manifold imperfection".[9] Throughout his life as a poet is revealed the tension between the necessity, in human sinfulness, of what Coleridge describes in 1815 as "modern" Calvinism, and the activity of the

5. Ben Knights, *The Idea of the Clerisy* (Cambridge, 1978), p. 41.
6. *Tradition and Renewal*, pp. 29-30.
7. Kathleen Wheeler, *The Creative Mind in Coleridge's Poetry* (London, 1981), pp. 31-33.
8. Letter to Thomas Boosey Jr. 25 February 1818.
9. *Confessions* Letter I.

poet who reveals in fragments those glimpses of Paradise which make it bearable. Grundtvig, on the other hand, in his "matchless discovery" of Christian conviction in 1823-4, is settled firmly within the insights of Luther, in their understanding of the living word of the Bible and the interconnection between Word and Sacrament.[10] His insights are altogether more ecclesiological, more communal and more conducive to hymnody's poetry of the congregation than Coleridge could ever achieve: but not necessarily more Christian. Both, perhaps, are poetically necessary.

I want to spend the rest of my time looking in some detail at two poems, one (perhaps Coleridge's greatest) *Kubla Khan* (1798) and the other Grundtvig's Sunday hymn, *We are God's house of living stones*,[11] as an illustration of what I have been saying.

Notoriously, from Coleridge's prose preface to the poem, *Kubla Khan* is a fragment of an opium dream which was interrupted as the poet slept in "a lonely farm-house" by a person "on business" from the nearby village of Porlock, who detained him for more than an hour and scattered his visions.

KUBLA KHAN
In Xanadu did Kubla Khan
A stately pleasure-dome decree:
Where Alph, the sacred river, ran
Through cavern measureless to man
  Down to a sunless sea.
So twice five miles of fertile ground
With walls and towers were girdled round:
And there were gardens bright with sinuous rills,
Where blossomed many an incense-bearing tree;
And here were forests ancient as the hills,
Enfolding sunny spots of greenery.

But oh! that deep romantic chasm which slanted
Down the green hill athwart a cedarn cover!
A savage place! as holy and enchanted
As e'er beneath a waning moon was haunted
By woman wailing for her demon-lover!
And from this chasm, with ceaseless turmoil seething,
As if this earth in fast thick pants were breathing,
A mighty fountain momently was forced:

10. See, A.M. Allchin, "The Hymns of N.F.S. Grundtvig" in *The Eastern Churches Quarterly* XIII, nos. 3 & 4. (1959), pp. 131-32.
11. "Kirken den er et gammelt hus" in *DDS*, no. 280.

Amid whose swift half-intermitted burst
Huge fragments vaulted like rebounding hail,
Or chaffy grain beneath the thresher's flail:
And 'mid these dancing rocks at once and ever
It flung up momently the sacred river.
Five miles meandering with a mazy motion
Through wood and dale the sacred river ran,
Then reached the caverns measureless to man,
And sank in tumult to a lifeless ocean:
And 'mid this tumult Kubla heard from far
Ancestral voices prophesying war!
    The shadow of the dome of pleasure
    Floated midway on the waves;
    Where was heard the mingled measure
    From the fountain and the caves.
It was a miracle of rare device,
A sunny pleasure-dome with caves of ice!

    A damsel with a dulcimer
    In a vision once I saw:
    It was an Abyssinian maid,
    And on her dulcimer she played,
    Singing of Mount Abora.
    Could I revive within me
    Her symphony and song,
    To such a deep delight 'twould win me,
That with music loud and long,
I would build that dome in air,
That sunny dome! those caves of ice!
And all who heard should see them there,
And all should cry, Beware! Beware!
His flashing eyes, his floating hair!
Weave a circle round him thrice,
And close your eyes with holy dread,
For he on honey-dew hath fed,
And drunk the milk of Paradise.
(1798.)

There is good evidence to suggest that the account of the poem's origin in the cottage near Porlock on Exmoor is an ironic, shrewd literary device of Coleridge's own making, the person on business an indicator that the finite, busy world will always put bounds upon infinite vision. Yet a "dim recollection"[12] remains, and that is enough to draw the reader back to the fragment of poetry with its mysterious indications of a vision that can never be fully recovered. The tomorrow is always yet to come. That *Kubla Khan* is a fragment may be a deliberate exercise of the imagination, necessarily incomplete and fragmentary, but, as Coleridge understands it, a repetition in the finite mind of the poet of the infinite act of divine creation.[13]

Kubla Khan foreshadows the theological and religious concerns of the older Coleridge. It begins with a paradise garden decreed by an emperor who is threatened by the past of his "ancestral voices". But the paradise which is threatened by Original Sin is found again by the poet and his vision which he has but to remember in order to re-create an image of the harmony and wholeness of the Paradise with which the poem concludes. In 1815, Coleridge wrote to the poet William Wordsworth that he hoped his poetry would have

affirmed a Fall of some sense, as a Fact, the possibility of which cannot be understood from the nature of the Will, but the reality of which is attested by Experience & Conscience.[14]

For Coleridge, the task of the poetic imagination is a theological one, "reviving" the symphonic vision and rebuilding Kubla's dome; paradise lost and regained.

Despite the oriental barbarism of its imagery, *Kubla Khan* remains firmly within the structural plot of the Judaeo-Christian tradition. It has frequently been pointed out that actually Coleridge is drawing on Plato, and particularly the *Ion*, with his images of the poet who draws milk and honey from rivers in paradisal gardens as their souls fly from flower to sweet flower, (e.g., Elisabeth Schneider, Kathleen Raine). But this is not to deny his "divine inspiration", since it is through the poetic imagination that Coleridge reaches up to and begins to articulate the theology which becomes so necessary for him. As a poet, his theology is "recognized", and not imposed.

In *Kubla Khan*, Coleridge prompts reflection in the reader by an interplay between a number of perspectives or visionary centres. In the last stanza, for example, he switches from first person to third person narrative; the poet with flashing eyes and floating hair, mysteriously and divinely inspired, is distanced from the visionary (in the first person) who delibera-

12. Coleridge's Preface, Line 30.
13. *Biographia Literaria*, Chap. 13.
14. 30 May 1815. Letters.

tely recollects and re-creates what once he saw. Different again is the dry and ironic third person narrative of the prose Preface. The effect of these parallel levels of perspective is to prompt the reader to reflect creatively upon his own reading, to perceive that his own limited vision and reductive rationality will supply a person from Porlock to cut short the "dream" which is released and completed only when, in the third stanza, the imagination and creative powers assume command and the poet is received in holy fear and reverence, and the vision becomes a religious experience.

It is not accurate to describe as is often done, *Kubla Khan* as being about the act of poetic creation. Rather, as a deliberate fragment, it has as its subject the poet's consciousness of his process of creation. He is looking at his language, what it is doing to him and what he is doing to it. The perceptual process is obviously not a response to an observed, external language. The lush descriptions are rather the transformation of subjective, internal experiences into public objects. For as the language becomes active in the processes of reading, its metaphor of mental process is drawn back in a new, creative and imaginative experience. That which the poem describes would not be were it not for the poem as-it-is-read.

The prose preface to *Kubla Khan*, with gentle irony, shakes the reader out of a literal reading of the poem which fails to perceive that the dream and the fragments are metaphors for what is happening to him. While the heightened consciousness of the poet may find, paradoxically, in his creative activity, a release by language from language, so that it may begin to intimate what is not there, a glimpse of Paradise or the tomorrow which is yet to come. (The phrase is borrowed by Coleridge from Theocritus).

I have suggested that the poetics of *Kubla Khan* are ambivalent – hovering between activity and passivity – between the sunny dome and the icy caves, the fertile sacred river and the lifeless ocean. In his essay *On Poesy or Art*, written much later, probably about 1818, Coleridge describes artistic creativity as both passive and active on "unconscious activity" and also "according to the severe laws of the intellect". It is, he suggests, "the co-ordination of freedom and law". From such creative activity alone can we be led closer to the nature of God, for the fragment which is the conscious intellect creates the impulse to move beyond the broken form to an infinity, so that, in a sense, the poem never really ends.

Coleridge never developed a strong sense of the historicity of the Christian tradition, nor of the community of the church. His was essentially an intensely private religious sensibility into which he was led by the formal enclosed and reflexive world of his poetry: from this was forged, with its moments of creative vision, the strict and disciplined belief of Coleridge's last years, lived under the awareness of his own sinfulness and infirmity.

Grundtvig, it seems to me, develops his poetic, similarly ambivalent or "deponent", from the opposite perspective. He was essentially a churchman and his hymns serve the public worship of the Christian community. Their poetic virtue lies not in intense introspection, but in fulfilling beautiful congregational expectation in the lively rehearsal of applied doctrine. If in Coleridge one moves through the poetry to belief, in Grundtvig one moves from belief into a durable poetry. I am hampered by having to use an English translation, but here is a hymn of Grundtvig which is a joyous statement of God's grace in the risen Christ:

> We are God's house of living stones,
> Builded for His habitation;
> He through baptismal grace us owns,
> Heirs of His wondrous salvation;
> Were we but two His name to tell,
> Yet, He would deign with us to dwell,
> With all His grace and His favour.
>
> Here stands the font before our eyes,
> Telling how God did receive us;
> Th'altar recalls Christ's sacrifice
> And what his table doth give us;
> Here sounds the word that doth proclaim
> Christ yesterday, today the same,
> Yea, and for aye our Redeemer.
>
> Grant then, O God, where'er men roam,
> That when the church bells are ringing,
> Many in Jesus' faith may come
> Where He His message is bringing:
> I know mine own, mine own know me,
> Ye, not the world, my face shall see:
> My peace I leave with you. Amen.[15]

In almost every respect Grundtvig's hymn is the opposite of Coleridge's poetry. If, in Coleridge, all comes from deep within in a willed creation dependent hardly at all upon the memory or reproduction of actual scenes or objects experienced, in Grundtvig everything is architectured from outside. Not a solitary but a communal experience, taking its common

---

15. From Kenneth Stevenson, *Jerusalem Revisited* (Washington D.C., 1988), pp. 98-99.

expression from the familiar images of the Bible, from theology and from the sacraments of the Church. As Grundtvig points out in a letter, it was

a chief failing with our Fathers, which we their children must try to correct, that they wished to deal with our Saviour each for himself and to possess him, which can never be the case, as the "Our Father" among other things should have taught them.[16]

Not only the community, theology and literature of the church, but its physical presence in the act of worship in its buildings – font and altar – is drawn into the poetic celebration. From their physicality we are drawn back to the memorial and anamnesis of the Passion and the eternal presence of Christ in history. Coleridge's poem is outside time: Grundtvig's hymn draws all time together. In each case we are brought to rest in the moment of the verse.

In the third stanza of the hymn, the temporal dimension is replaced by the spatial, which, in its turn, is drawn into the poetic moment. The gathering is completed in the Gospel words of Christ himself, and his final blessing in words also familiar from the church's liturgy. And in each poem we are brought to the still point of Paradise itself – one in the total absorption of the reader into the mysterious experience of reading and "pure imagination", the other in the mystery of communion with Christ realized within the diverse resources of the hymn. The poem of Coleridge and the hymn of Grundtvig share, it seems to me, an elusive quality, an indirectness and metaphorical quality which is both biblical and most profoundly poetic.

I am, of course, conscious of the limitations of reading and understanding of Grundtvig because of my lack of Danish and what strike me as on the whole rather flat translations of his work into English. Coleridge, however, as the subject of my doctoral thesis and a full-length book, has been a part of me for very many years. Nevertheless, I am prepared to say that I am struck by the similarities between these two extraordinary, many-sided and deeply religious men, and how these are reflected in two very different kinds of poetry which they wrote. In his essay *Grundtvig the Hymnwriter*[17] Christian Thodberg describes how, in the hymns, "the theological and poetic motives multiply, even though he always remains within his own universe of words and images".[18]

As I have suggested, Coleridge and Grundtvig have in common a

16. Allchin, p. 135.
17. *Tradition and Renewal*, pp. 160-96.
18. ibid., p. 189.

passionate concern for immediate, political and practical matters, while at the same time they are poets and *literary*, library men. They *create* a universe in language, from imagination and deeply felt matter of belief. It is the power of that literary universe which make Coleridge and Grundtvig so important, for it is a power to reflect indirectly and discretely a world and change a world. It is not the limited, *literal* quality of language whose referentiality is direct and simple. It is, rather, that literariness which denies the immediate presentation of thought or exercise of practicalities, but is dynamic to change and unsettle, in the very act of reading, in the activity of singing.

Grundtvig and the English Hymn of the Romantic Period

By J.R. Watson

In most studies of hymnology, there is little reference to parallel movements in the history of English poetry. The fact that Herbert's hymns were
influenced to some extent by Donne and the "metaphysical" mode, or that
Isaac Watts wrote at the same time as Dryden and Pope, is usually held to
be irrelevant. And yet, of course, the way in which these writers ap-
proached the business of writing hymns was not determined solely by
matters of worship and theology. Literary and philosophical assumptions
were also relevant: the writing of the hymns was affected by the total
environment in which the authors lived – the assumptions of the age both
politically and culturally, the conditions not only of the age but of the
literature and philosophy of the age.

The argument of this paper is that we must see the hymns written
during what we call the Romantic period – if we are to appreciate them
fully – in the light of the critical and creative preoccupations of that period.
This, I suggest, is true of the English writers, as it is also true of the hymns
of N.F.S. Grundtvig: so that one of the aims of this paper is to see parallels
between the work of the English hymn writers of the eighteenth and early
nineteenth centuries and the underlying preoccupations and techniques of
Grundtvig's hymnody. The conditions of production, in the case of Grundtvig, include not only his contacts with English hymn writers such as J.M.
Neale (recently discussed by Leon Litvack)[1] but also the intellectual and
emotional preoccupations of English Romanticism and English hymnody.

In considering the work of any writer, it is important to determine, as
far as is possible, the historical conditions under which his or her work was
produced. Of course, a total awareness of such things is impossible: the
contemporaneity of a writer's work, its complex (unconscious as well as
conscious) exclusions and inclusions, can never be fully recaptured. We
read a work, aware of its past, but also of our own present: indeed if we
are not careful, the tyranny of our own present will lead us into a reading

---

1.   Leon B. Litvack, "The Greek Hymn Translations and Adaptations of N.F.S. Grundt-
     vig and J.M. Neale", *Bulletin of the Hymn Society* no 183, April 1990, pp. 181-87.

that is a hermeneutical circle, so that we get from a text what we put in to it. It is a text which we still have and read, yet which also belongs to its own time and to the conditions under which it was produced. As Schleiermacher observed, "part of the intelligibility of each (work of art) derives from its original purpose":

a work of art is really rooted in its own soil. It loses its meaning when it is wrenched from this environment and enters into general commerce; it is like something that has been saved from the fire but still bears the marks of the burning upon it.[2]

The hymns of Grundtvig have been saved from the fire of oblivion by the recognition that they still have a function and purpose in worship and spiritual expression. Yet they bear the marks of the burning upon them in that they are characterized by Grundtvig's response to the needs of his own time, and in that time by certain features that are part of the matrix of European Romanticism. They share these characteristics with other writers of the same period, and some English examples and parallels are the subject of this paper.

I begin with the religious imagination. The word *imagination* is one which all students of Romanticism have learned to use with care, but which can be controlled for certain purposes by Coleridge's description of it in *Biographia Literaria* as being Primary and Secondary, and as being opposed to Fancy. It is essentially creative, and not aggregative; and in its Secondary form it is original. It does not add an idea to an image, or an interpretation to an illustration, but it creates and then re-creates. Its Primary act of creation is God-like, a repetition in the finite mind of the work of the infinite I AM; its Secondary action "dissolves, diffuses, dissipates, in order to re-create".[3] The Imagination is deeply implicated, as Kathleen Wheeler has shown, in the processes of Romantic irony, that "principle of artistic creation"[4] which involves the creative interaction between subjective and objective, between the finite and the infinite. The Romantic theorists knew that the act of poetic creation was an expression of a relationship between the ideal and the actual, the divine and the human; religious art fulfilled the desire of the Romantic theorists for unity and wholeness, recognizing the oppositions and yet reconciling them. Kathleen Wheeler quotes Solger:

2. Friedrich Schleiermacher, *Asthetik*, pp. 84ff.; quoted in Hans-Georg Gadamer, *Truth and Method* (New York, 1975), p. 148.
3. S.T. Coleridge, *Biographia Literaria*, chapter 13; in volume 7 of *The Collected Works of Samuel Taylor Coleridge*, Biographia Literaria, ed. James Engell and W.J. Bate (London, 1983), I. 304.
4. Kathleen Wheeler, *Sources, Processes and Methods in Coleridge's Biographia Literaria* (Cambridge, 1980), p. 65.

Philosophy, art, and religion are the three necessary parts of a harmonious culture; Philosophy without art is means without purpose; art without philosophy is end without beginning; and both without religion are utterly debased, vile and godless: philosophy becomes insolence and violence, and art arrogant amusement.[5]

So when Grundtvig describes the soul as a bird, in *Alt hvad som fuglevinger fik*, he begins with an idea from *Isaiah* 40:31, "They shall mount up with wings like eagles", but the original simile is dissolved, diffused, dissipated, to be re-created. The soul rises upward:

> My soul, thou art of noble birth,
> Thy thoughts rise upward from the earth
> As if on eagle pinions.
> Most lofty is thy upward flight
> When thou ascendest, robed in light,
> To heaven's fair dominions.

The soul in flight is what D.H. Lawrence would later describe as a constitutive symbol, sufficient in itself without having to be interpreted or allegorized. It is consonant with Coleridge's idea of the imagination as giving birth to symbol, rather than allegory. Allegory, which is the application of an interpretation to a narrative, is the product of fancy: symbol is the result of an imaginative vision, in which the symbols are "consubstantial with the truths, of which they are the conductors". As Schelling saw, the symbol both represented the idea which it represented and became a part of it: it can never be fully captured in a summary, because it is a living thing, what Coleridge (in writing about Holy Scripture) called "the living educts of the imagination". I would wish to set beside this Grundtvig's letter, as quoted by Professor Thodberg in his essay on *Grundtvig the Hymnwriter*:

As long as our hymns fail to express the living feeling that we have already passed over from death into life, that we have found the everlasting life in God's love and have drunk from the chalice of His salvation, but express only the memory of God's great and wonderful works among the children of man and the hope of redemption from the chains of vanity, then they remain flat and weak compared with what the song of God's servant Moses, and the psalms of David and Asaph meant to Israel's people who believed.[6]

Here Grundtvig contrasts "the living feeling" with the workings of me-

---

5.   ibid., p. 73.
6.   Christian Thodberg, "Grundtvig the Hymnwriter", in *N.F.S. Grundtvig, Tradition and Renewal*.

mory, which of course is precisely the distinction which Coleridge makes between imagination, which is "essentially *vital*", and fancy, which is "no other than a mode of Memory".[7] Memory is only part of the mental and emotional life, and the living feeling which Grundtvig speaks of involves the whole person.

Wholeness and the fragment

Wholeness is of great importance to the Romantic theorists. Coleridge spoke of poetry as "bringing the whole soul of man into activity", and for the German theorists Shakespeare became the great example of an artist who could combine subjective and objective. Like finite and infinite, subjective and objective were oppositions which could be reconciled in art. The language of that reconciliation was the symbol, which is itself "a living fragment of the experience or idea it seeks to represent".[8]

The word fragment is important, because (precisely because it is aware of wholeness) Romantic art recognizes the essential incompleteness of any utterance, and also because any fragment encourages interpretation and attempted understanding in ways which provoke thought. In the writing of hymns, I think that it is true to say that a distinct awareness of the fragmentary nature of literary expression is first found in Charles Wesley. His predecessors versified scripture, and explored devotional needs, as in the Communion Hymns of Isaac Watts or Joseph Stennett; but it was Charles Wesley who first displayed the true Romantic questioning, and the awareness of incompleteness:

> Where shall my wond'ring soul begin?
> How shall I all to heaven aspire?

Wesley begins by not knowing where to begin; he asks a question which he knows cannot be answered. And yet in asking the question, in the very statement of aspiration, he is making a statement about the self, and the self as poet. He can make the statement because he is, as the next lines tell us -

> A slave redeemed from death and sin,
> A brand plucked from eternal fire, ...

The verse points from the finite to the infinite; it does so in the full know-

7.   *Biographia Literaria*, ed. Engell and Bate, I. 305.
8.   Kathleen Wheeler (ed.), *German Aesthetic and Literary Criticism; the Romantic Ironists and Goethe* (Cambridge, 1984), p. 10.

ledge of what it is doing – writing a hymn, which came to be known as "the Wesleys' conversion hymn"; and it is a fragment of experience, the poet trying to come to terms with the experience of new birth and free grace. It is strangely parallel to Grundtvig's letter already quoted, with its reference to expressing

the living feeling that we have already passed over from death into life, that we have found the everlasting life in God's love and have drunk from the chalice of His salvation.

Wesley and Grundtvig were both voluminous hymn writers, and this, I suggest, points to the moment, the great question, as symbolic and consequently fragmentary. The asking of the question is a momentary response, and yet it is also a fragment which leads to hundreds of others. Charles Wesley sought to begin: the subject was so encompassing, that he could not find a place to enter it. And yet, of course, the very asking of the question is itself an entrance. What it also does, of course, is to pave the way for thousands of other inquiries: the relationship between the finite and the infinite, the human and the divine, is so complex and all-enveloping that any attempt to express it would be inadequate. Charles Wesley is wrestling, not only with the inadequacy of language, but with the inability of the soul to comprehend the infinite except in momentary insights, the fragments of symbolic utterance. His response is to seek for the infinite everywhere – to write poem after poem, using symbol upon symbol, in a vain attempt to grasp the unattainable. So he wrote some 8,000 fragments of hymns, and completed hymns; each is a response, or rather a re-phrasing, of the original question – "Where shall my wond'ring soul begin?" And, before he has finished, the question becomes not "Where shall I begin?" – but "Where shall I ever end?"

I would be bold to suggest at this point that Grundtvig's considerable output, while nowhere near the size of Charles Wesley's, was a similar attempt to reconcile the duality of the finite and infinite. "His works are so voluminous", says Canon Allchin, "that it is difficult to know where to begin".[9] Precisely: and in that voluminousness there is not only the spirit of an extremely energetic man, but also the spirit of the *saved* man, the man in all his fullness. We come back to the idea of *wholeness* in poetry: for Charles Wesley and for Grundtvig, there was a sense that in writing their hymns they were themselves, wholly themselves, expressing that which was their innermost nature. As Stephen Prickett has written, comparing St Augustine and Wordsworth:

9.   A.M. Allchin, *The Kingdom of Love and Knowledge* (London, 1979), p. 71.

the peculiar fascination and greatness of Augustine is that he could not separate the 'spiritual' from the whole of the rest of his mental development – any more than Wordsworth could separate the 'poetic'. Augustine, like Wordsworth, was in search of a particular quality of *wholeness* in his life; a wholeness for which his religious intuition gave him the perspective. He begins an exploration of *feeling* as a mode of religious experience that is rediscovered with the advent of Romanticism.[10]

One might want to raise a question-mark about the long gap between St. Augustine and the Romantics, particularly with reference to the religious poetry of Donne or Herbert. But Prickett is certainly right in wishing to draw attention to the importance of feeling as a mode of religious experience. "I felt my heart strangely warmed" was John Wesley's description of his 1738 "conversion". And the symbolic language which is used for this is that of the heart, traditionally the seat of the affections. It was what Wordsworth called "the human heart by which we live", with its tenderness, its joys and its fears. So, searching for the parallel effects of hymns and folk songs, Grundtvig wrote: "bygone times learnt that such songs speak loudly to the heart and lend the soul wings to fly high above earthly things".[11] As Canon Allchin has written, the word "heart" "speaks of a centre in men where feeling and thought, intuition and will are fused together into one",[12] and he argues that our current neglect of the heart is an impoverishment of our religious life. The Romantics would have called this a neglect of wholeness.

Wholeness and metaphor

It is significant that Allchin's comment comes in an essay entitled "the Spirit as Life-giver", because the Spirit, the Holy Ghost, has always been seen as entering the heart. Charles Wesley writes of it in terms of the traditional image of fire:

Refining fire, go through my heart...

Grundtvig's term is Hjerte-Dronning, heart-queen, a more resonant image than that of Charles Wesley, because it suggests also royalty, remote beauty, queenly presence, and magnificence. It is one example of the way in which Grundtvig, like the Romantic period hymn writers in England, excelled in metaphor. Imagination is, in Kathleen Wheeler's words, "the

10. Stephen Prickett, *Romanticism and Religion* (Cambridge, 1976), pp. 89-90.
11. *Poetical Writings*, pp. 299-300; quoted in Thodberg, "Grundtvig the Hymnwriter", p. 162.
12. Allchin, *The Kingdom of Love and Knowledge*, p. 72.

faculty which evolves metaphors",[13] and we can notice, in the hymn already quoted, that Grundtvig changes the mode of expression from the biblical simile ("They shall mount up with wings as eagles") to a metaphor which expresses the state of the flying soul. Such an employment of metaphor has two principal consequences.

In the first place, it encourages the mind in an active reading: because metaphors transfer meaning from one thing to another, the mind has to make the connection in order to accommodate the new idea. Our object, in reading religious metaphors, is to make sense of what is being said, and in that process the religious understanding is increased. An obvious one is the image of the building with a foundation, built on the Word of God. What is fascinating about this image is that it is both a symbolic rendering of the state of the soul and an instance from contemporary Denmark which Grundtvig uses as an example. The *Song-Work of the Danish Church* of 1836 refers not only to the revival of hymn singing but also to the ruined church tower at Copenhagen. For Grundtvig, the importance of such imagery is that it goes with his fear of abstraction.

This is the second consequence of the predominance of metaphor. It allows the intertexture of body and spirit in the imagery which is used to express both. The spiritual image, in particular, is rooted in the processes of physical life. Allchin quotes from *The World as Sacrament* a statement of belief which is founded on this fear of abstraction:

From this lack of understanding of the Holy Spirit comes our times' abstract conception of spirit and spiritual reality, and its material concept of freedom and personality, which where they are dominant make any living relationship between heaven and earth, God and man, and thus between Christ and us, evidently impossible.[14]

Grundtvig saw what Blake saw: the deadliness of single vision, whether it be abstraction for the Holy Spirit or materialism for the processes of humanity. What was required was the ability to unify the two, and metaphor and symbol do that, as Coleridge saw: his image is of the chariot with wheels from *Ezekiel* chapter 1:

These are the Wheels which Ezekiel beheld, when the hand of the Lord was upon him, and he saw visions of God as he sate among the captives by the river of Chebar. Whithersoever the Spirit was to go the wheels went, and thither was their spirit to go: for the spirit of the living creature was in the wheels also.

13. Wheeler, *Sources, Processes and Methods*, p. 59.
14. Quoted in Allchin, *The Kingdom of Love and Knowledge*, p. 87.

Coleridge is attempting to explain the way in which content and form are inseparable, but in the process he also finds himself blurring the distinction between inner and outer. The life of symbol and metaphor, the "living educts of the imagination" that are Holy Scripture, depend on the refusal to separate abstract and concrete, body and spirit. Hymn singing is itself a very good example of this: it involves the written text on the page but also the sound of that text when sung by a congregation. As Grundtvig wrote, "sound is the life of the Word and tone is the power of the sound which reveals the Spirit".[15]

Thus Charles Wesley's "Wrestling Jacob" is both a description of Jacob wrestling with the unknown and the soul struggling with God, who is Christ. It appears to be allegorical and typological, but in its presentation it becomes more than that, because it *enacts* the struggle in the present tense, emphasizing the tension, the human weakness, and the mercy of the Saviour: so that the struggle becomes at once a victory and a surrender, in the paradox which is at the centre of Christian action and understanding. Similarly, Cowper's celebrated image, which appears so grotesque -

> There is a fountain filled with blood,
> Drawn from Immanuel's veins;
> And sinners, plunged beneath that flood
> Lose all their guilty stains -

depends, if we are to read it properly, on a refusal to be abstract about redemption or materialistic about blood. It is a classic example of Grundtvig's perception that such abstract conceptions and material concepts are destructive. The hymn from which these lines come, "Praise for the Fountain Opened", is one which is concerned with redemption through the blood of Christ, but also with the sacrament of the Holy Communion, which is itself, of course, the most profound and dramatic example of the reconciling of finite and infinite: "This is my blood; drink this". As Grundtvig saw,

> on the Lord's Table...

> in the tent of the Word
> Heaven and earth are fused together.

15. Christmas Day sermon, 1822: quoted in Thodberg, "Grundtvig the Hymnwriter", p. 166.

Nature for the Romantic theorists, therefore, is not objectively described phenomena, because "all objects (*as* objects) are essentially fixed and dead".[16] Nature is the interaction of the inner and outer, the subjective and objective: it is at the point where spirit finds itself in substance, where the symbolic, and hence the fragmentary, is present in form. For the Romantic hymn writers, therefore, the Incarnation is a crucial event. The Word is made flesh, and the dayspring from on high hath visited us. Nature is transformed. The finest example in Romantic hymnody is probably James Montgomery's *Hail to the Lord's anointed*, where the third verse depends upon the image of the dayspring:

> He shall come down like showers,
> Upon the fruitful earth;
> And love, joy, hope, like flowers,
> Spring in His path to birth:
> Before Him on the mountains
> Shall Peace, the herald, go;
> And righteousness, in fountains,
> From hill to valley flow.

As spring after winter and as rain after drought, the presence of the Incarnate Christ is felt: but how do we explain the working of a verse such as this? in what way is it different from the kind of hymnody that has preceded it?

I think that the theories of the German and English aestheticians help to explain the processes, as I have tried to suggest above. In particular, they can assist us in three ways, to understand the treatment of nature, the self, and the spirit.

Nature

Montgomery's verse about the dayspring is about nature, and the spring: the April showers come, the flowers appear, and the frozen streams begin to flow from the mountains to the plains. Yet it is, of course, about the coming of Jesus Christ, not just at Bethlehem, although that is being celebrated here, but in a perpetual coming into the human heart. It is, like the struggle of wrestling Jacob, both physical and spiritual, a kind of psychosomatic process. In the coming of the dayspring, as in the Communion Bread and Wine,

---

16. *Biographia Literaria*, ed. Engell and Bate, I. 304.

the heavenly in the Spirit
And the earthly in the hand
Fuse together, basically one
As in the Word, so in the mouth
To the benefit of soul and body.

The process of fusing described here is fundamental to the theories of Romantic poetry, but also deeply involved in its practice. Montgomery's verse requires a reading that is simultaneously responsive to the heavenly and the earthly – to the effects of spring after winter, to the coming of Jesus Christ at the Incarnation, and to the perpetual influence of the dayspring from on high on the human heart. It is also a representation of the ideal: Montgomery is celebrating the coming of the Kingdom of God upon earth. In this he takes and uses Romantic idealism for his own religious purposes. He links the Romantic emphasis on the sublime and inspirational with his religious belief, and this takes him beyond reason to the intuitive. It is parallel to the reaction of the German Romantic theorists to the ethics of Kant, as described by Kathleen Wheeler:

Man's delight in beauty and the gradual refinement of his taste was seen not only as a worthy end in itself, but also as a means of inspiring him to knowledge of his transcendental self and thereby to knowledge of reality. Love of beauty led naturally to love of the good, so that the harsh demands of Kant's Stoic duty were replaced by an emotional yearning to live morally – an inner drive, rather than duty imposed from without and performed without the desire to do the good.[17]

In the same way Montgomery's vision of the coming of the Lord's anointed is inspirational rather than rational. His claim that the whole world will worship at the feet of God is something which can be intuited but not proved; and Romantic theory links with Christian doctrine to produce a particular kind of hymn:

Arabia's desert ranger
To him shall bow the knee,
The Ethiopian stranger
His glory come to see;
With offerings of devotion,
Ships from the isles shall meet,
To pour the wealth of ocean
In tribute at his feet.

17. Wheeler (ed.), *German Aesthetic and Literary Criticism*, p. 2.

I think that it is no good objecting to this on the grounds that it is unproved assertion; it is a particular mode of utterance which intends to speak of the world transformed and the self exalted. The key to this process is the Incarnation.

Montgomery is perhaps best known in this country for two hymns which are concerned with the Incarnation, *Hail to the Lord's anointed* and *Angels from the realms of glory*. The first, as we have seen, deals with the dayspring from on high; the second describes the coming of the angels, the denizens of the realms of glory, to proclaim the good news of Christ's birth to the shepherds. Both are symbolic fragments of what for Montgomery was the central experience, the transformation of the world by the entrance of God into history. So *Angels from the realms of glory* ends:

> Sinners, wrung with true repentance
> Doomed for guilt to endless pains,
> Justice now revokes your sentence,
> Mercy calls you – break your chains:
> Come and worship,
> Worship Christ, the new-born King.

The imagery is less ecstatic than that of *Hail to the Lord's anointed*: it comes from the Christmas psalm, *Psalm 85*, in which "Mercy and truth are met together: righteousness and peace have kissed each other". In the processes of reconciliation, opposites unite, as they do in the poetry of the Romantics, because that poetry pushes towards improbable connections, and not only in language: the old order of righteousness and mercy as separate things is dissolved, diffused, dissipated, and what is recreated is a new order of the two things together – neither losing its identity, but each fusing with the other.

Montgomery may be usefully compared with another English hymn writer of this period, Reginald Heber, Heber was born in 1783, and so was Grundtvig's exact contemporary: he finished up as a short-lived but exemplary Bishop of Calcutta. He is best known for his Trinity Sunday hymn, *Holy, holy, Holy*, and for his Epiphany hymn, *Brightest and best of the sons of the morning*, which begins and ends with the same verse:

> Brightest and best of the sons of the morning,
> Dawn on our darkness, and lend us thine aid;
> Star of the east, the horizon adorning,
> Guide where our infant Redeemer is laid.

By placing this verse at the beginning and end of the hymn, Heber accepts a certain circularity of movement, a return to the starting-place, which is quite unlike Montgomery's progressive structure. Heber's hymn is not about the transformation of nature but about the need for guidance: it is possible, I think, that Heber knew the importance of the Epiphany for Eastern Christians, and was aware of its Greek name *ta phota*, the lights. The hymn is therefore a prayer for guidance from the star, and from Christ himself. The first line must refer to the morning star, but also to Christ himself as the morning star: Heber is in touch with a tradition of devotional symbolism that goes back to earliest times.

In spite of the ingenuity of this first line, Heber is much less Romantic than Montgomery. His hymn is a prayer for enlightenment from a human being who knows that he lives in a fallen world. There is some attractive natural description in the hymn, but it is there to try to bring the detail of the scene to the eye, not to transform it:

> Cold on his cradle the dewdrops are shining,
> Low lies his head with the beasts of the stall;
> Angels adore him in slumber reclining,
> Maker, and monarch, and Saviour of all.

The subject of this verse is the traditional one of the human child who is also the king of the universe; but Heber keeps the two halves of the verse separate, and throughout the hymn he never attempts to reconcile the finite and the infinite in the way that Montgomery does:

> Say, shall we yield him, in costly devotion,
> Odours of Edom, and offerings divine,
> Gems of the mountain, and pearls of the ocean,
> Myrrh from the forest, or gold from the mine?

> Vainly we offer each ample oblation...

The hymn is exotic but not transformative; as in all of Heber's hymns it is conscious of the worshipper, praying and praising, but not changed into something different. His fervour is deliberately linked to a sober management of the spiritual life; and in his hymn writing, nature is not transformed. A good example is his hymn for the seventh Sunday after Trinity:

> When spring unlocks the flowers to paint the laughing soil;
> When summer's balmy showers refresh the mower's toil;
> When winter binds in frosty chains the fallow and the flood;
> In God the earth rejoiceth still, and owns his Maker good.

> The birds that wake the morning, and those that love the shade;
> The winds that sweep the mountain, or lull the drowsy glade;
> The sun that from his amber bower rejoiceth on his way,
> The moon and stars – their Master's name in silent pomp display.

Heber's language is little more than assertion, though with desperate attempts at giving life to nature, such as the reference to laughing soil. We might ask ourselves why it does not work; and I think the answer is that it is a crude animation of nature, without any sense of the interaction between the self and the external world. Heber's hymn, in fact, ends by brushing nature aside as irrelevant:

> The flowers of spring may wither, the hope of summer fade,
> The autumn droop in winter, the birds forsake the shade;
> The winds be lulled, the sun and moon forget their old decree;
> But we, in nature's latest hour, O Lord, will cling to thee!

The self

The heart occurs with great frequency in the hymns of Charles Wesley, and of Cowper, who worried about the state of his own heart:

> The Lord will happiness divine
> On contrite hearts bestow:
> Then tell me, gracious God, is mine
> A contrite heart, or no?

Cowper is exceptional among Romantic period hymn writers in his preoccupation with his own self: he is so concerned with what Vincent Newey, in his book on Cowper, has called the "psychodrama" of his own religious life, that he has little time for other things: unlike Heber, he is not concerned with the Christian Year, or the great festivals of the church, and the nearest he gets to an acknowledgment of public worship is his hymn *Jesus where'er thy people meet*, which was clearly intended for his own local situation as a member of John Newton's evangelical church. However, the force of Cowper's writing comes in part from this concentration on the individual predicament:

> Where is the blessedness I knew
> When first I saw the Lord?
> Where is the soul-refreshing view
> Of Jesus and his word?

What peaceful hours I then enjoyed!
How sweet their memory still!
But now I find an aching void
The world can never fill.

The "I" is important to a hymn-writer, because it declares the hymn to be an authentic and personal experience. Yet Cowper realises that it is also important to de-personalise Christian experience, and at one point he makes the decision to write in the third person:

Sometimes a light surprises
The Christian while he sings...

But few of his hymns approach the impersonal majesty of Grundtvig's hymns, influenced as they are by Greek or Lutheran examples. What is interesting about them, and about Montgomery's, is their openness, their vulnerability. They speak of individual temptation and personal problems. So Montgomery can write:

In the hour of trial,
Jesus, pray for me,
Lest by base denial
I depart from thee;
When thou seest me waver,
With a look recall,
Nor, through fear or favour,
Suffer me to fall.

Montgomery frequently allows himself to admit the possibility of failure and sin, and this is one of his more attractive features as a hymn writer. But he can also be brilliant at the metaphors for the self. In one hymn, *Forever with the Lord*, he introduces a rather awkwardly-expressed Platonic image of the soul pent in the body, and absent from God:

Here in the body pent,
Absent from Him I roam,

but this allows him to continue with a wonderful image of the soul on its journey:

Yet nightly pitch my moving tent
A day's march nearer home.

The tent is moving in time, rather than space; in the pilgrimage of life, every day brings the pilgrim nearer to heaven, so that

> my spirit faints
> To reach the land I love,
> The bright inheritance of saints,
> Jerusalem above!

Montgomery's image of the soul pitching its tent is an extraordinary and powerful one, I think because in the days when beds had curtains, the process of going to bed must have been a little like putting oneself to sleep in a tent. What is happening here is that just as in the earlier example Montgomery was transforming nature, so here he is transforming the self to a pilgrim journeyer, camping every night at a different location in time if not in space.

Montgomery is very different from Heber, whose propriety and reticence are everywhere evident. His hymn for Whitsunday does not ask for the fire which Charles Wesley demands, indeed specifically rejects it:

> We ask not, Lord, thy cloven flame,
> Or tongues of various tone;
> But long thy praises to proclaim
> With fervour in our own.

The rejection of speaking with tongues is in character with the serious refusal of Heber's hymnody to engage in the inspirational or enthusiastic manifestations of religion. So although he is a contemporary of Grundtvig, he is in fact far less original than some of those who were eighteenth-century writers, such as Wesley and Cowper.

The Spirit

It is not surprising that Canon Allchin's essay on Grundtvig is entitled *The Spirit as Life-giver*. It is, of course, about the perception of the work of the Holy Spirit in Grundtvig's work; but it also has the sense that the letter killeth, but the spirit giveth life. So Coleridge, in *The Statesman's Manual*, addressed himself to the question of living religion. Its crucial quotation is "As sure as God liveth", and the important word there is "liveth":

The understanding may suggest motives, may avail itself of motives, and make judicious conjectures respecting the probable consequences of actions. But the knowledge taught in the Scriptures *produces* the motives, *involves* the consequences; and its highest formula is still: AS SURE AS GOD LIVETH, so will it be unto thee![18]

Coleridge is arguing that there are deeper causes than motives of self-interest and self-preservation, mightier powers at work than expediency. And what he calls notions, and natural phenomena, are only useful in adding to our knowledge when they are, as he puts it "actualized by an idea":

Notions, the depthless abstractions of fleeting phenomena, the shadows of sailing vapors, the colorless repetitions of rain-bows, have effected their utmost when they have added to the *distinctness* of our knowledge. For this very cause they are of themselves adverse to lofty emotion, and it requires the influence of a light and warmth, not their own, to make them crystallize into a semblance of growth. But every principle is actualized by an idea; and every idea is living, productive, partaketh of infinity, and (as Bacon has sublimely observed) containeth an endless power of semination.[19]

Principles are actualized by ideas; ideas partake of infinity. Coleridge is as always arguing against the deadness of facts. Facts are not science, because science is imaginative, consisting "wholly in ideas and principles"; but there is a materialism, what Coleridge calls elsewhere in *The Statesman's Manual* a "mechanic philosophy" and which he links with the histories and political economy of his own day. In opposition to these are what he calls "principles" and "ideas":

The great PRINCIPLES of our religion, the sublime IDEAS spoken out everywhere in the Old and New Testament, resemble the fixed stars,... At the annunciation of *principles*, of *ideas* the soul of man awakes, and starts up, as an exile in a far distant land at the unexpected sounds of his native language, when after long years of absence, and almost of oblivion, he is suddenly addressed in his own mother-tongue.[20]

In this remarkable passage, Coleridge celebrates the soul's recognition of its own, the deep calling to deep, the internal to the external. In *The Ancient Mariner*, similarly, he portrays the mariner as "yearning" for the stars and the moon:

---

18. S.T. Coleridge, *The Statesman's Manual*; volume 6 of *The Collected Works of Samuel Taylor Coleridge, Lay Sermons*, ed. R.J. White (London, 1972), p. 21.
19. ibid., pp. 23-24.
20. ibid., p. 24.

In his loneliness and fixedness he yearneth towards the journeying Moon, and the stars that still sojourn, yet still move onward; and every where the blue sky belongs to them, and is their appointed rest, and their native country and their own natural homes, which they enter unannounced, as lords that are certainly expected and yet there is a silent joy at their arrival.

In Grundtvig's work this is parallelled by the beautiful *Zion's Song*, in which human beings return to their true selves: the question, which involves the heart,

> Who is there dares remember now
> The heart's sweet morning dream

is answered by the presence of the Holy Spirit, which descends to earth, where -

> ... from trunks of tender beechwood
> Under songs of nightingales
>
> We are building but a guest-room
> For a heavenly Eucharist.

In that guest-room, the soul of man, in Coleridge's words, awakes and starts up, as an exile being suddenly addressed in his own language. And so the Resurrection speaks to the human heart:

> In the dark earth the Saviour lay,
> Now on his throne he is sitting,
> Spirit and life are His Word to us,
> Joyful the tone of our singing.

It was this, as Professor Thodberg has very properly pointed out, that attracted Grundtvig to Montgomery's hymnody: the sense that the Holy Spirit accompanies the Word of God, and without it the Word is none other than lifeless words, a mode of Coleridge's "unenlivened generalized understanding".

The importance of the interaction of the internal and external presided over by the Holy Spirit is, finally, one reason for the split in the nineteenth century between poetry and hymnody, a split which I am inclined to date from the Romantic period. It was Reginald Heber, who had admired *Childe Harold's Pilgrimage*, who regarded the later work as the systematic and increasing prostitution of those splendid talents to the expression of feelings, and the promulgation of opinions, which, as Christians, as Englishmen, and even as men, we were constrained to regard with abhorrence[21]

and Montgomery, who was born in Ayrshire and liked to compare himself with Burns, wrote a poem comparing him to various birds, which ended:

> O had he never stooped to shame,
> Nor lent a charm to vice,
> How had devotion loved to name
> That bird of paradise!

One of Montgomery's biographers, Jabez Marrat, quoting these lines, adds sententiously:

Burns... would have been an unshadowed glory to his native land, and have given strains of lofty worship to its churches and homes, if he had been true to his nobler self, and had consecrated his powers in the service of Christ.[22]

What is disappointing here is the righteousness with which Burns is condemned, a view which reflects the mutual antipathy between the poet and the "unco' guid". What is even more unfortunate is the way in which the spirit of poetry, the imagination, comes to be seen in this period as sacred or as secular; so that at one end of the Romantic period it is quite natural for someone like Mrs Barbauld to write pious *Hymns in Prose* (1781), and at the other for Shelley to write (in 1816) a hymn which is called *A Hymn to Intellectual Beauty*.

What we find in Montgomery, as in Grundtvig, is an attempt to keep alive that transformation of nature in the context of the work of the Holy Spirit. What we find in Heber is a series of pictures, often elegantly presented; but the great strength of English Romantic poetry is found in the interaction of external and internal in modes that are essentially secular – Wordsworth's doctrine of nature, Keats' sense of transience, Shelley's intellectual beauty, Byron's liberty. What followed in Victorian hymnody was John Mason Neale and his antiquarianism, *Hymns Ancient & Modern*, and the split between religion and poetry which Matthew Arnold lamented; and one reason for that split, I suggest, may have been that in England there was no N.F.S. Grundtvig.

21. Andrew Rutherford (ed.), *Byron, the Critical Heritage* (London, 1970), pp. 236-37.
22. Jabez Marrat, *James Montgomery, Christian Poet and Philanthropist* (London, 1879), p. 7.

The Importance of Baptism in Grundtvig's View of Christianity

By Christian Thodberg

The most important theological and personal problem for Grundtvig was where and how does Christ become contemporary with his people, his Church? Both as a theologian and a historian Grundtvig had relied on the absolute authority of the Bible but historical-critical biblical scholarship had already in the eighteenth century been shaking the credibility of the Bible and this heightened Grundtvig's problem; where was God's living voice heard – how did God speak clearly and unambiguously to him, the individual Christian?

This is the background to Grundtvig's "matchless discovery" of the apostolic confession of faith (i.e., the apostles' creed) in 1825 – or to be more exact, not just the confession of faith but the renunciation of the devil and the confession of faith as they are used in the interrogative form in the service of baptism. It is generally maintained that in the apostolic confession of faith Grundtvig found the unshakable Christian foundation which he did not find in the Bible. It was thus that Grundtvig himself described the matchless discovery. But if one investigates the contemporary sermons more closely, one sees that earlier on, Grundtvig not only discovered baptism but also eucharist as places in the church's worship where God speaks to us *now*, as opposed to the scriptures which spoke to them *then*. In the rite of baptism it is the interrogative and responsive words and in the eucharistic rite especially in the imperative words in the institution narrative which have this function.(Take this and eat it... Do this in remembrance of me... Drink this all of you...) Grundtvig expressed this concisely in the programmatic lines, "Only at the font and the altar/ Do we hear God's word to us..."[1]

It is these words which in Grundtvig's view Jesus himself had proclaimed and had commanded his people to repeat till the end of time in connection with baptism and communion. It is these words and actions which demonstrate the church's continuity. Christian people are one and the same from Jesus' time till now; there is only one people, one church.

That did not mean, that the Bible, the Gospel, and preaching lost their

---

1. GSV, vol. V, no. 232, stanza 1.

significance in the church. On the contrary the imperative words of the rite give the key to preaching; they establish the links between the texts of the Bible and their contemporary proclamation.

When for example Grundtvig preached on the story of the widow's son at Nain (Luke 7:11-17) on Trinity XVI, 1836 he could maintain that Jesus' word to the widow, "Do not weep", and to the dead youth, "Rise up", cannot naturally relate to us; they were said to them then. Jesus' presence for us now is to be found in the words of the rite.

I declare, just as surely as Jesus Christ is God's only begotten son, and just as surely as the baptism we are baptized with and the holy communion to which we are invited are instituted by him, so he is also present wherever people are baptized, are fed and nourished, on his behalf with his Word, and it is he himself who speaks to those who hear his voice, he himself who asks, do you believe, he himself who says to the believer I baptize you in the name of the Father, the Son and the Holy Ghost, he himself who invites those who believe and are baptized to his table, and says to them, "Take this and eat it, this is my body which is given for you; drink of this all of you, for this is the cup of the new covenant in my blood, which is poured out for you for the forgiveness of sins." It is he himself, our Lord Jesus Christ who speaks this Word through the mouth of his servant who has been sent out for this very purpose, and whoever receives this word and keeps it in his heart as God's Word will discover that it is life and spirit, has the Spirit in itself which gives life, the Holy Spirit who is Christ's true representative on earth, and as the spirit of truth is one with the Lord. Yes, this is my Witness and therefore I have often said and I repeat that the Lord has met his people in the Spirit, as in today's Gospel he met the widow and her only son, has halted the bier and said to the church our mother, do not weep, and by awakening his Word from the dead through the means of grace he has awoken the church's hope and confidence which he in the end is himself, the Word of the living God.[2]

It is affirmed that "it is he himself who speaks" in the words of the rite. This stresses what great significance the rites of baptism and communion had for Grundtvig. This is why the position he took in the controversy about the baptismal rite is so important. The living word of which Grundtvig constantly spoke is to be found in an exemplary way in the words of the rite. They are the core of Grundtvig's view both of worship and of Christianity itself.

The meaning of baptism to Grundtvig appears amongst other things from his close concern with the particular elements of the rite and the

2. Christian Thodberg (ed.), *Grundtvigs Prædikener*, vol. IX (København, Gad, 1985), p. 310.

articulation of the rite as a whole. With the central place which Grundtvig's hymns have won in Danish worship, his view of baptism has come, so to say, to be sung into the congregations and thus his hymns have had a great influence on the conception of baptism.

Exorcism and the sign of the cross

For Grundtvig who through the whole of his life maintained "the old baptism", it was a stumbling-block that he had been the first child to be baptized in his father's parish in 1783 with the new, rationalistically influenced baptismal rite introduced in that year, that is to say a rite without the exorcisms (of which the first ran, "Go forth thou unclean spirit, make way for the Holy Spirit...").

Since I know that there was a change made in baptism the year I was born, so that I was baptized without the exorcisms of the devil, and with the new introduction of Bishop Balle, without so far as I can see that making any difference to the efficacy of baptism as between the fathers and myself. so I as a parent would naturally enough not raise any objection if the child was baptized with another introduction, as long as it was appropriate to faith and baptism, or if one simply omitted what I do not consider to be the more essential things. But if one left out more than I understand, and I know that it is very ancient at baptism, if not as ancient as baptism itself...[3]

Grundtvig knew well that making the sign of the cross was in general popular use as a magic act, but it was not so at baptism. The accompanying words make the decisive difference. In the baptismal rite under consideration these were, "Receive the sign of the holy cross both on thy face and on thy breast in witness that thou shalt believe in the crucified Lord Jesus Christ". For Grundtvig undoubtedly they meant more. For him was all-important that it was Jesus himself who spoke.

> Make a cross with the Lord's voice
> Before your face and your breast
> So that we can perceive
> That our Jesus is he
> Who despite the cross's death and shame
> Has the word of the Father[4].

3. *Udvalgte Skrifter*, vol. VIII (Copenhagen 1908), p. 70.
4. *GSV*, vol. I, no. 92, stanza 16.

The sign of the cross was a more distinct sign than exorcism and "was a suitable indication of the passover from the kingdom of darkness to the kingdom of God's dear son which for believers take place in baptism and for that, signing with the cross without the exorcisms is certainly the simplest and the best". But it is the accompanying words spoken by Jesus himself which makes the sign of the cross something special – not just in connection with baptism, but for Grundtvig also the sign of the cross as made on his face and his breast in his morning prayer. This cast light on a favourite hymn stanza in the Danish church.

> God's gentle fingers
> Made the cross on your forehead,
> The voice of God's only-begotten
> Made the cross on your breast
> Then no devil shall harm you;
> Now in your baptism,
> With the hope of salvation
> Both your soul and your heart can be bathed.[5]

The gentle fingers of God with the voice of Jesus make the cross on the forehead and breast baptism thereby driving away the devil. These are words which more than anything else in the Danish church have contributed to maintain the position of both the sign of the cross and the renunciation in the service. It is more difficult at first to understand the last three lines where what the sign of the cross means *now* is described. Usually it would be interpreted like this, "now in the strength of your baptism and the sign of the cross on your face and breast you can hold fast to the hope of salvation." But Grundtvig meant something more concrete. If we analyze his use of words more closely, we see that "hope of salvation" corresponds to "hope of glory" (Col. 1:27) "Christ in you the hope of glory" and in Grundtvig "the hope of glory" comes to be synonymous with the "Our Father". In other words, "Now in this moment, by praying the 'Our Father' you can repeat and renew the sign of the cross at baptism," and this corresponds to the fact that the "Our Father" prayed in Jesus' name is the principle theme in the hymn quoted above.

The Asking-Knocking Prayer

In his own way, Grundtvig stressed baptism as a sacramental action by

---

5.   "Sov sødt barnlille" in *DDS*, no. 488, stanza 2.

letting all the visible actions of the service represent a word of personal address from God.

> The hand does little in this matter
> Still less the arm,
> The sign of the cross is invisible
> On the brow and the breast
> And all that a visible hand
> Can do for the Spirit in the Lord's house
> Is faithful to the mouth's command
> To signify God's Word[6].

The next section was the Asking-Knocking prayer.

O almighty and everlasting God, Father of our Lord Jesus Christ, I beseech thee for this thy servant who prays for the gift of thy baptism, and who for spiritual rebirth implores thy eternal grace. Lord, do thou receive him, thou who hast said, Ask and ye shall receive, seek and ye shall find, knock and it shall be opened to you; do thou now give thy gifts to him who asks, open the door for him who knocks that he may receive eternal blessing in this heavenly flood that kingdom which thou hast promised to all through our Lord Jesus Christ.

This prayer played a corresponding role for Grundtvig.

> Up to Gods house we go
> And boldly knock.
> Open to us is our prayer
> We seek the Son of God.
>
> As quick as lightning
> The door is opened for us,
> In baptism by the Spirit and word
> Here stands our Saviour.[7]

The chief thing here is the promise of the immediate granting of the prayer of the one who knocks in baptism.

6. *GSV*, vol. I, no. 74, stanza 4.
7. "Op til Guds hus vi gå" in *DDS*, no. 376, stanzas 1-2.

The children's gospel and infant baptism

There followed in the baptismal rite the reading of the children's gospel (Mark 10:13-16):

And they brought young children to him, that he should touch them: and his disciples rebuked those that brought them. But when Jesus saw it, he was much displeased, and said unto them, Suffer the little children to come unto me, and forbid them not: for of such is the kingdom of God. Verily I say unto you, Whosoever shall not receive the Kingdom of God as a little Child, he shall not enter therein. And he took them up in his arms, put his hands upon them, and blessed them.

Grundtvig was an unconditional supporter of infant baptism.

> How dare they stand in the way!
> He himself calls the little ones
> Opens in his Father's name
> His saving embrace to them,
> Encloses in his heaven
> Everyone who is like them.[8]

Grundtvig argued insistently for the validity of infant baptism. Experience and the judgment of the ages witnessed that those baptized as children had received the gifts of baptism. Even Augustine who had himself been baptized as an adult preferred infant baptism, because the Holy Spirit finds no obstacle in children.

That children are not conscious of faith follows necessarily from the fact that they are not conscious of anything, but that they have life although they are not conscious of life is something that all can see, and since faith in the truth is nothing else but an open heart for truth, so children can undeniably have faith, although they are not conscious of it; and since all sin is willfulness which springs out of obstinacy, infants are rightly called innocent until their obstinacy awakens. It is in this way that I understand the Lord's word that the kingdom of heaven belongs to children and I can understand the Lord's word that the kingdom of heaven belongs to children and I can scarcely understand how Christians can fail to hear the Lord inviting their children to baptism when he says Suffer the little children to come unto me and forbid them not.[9]

In other places Grundtvig speaks even more clearly about the particular situation of children before God, for instance in his great poem, *The Land of*

8.   *GSV*, vol. I, no. 76, stanza 5.
9.   *Udvalgte Skrifter*, vol. VIII, p. 432-35.

the Living. The first three stanzas speak about the childhood memory of an eternal life surrounded by God's love and care. In other words every human being created in God's image has a memory of his own destiny. The next three stanzas describe the adults' frustrated but obstinate attempt to get back to "the beautiful land", something that remains a fleeting, disappointing, enchanting dream. Only an intervention of God's unconditional love (stanzas 7-13) can bring lost humanity back to "the land beyound the sea", precisely through baptism in which we become children again, i.e., the brothers and sisters of Jesus. Salvation is Christianity understood as "Christ-likeness".

The children's gospel and the Lord's Prayer

This view is strengthened for Grundtvig by the rite of baptism itself and in particular by the connection between the gospel reading (Mark 10:13-16) and the Lord's Prayer which follows it, and the way in which the two elements were linked together in the rite of that time.

... and he took them in his arms, laid his hands upon them and blessed them and so shall we do, helping this little child (these little children) to the same blessing with our devout prayer to God. (Here he lays his hand on the child's head.) Our Father who art in heaven...

When Grundtvig looks for a name or an image for the place of salvation, among the first to present themselves to him are God's embrace or God's arms. Thus he chooses the most familiar and human expression of confidence and love. It is there that we learn to know "Christ-likeness".

> The Lord stretches out his arms
> To bless the little ones;
> Come, children to Jesus' breast
> Learn to be like him[10]

To be in God's embrace is salvation already here in this life and also when death stands at the door.

> Sing and rejoice,
> Weep for joy,
> Those who rest in the saviour's embrace[11]

10. "Herren strækker ud sin arm" in *DDS*, no. 402.
11. "Klynke og klage" in *DDS*, no. 460, stanza 2.

Before death with its icicle-hand
Makes a cleft between dust and spirit
And takes away the heart's warmth
I shall gladly go to sleep
Like a child on its mothers breast
In your saving arms.[12]

Evidently enough the inspiration comes from the end of the children's
gospel. This idea could easily risk being understood as a mystical union
with God. This is not the case with Grundtvig; here as in other places he
links it with definite words.

If one investigates the use of words in Grundtvig's hymns, one discovers
the term "embrace" or "God's embrace" is very often connected with the
Lord's Prayer and with prayer in general. Thus we read in the hymn on the
Lord's Prayer

Mark this well in Jesus' name
We may pray every day
Like a child who in Jesus' arms
Can feel his love there,
And knows in himself, that all his hope
Is born from faith in his baptism
And grows with Jesus the child.

Remember then with mouth and hand
That "Lord Jesus" can only rightly
Be learnt from the Holy Spirit,
Whom all fools despise
He breathes life in Jesus' arms
He puts his prayer in our mouth.

If thus you pray your "Our Father"
The Spirit with the Father's voice
Entitles you to be a child with Jesus,
So that you are at home in God's house:
For only God's true children have a mouth
To call God their father
From the ground of the heart.[13]

Those who pray Our Father in Jesus' name really pray the prayer together

12. "At sige verden ret farvel" in *DDS*, no. 609, stanza 9.
13. "Stol du kun på dit Fadervor" in *DDS*, no. 553, stanzas 2-4.

with him and thus are placed like children in his arms, the arms in which they were placed at baptism. In those arms the child becomes Jesus' brother or sister and grows his Christian growth with him. Those who pray Our Father in Jesus' name become like children again (Matthew 18:3), but together with Jesus. For this reason this prayer has a special power. For the heavenly Father does not distinguish between the Son's prayer and our prayer, and the Holy Spirit gives wings to our prayer so that it can rise up to the heavenly Father.

> So God's Son teaches us
> His own childhood prayer
> Breathes into our breast
> His own childhood voice.
>
> God's Son with the Father's embrace
> Gives us the name of children,
> God says about our prayer,
> That comes from my Son.[14]

The content of the Lord's Prayer is also coloured by the fact that it is prayer made in the embrace of God, that is in the chosen place of divine love; in this there also lies an obligation for the baptized in relation to their neighbour as we see when we think about the prayer "Forgive us our sins as we forgive those who sin against us".

> Every time we pray Our Father
> We feel deep within us
> That grace will harvest what it sows,
> Will not be satisfied with less;
> Grace and truth in your breast,
> Must meet, if the voice of truth
> Is to move you as God's child.[15]

The connection in the baptism service between the end of the gospel reading and the following Our Father – between the embrace and the prayer – thus becomes especially significant for Grundtvig. The embrace in baptism becomes the place of salvation where the child Jesus prays his own prayer together with the child that is baptized, who thus again becomes a

14. "Op til Guds hus vi gå" in *DDS*, no. 376, stanzas 6-7.
15. "Nåden hun er af kongeblod" in *DDS*, no. 595, stanza 4.

child in relation to God. Grundtvig's hymns affirm this in worship time after time.

The questions

After Psalm 121:8 and the connecting link (1 Peter 13 and Romans 6:4) there followed in the rite the questions about renouncing the devil and the confession of faith.

> Dost thou forsake the devil?
>> Yes.
> And all his works?
>> Yes.
> And all his nature?
>> Yes.
> Dost thou believe in Jesus Christ his only begotten son...
>> Yes.
> Dost thou believe in the Holy Ghost...
>> Yes.

As has already been said, it is not the enunciatory form which is underlined in itself. It is as questions *at baptism* that they have weight for Grundtvig. Thus it is God himself who takes the word. What he spoke to men at the time when Jesus walked this earth does not concern us; he must address a special word to *us*.

> Therefore we are asked and baptized
> With our own name in his,
> With whose blood we are all bought
> For his cross and his crown.
> His word grants us life and peace
> With his word he unites us to himself
> With salvation at God's table.[16]

In Grundtvig's time the renunciations were under particularly critical review. Many preferred to forsake "evil" so as to direct the baptized to a moral way of life in the future. To forsake "evil", it was argued, is an altogether more practical thing than to forsake the devil! Behind this change from the devil to evil there lies a theological optimism which is in clear conflict with the biblical dualism of good and evil, which was a reality for

16. *GSV*, vol. IV, no. 280, stanza 6.

Grundtvig. For him, renunciation of the evil one, the devil, was the important thing, because he conceived baptism as an all-inclusive revolution in human life, which definitively brought the baptized into the kingdom of God; so this renunciation also must, at least in intention, originate with Jesus himself.

Certainly it is ludicrous from our point of view if people maintain that according to the bible our Lord Jesus Christ does not make forsaking the devil an essential part in his baptismal covenant, for even if the story of the temptation contained the bible's only information about the personal relationship between the Saviour and the Tempter, even so the Lord's "Begone, Satan" would be a guarantee enough that when he founded his kingdom on earth he would not forget to do something, which could keep his vicious enemy out of it, and that when he would take an oath of loyalty from his subjects he would also take their word of it, that they would not be like traitors and side with his enemy... so this is obviously a foundation condition which must belong to the very basis of Christianity.[17]

Grundtvig also strongly opposed those priests in his time who left out "descended into hell" when they came to this phrase in the second article of the creed; the descent into hell is good news for those who are anguished now as well as for those of the old covenant, who have not met God's Son.

> You article of faith, sorely hated,
> As light of life by the night of death
> Come to our hearts! There still
> Is enough of the darkness of night and death.
> Extinguish the strong scorn of the enemy.
> Release all that considers the good
> So that when saved and freed
> Joyfully from hell to heaven
> It may follow in your triumph.[18]

The questions in the renunciation and confession of faith ought not to be thought of as an examination; they are the promise of a heavenly gift.

So long as we consider our baptismal covenant or enunciation and confession of faith, as a human commandment, it lies heavily on our shoulders, demands much and grants but little; but when we consider it as our lord Jesus Christ's testimony about what we must believe and confess in order to live with him as he lives with

---

17. *Værker i Udvalg*, vol. VI (Copenhagen 1944), p. 234.
18. *GSV*, vol.I, no. 47, stanza 2.

his Father, as a legacy of him who will give rather than take, whose commandments are all great gifts, whose commandment is like his Father's, eternal life; when we consider them thus, then we see at once that they demand little and grant ineffably much. They demand only honestly and trust, but they grant all that they name; That is the Father, the Son and the holy Spirit; the creator as Father, the judge as brother, providence the almighty ruler as advocate, comforter and guide.[19]

To an overwhelmingly great gift one can only answer yes; even if baptism is considered by Grundtvig as a pact between two parties, he can go so far as to think that the Yes to the questions of renunciation and confession of faith is given by the Holy Spirit himself – with reference to the effata-ceremony in the Catholic rite.

> God's word to soul and body
> Itself says "Be opened",
> Do you forsake the lie
> And believe God's truth.
>
> It is his effata   (Mark 7:43)
> And the tongue replies Yes,
> God's voice like an almighty hand
> Loosens the tongue's bond.[20]

With these questions and answers, Grundtvig underlines that the baptized receives new life, receiving the creator as Father, Jesus as brother, the Holy Spirit as advocate and comforter. Baptism for Grundtvig is this total change of life.

Just as in the eucharist so also in baptism. The material element, water, receives a lover status than for instance was the case with Luther, the word has priority.

> The water-bath in the Word
> As the Lord, our hope,
> Girded with omnipotence
> Gives us a name in his baptism,
> Destroys our sin, renews God's image
> As surely as Jesus
> Is the Word of God on earth.[21]

19. *Grundtvig's Prædikener*, vol. VIII, p. 237.
20. "Op til Guds vi gå" in *DDS*, no. 376, stanzas 4-5.
21. *GSV*, vol.I, no.399, stanza 3.

Assurance

After the action of baptism itself, the prayer of the laying-on of hands followed, which Grundtvig also reckoned as part of the essence of baptism.

Almighty God, father of our Lord Jesus Christ, who has now given thee new birth by means of water and the Holy Ghost, and has forgiven thee all thy sins, strengthen thee with his grace to eternal life.

The last phrase in the prayer was Luther's polemical change of the Catholic form "May he anoint thee with oil of salvation in the same Christ our Lord to eternal life." Grundtvig would have gladly kept the Catholic form. He says about the form of the prayer and the rite:

It ought to be noticed that we have made some arbitrary changes in this necessary Assurance of the saving efficacy of baptism (naturally under the conditions of the covenant), and this error, however small it may seem, should certainly be rectified. First we say "By means of" water and the Holy Ghost, but the Church says "By" water and the Holy Ghost, and the bible upholds the rightness of this when it says "Unless a man is born again by water and the Holy Spirit he cannot enter into the kingdom of God" John 3:5. Next we say, "Has forgiven thee all thy sins" but the Church says "Has given thee the forgiveness of all thy sins", which especially at infant baptism sounds much better. Finally we only say, "strengthen thee with his grace", but the Church says, "Anoint thee with the oil of salvation in the same our Lord Jesus Christ" for eternal life, and this alteration was so unreasonable that it probably happened because the church's expression seemed to refer to actual anointing at baptism which the reformers had abolished[22].

In other words, Grundtvig would gladly follow what the Church, the Catholic Church, had kept; he would gladly have kept the concrete expression "anoint" even if only as a sign.

The greeting of peace

Even if Grundtvig does not say much about the prayer of the laying-on of hands at the baptism he says more about its content indirectly in relation to the following greeting of peace ("Peace be with you") as we shall shortly see. Grundtvig's interest in this greeting is very evident.

22. *Udvalgte Skrifter*, vol. VIII, p. 423-24.

Apart from this declaration, at least one more word belongs to the essence of baptism, and that is the Lord's blessing, "Peace be with you"; and that we have kept this at baptism is all the greater good fortune because our fathers with an extreme blindness, exchanged this word from the Lord's own mouth in all other ecclesial acts, for a scripture word from the Old Testament, the blessing the high priest gives to the Lord's children (the Aaronic blessing).[23]

That this is a word said by the Lord himself is clear from the New Testament (John 20:19, 26; Luke 24:36). And since the greeting of peace stands in this striking place in the baptism service, Grundtvig considered it as the true blessing, greatly preferring it to the Aaronic blessing which Luther introduced into the liturgy. Grundtvig tended therefore to minimize the Aaronic blessing:

> The Lord bless thee and keep thee
> The Lord make his face to shine upon thee and be gracious unto thee
> The Lord lift up the light of his countenance upon thee and give thee peace.

Grundtvig was obliged to use the blessing in the authorized services. A Norwegian church-goer at Vartov noticed with surprise that after the Aaronic blessing Grundtvig added almost as a protest "So, peace be with you".

When Grundtvig in hymns and sermons speaks about the blessing, it is the blessing of peace which he has in mind. For him they are one and the same, and first and foremost the blessing of peace corresponds to the content of God's peace as seen in the previous prayer, the unconditional promise of the forgiveness of sins to the baptized.

> ... The Lord's blessing at baptism, "Peace be with you", teaches us that being a Christian consists in finding peace with God and forgiveness of sins.[24]

That the content of the blessing of peace is defined by the preceding prayer which Grundtvig called the "assurance" can be seen from *DDS* 445, where there is a reference to the throne of grace, i.e., the place where atonement is found.

> There is a heavenly sound
> In the word: the lamb of God

---

23. Ibid., p. 424.
24. *Værker i Udvalg*, vol VI, p. 4-5.

For our salvation, our peace, our atonement
He bore our sin and shame.

In baptism he forgives me
All the guilt of my sin
In God's peace he washes me
And heals the wounds of death[25].

Thus it is that the greeting of peace, and the word "peace" in Grundtvig's hymns and sermons always carries an allusion to the forgiveness of sins as the strongest expression of God's salvation.

Grundtvig's original contribution to the nineteenth century

Grundtvig's view of the rite of baptism is one of the most important elements in his understanding of Christianity. In the nineteenth century Grundtvig was without comparison the person who concerned himself most intensely and thoroughly with his service. It was the starting point on the renunciation and confession of faith in baptism.

Furthermore, Grundtvig went against the tendencies of his time when he strongly underlined the dualism in the rite, which is both biblical and Lutheran, the dualism of God/devil, life/death, salvation/loss. It was for this reason that in contradiction to his contemporaries he would maintain the renunciation of the devil and the descent into hell in the creed.

But his original emphasis on the word in baptism as a word personally addressed to the baptized preserved baptism as a sacramental act in an extremely powerful way. In baptism the baptized definitely brought over soul and body into God's kingdom and thus granted eternal life; the resurrection of the flesh begins on earth.

In and with the introduction of confirmation into Denmark in 1736, as an action which with its questions reminded people of baptism, a certain rivalry grew up in the eighteenth and nineteenth centuries between baptism and confirmation. Baptism was being diminished into a mere introductory blessing whose full content first came into effect when the consciously believing person confessed their faith in God with their own commitment. In this there was the risk that baptism would lose its sacramental character when it was no longer seen as an expression of a positive choice of life and fellowship of destiny with Jesus but instead was reduced into an incorporation into the church, a dedication to a moral way of life and to a Christian education as a preparation for the examination of faith in confirmation. His

25. "O, hvor er nåde-stolen" in *DDS*, no. 445, stanzas 5-6.

old opponent, Professor H.N. Clausen, had maintained this on the basis of the Confessional Writings, when he said in 1825:

When these principles are referred to infant baptism, it is clear that the Protestant church cannot allow it any real sacramental efficacy, since faith (actus credendi) is lacking here as well as consciousness, but that the sacrament can be considered complete only with the confession of faith which come later.[26]

Bishop H.L. Martensen (1808-84), who was not uninfluenced by Grundtvig, took the question up in 1843 in *Christian Baptism Considered with Reference to the Baptist Question*, where he criticized Schleiermacher for maintaining that baptism and confirmation ought to come together.

When Schleiermacher who in so many respects has worked for the renewal of our consciousness of the church and in general must be named as the one who first restored the idea of a Christian society to us, advances such an assertion, such an attitude to the Baptist Church on his part can only be explained through the influence on him of the reformed concept of the sacraments, which he who in all main points shows himself to be nearer Calvin than Luther, had adopted. When it is affirmed that infant baptism first becomes complete at confirmation, that evidently follows from a change in the nature and use of the sacrament and a one-sided use of the protestant idea of faith which already earlier had been evident in the protestant church. The divine action which makes up the essence of the sacrament is complete in infant baptism and it is therefore a true and complete baptism whether confirmation follows or not.[27]

It was also logical enough that at the end of the eighteenth century and at the beginning of the nineteenth century in Germany for instance people began to suggest the use of adult baptism in the place of infant baptism. It was not so with Grundtvig. For him faith was decided by God's *presence*, which was identified with the most basic confidence that can be imagined, something which the infant grasps better than the adult. When people in England suggested that the parents should decide whether the child should be baptized as an infant or not, Grundtvig remarked,

... but I would not recommend such a postponement, for I believe that one is best suited for baptism before one knows one's right hand from one's left. I know that I will seem an unreasonable view to some of my fellow Christians, for even those that

---

26. *Catholicismens og Protestantismens Kirkeforfatning, Lære og Ritus* (Copenhagen 1825), p. 451.
27. *Den christelige Daab* (Copenhagen 1843), p. 80-81.

accept the validity of infant baptism, are inclined to maintain that adult baptism is preferable, so that when the "learned people" ("de Høilærde") do not generally adopt this policy, that is evidently only because they fear that people would not accept baptism when they were grown up and that then it would be necessary to use force as in the time of the papacy. That cannot be my reason for discouraging the postponement of baptism for it is precisely my wish that no one should ever be baptized that does not have the heart to believe, and so I not only hate compulsory infant baptism, but consider it improper to baptize children of parents other than those who so far as we know are believing Christians and will do their best to see that "the children will grow in Christ, as in baptism they were grafted into him"; but even in these circumstances I prefer infant baptism, for the simple reason that all birth, spiritual as well as bodily, happens most easily when we are smaller, and the farther we grow the bigger we get.[28]

Or, as he says in a hymn

> From the mouths of babes and children
> For the word Peace be with you
> May praise be given to God always.
> At the baptism of infants
> He reveals to the babes
> What the wisdom of the world and of reason
> Seeks after in vain.[29]

For Grundtvig infant baptism was a sacramental act, a total revolution of life. Each part of the rite (signing with the cross, the knocking-asking prayer, the Lord's Prayer, the words of baptism, the Assurance, and the greeting of peace, contains the whole meaning of baptism and the sequence of the parts of the rite comes, as we have shown, to colour his particular world of Christian concepts in a decisive way. For him, the particular elements of the rite, were not accidental.

If anyone says it is a matter of indifference what prayers are used in the rite and what usages find their place in baptism, then we must certainly protest, partly because all that is essential to baptism may be found in the papist Church-state, but almost not in evidence, and partly because we cannot give up something which has the stamp of the Holy Spirit on it and has lived through the church and arrived at us.[30]

28. *Udvalgte Skrifter*, vol VIII, p. 433-34.
29. "Af diendes og spædes mund" in *DDS*, no. 400, stanza 1.
30. *Udvalgte Skrifter*, vol. VIII, p. 425.

Grundtvig held fast to infant baptism, but baptism meant something not only for infants. The "child" could also be an adult in his or her deep powerlessness and depression. In such a situation, to relive the rite became a strength and a pastoral help. As we can see from hymns like *DDS* 488 and 519, hesitant prayer and knocking at God's door are met by God's ceaseless care and reassurance. The one who is in anxiety prays himself back into the embrace into which he or she was placed at baptism and so can pray the Our Father with the authority of Jesus. The unquiet heart finds peace with the forgiveness of sins.

> Do we not have, even being few,
> The most beautiful hope?
> What did our Lord
> Say to us in baptism?
> Was it not the Word which comes,
> Only to those that enter God's heaven:
> Peace be with you all, peace be with each one.[31]

Baptism and its ritual form was a constant theme in Grundtvig's hymns. People sometimes maintain that the Danish hymn-service is liturgically poor compared with that is to be found in other churches. But when Grundtvig's hymns are used the congregation can sing about baptism and its sacramental reality in a way which disproves this assertion. Therefore Grundtvig's view of baptism belongs inseparably to the history of Danish worship as one of its vital elements. With his viewpoint, as has already been said, Grundtvig went against the stream of his own time and thus came in an important way to influence the debate which followed later in the nineteenth century.

It was Grundtvig first and foremost who reacted against all attempts to water down the Lutheran rite of baptism. This happened because of Grundtvig's matchless discovery of the confession of faith in 1825, and the rite of baptism became, so to say, his constant sermon text, a theme which he developed and deepened throughout his life, especially in his hymns. He understood baptism as a divine transformation of life in which the baptized receives God as Father and fellowship of life with his Son through the Holy Spirit, who guides us on the way which leads to eternal life.

For Grundtvig the shape of the baptismal service was itself a constant inspiration. In his periods of deep depression he found his way back to faith by reliving the way from the knocking and asking of the child in

---

31. "Urolige hjerte"in *DDS*, no. 39, stanza 2.

baptism to the Lord's Prayer in Jesus' name, which brought him back again into God's embrace and to the recollection that it was God's voice which had given him power to say yes to the renunciation and confession of faith and it was God's own hand which had baptized him and had pronounced peace with the forgiveness of sins over him. The rite had such a powerful pedagogical and pastoral character that it could preach by itself.

In connection with baptism the dualism between heaven and hell, between God and the devil became his own choice, his own life and death struggle, as it had been for Luther. Over against the theology of his time, represented by the speculative German theologian, P.K. Marheinecke (1780-1846), who maintained that the great opposition in life is between thinking and being, Grundtvig maintained his position in a famous conversation in 1836. "Grundtvig would not admit this and said that he feared to do so. 'Why are you afraid,' said Marheinecke. Grundtvig answered, 'I fear for myself. For me the basic opposition is between life and death'."[32]

It was this existential stance which set its mark on his attitude towards baptism and its rite. He defended the rite which he himself had been baptized with even though it lacked the exorcisms which underlined the dualism between God and the devil. In return he defended the sign of the cross and the renunciations; he did not doubt the devil's existence and defended the phrase of the creed, "He descended into hell". He emphasized baptism as the place of the unconditional forgiveness of sins and understood the final greeting of peace as the real blessing. He understood the Holy Spirit as the person who after the ascension was the church's governor on earth. He advocated infant baptism with unusual force, because the life choice with Christ which takes place in baptism must necessarily include the whole of human life from first to last and from this it followed that he found in the child's world of concepts the divine image of Christ which adults as a rule have lost.

In this way he brought to life a classical orthodox theology but in an original and personal way which had his own experience of life as its background. This effort brought about a low church sacramental revival which empowered lay people to make a strong revolt against the dominant rationalist theology and churchmanship of the period.

Above all, baptism and the rite of baptism was an inspiration for Grundtvig's hymn writing. The structure of the service represented the way of salvation step by step and the words and actions of the rite time and again provide the key to understanding the hymns. Grundtvig's hymns,

32. Steen Johansen and Henning Høirup (eds.), *Grundtvigs Erindringer og Erindringer om Grundtvig* (Copenhagen, 1948), pp. 179ff.

unlike other hymns, do not deal with eternal theological truths but are always concerned with God's powerful actions in the history of salvation. His hymns reflect a drama, a history of God's constant intervention in the story of humanity. Grundtvig's hymns are sacramental through and through, because something happens in those who sing them. The Christian is lead by the hymns from the deepest doubt and depression to the fulfillment of salvation in God's kingdom, because the history of salvation in the macrocosm is repeated in the microcosm – in the history of each particular human being. Through Grundtvig's hymns his theology has been sung into the congregations of his church. They have become, so to say, the Danish church's "liturgy" and thus a remarkable parallel to the liturgy of the Eastern Church in which also the church's faith and theology is articulated.

Grundtvig's Hymns from an Anglican Point of View

By Kenneth W. Stevenson

1. Some contextual questions

The Anglican and Danish Lutheran Churches have very different cultures, even though they are cousins in what might be called the Reformed Catholic tradition. Anglicans set great store by prose-literature, hence the way we value the Book of common Prayer and the Psalter, and our long tradition of literature in the prayers of public and private worship which has continued in the intervening centuries since the Reformation. Indeed, in a recent study of contemporary worldwide Anglican worship,[1] it is apparent that this emphasis on the spoken words of the liturgy is still distinctly Anglican. For many clergy, the Psalter is the backbone of their spiritual life, since it forms a major part of the daily offices of Morning and Evening prayer. It goes without saying that this tradition lives on, albeit in a new form, in the revisions of the Prayer Book in our own century.

For Anglicans, hymnody is a relative newcomer to popular religion. Much as I enjoy hymns and value their place in church services, it cannot be emphasized too strongly that their use is not native to Anglicans in the way it is for Lutherans.

Before hymns became a popular part of Anglican liturgy in the early 19th century, metrical psalms held an important place, probably because these were easier to sing than prose-psalms, and have a directly biblical base. But there was still suspicion of the longer metrical forms of the psalms of the Continental Calvinist tradition. Queen Elizabeth I is reported to have referred to them as "Genevan jigs", probably because of their jerky melodies. These metrical psalms, of course, became the backbone of English Free Church praise as well as that of the Church of Scotland. The 18th century explosion of hymn-writing which is focussed in the work of John and Charles Wesley has a distinctively Lutheran feel to it, since here we have hymns that are partly original songs of praise, partly free adaptations of the psalms, partly sacramental songs, and partly translations from earlier classics.

---

1. See Kenneth Stevenson, Bryan Spinks (eds.), *The Identity of Anglican Worship* (London, 1991).

All of this distances Anglicans considerably from the Danish tradition, so loyal to Luther's *Deutsche Messe*, where the song of the congregation forms an essential part of the liturgical action. I have often contrasted in my mind the sometimes cavalier way in which hymns are chosen in Anglican Churches with the great care lavished upon this activity in Denmark. The Danes have a liturgy that speaks volumes about this. Bell-ringing calls the people to worship; the liturgy begins with an organ voluntary; but it is only after the introductory prayer by the "choir-deacon" ("kordegn") that the people can sing, duly made ready for that activity after this prayer of approach. Sacred song is *built up to* in the Danish liturgy because it is an integral part of it. While music is much valued in Anglican worship, it is not in the same league. That might suggest that, if Grundtvig had been an English country parson in the 19th century, his hymnody might not have caused the problems of authority which he encountered in his native country. I would hazard a guess that he would still have composed English hymns, but he would also have composed prayers, whether for private devotional use, or to supplement the already-existing official forms.

Another contextual issue that strikes the Anglican is the standing which Grundtvig has in the Danish hymn-book itself. In England, there are prominent hymn-writers who have left their mark on our various hymn-collections, but we have nothing like the prominence given to any single author which the Danish hymn-book accords to Grundtvig. Even allowing for the fact that getting on for half of the hymns that bear his name in the hymn-book are translations or paraphrases of older hymns, the only conclusion that can be reached when faced with this enormous output is that Grundtvig must have done something very special to the Danish spirit to set him, in effect, higher than Luther, and the two other great Danish hymn-writers, Thomas Kingo (1634-1703) and Hans Adolf Brorson (1694-1764). It maybe that in time adjustments will be made to this. There are no doubt those who would like to revise the present Danish hymnbook. But the fact remains that the great man, in all his very Danishness, occupies this unique place. And while Isaac Watts and the Wesleys are hailed in England as great poets, in no way can our hymnwriters be said to have contributed to the development of English literature in the way that the great hymn-writing tradition represented by Kingo, Brorson, and Grundtvig has done in Denmark, to which we must also add such writers as Hans Christensen Sthen (1544-1610) and Bernhard Severin Ingemann (1789-1862).

When I drew up a list of all the Grundtvig compositions and translations and paraphrases which appear in the Danish hymn-book, and made some comparisons with the later English scene, certain features sprang to mind. As an author, Grundtvig's productions bear a markedly liturgical character. By that I mean that they are not exercises in individual piety or personal reflection. They all bear a strongly *ecclesiological* weight. They are songs of the Church, collectively confident in God's presence. Whether they are the psalm-paraphrases, the gospel-narratives, or the hymns of Christmas, Holy Week, Easter, or Pentecost, they are the songs of an expectant people. These hymns do not revel in existential *angst*, although they do explore the human condition (*Er du modfalden, kære ven?*, Are you downcast, dear friend?).[2] And as a translator, there are different patterns which emerge from this work, apart from the obvious fact that 1837 was a key-year in Grundtvig's development. He re-translates (some would say murders!) some of the hymns of Kingo, and many of the old classical Danish translations of sixteenth-century German-Lutheran hymnody, including Luther himself. The motivation here, surely, is to reappropriate the past, in a way comparable to the concerns of the English Tractarians, like John Mason Neale, who in 1852 published the first edition of his *Mediaeval Hymns and Sequences*. There are also, like Neales's work, Grundtvig's translations of mediaeval Latin originals, spread right through the Church year (e.g., *Glæden hun er født i dag* = *Dies est Laetitiae*, for Christmas);[3] and also of Greek hymns, perhaps with an accent on Easter (e.g., John Damascene's Easter Canon, in *Hør vor helligaftens bøn!* = *Hear our holy evening prayer*).[4]

When it comes to the English hymn-writers who inspired him to translate, the observation is unmistakable that most of the authors were not Anglican. Isaac Watts (e.g., *Syng højt, min sjæl, om Jesu død* = *I sing my Saviour's wondrous death*)[5] was a Congregationalist; James Allen (e.g., *O lad din Ånd nu med os være* = *Jesus, we lift our souls to Thee*)[6] was Free Church, of an indeterminate sort; and James Montgomery, perhaps one of the most prolific hymn-writers after the Wesleys (he wrote about 500, and inspired Grundtvig with *Følger med til urtegården* = *Go to dark Gethsemane*)[7] was a Moravian.

Had Grundtvig been writing half a century later, by which time Anglican hymnody will have emerged more fully in a distinctive manner, there might have been more Anglican names on his list of sources.

From an Anglican point of view, then, Grundtvig wears two hats. As an author he can be compared with a prolific Free Church hymn-writer like Montgomery. As as translator, he can be compared with a scholar like Neale. But he is much bigger than either of those two. He is more than the

---

2.   *GSV* IV 210 = *DDS* 511.
3.   *GSV* I 164 = *DDS* 88.
4.   *GSV* I 217 = *DDS* 188.
5.   *GSV* I 250 = *DDS* 183.
6.   *GSV* I 369 = *DDS* 401.
7.   *GSV* I 247 = *DDS* 156.

explorer of religious experience of his own time and the reappropriator of the forgotten past. It is now time to look in more detail at some of the striking theological features in his work.

2. Some outstanding themes

It would be tempting to try to make some elaborate and objective assessment of Grundtvig from a theological point of view. All I want to do, however, in the limitations of this essay, is to draw attention to several outstanding themes, as these come across to an Anglican who, for family reasons, has known and loved the Danish Church all his life. These themes may be about what Grundtvig has to say to Anglicans, even to the Anglo-Saxon world in general. As will become obvious, they include some important areas of theology and spirituality that are in danger of neglect, or else are being looked at afresh in our own time.

Natural imagery
I want to begin with a piece now regularly used in the Danish Church as a hymn for Easter, *Paaskeblomst, hvad vil du her?*[8] Originally this was a lyric written for an Easter play, but even so its imagery seems at first very strange, being taken entirely from the natural world. Surely the Danish Lutheran tradition can do better than this piece of sentimentality, which on first hearing reminds us of a Harvest Festival, with all the romanticism associated with landscape gardening, and the produce of the soil.

But in time I have learned to appreciate the subtlety of this unusual hymn. The poet strains natural imagery but he never quite breaks it. Here are a couple of verses in an inadequate English translation:

> Easter-flower, why are you here?
> Humble flower from village garden
> with no perfume, sheen or beauty.
> To whom are you a welcome gift?
> Who do you suppose would wish
> to press you tenderly to their breast?
> Do you think a bird would dare
> to think of you in Denmark's woods?
>
> Not in balmy summer-air
> did you bloom in sheltered bed
> so that you got rose's scent

8.   *DDS* 206.

> or the lily's silver leaves –
> rather in winter-storm and rain
> out of the barren soil you sprang;
> only those rejoice to see you
> who hold dear what you signify.

It must be repeated, this was *not* written to be a formal Easter hymn. But no Dane today regards Easter as complete without having sung it in Church.[9] We just do not have anything like this in England. Yet it speaks across the cultures. Grundtvig's enthusiasm for building on the tradition of using natural images from the country-side that Danish hymnody knew already (in this case, the "Easter-Flower", the common daffodil) *and* of making the gospel-message contemporary ("*Denmark's* woods") seems far from much of 19th century England, parts of it already heavily industrialized by the time of Grundtvig's first visit there. But the *method*, strange as it first appears, is one where medium never determines message. Grundtvig never sentimentalizes the flower, for the Easter gospel emerges from it beautifully articulated. It is not a style to espouse deliberately. But when it comes across as brilliantly as that, for a festival that needs to be brought into nature, *and* in a tradition that at times drives a wedge between creation and redemption, one can only stand back and admire it.

Sunday-Theology

This forms a recognizable unit in the Danish hymn-book. Grundtvig was not alone in building on this theme. Isaac Watts himself wrote a metrical version of Psalm 118:24-26 which is, in effect, a free Christological expansion of the original:

> This is the day the Lord hath made,
> he calls the hours his own;
> let heaven rejoice, let earth be glad,
> and praise surround his throne.
>
> Today he rose and left the dead,
> and Satan's empire fell;
> today the saints his triumphs spread,
> and all his wonders tell.
>
> Hosanna to the anointed King,
> to David's holy Son.

---

9. Professor Christian Thodberg preached a sermon on Danish radio, ending with an exposition of this hymn, from Aarhus Cathedral, on Easter Monday, 1989.

O help us, Lord, descend and bring –
salvation from thy throne.

Blest be the Lord, who comes to men
with messages of grace;
who comes, in God his father's name,
to save a sinful race.

Hosanna in the highest strains
the Church on earth can raise;
the highest heavens in which he reigns
shall give him nobler praise.

If one compares this composition with what Grundtvig achieved, one sees straight away that Grundtvig, though doubtless aware of Watt's work at this point, has his own agenda, which is worship, sacrament, glorying in God's Word. He wants to see God's people gather for feeding and spiritual nourishment:

This is the day which the Lord hath giv'n;
Greatly his people rejoices;
Open today are the portals of heav'n;
Lift now in gladness your voices,
For on this day of rejoicing
Jesus ascended with glorious might,
Sent us his Spirit with grace and light,
Gladly his praise we are voicing.

Grant us, Lord Jesus, Thy wisdom and grace;
Enter this Sunday thy dwelling,
Millions unnumbered from every race
Happy Thy praises are swelling.
Yea, may we praise Thee with gladness!
Freely Thy Spirit attend our need,
Blessing Thy people in word and deed,
Bringing rejoicing for sadness.

Lend us, O Saviour, Thy high-altar's fire
As in Thy house we assemble,
With Thine own presence our spirits inspire
Till we in ecstasy tremble;
Ever our joy is increasing.
Easter and Whitsun from Christmas grew:
Thus shall each Sunday our joy anew
Spring from thy mercy unceasing.

Quicken and strengthen Thy people today;
Bless them, O Lord, at Thine altar.
Lend us thy wisdom and counsel, we pray,
Sanction thy gospel and psalter.
Yea, may we know by Thy Spirit:
We are Thy people to grace restored;
Full of compassion art Thou, O Lord;
Christians Thy glory inherit.
(= *Denne er dagen som Herren har gjort*)[10]

This kind of Sunday spirituality has never been strong in Anglicanism, because of the corresponding emphasis laid on the annual commemoration in the Liturgical Year. The work of the Liturgical Commissions of the Church of England since the production of the 1980 *Alternative Service Book* has been concerned with enriching that yet further, first with the 1986 *Lent Holy Week and Easter Services and Prayers*, and secondly with the 1991 *The Promise of His Glory: Services and Prayers from All Saints to Candlemas*. Anglicans have long taken the Easter and Christmas Cycles of the Church Year seriously. But the time will come when this will have to be offset by a stronger accent on every Sunday as Easter and Pentecost. The popularity of Vigil liturgies, which are, as it happens, a prominent feature of *The Promise of His Glory*, may well lead into such a development. It is conceivable that Grundtvig's hymnody could help to unlock some of the riches of the patristic past and adapt it to Anglican culture.

Christmas and divine sonship
There is a liturgical law propounded by Anton Baumstark, the founder of comparative liturgiology, that the liturgy is at its most conservative on special occasions. One can apply that "law" to almost any rite and it works. It certainly holds true of Christmas, where innovating clergy are soon told what "always" happens in Church by anxious parishioners. There is, then, a natural conservatism about Christmas-spirituality, but one wonders exactly how wholesome it is. For there are in the older Christian tradition two sides to Christmas. One is about commemorating the birth of Jesus, and the other is about the fact that we are God's adopted children. When Thomas Cranmer put together Prayer Book collects, he used various sources, thought he was normally guided by the corresponding Latin original in the Missal. But when it came to Christmas, he went his own way:

10. *GSV* I 134 = *DDS* 368.

Almighty God, who hast given us thy only begotten Son to take our nature upon him, and as at this time to be born of a pure Virgin; Grant that we being regenerate, and made thy children by adoption and grace, may daily be renewed by thy Holy Spirit; through the same our Lord Jesus Christ, who liveth and reigneth with thee and the same Spirit, ever one God, world without end.[11]

In the composing of this collect, Cranmer seems to have had the same priorities as Grundtvig. Both rely on ancient tradition. But it is interesting to note that Cranmer felt the need to emphasize that latter aspect – *our daily* renewal in divine sonship as a consequence of the *annual* commemoration of Christ's birth. There are several instances where Grundtvig employs a similar device in order to hold together these two aspects of Christian theology, most notably in his translation of *Puer natus in Bethlehem* (*Et barn er født i Bethlehem*).[12] As Christian Thodberg has pointed out, the last three stanzas are changed in order to maintain a balance in the whole hymn between the baby that has been born and the consequences of that birth – – divine adoption:

> God's children we become again,
> Our Christmas is in heav'n domain.
> Hallelujah!
>
> On starry carpets azure-blue,
> We gladly come to worship you.
> Hallelujah!
>
> God's angels teach us with delight
> To sing like them on Christmas night.
> Hallelujah![13]

Baumstark's law applies as much to spirituality as it does to what is actually done in the Church. One suspects that the basic starting-point in both Danish and Anglican traditions is that Christmas is about the birth of a baby in Bethlehem. But how widely known is this other, deeper dimension? Both Cranmer and Grundtvig felt the need to draw attention to the

11. See F.E. Brightman, *The English Rite I* (London: Rivingtons, 1915), pp. 220f., for parallel texts of Latin collect, 1549, 1552, and 1662.
12. *GSV* I 163 = *DDS* 85.
13. See Christian Thodberg, "Grundtvig the Hymnwriter", in *N.F.S. Grundtvig, Tradition and Renewal* (Copenhagen, 1983), pp. 160-196 (pp. 162f on divine sonship, and 184ff on pneumatology, see below).

other side of the picture – one could almost say, the consequences. Popular piety, a conservative business, finds it much easier to dwell on the birth of Jesus than the appropriate new birth given to us all.

The atonement

It is truly remarkable that Grundtvig should have written so many Easter hymns. The repertoire of passion-tide hymns (if it is really right to draw the two categories apart anyway) is not by comparison so full. But there is one which reaches across the centuries and traditions, *Herren god, som uden grænser*[14] (Good Lord, who without boundaries) because it is fundamentally about *God*. God loves without boundaries and wants everyone to share his gifts. But it is not a smothering generosity of something easy. We are bidden to share in everything that is his, which includes his death and glory. Although the hymn is addressed to Jesus (Good Lord), the way in which the Son and the Father are coidentified at the end makes it clear that both the suffering and the redemption are the work of God the Father himself.

In the century and a half since Grundtvig wrote the hymn, there have been World Wars, and the threat of the Holocaust that we all dread. And since then, too, there have been Benjamin Britten's *War Requiem*, Guido Rocha's sculpture, *The Tortured Christ*, and, to cap it all theologically, Jürgen Moltmann's *The Crucified God*. Grundtvig is sometimes near the kind of religious experience and reflection represented by these developments.[15]

Pneumatology

Of the forty hymns listed under *Holy Spirit* in the Danish hymn-book, Grundtvig had a hand in fourteen as a translator, and twelve as a composer, which makes twenty-six in all – 65%, well above average. Translations from English originals number four. There are four Mediaeval Latin. The remainder are older Lutheran hymns, with one exception, which is Greek.

But it is in his own compositions that he feels freest. *Var I ikke galilæer* (Were you not Galileans) brings out in fullest measure his love of paradox. It almost reads like a passage from a Chorus in a Greek tragedy, where slightly off-stage a group of people comment on what is going on and speculate on what the next move might be. The hymn ends, as one might expect, with a firm rejoicing in the givenness of the Spirit. *Talsmand, som på jorderige* (Paraclete, who to the earth) reflects on the Spirit being unlike any

---

14. *GSV* III 114 = *DDS* 153.
15. See Jakob Fløe Nielsen, "Kristologien i Grundtvigs salmer", in *Grundtvig Studier* 1989-1990 (Copenhagen, 1990), pp. 121-140.

"spirit" known in the Old Testament, and *Du, som den store pinsedag* (You, who on the great Pentecost) refers to us as orphans without the Spirit – another way of looking at divine sonship.

There is one theological feature that has an indirect relationship with some developments within Anglicanism, and some other Churches, too. We have already noted Grundtvig's adaptation of Luther's *Puer Natus. Nun bitten wir den Heiligen Geist*, the classic Luther hymn to the Holy Spirit, undergoes significant changes, too, at Grundtvig's hands, for *Nu bede vi den Helligånd*[16] (Now pray we to the Holy Spirit) expressly addresses the Holy Spirit in such a way as to avoid implying that the Spirit was absent before the hymn was sung! Thodberg's researches continue to provide surprises.

By one of those historical ironies, there is a certain restlessness about the way in which the Spirit is invoked in the Anglican Prayer Book tradition in the confirmation rite. Anglicans retained the Mediaeval practice of episcopal confirmation, with the laying-on of hands restricted to the bishop. It also retained much of the mediaeval rite itself, notable among which is the old Latin Confirmation Prayer, with its invocation of the gifts of the Spirit (Isaiah 11:2). The Latin text and the English version in the First Prayer Book (1549) use the words *"immitte in eos septiformem spiritum sanctum"* (*"Send down* from heaven .... thy holy ghost ...."). But in 1552 this was changed to *"strengthen them* ... with the holy ghost ...". And the 1980 version of the prayer in *Alternative Service Book* has "Let your Holy Spirit *rest upon* them."[17]

There are many debates about Christian Initiation among the Western Churches today, Catholic as well as Protestant. There are, too, many questions about the traditional practice of Confirmation as a combination of the three features of (a) a rite of mature commitment, and (b) admission to Communion, and (c) a rite which is restricted to the bishop, and is therefore an expression of his ministry. It is fascinating to observe at this point a similar tension over how the presence of the Spirit is expressed in the lives of Christians. The message of Grundtvig is to combine the *fact* of the givenness of the Spirit with an *insistence* that the Spirit enables the Church to function in terms of worship and service, not in some metaphysical, ideal world, but in the world ordinary men and women inhabit now.

Eucharist

One of the first things I was told about Grundtvig when I was a teenager was the famous "bath and board" reference in his hymns alluding to the

16. *GSV* I 30 = *DDS* 246.
17. See Brightman, II, pp. 794f.

two dominical sacraments. I was given the distinct impression from my Danish mother that this was not quite the proper way to speak of them! This may have been the result of some lingering suspicion from my various Lutheran clerical forebears that Grundtvig might have gone a little too far in his desire to make the sacraments accessible to people in such direct terms. But it was clearly a favourite technique of his to make the link between baptism and eucharist, and to build up a sense that font and altar should be part of the everyday reflection of the Christian.

Another area where Grundtvig comes over as a pioneer is the way in which he alludes in a beautifully convoluted manner to the eucharist as a thank-offering. Sacrifice has long been a kind of "no-go area" for much of Western Protestantism. But in one of his hymns to the Holy Spirit (*I al sin glans nu stråler solen* (In all its lustre now shines the sun)) we encounter the expression "takkesangens offerskål", ("thanksong's offering"). In terms of comparative liturgy, this is a way of restoring to the eucharist a more general, corporate, and primitive understanding of the Lord's Supper as a spiritual sacrifice.[18]

The eschatological aspects of Grundtvig's teaching, too, come across in the way he constantly puts the earthly and heavenly together. This is a theme developed in a different way by some of the classical Anglican theologians, notably Jeremy Taylor (1613-67).[19] Taylor maintains that the earthly altar (of the eucharist) is a copy of the heavenly, building upon a Christology based on Hebrews 7:23ff. Grundtvig, who has other priorities, sets the eucharistic action in the context of God's eternal action now. *Du er vor skat, O Jesus sød* (you are our treasure, sweet Jesus) is perhaps one of his most beautiful meditations on the Lord's Supper, because of the succinct eloquence of the poetry.[20] The worshipper is led through a series of reflections upon Jesus' words and actions in the Upper Room, yet it is all firmly set in the context of the ongoing discipleship of the Church. The union of the earthly and the heavenly in the eucharist is a theme that recurs in Anglican writing. *Du er vor skat* ends on a predictable Grundtvig double-motif of the gift of the Spirit and the worship of heaven. The methods of the Anglican Taylor and the Lutheran Grundtvig may be different, but their potential in terms of sacramental realism are not that far apart.

---

18. *GSV* III 266 = *DDS* 247.
    See A.M. Allchin, "N.F.S. Grundtvig: the Spirit as Life-Giver", in A.M. Allchin, *The Kingdom of Love and Knowledge* (London, 1979), p. 79, and whole essay, pp. 70-89; and Kenneth W. Stevenson, *Eucharist and Offering* (New York, 1986), pp. 233. Grundtvig's broadened view of sacrifice is close to ours.
19. See H.R. McAdoo, *The Eucharistic Theology of Jeremy Taylor Today* (Norwich, 1989).
20. *GSV* III 192 = *DDS* 426.

It is worth enlarging further on Grundtvig's eucharistic theology, because it is symptomatic of the way in which he can be described at one and the same time as a very 19th century Dane, and also as a writer and thinker of universal significance. From the many examples that could be chosen to illustrate these characteristics, for the purposes of ease and clarity, we shall use one particular hymn: *Herre, hvor skal vi gå hen?*[21] (Lord, where shall we go from here?). No fewer than seven features are recognizable from this superb, quintessentially "Grundtvigesque" composition.

Grundtvig is *biblical*. The whole hymn is a sweeping meditation on John 6:68 – Peter's question to Jesus, "Lord, to whom shall we go?" Without being in any sense fundamentalist, the author is a man of the bible, soaked in its language and drama. It takes the confession of faith (John 6:69) in verse one; the "harsh word" (John 6:60) in verse two. It then goes on to reflect on the bread of life (John 6:35), verse three, and the experience of Communion itself as a rising from the dead (John 6:39) in verse four. The final two verses explore the very Johannine themes of service and union with Christ.

Grundtvig is *liturgical*. The whole hymn is a rare example of liturgical theology itself. The biblical base just explored could be answered by a corresponding one taken from the Danish eucharist. The first two verses cause the communicant to enter the sanctuary, while in the third verse reference is made to the Institution Narrative, of central importance in the Lutheran rite. In verse four, as has been pointed out, the act of communion is alluded to, and this is done with reference to the physical act of rising up from the altar rail as a sign of resurrection. The final two verses dwell on the response to communion, both individual and corporate, and to the indwelling presence of Christ.

Grundtvig is also *apologetic*, in the technical sense of the term. In the two opening and two concluding verses, the hymn explores an underlying theme of John 6, that the gospel can be hard, that there are going to be some people who find faith difficult, so difficult, in fact, that they may refrain from receiving communion, to say nothing of refusing to come to Church altogether. Grundtvig's boldness in affirming this reality is an important truth which the modern, comfortable congregation forgets at its peril.

Grundtvig is *individual*, to the point of being idiosyncratic. In the stark use of the imperative formulae, "eat" and "drink", and others like them, he not only challenges the worshippers, but makes the actions described

21. *GSV* I 100 = *DDS* 418.

contemporary and real. Imperative formulae are not new in liturgy, but Grundtvig gives them a particularly poignant style and meaning, here almost aggressive.

Grundtvig is *Lutheran*. One finds in this hymn the traditional Lutheran emphasis on the cross, the sacramental actions as enjoined by Christ, as well as the powerful emphasis on Christ's presence. This is given liturgical expression by Luther himself in his eucharistic hymn, *Jesus Christus unser Heiland*, and his Post-Communion Prayer, both of them to be found in the 1526 *Deutsche Messe*; and the Post-Communion Prayer is the same, in all essentials to the one known by Grundtvig in Denmark. It is still in use today.

The final verse of our hymn, in particular, reflects on that prayer, too. Grundtvig is concerned to *integrate Word and Sacrament* in the discourse, celebration, and experience of the Church, hence the deliberate repetition of the term "ord", "Word", which occurs four times in this hymn; first in reference to Christ, in whose mouth are the words of life, contrasted with the "harsh" word (death), and then, in the following verses, back again to Christ, on whose word the eucharist has its very existence. This is not the dry, cerebral word of certain exaggerated forms of Western Protestantism, but rather the living word of Easter.[22]

Grundtvig is also *ecumenical*, not in the sense of being a regular worshipper at other Churches' eucharists in his time. For him, that would be (in some cases at least!) unthinkable. Rather, I mean Grundtvig as possessing a sense of historical perspective, which was informed by his reading of such sources as the Early Fathers. Behind the words of this hymn is a desire to stand back from the various divided traditions of the whole Church in order to make some universal statements in poetic form about the meaning of the eucharist. For example, he sees the Lord's Supper as both a meal in its own right and also a true celebration that stands under the shadow of Good Friday and in the sunlight of Easter Day. How he loves such paradoxes! Christ is present in a personal (though not mechanical) way, and the grace that is made available at the eucharist is costly. Presence and sacrifice only make sense when they are seen to be one and the same, because they concern fundamental truths – about the nature of God and basic human thirst for and need of him.[23]

Put together, these characteristics of Grundtvig place him firmly within

22. See Jens Holger Schjørring, *Grundtvig og Påsken* (Copenhagen, 1987), for a discussion of this important theme.
23. See Regin Prenter, *Skabelse og Genløsning. Dogmatik* (Copenhagen, 1962, p. 529, particularly the telling sentence, "I dette offermåltid er realpræsens og offer eet" ("In this meal-offering are real presence and offering one").

the prophetic movements of the 19th century. From those movements, so very much that is good and true in our own time has looked for inspiration.

Narrative Hymnody

Hymns that recount directly, with poetic expansions, a passage from scripture are few and far between in the Anglican tradition. Nahum Tate's *While shepherds watched their flocks by night* is one English example. Kingo, too, wrote in this vein. But Grundtvig's catalogue in this regard is, surely, exceptional. *Der sad en fisker så tankefuld*[24] (There sat a fisherman so full of thought – Luke 5:1-11), *Ånden opgav enkesønnen*[25] (the widow's son gave up his spirit – Luke 7:11-17), *En sædemand gik ud at så*[26] (A sower went out to sow – Luke 8:4-15), and others, besides, stand out as both unfamiliar in style and welcome as meditation. Clearly intended for specifically liturgical use, they serve the triple purpose, of bringing the gospel-lection further to the fore, giving the preacher an effective backdrop, and adding a touch of variety to the service. In *Ånden opgav* are all the human dimensions, central to which is the relationship between Jesus and the mourning mother whom Jesus goes to meet in the funeral procession, thus breaking all Jewish conventions. But we are not left watching: the last verse asserts Christ's Lordship over life and death and hints that when it comes for us to die, he will be with us.

Apart from the pastoral and doctrinal sensitivity shown in these hymns, there is a question of methodology. "Story-theology" has been in vogue in recent years, and a whole area of investigation between theology and literature has developed (see the essay by David Jasper). Central to this development within Anglicanism has been the recovery in the liturgy of the full recitation of the "mighty acts" of God in the eucharistic prayer; and this has happened worldwide in all Anglican revisions of the liturgy this century, though the roots of the recovery go back much further to the patristic age. In our tradition, where hymn-singing is manifestly popular but not (at least in theory) integral to the service, it is important that the *narrative* aspect of the eucharist is given its proper emphasis. As we observed over Christology, it is crucial that the eucharist is seen to be more than just a group of people gathered in one particular place, but a community linked to others, both geographically, historically, even eternally.

And the point goes further. In the English-speaking world, we are

24. *GSV* II 74 = *DDS* 127.
25. *GSV* II 79 = *DDS* 130.
26. *GSV* I 146 = *DDS* 134.

witnessing a spate of different versions of the bible, and at the same time many different people taking part in services, in the interests of popular participation. This is a natural reaction to an era where there was only one version (the Authorized Version) of the scriptures, and the spoken parts of the service were almost exclusively in the hands of the clergy. But these developments need to be backed up by considerable familiarizing with the whole spirit of the bible and its narrative-character, among a people who may not be as knowledgeable about the bible as previous generations. Perhaps such narrative-hymnody might find a place as a means of reflecting on the Christian story.

Psalms

There are around ten Grundtvig hymns in the Danish hymn-book that are based directly on Psalms. Metrical psalms were, as we have seen, sung in both Anglican and Free Churches from the Reformation onwards. Calvinist influence ensured that the two main versions, whether that of Sternhold and Hopkins (1562) or Tate and Brady (1696), were those which were generally used, since they reproduced the biblical original faithfully, and did not err into the Christological domain, like the heretical Lutherans! As English Nonconformity grew apace, and as the Methodist revival in the 18th century itself sprang up, other types of metrical psalmody, and (of course) hymnody itself, developed into a native English culture.

For this reason, Grundtvig's metrical psalmody is the feature of his hymnody that is the least striking. But it is still of special interest. He avoids Christology altogether, preferring the liturgical context itself to provide that dimension. For example, *Hyggelig, rolig, Gud, er din bolig*[27] (Cosy, quiet, O God, is your dwelling – Psalm 84), when sung during the distribution of Communion is an affirmation that the eucharistic celebration is the dwelling of God that is the object of praise and thankfulness. Similarly, *Giv mig, Gud, en salmetunge*[28] (Give me, God, a hymnsinging tongue) is an eloquent expression of the start of the Danish liturgy as it builds dramatically to the point at which the congregation's song of praise can begin.

Baptism

Grundtvig's emphasis on the two dominical sacraments produced its own kind of liturgical movement, which in turn served to draw baptism away from the margins of churchlife to enter the mainstream of worship, just as

27. *GSV* I 61 = *DDS* 378.
28. *GSV* I 62 = *DDS* 4.

it is doing in so many other churches in our own century. This was the clear intention of Thomas Cranmer, who did his best to recommend a more "public" context for the celebration of Baptism. Such a move was, of course, compromised by the way in which baptism had been celebrated for a number of centuries, in many cases the only "public" link being the fact that the water had been blessed at the Easter Vigil, hence those grandiose font-covers of the later Middle Ages, to prevent the holy water being fouled or stolen.

Another debate on Christian Initiation is going on in those Churches, Catholic and Protestant, that have inherited a historic link with the society in which they live. The question is raised as to whether baptism is for everyone, or whether it is only for the children of "believing" parents, and for "believing" adults (an increasing proportion of baptism candidates). If that is so, what criteria should be set to decide who is "believing" and who is not? Other attendant questions concern how to give ritual expression to the commitment of young people who, perhaps after infant baptism, and confirmation, lapse from church life. They may then undergo a powerful conversion-experience and sometimes wish to be "rebaptized" in a pool, by submersion. Anglican baptismal hymnody is on the whole paltry, though recently there have been brave attempts to make up for lost time, especially as baptism is increasingly held during the main Sunday service, when hymns are obviously necessary, whereas in previous times it was celebrated on a Sunday afternoon, at a liturgy without music. Can Grundtvig address this situation?

In one way, he cannot. Our times are different. But there are two areas where he might be of some help as his hermeneutic comes to the fore. The first is the theme of divine sonship. In the famous hymn, *Sov sødt, barnlille* (Sleep sweetly, little child)[29], the adoption of the child by God in Christ is explored, under the guise of an apparently sentimental view of the scene. Anglican teaching on rebirth and adoption at baptism is secondary, if not downright neglected. Much popular understanding of baptism in Anglicanism today concentrates on the dramatic Christological image of dying and rising (Romans 6:3-11) to the exclusion of rebirth and adoption (John 3:5).

The second concerns the dual features of baptism as *anamnesis* (memorial) and *epiclesis* (invocation). Both these are stressed in the Prayer Book rite

29. See Thodberg, op. cit., p. 247. Just to illustrate the use of this composition, it was sung at the Consecration of Niels Holm as Bishop of Ribe on Sunday 12th January, 1992, following a sermon by the new Bishop on the day's text, 10:13-16 (Jesus taking children into his arms, also a pericope from the Danish Baptismal rite).

of baptism and the revised liturgies. And yet we still walk to the font thinking that we are baptizing because Jesus was baptized, in memory of him, and without a counterbalancing invocation of the Spirit on the future life of the baptized. *Alle min kilder* (All my sources) and *Kom hid kun med de små* (Come her only with the little ones) combine precisely these features. Perhaps Grundtvig's real genius lies even deeper, because of the way he alludes to baptism in hymns that have no direct bearing on baptism at all; and these allusions are intended to help make the connections which build up healthy pieties about the sacraments. Grundtvig had a remarkably corporate view of baptism, derived from Luther and the Fathers.

Liturgical allusion
Not being a native Dane, I do not know either Grundtvig's hymns or the Danish liturgy well enough, but a case could be made for showing how Grundtvig saw the liturgical prayers in a close relationship with the hymns. The final line of *Kirken den er et gammelt hus* (The Church is an old house) quotes the greeting of Peace at baptism and eucharist, and, of course, the endings of a few of the New Testament epistles. *Gud Helligånd, vor trøstermand* (God the Holy Spirit, our Comforter) quotes from the opening prayer of the "kordegn" ("Choir-deacon"). *Syndernes forladelse* (The forgiveness of sins) are the opening words of a hymn – and a quotation from the end of the Apostles' Creed, the one in normal Sunday use in the Danish liturgy. Perhaps the liturgical character of Grundtvig's hymnwriting reaches its peak in the fact that it is *his* version of the *Agnus Dei* that now stands in the eucharistic rite (*O Du, Guds Lam*). Strangely, it is the reverse process that is now beginning to happen in England, as new prayers are written which are intended to embody resonant language. In one eucharistic prayer,[30] recently drafted, three insertions for use at Easter have been inspired by hymnwriters:

First, John of Damascus: "You delivered them from slavery, and brought them to the promised land."

Second, Charles Wesley: "By his victory over the grave he burst the gates of death for ever."

---

30. See *Patterns for Worship: A Report by the Liturgical Commission of the Church of England* (London, 1989), p. 247. For parallel texts and discussion of the Ingemann hymnn, *Igjennem nat og trængsel* (= *Through the night of doubt and sorrow*), see Maurice Frost (ed.), *Historical Companion to Hymns Ancient and Modern* (London, 1962), p. 301.

Third, Bernhard Severin Ingemann: "Through the night of doubt and sorrow that the light of his risen presence may brighten the path before us."

Perhaps Grundtvig may come in time to be employed as a similar liturgical source for future compositions.

3. Conclusion

In conclusion, the question must be raised, what does an Anglican, or an English person, or indeed anyone from the English-speaking world unfamiliar with Grundtvig do when faced with this giant?

One possible course of action is to attempt to translate some of these hymns. This has proved a difficult task, because of the sheer force and power of the language. Danish is an expressive enough tongue as it is, and the Danish hymn-tradition is full of short, jerky combinations of rhythms, matching those Chorale-type melodies. There have been some brave attempts to make such a leap. Translating is an enriching experience, because it involves the mother-country lettinggo of the original, and allowing it to find a new life on fresh terrain. It could be that in the process, new meanings will be found, or inspired, in the work of this remarkable of Danish writers.

Another course of action is to attempt to turn some of Grundtvig's hymns into liturgical prose, which would be a very Anglican exercise. Although this may sound a surprising task, it has been done before. All the greatest prayer-writers of the past relied on sources, however indirect, and it is one of the liturgiologist's more delightful tasks to look for new frontiers of source and parallel when studying new (or not so new) texts. It could be that Grundtvig might supply fresh insights into one or other of the main themes enumerated in this survey.

But for the writer of this essay, the main fruit of studying Grundtvig is to admire and bask in his very Danishness. And that above all means going back to Denmark yet again, and sitting in a Danish Church, with a bright and finely-tuned organ in the west gallery, and joining in the People of God's sacrifice of praise – with Grundtvig's own, native "salmetunge".[31]

31. See, in general, Kenneth Stevenson, "Theology across the Nordic Seas", *Theology* 95 (1992), pp. 189-193.

Grundtvig's *The Church's Retort* – in a Modern Perspective

By Theodor Jørgensen

By way of introduction, I want to clarify my intention in reading Grundtvig's pamphlet from 1825 in a modern perspective. In *The Church's Retort* Grundtvig presents, programmatically if briefly, his "View of the Church" for the first time. He does so in a violent clash with Professor H.N. Clausen whom he sees as a representative of rationalist Protestantism, from which, as a clergyman in the Church, he wishes to dissociate himself for the sake of that Church; cf. the preface:

In order ... to make clear that my polemics are neither personal nor purely academic but are as purely a church matter as possible, I have called this polemical letter *The Church's Retort*. By this I submit my concern to the judgment of universal Christendom and not merely to the judgment of the literary world.[1]

In the same preface, written on the day of Irenaeus, August 26, 1825, he also emphasizes that the inspiration he had received from Irenaeus was significant for his conflict with Professor Clausen. As a motto for the whole pamphlet he takes a quotation from *Confessio Augustana*, art. VII: "Una sancta ecclesia perpetuo mansura sit" (One holy church will be and remain forever). All this makes it natural to read Grundtvig's pamphlet as a defence of a church life deeply rooted in tradition and history. It makes his relationship with the early church interesting as well as his high evaluation of the church's worship and sacraments. In this perspective Grundtvig can be seen as an exponent of the movement of restoration that is known throughout Europe in the first half of the 19th century. It is in this way that the Danish High Church Movement has always wanted to think of Grundtvig. But this view is too narrow and one-sided. And it is also an unprofitable view. It fails to make use of the possibilities of understanding with which Grundtvig, who was entirely and completely a man of the 19th century, presents us, when in the 20th century we have to make up our own minds about questions dealing with the relationship between Christianity and the present. Even where Grundtvig settles the score with his own age,

---

1. N.F.S. Grundtvig: *Selected Writings*, ed. by Johannes Knudsen (Philadelphia 1976).

he does so as a representative of that age. With all the ironical comments he has to make about Protestantism, he is in that respect a Protestant himself. It is as a Protestant that he carries forward the legacy of the early church, of the Christian poetry of Anglo-Saxon England, of Luther and the Reformation, and it is in this modern perspective that a reading of *The Church's Retort* seems to me to be most profitable.

Well aware of what a complex problem modernity is, I shall nevertheless point to some views that are typical of the present time and which were also central to Grundtvig's thinking. Moreover, I am of the opinion that these views are at the same time, for better or worse, a result of the *Wirkungsgeschichte* of Christianity.

1. Faith must be a matter of experience because it concerns the salvation and thus the integrity of the individual. Therefore, the relevance of the content of the Christian faith must be verifiable in the life experience of the individual. Grundtvig here usually refers to the amicable relationship which exists between Christianity and humanity. But it is a further precondition that man's autonomy is accepted. Man can only endorse what he can recognize as truth from his own inner conviction. What is involved here is a legacy of the Reformation's rejection of the idea of any human intermediary between God and man. But this means that faith is a matter of freedom, and this Grundtvig never tires of emphasizing. Only in freedom can the individual accept the unconditional commitment of faith which is equivalent to certainty of faith.

2. Faith must be a matter of certainty. The emphasis on the necessity of the certainty of faith, which is characteristic of the theology influenced by the Reformation, is closely connected with the necessity of the experience for faith. The experience of the individual is particular and incidental to that individual. It is finite and may thus be arbitrary. This raises the problem of relativity from which nobody is exempt, and this is why certainty becomes so necessary for faith. In his own relative experience man cannot find the foundation for certainty. It must be sought outside him. The collective experience, as it takes shape in history, may be important for the individual here, inasmuch as the collective experience may have both a corrective and an affirmative effect. But in itself it does not suffice. It too must have something to relate to, to substantiate it. It is the classical theological problem of the relationship between *verbum externum* and *verbum internum* which underlies the problem of certainty, or the question of *fundamentum fidei*. This takes us to the third view.

3. Faith must have criteria for its Christian identity. A need for such criteria has always existed, since Christendom has always debated what is true Christianity. The New Testament offers early evidence of this. But in our time the identity problem has become more acute as a consequence of

the emphasis which Protestantism places on faith as a matter of experience and certainty. This emphasis, in my view, explains much of the constant tendency in Protestantism to split up into a countless number of denominations because it involves the temptation to present a particular creed as absolute. The absurdity of this development is seen in its relativistic effect which in the end makes the church affiliation of the individual a question of personal taste, where non-theological factors may determine the choice. It is in this connection that the signs of the Christian Church, *notae ecclesiae*, acquire such importance.

4. In answering this question, theology, of course, plays an important role. But which role, and with what authority? The plurality of creeds which has always been, and must be, characteristic of Christianity, is reflected, of course, on the theological level, even though the work of theology aims at finding criteria for Christian identity which will delimit that plurality. If the theologians are to have the decisive voice in the question of what is true Christianity, will not the layman be in a still worse position? And does not the authority crisis, which university theology by and large suffers from today at least as far as its relations with the Church are concerned, indicate that the relationship between church and theology is anything but clear?

Grundtvig's pamphlet *The Church's Retort* can be read as expressing an attitude to these four questions, and thus as a contribution to a more general debate, which we are right in the middle of even today.

But before going more deeply into this subject, it is appropriate to describe briefly the occasion and content of the pamphlet. The occasion was a bulky work by the young professor of theology, H.N. Clausen, entitled *Catholicismens og Protestantismens Kirkeforfatning, Lære og Ritus* (Catholicism and Protestantism: Their Constitution, Doctrine and Ritual), which appeared in August 1825. H.N. Clausen had been studying in Berlin where he was greatly influenced by Schleiermacher, whose theology is as a consequence clearly traceable in the work just mentioned, not least as far as its concept of the church is concerned. H.N. Clausen was a professor of dogmatics and New Testament exegesis at the University of Copenhagen, and he exercised a considerable influence on the students. Clausen's book infuriated Grundtvig. In less than a week he had composed his Retort, which was published in the beginning of September. What was it that made Grundtvig fly into such a rage? In the Preface he makes the following summary:

Professor of theology H.N. Clausen has in his above-mentioned book expressly and strongly declared that he will tolerate no other source of knowledge and Rule of Faith in the Christian church than the Scriptures. He has with equal firmness declared that the Scriptures are uncertain and contradictory. The consequence of this undeniably is that he rejects the original confession of faith of the Christian church which has been confessed for centuries, as unknown and unrecognizable. Inasmuch as he does not only invoke the Christian name, but also claims to be an interpreter of the Scriptures, who teaches others what he himself does not know, namely what true Christianity is, then he is either deceiving his readers and followers, or he is blind to obvious truths...[2]

What makes Grundtvig so indignant is the unhistorical concept of the church that, in his opinion, Clausen displays, and which turns the congregation into a sort of reading circle, which must accept the differing and often contradictory interpretations of the Scriptures offered by theologians as criteria of true Christianity. Against this unhistorical church view, Grundtvig puts his own:

The Christian church is no empty or disputable fancy; it is an obvious reality, a well-known historical fact, which can neither be shaken nor destroyed by the protests of the world".[3]

In the actual pamphlet this idea is further elaborated so as to form what is known as Grundtvig's "View of the Church". Grundtvig sees it as a historical fact that through all the centuries since the time of Jesus, the Church has been recognizable by its confession of faith and by the means of grace, baptism and communion. Grundtvig speaks about

the unshakeable fact that there has been and is now one Christianity on earth, distinguished from everything else by its matchless confession of faith. On all tongues and in many and marvellous ways it has proclaimed and still does proclaim faith in Jesus Christ, the crucified and arisen, as the certain and only way to salvation for sinners, a way that leads through baptism and communion to the kingdom of God and the land of the living.... The means of grace and the corresponding confession of faith are the only features which all Christians, in all situations, in all congregations, and at all times have had in common. This has identified the Christian church for its friends and enemies and united the congregation...[4]

The two views of the church that are at variance here, are on one hand a church view which has its foundation in a doctrinal concept of the church (H.N. Clausen's church view), and on the other hand a view of the church

2.   op.cit., p. 13.
3.   Preface, op. cit. p. 12.
4.   op.cit., p. 18.

which invokes the evidence of history, i.e., the concrete historical experience of the individual. A doctrinal definition of Christianity as a religion is here contrasted with a multidimensional understanding of Christianity, corresponding to Professor Ninian Smart's analyses of religion:

Religion is a six-dimensional organism, typically containing doctrines, myths, ethical teachings, rituals, and social institutions, and animated by religious experiences of various kinds.[5]

In Grundtvig's view, the place where this concrete experience of Christianity in its multi-dimensionality occurs, is in the worship of the church.

In what follows, taking my point of departure from the above-mentioned four viewpoints, I shall describe and discuss Grundtvig's arguments in *The Church's Retort*, but I shall take the liberty of including later discussions by Grundtvig of his view of the Church.

1. Faith must be a matter of experience

It is impossible here, of course, to elaborate Grundtvig's concept of experience and to relate it to the epistemological problems that are generally connected with the concept of experience. I shall only point to the fact that Grundtvig's emphasis on faith as experience serves a double purpose: On the one hand, there is the incorporation of faith in supraindividual aspects of life, above all in history, and on the other hand there is faith as the individual's most fundamental act of life. In experience, the external and the internal, the collective and the individual, the spiritual and the physical, the heavenly and the earthly are held together.

Grundtvig places the emphasis on the first concept in each of the pairs mentioned, not in order to deprive the second concept of its full significance, far from it, but in order to emphasize the incorporation into the whole of the individual human life or – theologically speaking – its condition of being created. In *The Church's Retort* Grundtvig uses the concept of experience polemically against H.N. Clausen's view of constructional reason. While Clausen wants to make a constructed doctrinal concept of the church to the basis of his reasoning – the church as a community intended to promote general religiousness – , which Grundtvig scorns as a castle in the air, Grundtvig invokes the evidence of the experience of a church, which has existed for many hundred years, and which has always

---

5.   The Religious Experience of Mankind, 1971, p. 31, quoted here from S.W. Sykes, *The Identity of Christianity* (London, 1984), p. 28.

been in fundamental agreement about what characterized it as Christian. The evidence of experience is the evidence of history, which grows in authority with the years. And it is most deeply in agreement with true reason as against false, mortal reasoning, since

truth is always seen to be a day older than falsehood, because the lie cannot possibly begin to speak until it has something to contradict, to protest against: until it has something true to deny.[6]

Truth, then, is always prevenient and is therefore only accessible to experience. It must be sensed, heard.

Grundtvig's concept of experience is founded in his anthropology and theology. In a treatise from 1817 he writes:

Through the sense of hearing we experience not only something physical – the sound – but also something spiritual – the word; for the word is nothing but the spiritual that enters the sphere of experience and reveals itself to spirits ... it is un-deniable evidence of the intimate connection between spirit and body which reveals itself even in the world of the senses: an unshakable wall against all idealism, all refusal of the sensible reality of the bodily.[7]

Experience is sense-perceiving understanding and understanding sense-perception, it is in itself a psycho-somatic function and as such precisely human experience. For according to Grundtvig, man is himself "a divine experiment, which demonstrates how spirit and dust can interpenetrate one with another and be transfigured in a common, divine consciousness".[8] The proof of this divine origin is for Grundtvig above all in human language, i.e., language not only understood as the ability to speak, but as the particular language, the living words that man has on his tongue and by which he can achieve great things. And the word itself, like the whole human being, is this unity of dust and spirit, of sound and sense. To Grundtvig, words are always spoken words. Written words – though necessary in certain situations – are a deformation of language. For the human word is the echo of the Creator's word, and that was a spoken word. Correspondingly the organ of language, its speech as well as its understanding, is the heart, not the reason. The spirit speaks or sings with "the tongues of the heart of dust".[9] And only the heartfelt understanding,

---

6. *US* IV, p. 417.
7. *US* III, p. 413.
8. *Selected Writings*, p. 26. The introduction to Norse Mythology, 1832.
9. "Lyksaligt det Folk", Blessed Be the People, stanza 1. *GSV* IV, p. 351.

i.e., the loving understanding, is real understanding: "..and he has never lived / Who deeply understood / What first he did not love".[10] It is in the heart that man is most himself, not in the reason. It is with the heart that man knows about his own life as lost, and it is with the heart that he longs for and dreams about another whole existence. Therefore, the heart is also the seat of faith in God's salvation in Christ and of the two other signs of life, hope and charity. Only with the heart does man experience the amicable interchange and interaction between Christianity and humanity.

Grundtvig's defence of man's freedom, also in the choice of faith, and thus of man's autonomy is, characteristically, not a defence of the autonomy of reason, but of that of the heart. By rationalism Grundtvig had been taught more than enough about the way in which the autonomy of reason might degenerate into a patronizing attitude on the part of reason towards the individual, and it is this same patronizing attitude which he so savagely fights against in Clausen in *The Church's Retort*. Conversely, the defence of the autonomy of the heart is a defence of every single individual's immediate relationship with God in an independence which is maintained on the condition of man being created and thus being mortal. This must in no way be misunderstood as suggesting an anthropological foundation of our relationship with God. Rather, the opposite is the case. The autonomy of the heart, understood as its immediacy to God, is matched by God's sovereignty in His approach to man by virtue of His word, which is Christ. It is because God does not allow Himself to be bound by intermediaries that man is not bound either:

We are, we become / We live and we move / in Christ, God's living word; / Take the word in your mouth, / and love it to the end! / Then with you He lives in the name.[11]

2. Faith must be a matter of certainty

The immediacy of faith is its certainty. Liturgically this finds expression in the response: Amen! "It is true. It is so!" The message heard and the sacrament received is heard and received as Christ, the living word of God. The only problem is that this immediacy arises in a process of transmission. The message comes to me as the word of another person, the sacrament is administered to me by another person. Is not, then, the certainty a highly fragile thing? The awareness in our times of this historical transmission and

10. "Gylden-Aaret 1834", stanza 41, *US* VIII, p. 18.
11. "Trods Længselens Smerte", Despite the Pain of Longing, stanza 3. *GSV* V, p. 531.

of the relativity inherent in it is probably one of the greatest contemporary challenges to faith as certainty. This problem is already reflected in the *sola* formulations known to all from the time of the Reformation: *Solus Christus*, *sola fide, sola scriptura*, and the connection between them, the two first *sola* formulae representing the immediacy of faith, and *sola scriptura* representing the transmission to which faith is subject. But at the same time the Reformation principle of scripture contrasts the transmission by Holy Scripture to the transmission by tradition in the Church, fully aware of the necessity of this contradiction if *solus Christus* and *sola fide* are to be maintained. But this contrast can no longer be maintained in the form given to it in the Reformation Age on the background of the knowledge with which exegetical scholarship has provided us today. If nevertheless one continues to do so, as Clausen did, it leads to the consequences that so angered Grundtvig. Grundtvig maintains *solus Christus* and *sola fide*, but abandons *sola scriptura* as the basis of transmission of faith, or as a rule of faith, and he does so for the sake of the certainty of faith. To Grundtvig, Clausen's view which is as follows is absurd. Unlike the Roman Catholic Church, which builds on the evidence of history, the Protestant Church builds on Holy Scripture as the only rule of faith. It is the normative expression of the teaching and spirit of Christ and thus the foundation of the Christian faith as an animating principle in which the Church must as far as possible render itself superfluous in favour of the teaching and spirit of Christ. Even though Clausen maintains the *sufficientia* of Holy Scripture and its *perspicuitas*, he points, at the same time, to all the various kinds of the uncertainty in the text which cause problems in its interpretation, and lead to constant conflicts in the Christian world. The intolerableness of Clausen's view, as Grundtvig sees it, is that Christianity and the Bible acquire a demonic character, being at once true and false, and that the Christian laity is abandoned to the mercy of the new exegetical papacy, which precludes any certainty of faith. If this is the consequence of the reformers' understanding of the church and its foundation, they have been mistaken. And Grundtvig himself accepts the consequences of this and so abandons Holy Scripture as *regula fidei*.

What then does Grundtvig substitute for it? He refers to the apostolic confession of faith and to the means of grace, baptism and communion, which must be the distinctive marks of any church that wants to call itself Christian. Grundtvig makes this assertion

not just as a theologian, not just as a clerical scholar, but above all as a believing member of the great universal Christian Church, which not only through the apostolic confession of faith and the means of grace distinguishes itself from Jews,

Turks, and Heathens, but above all secures for its believing members absolution for their sins and salvation in the name of Jesus Christ.[12]

In order to understand Grundtvig properly, it should be carefully noted that Grundtvig speaks about the *Apostolicum in connection with* baptism and communion. In the same place Grundtvig characterizes the *Apostolicum* as "the exclusive condition [of the Church] for admission into the community", whose "salutary power" corresponds to that of the means of grace. Obviously then Grundtvig does not see the *Apostolicum* as a dogmatic confession. In that case, he might rightly be criticized for reductionist tendencies, substituting the *Apostolicum* for Holy Scripture as a rule of faith, and the papacy of the exegetes would be replaced by that of the dogmaticians which would certainly not make for fewer problems. What then is Grundtvig's understanding of the apostolic confession of faith?

I think in this connection we should also take note of what is implied in the motto, already quoted, taken from the *Confessio Augustana*, art. VII: "Una sancta ecclesia perpetua mansura sit". The passage continues: "Est autem ecclesia congregatio sanctorum, in qua evangelium pure docetur et recte administrantur sacramenta". On closer inspection it is actually possible to read the non-polemical parts of *The Church's Retort* as an interpretation of *CA* VII. As far as the confession is concerned, this comes to mean that it takes the place of the Gospel, in Grundtvig's view. The apostolic confession of faith is the Gospel inasmuch as it is proclaimed, and preached, and this happens above all in baptism. The *Apostolicum* is the word of the covenant from God, through which God concludes a pact with the individual. Through this word of the Covenant, God so to speak extends his covenant history to each individual, spanning all time from the creation of the world to the rebirth of the world on the Day of Judgment and the eternal life. The pivotal point of this covenant history is the Word of God, became man, Jesus Christ, his death and resurrection, in whom everything is gathered together. For Grundtvig, the confession of faith has a sacramental character. Therefore he is able to characterize it as the word from the mouth of Christ, which as we open our mouth to speak it and embrace it with our heart unites us with him in community:

He speaks to the heart / He comforts the heart / He answers as God to His name; / when warmly the heart / embraces the Word / we take our Saviour into our arms.[13]

---

12. *US* IV, p. 416.
13. "Trods Længeselens Smerte", Despite the Pain of Longing, stanza 5; cf. Rom 10:6ff. *GSV* V, p. 532.

This view of the apostolic creed does not depend on whether or not it can be traced back to Jesus Himself, as Grundtvig at one time thought that it could be. It is exclusively dependent on the living presence of Jesus, risen from the dead, in the worship of the church through baptism and communion. Therefore, Grundtvig can add to the creed as words from Jesus' mouth the ritual words of baptism and holy communion and moreover the Lord's Prayer and the Greeting of the Peace, both of which form part of the ritual of baptism. The inevitable process of transmission, from which the immediate certainty of faith arises, is then baptism and communion along with the creed and the Lord's Prayer, in a sacramental sense. In other words: In His living presence, Christ Himself is the transmittor, and thus immediacy is granted. This also appears from the way in which Grundtvig attaches the manifestations of life to the words from Jesus' mouth. Faith corresponds to baptism, hope to the Lord's Prayer, and love to communion. These three manifestations of life, again, have their signs of life in confession of the faith, in preaching, and in singing of praise, respectively. In these signs of life man's Godlikeness in the echoing word has regained its true worth. Christian life is the life of Christ growing in us, where faith grows through hope into perfection in charity, and is nourished in the community with Christ in the church's worship. But this growth is the work of the Holy Ghost.

The *Regula fidei*, according to Grundtvig, is thus Christ Himself in His living presence in the word of faith and the words of the sacrament. But it is undeniably a rule of faith which is difficult to handle in the question of Christian identity, and this Grundtvig by no means denies. Rather, that is his intention.

3. The criteria of Christian identity

Towards the end of *The Church's Retort*, Grundtvig enters into a vehement discussion with Clausen about the oath that clergymen in the Danish Church are required by law to take in connection with their ordination. Grundtvig's and Clausen's attitudes are illustrative of the question of the criteria of Christian identity. The central wording of the oath is as follows:

I promise: with my utmost strength, honestly to impress on my audience the heavenly teaching contained in the prophetic and apostolic scriptures and in the confessional documents of the Danish congregations.

Clausen's objection to the oath was that by signing it, one committed oneself to the letter, without anything having been said clearly about the spirit in which the confessions were to be interpreted. But the vague wording of the oath at least meant that every clergyman could still commit himself to it without hesitation. However, Clausen himself would have preferred an oath which was more meaningful and clearer than the present one, for, he argued, it could not possibly be intended that everything in the symbolical books was to be accepted as heavenly teaching. What Clausen missed was a more precise definition of the spirit of Protestantism and of the symbolic books. Such precision could be achieved if a confession was attached to the oath stating that Holy Scripture is the only norm of faith, that this principle of Protestantism is the true principle of the church, and that the Protestant church is faithful to this principle when it rejects the doctrine of justification by works and the doctrine of the seven sacraments, this confession to be followed by a declaration of obligation to teach according to this belief. Thus, Clausen maintained, what was permanent and what was variable in the essence of Protestantism would be clearly indicated. The Christian doctrines, which must be regarded as direct results of the Protestant principle of interpretation and thus as axioms of Protestant Christianity, would be established.

It is obvious that Clausen takes his place in a tradition within Protestant theology which wants to find criteria for Christian identity and more particularly for Protestant identity on the basis of a determination of the essence of Christianity or of a definition of Christianity's basic view, its principle, its spirit, or whatever term one chooses to use. The characteristic doctrines or axioms must not be viewed as a minimum of fundamental articles in a Christian dogmatic system, but precisely as criteria for establishing Christian and Protestant identity, serving as rules of interpretation. Here Christianity is understood as a direction of faith, a basic religious view, which has come to create a community in the church, and permeates the rest of society through its view of life.

It goes without saying that Grundtvig has to react sharply against this, for there is an essential difference between Christianity understood as a fundamental view, and Christianity understood as Church in the sense of the living presence of Christ in the word of faith and the sacraments in the midst of His confessing congregation. In its vehemence, Grundtvig's answer to Clausen is not very clear, but I want to point out a couple of points as particularly relevant.[14] For one thing, Grundtvig notes that the clergyman's oath goes on to say "that I shall not only avoid and abhor the teaching that conflicts with the word of God, but shall also fight it with all my might". We have seen what "the word of God" represents to Grundtvig, that is Christ Himself. As the servant of the congregation the priest's

14. *US* IV, p. 422ff.

duty is to preach this unchangeable word in order to enlighten and to edify. And the letter in the prophetic and apostolic scriptures and the confessional documents is binding in the sense that the clergyman promises in the oath "to preach everything that in the scriptures mentioned *appears to be heavenly* divine *teaching,* as *such...*" God's word must be preached as God's word. As far as the principle of scripture is concerned, Grundtvig claims that the scripture itself is misunderstood if it is regarded as a rule of faith. In Holy Scripture this can actually only apply to the Law of Moses. Moreover, the claim that the principle of scripture is "the only rightful one in the true church, that is that the letter was everything, the spirit and the living word in the Confession was nothing" must be refuted by every Christian as "book idolatry". Finally Grundtvig considers it "bedlam talk" on Clausen's part when he claims that the scriptura principle of Protestantism is faithfully observed if only the doctrine of justification by works and the doctrine of the seven sacraments are rejected.

It appears clearly from Grundtvig's argumentation that he does not understand Clausen's viewpoint so to speak from within, which, all the same, he can hardly be blamed for. Grundtvig does not see that, with his point of departure, Clausen is quite consistent. If Christianity is made into a fundamental view, expressed in the teaching and spirit of Jesus, it is a consistent step to go back to the sources that bear witness to their origin, and to use them all the time as a reference point in a renewed consideration of the fundamental Christian view or of the essence of Christianity. At the same time the most recent discoveries of the historical sciences must be taken into account in using the scriptures as a source. There is nothing contradictory in that. But this type of reasoning is so essentially different from Grundtvig's way of thinking that they were bound to clash.

I have already defined Grundtvig's position above: the *Regula fidei* or the criterion of Christian identity is Christ Himself in his presence in the confession, understood as the word of the covenant and the word of faith, and in the sacraments. In other words: The criterion is the liturgy as actually celebrated. It is a criterion of a very different kind from Clausen's. While Clausen's is a theological dogmatic and in that sense an intellectual criterion, Grundtvig's criterion has been deduced from the historical experience of the individual and of Christianity. That is why he emphasizes so energetically in the discussion with Clausen that "the Christian Church is an obvious reality, a well-known historical fact", which has never doubted what constituted it as a Christian church, which it has expressed and expresses by making the apostolic confession of faith into the condition of baptism, and by referring to baptism and communion as sources of Christian life. But is it not, then, *sensus ecclesiae* understood as *consensus ecclesiae* that becomes the overall criterion, which then, in turn, must be characterized as catholic? Grundtvig would deny that most categorically. The reference to the one Christian church as a historical fact is synonymous, in his view, with the worship of Christ as the only Lord of the church. And he repeatedly emphasizes to Clausen that it was precisely the intention of the reformers to defend this one true church, from its beginning, against the aberrations of the Roman Church. Thus he can say: "The historical evidence of experience is the only thing that honours Christ, the Bible and Luther".[15] To Grundtvig, the historical evidence of experience is identical with the experience of the celebration of the church's liturgy in a diachronic and synchronic perspective.

This is such an important aspect in a modern reading of *The Church's Retort* that I would like to elaborate it further. I shall do so with the help of a viewpoint, taken from Stephen W. Sykes' highly readable book *The Identity of Christianity* (1984) which seems to me to be deeply related in its basic attitude to Grundtvig's "church view". Sykes claims that it is impossible to avoid disagreements in the communication of the content of the Christian faith, since such disagreements arise precisely in the effort to maintain Christian identity. The decisive question is how to deal with these disagreements, and not least what role is played by the theologians here. This is also a fundamental question in *The Church's Retort*. Sykes emphasizes that it must be possible to maintain a unity in Christianity in a synchronic and diachronic sense, which thus becomes clear in the *answer* that Christians give about this unity, regardless of the fact that the answers may differ in their wording. If the opposite is the case, Christianity would be split up into a number of mutually disparate groupings. And Sykes' argument for the existence of such unity is that precisely the disagreement in the mutually conflicting theologies would be unintelligible if they were not seen in relation to this unity, which cannot, for good reasons, be a dogmatic unity. The unity is the person of Jesus himself in his special relationship with God. Sykes lists three points as essential for this presupposed unity in disagreement:

1. In Jesus, in his life and deeds, God must have created something decisively new, the foundation of a new existence, the Christian existence.

2. The God who created this new existence, in creating Jesus, is also the God of creation, who, in the beginning, created heaven and earth and continues to maintain his creation.

3. As God is the God of the beginning, he is also the God of consummation. In the death and resurrection of Jesus, God is proclaimed as the

15. *US* IV, p. 405.

master of death, also the death of the individual, since consummation is prefigured in the resurrection of Jesus.[16]

The important perspective in this formulation of Christian unity is that God and the world are kept together in Jesus, and thus the existence of the individual and of the human race are also kept together with God in Jesus. This is the diachronic and synchronic unity that Sykes speaks about, which only makes sense if all history is included in God's history for the world. This is precisely what Grundtvig means by the historical evidence of experience. Here the two dimensions are held together which in dogmatic language are termed *fides quae creditur* and *fides qua creditur*, and which Sykes defines as outward tradition and inward tradition, or the external and the internal dimension of Christian faith. To Grundtvig, the external dimension finds its primary expression in the confession of faith and the sacraments, but also in the evidence of scripture about the Lord of the Church who is present, living, in the community of the liturgy as celebrated. And to Grundtvig the internal dimension is the new life in Christ which finds expression in the manifestations of life, in faith, in hope and in charity. Sykes has analogous formulations. And Sykes' conclusion might also have been Grundtvig's in the view of Christian identity: "It is in the process of interaction between this inward element and the external forms of Christianity that the identity of Christianity consists".[17] For this process is only accessible through the historical evidence of experience. To Grundtvig it is particularly perceptible in the life signs of the congregation through the course of time, in the confession, the preaching, and the singing of praise of the church service. And in order to make this diachronic experience synchronic in the context of the service of the Danish Church he transformed Old Testament and New Testament psalms and hymns and Greek, Latin, Old English, English and German hymns and poems into Danish hymns, corresponding to his understanding of the history of the church as the history of a series of Christian churches belonging to different people. In his hymns Grundtvig transformed the understanding of Christian identity, contained in his church view, into liturgical practice.

4. Church and Theology

Is there any room left for theology in this view of the church? Is it any longer necessary for the church? The church view is, of course, in itself a

16. Cf. Sykes, p. 257, and the whole of chapter 10, pp. 239-261.
17. op.cit., p. 261.

kind of theology involving decision about what constitutes the true unity and identity of the church. It is a theology of the church's worship. But the question remains justified. What function is left to theology? It has no constitutive function since the confession of faith is not understood as a dogmatic confession and since Holy Scripture is not perceived as the foundation of faith. Thus, the importance both of dogmatics and exegesis has certainly become a relative matter.

No congregation can know, gather, and confess everything in Scripture, and none of us can die in the name of *Jesus Christ* on the strength of our own interpretation of Scripture, or of any man's word, which does not have God's visible evidence such as the original confession of faith had for the Church-Fathers.[18]

It is not theology which has the power to make Christ come alive to the congregation by translating and interpreting texts from the past and bringing them into the context of the present. Only "God's visible evidence", Christ as the word of faith, has that power. Grundtvig turns hermeneutics upside down, so to speak. It is Christ, who in his living presence in the congregation by the Holy Ghost overcomes Lessing's gap between past and present by turning His own earthly past, as it is witnessed in Scripture, into Himself as present. Therefore, in the controversy with the theology of rationalism and with Clausen, Grundtvig can call on all those who

truly want to be Christians...that we, so to speak, turn back to the choir, reach out our hands across the font to each other and to all those who have passed away in the Lord, and exchange the kiss of peace before the altar, in the one bread and the one chalice; that we abandon as brethren all quarrelling about what is doubtful ... Indeed, Christians! wherever you live, it is time that we unite again round the Christian faith, that which layman and scholar had in common, and which (NB!) those Christian teachers, however different in their thinking, such as a Justin Martyr and Irenaeus, Ansgar and Luther, Reinhard and Balle had in common and which is then undeniably the fundamental Christian faith, let us unite round it, and tolerate in each other (NB!) all theological difference that are reconcilable with it...[19]

In comparison with what the choir of the church symbolizes, fundamental Christianity, theology comes in second place. It is its limitation, but also its freedom that allows for differences. Not only may theology have differences, it actually must, in the role it has in second place. Grundtvig makes

18. *US* IV, p. 418f.
19. ibid.

this clear by distinguishing between church and school or church school. The church is bound by "God's visible evidence":

No rule of interpretation except this that Scripture must be understood in accordance with the confession, and cannot be understood except by believers with the assistance of the Holy Ghost, no rule of interpretation except this has the divine and human evidence of the apostolic church and history.[20]

The Church is committed to this rule of interpretation. This is the hermeneutical consequence of commitment to the living Christ. Elsewhere Grundtvig expresses this by saying that the scripture is placed on the altar and must be read and interpreted accordingly. But then, in the context just quoted, Grundtvig goes on to say that the church must

let the school be free in all other matters, let its theologians and scholars deliberate, and allow them to quarrel if they so desire, as long as they admit that Holy Scripture is enlightening and edifying to all Christians, towards the goal of faith and wisdom, set by the Lord and as long as they do not try to cause dissension between Scripture and the fundamental confession of faith of the church, by doing which, naturally, they would exclude themselves from the Church and from the Church school.[21]

In a sense theology is subject to the same commitment as the church, and that is to say to the same criterion of Christian identity if it wants to call itself Christian, but within the limits of this commitment it has not only a right, but also a duty to diversity and changeability. If theology refuses to submit to this commitment, it may, in Grundtvig's opinion, continue its work at the university if it so desires, and call itself by any name it chooses, be it Protestant, Rationalist, even Lutheran, but it is not Christian and it has no place in the church school.

But what precisely, according to Grundtvig, does the function of theology consist in, then, in its relationship with the church? As has been mentioned Grundtvig expresses his opinion about this through the concept of the church school. The school always has an enlightening function whether it is a church school or a folk school. And enlightenment, to Grundtvig, is synonymous with enlightenment for life. The church school cannot *communicate* the new life in Christ; only Christ Himself can do so in the church through baptism and communion. But the church school or theology can *enlighten* the new life in Christ for the congregation. And in

20. ibid., p. 419.
21. ibid.

that connection Grundtvig can attribute all the importance to Holy Scripture that he denied it as a foundation of faith and of the church. Scripture, and in particular the New Testament, which Grundtvig likes to call "the Apostolic Scripture",

makes such an unspeakable contribution to the enlightenment and rightful Christian explanation of the covenant of baptism that we must now find it absolutely indispensable for that purpose.[22]

The New Testament is the Apostolic evidence of faith. It expresses the *answer* that the Apostles and the earliest congregation gave to Christ as the living word of God, and thus necessarily contains the diversity that is part of all life, including new life in Christ. This diversity is even an advantage when the New Testament serves its purpose by contributing to the enlightenment and explanation of the covenant of baptism. As a book serving to enlighten, Scripture also has a critical, authoritative function. It is wrought by the Spirit, not, of course, in any literal sense, but as so far as its content is concerned. Therefore it may be a touchstone for the congregation when they have to distinguish "the impulses of Christ's Spirit from all others". But Grundtvig emphasizes that the Spirit has prepared Holy Scripture to be such a touchstone "for His own free use... in which His tools (i.e., the teachers of the church school or the theologians) can find confirmation of the impulses of the Spirit, like the Lord himself in His years of growth".

The analogy with Jesus' own relations with Scripture during His years of growth is worth noticing here. Scripture served as a book of enlightenment for Him, to help him become aware of the impulses of the Spirit. The freedom of theology in the church school corresponds to the free use by the Spirit of Holy Scripture. For it is in no way Scripture which is turned into living words on our tongues by the Spirit's free use of it, but the "Word of Mouth" underlying Scripture. As a book of enlightenment, the scripture can never be anything more than a work of reference, compared with Christ Himself as God's living Word. What theology is committed to in relation to Holy Scripture is the understanding of it as evidence, as reference, and nothing more. In that respect, the theologian must not place himself above the scripture in wisdom,

while in the congregation, he remains as free in his attitude to Scripture, its use and interpretation, as the Spirit is, and as the congregation is to the Spirit, the priest, and the prophet.[23]

---

22. *US* IX, p. 387.
23. For the whole of this context, cf. *US* IV, p. 732.

It is the theologian's task to enlighten and clarify Christian existence today, as it is created by Christ's living presence in word and sacraments. And Christian existence today must necessarily in many respects assume a different form from Christian existence in the first Christian congregations, for example, not least when the historical evidence of experience is included. In other words, Grundtvig defends an understanding of theology as contextual theology, closely connected with his view of the liturgy and of the church and his view of history. And in a contextual theology there must necessarily be diversity, disparities, and even conflict. If this was not the case, theology would not live up to the demands for enlightenment for life that the church poses. While the church must stand firmly on its foundation, Christ, the school must change with life, because life never stands still, yet always remaining firmly committed to the foundation.[24]

What, then, is the particular task of theology, seen in relation to the question of Christian identity? According to Grundtvig, it should certainly not assume the position of pope in the church by usurping the authority to establish what true Christianity is. Christian identity is vouched for by Christ, for He is Himself synonymous with it. It can only be experienced and must constantly be experienced in the meeting with Christ's presence in the word and the sacraments. And this experience of the liturgy as celebrated is something else and more than an intellectual experience. But it can be the subject of intellectual explanation, and this work falls within the scope of theology, for Christian faith is not obscure. In Christ truth has been revealed, as we know. One of the scriptural passages that Grundtvig repeatedly alludes to, directly and indirectly, in his prose and poetry is Joh. 1,4: In him was life; and the life was the light of men. This passage is behind the term that Grundtvig likes to use about Christ: *brightly alive* [lyslevende]. And it is his theological justification for the work of the school as enlightenment for life. The function of theology in relation to Christian identity is to throw light, at any time and in the various contexts of time, on the life which has been granted by Christ, and to do so in constant interchange and dialogue with whatever questions and reflections about human life may otherwise occupy the minds of people at any given time. The task of theology is to unfold the view of life and the practice of living which follows from a Christian life in faith, hope, and charity. That this task can only be accomplished in freedom, and must necessarily hold diversities that may also be at variance with each other, is a matter of course.

24. cf. *GSV* III, p. 150.

Conclusion

What relevance may Grundtvig's "church view" have for us today? At least it sharpens our awareness of the problem of the situation of Christianity in those societies today where the view of life or the religion of the individual has become a question of that individual's choice, in other words the situation of Christianity in a pluralistic society. Choices are always made on the basis of a deliberation, a reflection, which, as Grundtvig would have it, takes place in school. But a basic feature of Grundtvig's "church view" is, as we know, precisely that nobody can be taught or enlightened about how to arrive at a Christian faith. It must be experienced and granted in the context of the church's worship. The school can prepare the way for the experience of faith by clarifying aspects of human life that open up people's understanding of Christianity. Grundtvig himself attached much importance to this when he emphasized the necessity of acquiring an insight into human life, before one could achieve insight into Christianity. But any communication of faith by teaching is impossible.

What, then, do we do today at a time when many people feel alienated from the services of the Christian church and few, accordingly, take part in them? And when the individual person wants to see the particulars of the Christian view of life demonstrated so to speak in competition with others, before the choice of faith is made? In my view, modern theology offers two ways forward in the effort to take up this challenge. One way is to make the liturgical and sacramental experience more comprehensible, partly in order to motivate people to make that experience for themselves, partly in order to help the church to celebrate its church service in better agreement with its content. Such a "theology of worship" seems to me to be represented by Geoffrey Wainwright's *Doxology* (1980) and also by the reflections made by S.W. Sykes in the book already mentioned, which, with an inherent logic, concludes with a final chapter about *Worship, Commitment and Identity*. In my view this way is a continuation of what Grundtvig defended as his "church view". Its difficulty consists in the crisis which worship finds itself in today, and which theology cannot solve. Only the church can do that since it is connected with the life of the Church.

The other way is to distinguish consciously between the church as a religious community and Christianity as a world view, on the basis of the recognition that even today Christianity as a view of life has a direct and indirect influence in the society that reaches considerably further than that of the church, and that it is possible to argue for it in a way so as to create a convincing foundation for a choice of faith. It has been fully accepted here that the relation between faith and a world view has been reversed on the conditions of modernity. This does not in any way mean that the liturgical and sacramental dimension is not included in this process of thought, but it is included as part of the view. It seems to me that W. Pannenberg's theology is representative of this way, as it is expressed for example in his recently published *Systematische Theologie*, volume I. (1988) But Pannenberg clearly fulfills the condition set up by Grundtvig for a Christian theology, i.e., that it must be committed to the Christian revelation.

I for one choose the first way, but cannot deny that the other way holds insights and possibilities that prove their justification, not least in apologetic contexts. And the two ways represent the diversity which is not only permissible, but necessary in theology.

As for Grundtvig's "church view" in an English perspective, I am not the right person to speak about it; an Englishman must do that. But I do not mind offering an opinion. The Anglican will perceive a profound agreement with Grundtvig's understanding of the church's worship and his view of history and also with his view of Holy Scripture compared with the spoken word, but he will miss the ministry as an essential characteristic feature of the church and a more detailed theological foundation of the church as an institution. Precisely these lacks will, however, appear attractive to Free Churchmen in their different denominational variations, while Grundtvig's view of Holy Scripture may seem problematic to some of them. In both regards, Grundtvig's "church view" probably turns out to be unmistakably Lutheran. Let me finally make this clear by quoting a stanza from one of his church hymns, *The Church, It Is an Ancient House*,[25] a stanza which has unfortunately been left out in *The Danish Hymn Book*, possibly because it was a little too provocative, even for the clerical members of *The Danish Hymn Book* commission:

> Never forgotten shall be in the North
> The Church of living stones,
> Which on the strength of the Word of God
> Are united by faith and baptism!
> As a builder of a church, the Spirit is best,
> It needs a king no more than a priest
> The Word only hallows the House!

---

25. *GSV* I, p. 81.

Reason and Religion.
A Wesleyan Analogue to Grundtvig on Modernity and the Christian Tradition

By Geoffrey Wainwright

In the Anglican church Grundtvig found only rigid torpor and empty forms. On his last English visit, in 1843, it was if anything the Methodists who interested him (Hal Koch, *Grundtvig*).[1]

Locating the Conversation Partners

As a Christian theologian, N.F.S. Grundtvig engaged with modernity, it appears from the chapters by Theodor Jørgensen and Jens Holger Schjørring, through recourse to the tradition of the Church; and he was able to do so, precisely because modernity itself was, at least in part, an effect of Christianity, a product of the *Wirkungsgeschichte* of the faith. Tensions arise, however, between Christianity and modernity because modernity has *also* other sources than the Christian faith, and these in turn can have a distorting effect on the way Christianity is viewed and indeed held (as would have been the case with the "rationalist Protestantism" of Professor H.N. Clausen that combined a *sola Scriptura* position with an admission of the "uncertain" and "contradictory" character of the Scriptures). The trick, for Grundtvig in his time and for us in ours, must be to affirm and integrate those features of our culture that derive from Christianity and may enrich the Christian tradition, while at the same time we reject the anti-Christian elements and demonstrate their wrongness. This twofold (or fourfold) procedure – of assimilation and refusal (or affirmation and integration, rejection and rebuttal) – is necessary for apologetics, evangelism and doxology, if the way is to be cleared, humanly speaking, for the grace of God to abound to more and more people and for the eucharistic chorus thereby to swell (cf. 2 Corinthians 4:15).[2] It requires us in our generation,

1. Hal Koch, *Grundtvig*, translated from the Danish by Llewellyn Jones (Yellow Springs, Ohio, 1952), p. 103.
2. I am suggesting that what H. Richard Niebuhr, in *Christ and Culture* (New York, 1951), presents as five "typical" *attitudes* on the part of diverse Christian thinkers or groups towards culture *as a whole* can also serve as a grid for evaluating different

like the Church in each generation, to clarify the nature of the gospel and the faith; to discern the diachronic and synchronic identity of the believing and proclaiming community; and to risk making judgments as to where the kingdom of God is to be found. It is perhaps the principal duty of reflective theology to assist the Church and its pastoral leaders in these tasks.

Temporally to delimit "modernity", *die Neuzeit*, is difficult. In some intellectual and artistic circles on both sides of the North Atlantic, it is currently fashionable to speak of "the post-modern", and some would even say that we have already entered the next stage after that, however denominated; but such acceleration in journalistic historiography is to overprivilege – even granted an ostensibly unprecedented rapidity in superficial change – the ephemeral (and precisely *our* day in the sun) against the deeper and slower-moving "period" or "epoch" (*Konjunktur*) of "modernity", let alone the deepest levels of the human story, where anthropology is constant or nearly so.[3] My wager, for the purposes of present reflection, is that Grundtvig and ourselves live in what can still be significantly called a single period of history, and indeed that this period stretches back at least as far as John Wesley.[4]

It would, of course, be unwise to ignore altogether the differences of time and place. Philosophically, Wesley (1703-91) both was affected by and responded to the Enlightenment in its English form, characterized as it was by a Lockean empiricism and a Deistic worldview; religiously, Wesley was both helped by and became critical of German pietism in a Moravian or Herrnhut version; ecclesiastically, Wesley inherited the Reformation in its

---

components within a *particular* culture. In that case, Niebuhr's preferred fifth "type" – the transformation of culture by Christ – could occur by a process of sifting and choice such as John Henry Newman ascribed to the assimilative power of tradition: "Facts and opinions, which have hitherto been regarded in other relations and grouped round other centres, henceforth are gradually attracted to a new influence and subjected to a new sovereign. They are modified, laid down afresh, thrust aside, as the case may be. A new element of order and composition has come among them; and its life is proved by this capacity of expansion, without disarrangement or dissolution. An eclectic, conservative, assimilating, healing, moulding process, a unitive power, is of the essence, and a test, of a faithful development", *Essay on the Development of Christian Tradition*, II. v. 3; paperpack edition (London and New York, 1960), p. 135.

3.   For these "levels" of history, see Edward Schillebeeckx, *Jesus: An Experiment in Christology* (New York, 1981), pp. 576-582 (translation of *Jezus, het verhaal van een levende*, Bloemendaal, 1974, section IV.1.1).

4.   Up to now, the "post-modern" seems to me to consist of no more than the internal self-criticism of the modern. If the post-modern really does turn out to be a new epoch, it appears on present showing to retain so much of the modern that it will at most be its *Aufhebung* rather than a fresh start.

Anglican variant and sought to revitalize the Church of England according to the Prayer Book and the Homilies. Grundtvig's Denmark, two or even three generations later (1783-1872), was in some ways undergoing an Enlightenment that, across the German border, had both taken a Kantian turn and suffered a Romantic reaction. His church and people had been stamped by the Lutheran Reformation, and the vision which Grundtvig sought to implement for the Church of Denmark and the Danish nation would inevitably bear certain characteristics of Luther and his reception northwards. We live two hundred years after Wesley's death, and one hundred and twenty after Grundtvig's. Denmark is separated from Britain by the North Sea, and both are separated from the United States by the Atlantic Ocean, two stretches of water where the weather can be notoriously rough. My own situation is further complicated by the fact that I was raised a British Methodist and remain a minister of the British Methodist Church, even while living for the past decade and a half in a country where, at least since American independence, Wesley has been "received" in an ecclesiastical and cultural context that differs in complexity and style from his native land and mine. For all these reasons, the most that can be expected is an "analogy" between Grundtvig and Wesley, coming from a theologian who constantly struggles to keep Wesley's mark upon the latter's only half-intended ecclesiastical progeny (Wesley sought to remain Anglican, even while his para-church structures made an eventual ecclesial autonomy almost inevitable), while at the same time displaying that ecumenical openness and concern that is evinced precisely in, say, Wesley's sermon on the "Catholic Spirit" or in his "Letter to a Roman Catholic".[5] A sufficient commonality between Grundtvig and Wesley, while not neglecting certain differences between them, may help us to discern a viable range of nuanced options for ecclesial practice amid the modernity that continues to affect and challenge us all.

Wesley has recently been presented, in a rather controversial intellectual and theological biography, as a "reasonable enthusiast".[6] In that title, Henry Rack certainly links – in a tension-laden though hopefully not oxymoronic way – two characteristics of Wesley that Wesley himself might almost have preferred to designate according to the titles of his two

5. Sermon 39, "Catholic Spirit" (1750), in *The Works of John Wesley*, vol. 2, *Sermons II:34-70*, ed. Albert C. Outler (Nashville, 1985), pp. 79-95; "Letter to a Roman Catholic" (1749), in *The Works of the Rev. John Wesley, A.M.*, ed. Thomas Jackson (London, 1829-31; reprint Grand Rapids, 1984), vol. X, pp. 80-86, and in a modern edition by Michael Hurley, *John Wesley's Letter to a Roman Catholic* (London, 1968).
6. Henry D. Rack, *Reasonable Enthusiast: John Wesley and the Rise of Methodism* (London, 1989).

apologetic "Appeals" to "Men of *Reason* and *Religion*".[7] "Enthusiasm" was what Wesley's high-and-dry critics in his own day accused him of, when he saw himself rather as simply encouraging "vital religion" or "real Christian experience", whose "reasonable" nature he himself was persuaded of – provided, of course, "reason" was not limited, as by the very definition of some of his contemporaries, in such a way as to exclude transcendent revelation and grace. The original and normative gospel and faith were to be found, according to Wesley, in the Scriptures (one of the most important of his "standard sermons" expounded "The Scripture Way of Salvation"[8]), to which, above all, the earliest centuries and the English Reformers had been faithful. Methodism was but "the true old Christianity",[9] partly recovered at the Reformation and now commendable to all "men of reason and religion" in face of its regrettable decline in the England of his day.

Scripture, tradition, reason, and experience: those are the four factors which recent scholarship has detected in the shaping of Wesley's thinking and practice. In setting the standards for "our theological task", the 1972 *Discipline* of the United Methodist Church in turn noted that the Methodist pioneers believed there to be

a "marrow" of Christian truth that can be identified and that must be conserved. This living core, as they believed, stands revealed in *Scripture*, illuminated by *tradition*, vivified in personal *experience*, and confirmed by *reason*.[10]

For a brief while in the 1970s and 1980s, this fourfold strand became popularly known in American Methodism as the Wesleyan or Methodist "quadrilateral" (no less a figure than Cardinal Ratzinger told the present writer he had heard of the Methodist *Viereck*); but in so far as this expression may suggest an equal authority given to all four on a level plane, it is historically and theologically misleading, and much more careful attention is needed concerning the complex interplay and permutations among the four "sources" or "authorities". Nevertheless, this fourfold formulation, of Wesleyan or Methodist provenance, will be used, in an

7.   Scholarly edition of the "Earnest Appeal" (1743) and the "Farther Appeal" (1745) in *The Works of John Wesley*, vol. 11: *The Appeals to Men of Reason and Religion, and Certain Related Open Letters*, ed. G.R. Cragg (Oxford, 1975).

8.   Sermon 43, "The Scripture Way of Salvation" (1765), in *Works*, vol. 2, ed. Outler, pp. 152-169.

9.   Journal, Sept. 16, 1739, in *The Works of John Wesley*, vol. 19, *Journal and Diaries II: 1738-1743*, ed. W.R. Ward and R.P. Heitzenrater (Nashville, 1990), p. 97.

10. *The Book of Discipline of the United Methodist Church 1972*, (Nashville, 1973), paragraphs 68 and 70, pp. 39f., 75-79.

admittedly oversimple way, to identify some features by which Wesley and Grundtvig may be compared in their approaches to the issues of Christianity and modernity, with a view to detecting the range of tolerable options open to us as their respective heirs. Given the limitations of my own knowledge of Grundtvig, the weight will fall on the Wesleyan side of the analogy, and it will be up to those more familiar with Grundtvig, and especially those Danish readers who understand themselves in his line, to complement and correct what I say of Grundtvig[11] and to judge how far the range of compatible attitudes to modernity really extends for us at present.

We shall begin with reason and experience, for it is in those areas that the challenge of modernity is usually first encountered. Then we shall look at scripture and tradition, for those are the inherited resources upon which Christianity must draw if it is to retain its historic identity.

The Status and Use of Reason

Wesley's life spanned a century that considered itself the Age of Reason, even if it was only in 1793 that Reason became cultically enthroned for a few months in the cathedral of Notre Dame in Paris. That apotheosis, signifying the self-worship of humankind in its immanent powers, was but the logical entailment of the relegation of God from the world undertaken by the English Deists at the beginning of the century (John Toland's *Christianity Not Mysterious*, 1696; Matthew Tindal's *Christianity as Old as Creation*, 1730). Wesley would have no truck with the Deists and the dismissal of God to which their reasonings brought them: true Christianity was distinguished from Deism by the Atonement, by the original sin which made the latter needed, and by the Incarnation through which the Triune God made it possible. Thus Wesley wrote to Mary Bishop in a letter of February 7, 1778:

Nothing in the Christian system is of greater consequence than the doctrine of Atonement. It is properly the distinguishing point between Deism and Christianity....

---

11. Apart from brief extracts from his writings in English and German-language biographies, I have been able to read of Grundtvig himself only his "What Constitutes Authentic Christianity?" first published in four instalments in the *Theologisk Maanedsskrift* in 1826, and translated from volume 4 of the *Udvalgte Skrifter* [1906] by Ernest D. Nielsen (Philadelphia, 1985); and *N.F.S. Grundtvig: Selected Writings*, ed. Johannes Knudsen (Philadelphia, 1976). Otherwise I have relied heavily on the interpretations offered by Theodor Jørgensen and Jens Holger Schjørring in their contributions to the present book. This seems justified in that they, too, are concerned with the relation of Grundtvig to modernity and to tradition.

Give up the Atonement, and the Deists are agreed with us.... What saith the Scripture? It says, "God was in Christ, reconciling the world unto Himself"; that "He made Him, who knew no sin, to be a sin-offering for us".... But undoubtedly, as long as the world stands, there will be a thousand objections to this scriptural doctrine. For still the preaching of Christ crucified will be foolishness to the wise men of the world. However, let *us* hold the precious truth fast in our heart as well as in our understanding; and we shall find by happy experience that this is to us the wisdom of God and the power of God.[12]

The reference to "understanding" suffices to show that Wesley was not thereby abandoning intelligence. To the contrary: in his "Earnest Appeal" to "Men of Reason" he acknowledged and affirmed that "so far as [a man] departs from true genuine reason, so far he departs from Christianity".[13] That is because Christianity is

a religion evidently founded on, and every way agreeable to, eternal reason, to the essential nature of things. Its foundation stands on the nature of God and the nature of man, together with their mutual relations. And it is every way suitable thereto. To the nature of God, for it begins in knowing him – and where but in the true knowledge of God can you conceive true religion to begin? It goes on in loving him and all mankind – for you cannot but imitate whom you love. It ends in serving him, in doing his will, in obeying him whom we know and love. It is in every way suited to the nature of man, for it begins in man's knowing himself: knowing himself to be what he really is – foolish, vicious, miserable. It goes on to point out the remedy for this, to make him truly wise, virtuous, and happy, as every thinking mind (perhaps from some implicit remembrance of what it originally was) longs to be. It finishes all by restoring the due relations between God and man, by uniting for ever the tender father and the grateful, obedient son; the great Lord of all and the faithful servant, doing not his own will but the will of him that sent him.[14]

Within that divinely-posed ontological context of "eternal reason," reason may appropriately denote the human "faculty of reasoning, of inferring one thing from another".[15] In matters of religion, all depends then on the right use of reason, which is a God-enabled use of a God-given faculty:

We therefore not only allow, but earnestly exhort all who seek after true religion to use all the reason which God hath given them in searching out the things of God. But your *reasoning justly*, not only on this but on any subject whatsoever,

12. *The Letters of John Wesley*, ed. John Telford (London, 1931), vol. VI, pp. 297-299.
13. "An Earnest Appeal to Men of Reason and Religion", 27 (Cragg edition, p. 55).
14. ibid., 28-29, p. 55.
15. ibid., 30, p. 55.

presupposes *true judgments* already formed whereon to ground your argumentation.... [And] before it is possible for you to form a true judgment of them, it is absolutely necessary that you have a *clear apprehension* of the things of God.... And seeing our ideas are not innate, but must all originally come from our senses, it is certainly necessary that you have senses capable of discerning objects of this kind – not those only which are called "natural senses", which in this respect profit nothing, as being altogether incapable of discerning objects of a spiritual kind, but *spiritual* senses, exercised to discern spiritual good and evil. It is necessary that you have the *hearing* ear and the *seeing* eye, emphatically so called....And till you have these internal senses, till the eyes of your understanding are opened, you can have no apprehension of divine things, no idea of them at all. Nor consequently, till then, can you either judge truly or reason justly concerning them, seeing your reason has no ground whereon to stand, no materials to work upon.[16]

Once the Holy Spirit has revealed the things of God and bestowed the gift of faith, there is room for the believing mind to engage in more particular "chains of reasoning or argumentation, so close, so solid, so regularly connected" as may be found, for example, in the Epistle to the Hebrews.[17]

Doxologically, faith is maximized in comparison with unaided sense and reason:

Author of faith, eternal Word,
Whose Spirit breathes the active flame;
Faith, like its Finisher and Lord,
Today as yesterday the same:

To Thee our humble hearts aspire,
And ask the gift unspeakable;
Increase in us the kindled fire,
In us the work of faith fulfil....

The things unknown to feeble sense,
Unseen by reason's glimmering ray,
With strong, commanding evidence
Their heavenly origin display.

Faith lends its realizing light,
The clouds disperse, the shadows fly;

16. ibid, 31-32, p. 56f.
17. ibid., 30, p. 56.

Th' Invisible appears in sight,
And God is seen by mortal eye.[18]

None of the above, adapted as it is from a Lockean epistemology, may be too far from Grundtvig. Grundtvig rejected "abstract philosophical rationalism" (Schjørring); he set "true reason", which recognizes the "older" truth, against "autonomous" or "false, mortal reason" (Jørgensen). And what Grundtvig had to say anthropologically about language may, in its theological application, give a better account than Wesley himself – if there is in him a tendency finally to depreciate the physical senses – of the part played by preaching, and by the responsive confession of faith, in the juncture of body and spirit and in the communication between God and man: "Through the sense of hearing we experience not only something physical, the sound, but also something spiritual, the word."[19] Then, too, according to Grundtvig, theological reasoning has its place, within the framework of the *regula fidei*, in the refutation of heretics (as Schjørring recalls in connection with Grundtvig's translation of the fifth book of Irenaeus' *Adversus Haereses*).

In the self-criticism of the modern which (I bet) the "postmodern" represents, rationality has once again become an important issue. "According to *which* rationality?" is a question that Alasdair MacIntyre has shown always needs to be asked, when reason is invoked or reasoning is practised.[20] Against any too facile claims made by the Enlightenment in favour of an empirically universal reason, MacIntyre rightly argues that reasoning is always diachronically and synchronically "situated" – in a tradition and a community. Taken too far, however, that line could lead precisely to the epistemological scepticism that results from overprivileging the alleged "interest" of a putative knower over against what is there to be known, or to the spatial and temporal fragmentation of thinking that makes many "postmoderns" finally irrationalist.

The Christian story and confession offers rather a framework within which to account for the ontological consistency of true reasoning (thanks to the creative work of the Logos of the unique and universal Creator), the

18. Hymn of 1740 by Charles Wesley (1707-1788), figuring as no. 92 in the 1780 *Collection* (edition as in note 26, p. 194 s.) For Methodists, "Wesley" often functions as a collective noun including both John and Charles, although strictly the unqualified use refers to the elder brother alone. Danish readers may like to be initiated into a shibboleth: traditional British Methodists know that the pronunciation of Wesley is Wessley; only Anglicans and Americans say Wezley.
19. The point is set in its fuller context by Jørgensen's discussion.
20. Alasdair MacIntyre, *Whose Justice? Which Rationality?* (Notre Dame, Indiana, 1988).

empirical distortions of knowledge and argument that are due to the self-interest of human thinkers (which manifests original sin and its persistence), and the hope for a final harmony between all true knowers and the truly known (when the reconciliation wrought through the redemptive work of Christ will have extended according to the fulness of God's purposes). According to the Christian faith, the *universality* which was too abstractly and unproblematically assumed by the Enlightenment and the *particularity* which the "postmoderns" exalt at the expense of coherence meet in the *concrete universal* of the Word made flesh as Jesus of Nazareth. Of all contemporary theologians, T.F. Torrance has perhaps done most to show the correspondence – when both are seen as participation in the given structures of being – between the Christian faith and the procedures of the natural sciences which have produced the most significant achievements of modernity.[21] Torrance indeed holds that modern scientific method is historically dependent upon an attitude to the world that derives from the biblical faith. Persuasively proposed, such a connaturality, or even dependence, between faith and science affords a promising instrument for apologetics and evangelism amid modernity. And in turn, whatever in the fruit of modern science will pass muster by an evangelical ethic can be integrated into the Christian tradition.

Finally under reason may be mentioned an issue which is internal to Christianity and chiefly concerns the latter's "modernist" practitioners. It is the relation of what Wesley calls "doctrine" and "opinion", which broadly overlaps the question that Grundtvig might designate as "faith" and "theology". It must at once be stated that by "doctrine" Wesley does not mean what Grundtvig might call a "dead system" (or "mere orthodoxy", as Wesley might put it); rather "doctrine" for Wesley is the *fides quae creditur*, the content of the *fides qua creditur*, which is itself a living faith. In matters of theology, Wesley is largely content to "think and let think" – but only "in *opinions* that do not strike at the root of Christianity".[22] On the other (or rather the same) hand, in a generously ecumenical text Wesley declares that "a man of truly catholic spirit is fixed as the sun in his judgment concerning the main branches of Christian *doctrine*".[23] This appears quite close to what Grundtvig means by letting the Church rest on the "firm, unshakeable foundations" of the apostolic faith, while allowing "freedom

21. See Thomas F. Torrance, *Theological Science* (London, 1969); *God and Rationality* (London, 1971); *Christian Theology and Scientific Culture* (Belfast, 1980); *The Ground and Grammar of Theology* (Belfast, 1980); *Reality and Scientific Theology* (Edinburgh, 1985).
22. "The Character of a Methodist" (1742), in *Works* (ed. Jackson), vol. VIII, pp. 339-347, in particular p. 340.
23. "Catholic Spirit" (1750), in *Works*, vol. 2 (ed. Outler), p. 93.

of thought in the school of theology" (Schjørring), tolerating and even encouraging "all theological difference that is reconcilable with the fundamental Christian faith" (Jørgensen).

Such views certainly permit the "exploratory" work that is dear to modern theologians as they seek to engage with the (relatively) "new" questions put by the changes in culture. But it is also clear that, for disciples of Wesley and Grundtvig, a Christian theologian will stay within the ground-plan of the *regula fidei*, and that speculative construction must not exceed what the apostolic foundations of faith and doctrine will support, nor must these foundations be undermined by critical cavils drawn from an essentially different world-view.

The Place and Value of Experience

According to Jørgensen, faith for Grundtvig

must be a matter of experience, because it concerns the salvation and thus the integrity of the individual ... The Christian faith must be verifiable in the life experience of the individual ... It is a precondition that man's autonomy be accepted. Man can only endorse what he can recognize as truth from his inner conviction.

Faith is "the individual's most fundamental act of life". Yet the arbitrariness of individualism is avoided: "The autonomy of the heart, understood as its immediacy to God, is matched by God's sovereignty in His approach by virtue of His Word, which is Christ"; and that "brightly-alive" Word comes to humans in the historic community which it continues to create, namely the Church. The certainty of faith thus has its origin outside the believing individual – in the *verbum externum*, which is Christ himself who comes to expression in the Apostolic Confession and the Means of Grace.

For Wesley, too, Christianity is, in eighteenth-century terminology, "an experimental religion". Whereas Grundtvig at times appears to locate at the level of creation the human freedom to receive the gospel (as may be implied in what he has to say about the gift of language or in the polyvalent motto "first a man, then a Christian"), Wesley sees fallen humanity dependent, for its openness to accept the gospel, upon a sufficient restoration of freedom that has taken place only in virtue of the redemptive work of Christ: "Every man has a measure of free will *restored* to him by grace."[24] Although there may then be different "degrees of faith" (the fearful "faith

---

24. Wesley, *Works* (ed. Jackson), vol. X, p. 392. The context makes clear that this is by *redemptive* grace, in contrast to fallen human nature where "the will of man is free only to evil".

of a servant", the confident "faith of a son"), it is, according to Wesley, "the general privilege of believers" to be "assured" of their present state of salvation (which is no guarantee against backsliding or forfeiture). That assurance is given by "the witness of the Spirit with our spirit, that we are children of God, whereby we cry 'Abba, Father'" (Romans 8:15f. is a frequently cited text). Wesley can, of course, also speak in christological terms of Christ living in the believer and the believer's being conformed to Christ.[25]

Doxologically, the most significant expression of Wesleyan experientialism is the principal and resumptive *Collection of Hymns for the Use of the People called Methodists* (1780), where

the hymns are not carelessly jumbled together, but carefully ranged under proper heads, according to the experience of real Christians. So that this book is in effect a little body of experimental and practical divinity.[26]

The introductory first part is given to "exhorting and beseeching to return to God", "describing the pleasantness of religion, the goodness of God, death, judgment, heaven, hell", and "praying for a blessing". Part two briefly contrasts "formal religion" and "inward religion". Then the heart of the book comes in the next two sections: part three is devoted to "praying for repentance, for mourners convinced of sin, brought to the birth, convinced of backsliding, recovered", and part four to prayer "for believers rejoicing, fighting, praying, watching, working, suffering, groaning for full redemption, brought to the birth, saved, interceding for the world". The fifth and final part is "for the Society, meeting, giving thanks, praying, parting". Thus the emphasis falls on the way in which, within the fellowship of the Methodist Society, the individual is brought from sin through faith to salvation, corresponding to Wesley's statement that "our main doctrines, which include all the rest, are three, that of repentance, of faith, and of holiness".[27] In the 1780 *Collection*, the objective existence, work and presence of God are literally "taken for granted", and the interest centres on their achievement in the believer's justification and sanctification. Even

---

25. See Jürgen Weissbach, *Der neue Mensch im theologischen Denken John Wesleys* (Stuttgart, 1970); A.S. Yates, *The Doctrine of Assurance, with special reference to John Wesley* (London, 1952); H. Lindström, *Wesley and Sanctification: A Study in Salvation* (London, 1950).

26. Scholarly edition in *The Works of John Wesley*, vol. 7, *A Collection of Hymns for the Use of the People called Methodists*, ed. F. Hildebrandt and O.A. Beckerlegge (Oxford, 1983). The quotation is from Wesley's preface (here p. 74).

27. From "The Principles of a Methodist Farther Explained", *Works* (ed. Jackson), vol. VIII, p. 472.

in the many hymns, published in other collections, which Charles Wesley wrote for the great festivals that celebrate the Nativity, Passion, Resurrection and Ascension of Christ and the gift of the Holy Spirit at Pentecost, the present engagement of the worshipping believer is always prominent.

In his "Earnest Appeal" to "Men of Religion", Wesley is concerned that they pass from "the form" to "the power of godliness".[28] Correspondingly, he will not remain content with accurate statement of doctrines or with intellectual assent to them. With regard to the Trinity, for example, he endeavours to show, more experientially, that "the knowledge of the Three-One God is interwoven with all true Christian faith, with all vital religion":

I know not how anyone can be a Christian believer till "he hath" (as St. John speaks) "the witness in himself"; till "the Spirit of God witnesses with his spirit that he is a child of God" – that is, in effect, till God the Holy Ghost witnesses that God the Father has accepted him through the merits of God the Son – and having this witness he honours the Son and the blessed Spirit "even as he honours the Father". Not that every Christian believer *adverts* to this; perhaps at first not one in twenty; but if you ask any of them a few questions you will easily find it is implied in what he believes.[29]

Now experience, whether empirical or existential, has been much valued in modernity, and it might appear that Wesley and Grundtvig were, in their insistence on the experiential dimension of faith, not only children of their age but also (and thereby) apt for apologetics and evangelism in the service and line of the Christian tradition. But matters are not quite so simple: much depends on the precise place of experience in historic Christianity. George Lindbeck has recently argued that there is, in typically "modern" Christianity, an experience with experience that in fact *reverses* the sequence and priorities of an older, more original and therefore more authentic, Christianity. In modernity, religious interests easily "take the experiential-expressive form of individual quests for personal meaning":

The structures of modernity press individuals to meet God first in the depths of their souls and then, perhaps, if they find something personally congenial, to become part of a tradition or join a church.[30]

28. "Earnest Appeal", 47-52 (Cragg edition, pp. 62-65).
29. Sermon 55 (of 1775), "On the Trinity", in *Works*, vol. 2 (ed. Outler), pp. 373-386, in particular p. 385.
30. George A. Lindbeck, *The Nature of Doctrine: Religion and Theology in a Postliberal Age* (Philadelphia, 1984), in particular p. 22. In the fourth instalment of *What Constitutes Authentic Christianity?* (see note 11), Grundtvig makes a marvellous preemptive strike against "experiential-expressivism" by showing how the admixture of sin in

In my judgment, both Grundtvig and Wesley remain exempt from this flaw on account of their firm recognition of the *extra-nos* origins of faith; and both of them can be accommodated within the "cultural-linguistic" understanding and practice of Christianity which Lindbeck advocates as both ancient and *post*-modern, but the demonstration of that will have to await an exposition of their views on scripture and tradition in the next two parts of this chapter.

Meanwhile it may just be necessary to reaffirm, in face of some forms of would-be *post*-modernism, that the individual and his or her personal experience were important in Wesley and Grundtvig and *will always remain so* in a faith which believes that even the hairs of our head are numbered by God. The "decentring of the subject" occurs, for Christianity, not in the subject's fragmentation or even dissolution but rather by the coming of one "from outside" to visit and dwell "within us":

> Vi ere, vi bleve,
> Vi røres, vi leve
> I Christus, Gud levende Ord;
> Tag Ordet i Munden,
> Og elsk det fra Grunden!
> Da hos dig i Navnet han boer[31]

– and that presence is a transformative one:

> Heavenly Adam, Life divine,
> Change my nature into Thine;
> Move and spead throughout my soul,
> Actuate and fill the whole;
> Be it I no longer now
> Living in the flesh, but Thou.[32]

people's unformed desires for salvation subjects them to self-deception in their religious constructions (pp. 98-101 in the English translation).

31. Third stanza of "Trods Længselens Smerte", from Grundtvig's *Sang-Værk* (1837), no. 60; textual history in Anders Malling, *Dansk Salme Historie*, vol. 5 (Copenhagen, 1966), pp. 56-58. English translation in Jørgensen's chapter above.

32. Charles Wesley, "Since the Son hath made me free", fourth stanza (1739 and 1778 versions of the hymn). From *A Collection of Hymns for the Use of the People called Methodists*, No. 379 (eds. Hildebrandt and Beckerlegge, p. 552).

The sufficiency or subservience of Scripture

Wesley called himself "homo unius libri". That "one book" of the Bible constituted for Wesley not so much the "boundary of his reading" as "the center of gravity in his thinking",[33] and there can be no doubt that he attributed a strong instrumentality to the Scriptures in the process of salvation:

I am creature of a day, passing through life as an arrow through the air. I am a spirit come from God and returning to God; just hovering over the great gulf, till a few moments hence I am no more seen – I drop into an unchangeable eternity! I want to know one thing, the way to heaven – how to land safe on that happy shore. God himself has condescended to teach the way: for this very end he came from heaven. He hath written it down in a book. O give me that book! At any price give me the Book of God! I have it. Here is knowledge enough for me. Let me be *homo unius libri*.[34]

The written word remains subordinate to the work of the incarnate Word ("he came from heaven"), and it is significant that the passage just quoted comes from the preface to Wesley's *Sermons*, for in preaching, the *viva vox evangelii* is heard.[35] Yet scripture itself, as Wesley retained from the Anglican Articles of Religion, "containeth all things necessary to salvation".

Being already over seventy years old when Lessing published the Wolfenbüttel fragments of Reimarus, Wesley remained largely innocent of the "higher criticism". He knew, however, that the scriptures needed exegesis, and to help his preachers and his people he produced his *Explanatory Notes upon the Old Testament* and, in a text that became constitutionally embedded in Methodism, the *Explanatory Notes upon the New Testament*.[36] Where any text appeared "dark or intricate", Wesley followed the traditional procedures for seeking understanding as he had outlined them in the preface to his *Sermons*: first he prayed to the Father of lights for illumination, and then

---

33. A dictum of George Croft Cell, quoted by Thomas C. Oden, *Doctrinal Standards in the Wesleyan Tradition* (Grand Rapids, 1988), p. 82.
34. From the preface to Wesley's "Sermons on Several Occasions". Scholarly edition in *The Works of John Wesley*, vol. 1, *Sermons I: 1-33*, ed. Albert C. Outler (Nashville, 1984), in particular p. 104f.
35. See the text "Of Preaching Christ" (1751 and 1779), in *The Works of John Wesley*, vol. 26, *Letters II: 1740-1755*, ed. F. Baker (Oxford, 1982), pp. 482-489.
36. The Notes on the New Testament, indebted particularly to J.A. Bengel, date from 1755, and those on the Old Testament, indebted to Matthew Henry, from 1765. Wesley's prefaces to the two sets of Notes are printed in *Works* (ed. Jackson), vol X, pp. 235-239 and 246-253.

I search after and consider parallel passages of Scripture, "comparing spiritual things with spiritual". I meditate thereon, with all the attention and earnestness of which my mind is capable. If any doubt still remains, I consult those who are experienced in the things of God, and then the writings whereby, being dead, they yet speak. And what I thus learn, that I teach.[37]

This pre-critical approach easily allowed for the doxological use of the scriptures in hymns, in which interwoven texts depict the basic patterns of the Christian faith in ever-changing varieties of colour. The following example from Charles Wesley's "Spirit of faith, come down" (of 1746) is characteristic:[38]

No man can truly say	
That Jesus is the Lord,	(1 Cor 12:3)
Unless Thou take the veil away,	(2 Cor 3:12-18)
And breathe the living word;	(Mt 4:4; Jn 20:22)
Then, only then, we feel	
Our interest in His blood,	
And cry with joy unspeakable:	(1 Pet 1:8)
Thou art my Lord, my God!	(Jn 20:28)

Such procedures also allow the scriptures to be read for their fourfold meaning, as in the medieval senses of the historical, the doctrinal, the moral and the anagogical.

For Grundtvig, too, sermons and hymns, "the preaching and the songs of praise", were vital to the communication of God's Word, although (according to the interpretation of both Jørgensen and Schjørring) he appears to make the scriptures subservient to the ancient creeds and the continuing confession in ways that would have struck Wesley (I think) as tending to undermine the normativity of the scriptures themselves over against any subsequent witness to Christ. Perhaps, by his positive emphasis on tradition, Grundtvig was already also, on the defensive front, making moves to counter the problems that would arise when the combination of a *sola scriptura* position with a critical approach to the Bible, occurring already in Clausen, would finally expose Protestantism to the revisionary proposals of a D.F. Strauss. In any case, Grundtvig apparently felt confident enough to be "open to the historical interpretation of biblical texts" even when this displayed "a tendency towards modern criticism" (Schjørring). Lessing's historical and hermeneutical "ditch" could be bridged by the

37. As in note 34, p. 106.
38. No. 83 in the 1780 *Collection* (as in note 18), p. 182f.

living presence of Christ, by the traditionary process of the Church, and by an anthropological constancy that allowed biblical personages to figure as "examples of basic human characteristics" whose stories thereby remained susceptible to an "existential interpretation" (Schjørring).

The difference between Grundtvig and Wesley may be epitomized in the fact that Wesley calls the Bible "the Book of God" (and speaks in strong terms of the divine "inspiration" of the writings), whereas Grundtvig, even (or precisely) when he is dealing with the rationalistic criticism of "our present-day scholars", sees the historical books of the New Testament as "first and foremost ... a human testimony about the founding of the Christian church". As "the oldest church history", they provide "a truthful and dependable history of the life and teachings of Jesus Christ and his chief apostles, and of the initial beginning of the expansion of their teaching".[39] While it is possible to interpret Wesley and Grundtvig in a convergent way (by stressing the congruence between the divine revelation or inspiration and the human witness or record), they clearly make a difference of emphasis – and Grundtvig's "church-historical" approach facilitates his high valuation of the Apostles' Creed and later confessions and prepares the way for a more "continuous" view of the Christian tradition than Wesley, as we shall see, allows.

How, now, may Wesley and Grundtvig offer us common or distinctive help for the appropriation of the scriptures in modernity or post-modernity? I would judge that modernity has precluded any return to a method of dealing with the scriptures that *ignores* historical investigation. Here Grundtvig's "openness to the historical investigation of biblical texts" is basically correct. Belief in the Incarnation makes it both necessary and possible to seek out "wie es eigentlich gewesen". But such investigation need not, and should not, be constrained by Humean or Troeltschean limits that rule out "miracle" by a combination of scepticism and a closed-causality view of reality. W. Pannenberg's treatment of the Resurrection provides an excellent example of better procedures.[40]

Yet I should not wish to follow Grundtvig too readily in his seeming "demotion" of the scriptures in relation to ancient creeds and continuing confession – precisely because the scriptures have proved themselves better guardians of the traditional faith than either a creed left drifting from its scriptural moorings or typically modern attempts to "save" the gospel by

---

39. What Constitutes Authentic Christianity? p. 108. This "church-historical" view was Grundtvig's "matchless discovery" of the mid-1820s, and he stayed firm in it. After the "crisis" of 1810-11 he had gone through a "biblicist" phase.
40. See Wolfhart Pannenberg, *Grundzüge der Christologie* (Gütersloh, 1976 (5th ed.)), pp. 47-112.

"demythologization". Although, historically, oral and practical tradition preceded the New Testament scriptures, and although the confession and preaching of the apostolic faith developed in parallel with the development of those scriptures, yet I judge (standing in the line of Wesley) that ancient creedal confessions and epitomes of the apostolic preaching must, theologically, be seen as summaries of the scriptures before they can be seen, as it were independently, as their hermeneutical key. Otherwise the creeds, by their very brevity, become too easy game, in the modern period at least, for the reductionism inherent in "doctrinal criticism" (so, on the Anglican side, G.F. Woods, M.F. Wiles, and, yes, D. Cupitt); and the "regula fidei" or "kanon tes aletheias" of an Irenaeus, by its selective concision, might seem to excuse (on the Lutheran side) a Bultmann's procedure of narrowing the kerygma to (say) justification by faith, now modernized as authentic existence. The thick and complex texture of the scriptures themselves keeps them resistant to truncation and allows them to go on providing a variety of resources for contemporary proclamation and confession.

Several features currently seen as characteristic of "post-modernity" should help to regain a hearing for a view of the scriptures in some ways closer to the Wesleyan (although, of course, secular scholars would want to prescind from questions of the divine inspiration and salvific purpose of the Bible). Interest in "text", and particularly in the integral form of texts, meshes with the "canon criticism" by which some North American exegetes have sought again to read the parts of scripture according to their place in the ecclesially received whole.[41] Reader-response criticism allows new attention to the *Wirkungsgeschichte* of the scriptures (remember G. Ebeling's thesis of "church history as the history of the exegesis of holy scripture"![42]) and opens up the possibility of multiple "readings" along the lines of the four medieval "senses" of scripture. Without seeking to turn the clock back,[43] there is now an available option to penetrate through and beyond historical criticism to a "second naïveté" (P. Ricoeur). In any case, the notion of myth is enjoying something of an intellectual comeback in post-modernity, even (and indeed most significantly) among the natural

41. For example, B.S. Childs, *Introduction to the Old Testament as Scripture* (Philadelphia, 1979), and *The New Testament as Canon: An Introduction* (Philadelphia, 1985).
42. G. Ebeling, "Kirchengeschichte als Geschichte der Auslegung der Heiligen Schrift" (1946-47), in *Wort Gottes und Tradition* (Göttingen, 1964), pp. 9-27.
43. That is the implicit weakness in the otherwise appealing article of David Steinmetz, "The superiority of pre-critical exegesis", in *Theology Today* 37 (1980-81) pp. 27-38.

sciences.[44] George Lindbeck, in his "cultural-linguistic" approach to Christianity, has boldly revived the notion of a scriptural world being able to absorb the universe:

For those who are steeped in them, no world is more real than the ones [the canonical scriptures] create.... [A scriptural world] supplies the interpretive framework within which believers seek to live their lives and interpret reality.[45]

According to Lindbeck, ecclesial doctrine then functions to set the "rules" by which this should take place; and therewith we return to the notion of the *regula fidei* and the tradition of the Church.

The Promise and Problem of Tradition

Grundtvig, it is generally agreed, held a strong view of ecclesial tradition. Behind "the historical continuity of the Church", the "long chain of tradition", lies a "divine power", the signs of whose presence and the means of whose action are principally the Apostolic Confession and the Means of Grace; these "essentials of the Church are safeguards of what is primordial, unchangeable and recognizable in the Church" (Schjørring). As Jørgensen points out, this comes very close to article VII of the Augustana: "Est autem ecclesia congregatio sanctorum, in qua evangelium pure docetur et recte administrantur sacramenta." Grundtvig's favourite witnesses in and to Church tradition were Irenaeus, Luther and "our Lutheran forefathers", although his hymn-translations show him willing to draw doxologically upon Christians from a very wide range of times and places.

Living as he did before the Romantic movement, Wesley did not hold such an "organic" view of ecclesial tradition as may be found in J.A. Möhler, J.H. Newman, and perhaps N.F.S. Grundtvig.[46] True, he retained the Apostolicum doxologically from the *Book of Common Prayer* in the morning and evening prayer of *The Sunday Service of the Methodists* prepared for North America; and he respected and used the Nicaenum and

---

44. See, for instance, K. Hübner, *Die Wahrheit des Mythos* (Munich, 1985), and "Der Mythos, der Logos und das spezifisch Religiöse", in H.H. Schmid (ed.), *Mythos und Rationalität* (Gütersloh, 1988), pp. 27-43.
45. G.A. Lindbeck, *The Nature of Doctrine*, p. 117.
46. One of the reasons for Ted A. Campbell's scepticism concerning the finding of "the modern Methodist quadrilateral" (see early in this chapter) in Wesley himself lies in the absence from Wesley of a positive notion of tradition "in a post-Tractarian or modern ecumenical sense of the term" as "describing God's work in the Church after the scriptural period"; see "The 'Wesleyan Quadrilateral': The Story of a Modern Methodist Myth", in *Methodist History* 29 (1990-91), pp. 87-95.

the Athanasianum doctrinally as the formal and substantive "rules" of the Christian faith: his exposition of "the faith of a true Protestant" in the *Letter to a Roman Catholic* consists in an expansion on the Nicene-Constantino-politan creed;[47] and he valued the Athanasian Creed's "explication" of the Trinity as "the best I ever saw".[48] Wesley also appealed to the writings (incorporating some of them into his *Christian Library*, 50 volumes, 1747-55) and life of the "Primitive Church" of the first *three* centuries as a period of great, though not total, purity which the English Reformers had sought to repristinate.[49] Moreover, in the *Earnest Appeal to Men of Reason and Religion*, Wesley draws on Anglican Article XIX (so close to CA VII) to define the Church as essentially "a company of faithful (or believing) people, *coetus credentium*", with the properties "that the pure word of God be preached therein, and the sacraments duly administered". "Assembling together", they are "visible"; "scattered abroad", "dispersed up and down", they are (curiously, in Wesley's terminology) "invisible". In any case, "the Church of England" is "the *faithful people*, the *true believers* of England".[50] Yet those words, which Wesley himself italicizes, start to hint at a different ecclesiology, and a different view of tradition, than Grundtvig's. While without the preaching and hearing of the pure word of God "faith would languish and die", and while the sacraments are "the ordinary means whereby God increases faith", yet the essence is a "living faith, without which indeed there can be no church at all" – and, for Wesley, "living faith" has as its *indispensable expression* Christian character and works.[51]

47. See above, note 5. For an analogy between Wesley's procedure here and that of the current "Apostolic Faith Study" in WCC Faith and Order, see G. Wainwright, "Methodism and the Apostolic Faith" in M. Douglas Meeks (ed.), *What Should Methodists Teach?* (Nashville, 1990), pp. 101-117. Wesley's omission of the Nicene Creed from the Communion office in *The Sunday Service of the Methodists* is thus much more probably attributable to his passion for liturgical abbreviation than to material dissatisfaction with the text.
48. So in the sermon "On the Trinity" (see above, note 29). Wesley's omission of the Anglican Article VIII ("Of the Three Creeds") from the Articles of Religion he prepared for North America is most likely due to his objections, common among eighteenth-century and later Anglicans, to the "damnatory clauses" in the Athanasianum.
49. See Ted A. Campbell, *John Wesley and Christian Antiquity* (Nashville, 1991).
50. "An Earnest Appeal", 76-78 (Cragg edition, p. 77f).
51. This comes through, for instance, in the "Letter to a Roman Catholic" (see above, note 5), 13: an exposition of the *fides quae creditur* is followed by a description of the *fides qua creditur* and matching conduct ("A true Protestant believes in God, has a full confidence in his mercy, fears him with a filial fear, loves him with all his soul … and serves him truly all the days of his life … A true Protestant loves his neighbour…").

Wesley, in fact, largely shared the "radical" view of a fall, or at least a precipitous decline, of the Church that set in at "that evil hour when Constantine the Great called himself a Christian".[52] A sermon on "The Mystery of Iniquity" declares that

persecution never did, nor could give any lasting wound to genuine Christianity. But the greatest it ever received, the grand blow which was struck at the very root of that humble, gentle, patient love, which is the fulfilling of the Christian law, the whole essence of true religion, was struck in the fourth century by Constantine the Great, when he called himself a Christian, and poured in a flood of riches, honours, and power upon the Christians, more especially upon the clergy.... When the fear of persecution was removed, and wealth and honour attended the Christian profession, the Christians did not gradually sink, but rushed headlong into all manner of vices.... Such has been the deplorable state of the Christian Church from the time of Constantine till the Reformation. A Christian nation, a Christian city ... was nowhere to be seen; but every city and country, a few individuals excepted, was plunged in all manner of wickedness.[53]

The Reformation itself, according to Wesley, was only partially successful. Then his "Farther Appeal to Men of Reason and Religion" contains, in its second part, a descriptive catalogue of the vices that currently abounded in England and, in the third part, an account of the "call to repentance" with which Methodism began to execute its vocation to "spread scriptural holiness through the land", and some evidence of its success.[54] All this makes for a much more "episodic" view of the history of Christianity than is suggested by Grundtvig's "historical continuity" and "the long chain of tradition".[55]

Since baptism is generally regarded as the sacramental initiation into the tradition, the differences between Wesley and Grundtvig on tradition may be expected to come to significant expression in their respective views on

---

52. Sermon 121, "Prophets and Priests" (also known under "The Ministerial Office", 1789), in *The Works of John Wesley*, vol. 4, *Sermons IV:115-151*, ed. A.C. Outler (Nashville, 1987), in particular p. 77. For nuances in Wesley's view of the "Constantinian fall", see Campbell (as in note 49).
53. Sermon 61, "The Mystery of Iniquity" (1783), in *Works*, vol. 2 (ed. Outler), in particular pp. 462-464.
54. "A Farther Appeal" (ed. Cragg, as in note 7).
55. Wesley's dismal view of the earthly history of Christianity is somewhat mitigated by his belief in a transcendental communion of the saints embracing "all the living members of Christ on earth, as well as all who are departed in his faith and fear" ("Letter to a Roman Catholic", 9, as in note 4); see G. Wainwright, "Wesley and the Communion of Saints", in *One in Christ* 27 (1991), pp. 332-345.

baptism, and some clarification on this matter may also help the English and Danish churches as to the policies they pursue in a social, cultural and religious situation that is at least as problematic as those obtaining in the days of Wesley and Grundtvig respectively. In Grundtvig, baptism always figures in tandem with communion as "means of grace", and he appears never to call in question the general practice of baptizing infants in a multitudinist folk-church. Wesley, too, accepted the Anglican practice of infant baptism and appears never to have abandoned the belief that its subjects were thereby sacramentally regenerated.[56] But the stress in his preaching on the empirical need for *post*-baptismal "new birth" always shocks Lutherans accustomed to the "Baptizatus sum". Thus:

Say not then in your heart, I *was once* baptized; therefore I *am now* a child of God. Alas, that consequence will by no means hold. How many are the baptized gluttons and drunkards, the baptized liars and common swearers, the baptized railers and evil-speakers, the baptized whoremongers, thieves, extortioners!... To say then that ye cannot be born again, that there is no new birth but in baptism, is to seal you all under damnation, to consign you to hell, without any help, without hope.... Lean no more on the staff of that broken reed, that ye *were* born again in baptism. Who denies that ye were then made "children of God, and heirs of the kingdom of heaven"? But notwithstanding this, ye are now children of the devil; therefore ye must be born again.[57]

On a visit to Denmark just a few years ago, I was told there were three things one must never question: NATO, the Queen, and infant baptism. Is then the Church of Denmark (still – if it ever was) able to count on a kind of delayed catechesis being provided in the free-schools, folk-high-schools, and finally church-institutions in order to initiate growing children and young adults into the liturgical and moral existence for which their baptism in infancy marked them out (first baptized, then human, finally Christian – as it were)?[58]

---

56. See Bernard G. Holland, *Baptism in Early Methodism* (London, 1970). It must, however, be admitted that the notion gradually "fades" in Wesley.
57. Sermon 18, on "The Marks of the New Birth" (1748), in *Works*, vol. 1 (ed. Outler, as in note 34), pp. 415-430; cf. Sermon 45, "The New Birth" (1760), in *Works*, vol. 2 (ed. Outler, as in note 5), pp. 186-201.
58. "The school should not be a church, but on the other hand Grundtvig never doubted that a living school would act as a preparation for Christianity, as a church porch ... 'Let each upon this earth then strive / True man to be, / Open his ear to the word of truth / And render God his glory! / If Christianity be truth's way, / And he is not a Christian today, / He will be by tomorrow'" (Koch, p. 143, including a stanza from Grundtvig's poem "Man first, then Christian".)

In England, at least, modernity has brought a far greater disruption to any such pattern: the number of infant baptisms among Anglicans per 1,000 live births in the general population fell from 672 in 1950, to 554 in 1960, to 466 in 1970, to 365 in 1980, to 288 in 1988. Over the same period, the number of Easter communicants has also declined, although at a noticeably slower rate on account of the time-lag, from 2 million (of a total population aged fifteen and over of 32.3 million) in 1950 to 1.58 million (of 38.8 million) in 1988.[59] In an effort to close the gap between the number of the baptized (which is any case shrinking on account of social and cultural factors) and the number of believing and practising Christians, some voices in the Church of England are calling for greater discipline in baptismal use; but other Anglicans reject any move which might seem to turn the Church of England into a mere voluntarist "denomination" like (say) the Methodists. Meanwhile, on the Western side of the Atlantic, a parish priest in the Orthodox Church of America tells me his practice is to baptize infants only when he would be willing to baptize their parents or sponsors (were they not baptized already). That may be a lesson for Danes, English and Americans, Lutherans, Anglicans and Methodists, to relearn from the Ancient Church that was so much admired by Wesley and by Grundtvig in their respective ways.

Identifying a Eucharistic Church

Between Grundtvig and Wesley we have discovered both commonalities and differences in respect of reason, experience, scripture and tradition and the place of these in the engagement between Christianity and modernity. In conclusion, it may be suggested that the commonalities come to best expression in the sacrament of the Lord's Supper, which, in addition, provides not only a framework in which the differences between Wesley and Grundtvig can be moderated but also a paradigm of understanding and practice for the Church in its cultural, worldly setting.

The Lord's Supper was vitally important for both Wesley and Grundtvig. Wesley's lifelong observance and advocacy of "constant communion" was merely sealed when, in writing in 1784 to the "brethren in North America", he advised "the elders to administer the Supper of the Lord on every Lord's day".[60] In 1745, John and Charles Wesley produced a

59. Figures from *The Church of England Year Book 1991* (London, 1991), p. 400f.
60. *The Letters of John Wesley* (ed. Telford, as in note 12), vol. VII, p. 239. See also J.C. Bowmer, *The Lord's Supper in Early Methodism* (London, 1951), where it emerges that Wesley took communion on average every four or five days in an age when parish practice in England averaged four celebrations a year.

collection of 166 *Hymns on the Lord's Supper* to enhance the Prayer Book order.[61] At a time when the Danish church, in its pietism or its rationalism, failed to show much interest in the sacraments, Grundtvig insisted on baptism and the supper as dominical means of grace, and his hymns abound with references to "bath and board", "font and table".

Let us then attempt the constructive statement of a eucharistic ecclesiology that incorporates and reconciles some of the strongest features of Wesley and Grundtvig: At the Lord's Supper, as the baptized and believing congregation gathers in the Lord's name, the combination and interplay of scripture reading, preaching, confession of faith and prayer allow the living Word to be heard. Here, in Christ, the congregation finds itself in communion with the whole company of heaven and all those who at all times and in all places have joined in the unending songs of praise. Here every believer, in the fellowship of the Church, may have his or her experience shaped, and character formed, by the scriptural and traditional experience of the Christian community as it receives the Father's blessings through Christ in the Holy Spirit and, as sons and daughters in the Son, by the Holy Spirit cries "Abba, Father" and produces the fruit of the Spirit to God's glory; here participants are fed body and soul by Christ and taste in advance the joys of heaven.[62] Here Christians learn doxological thinking, in which their reasoning is trained by the Logos, who became incarnate in Jesus Christ and was crucified and raised, and they learn to discern the signs of God's kingdom and corresponding ways of action in the world.[63]

In the last generation or two, there has occurred a growing ecumenical awareness and practice of a eucharistic ecclesiology that must rejoice the hearts of Wesley and of Grundtvig. While, in this life, a eucharistic community may always run the risk of self-righteousness, which needs to be countered by the remembrance that participants come as forgiven

---

61. See J.E. Rattenbury, *The Eucharistic Hymns of John and Charles Wesley* (London, 1948).
62. The eschatological prospect is strong in section III of the Wesleyan *Hymns on the Lord's Supper*: "the sacrament a pledge of heaven" (nos. 93-115). In the *Danske Salmebog*, no. 54, Grundtvig speaks of "the word of grace, which comes to us at the Lord's table, inviting us to come and sit down eternally in the joy of the Lord"; and no. 243 echoes Luke 13:29. See, more broadly, Geoffrey Wainwright, *Eucharist and Eschatology* (London, 1971; New York, 1981 (updated)).
63. "A responsibly celebrated eucharist exemplifies *justice* because grateful people are all equally welcomed there by the merciful Lord into his table fellowship, and all together share in the fruits of redemption and in the foretaste of the new heavens and the new earth in which right will prevail (cf. 2 Pet. 3:13) ... The eucharist, responsibly celebrated, exemplifies *peace*, because reconciled people are there at peace with God and with one another (cf. Matt. 5:23f.)" (G. Wainwright, "Eucharist and/as Ethics", in *Worship* 62 (1988), pp. 123-138, in particular p. 135f.).

sinners, penitent and believing, yet the sharpening of the contours of ecclesial identity that takes place at the Lord's Supper has great potential for the clarity of the Church's witness to the world, whether ancient or modern.[64]

64. Danish Lutherans and English Anglicans will have to ask themselves, more than English or American Methodists need to, how such a eucharistic ecclesiology, with its resonances of the "gathered church", relates to their inherited pattern of an "established" church. Hal Koch writes that Grundtvig made a "precise distinction between the state church and the true church of Jesus Christ. The former is only 'a civil institution', but in it Christ's church may abide as guest. All that may reasonably be demanded of the state church is that it provide good living conditions for the true church" (Koch, p. 174). *Not* that the "free churches", for their part, are out of the woods: "Thoughts of withdrawing from the [state] church and forming free congregations were again present to Grundtvig in his latter days. Only, he pointed out, one must of course realize that a free congregation gives no better guarantee than the state church that it is actually God's congregation there assembled. The free congregation can no more be indentified with the true congregation out of hand than any other. The latter is neither palpable nor demonstrable, but is recognized through its signs of life, which are confession, songs of praise, and preaching" (Koch, p. 175).

Church Continuity and the Challenge of Modernity: Grundtvig, the Oxford Movement and Rationalist Theology

By Jens Holger Schjørring

When Grundtvig published the first volume of his Song-Work for the Danish Church his view of the Church had fallen into place in a consistent pattern of theological insight. This clarification was the result of many years of struggle, which included important intermediate positions. *The Church's Retort*, seen within Grundtvig's development in the 1820's, is probably the most decisive episode on his way towards clarity.[1]

Grundtvig's theology, as presented in his hymns and sermons, is an impressive achievement of doxological thinking within the framework of liturgical practice. This is true, not only when it is seen within a larger historical and contemporary perspective.

In order to recognize the real impact of some of these ideas we have to extend our analysis beyond narrow national and historical limitations. As a starting point for a systematic and international comparison it is worthwhile paying attention to Grundtvig's position in 1837 with special regard on the one hand to his reaction to the radical theology expressed by the German David F. Strauss and his connection with the Oxford Movement on the other. Thus we shall be able to consider Grundtvig's view of the continuity of the Church and the challenge of modernity when seen from a theological way of thinking that is marked by deep liturgical rootedness.

This task however cannot be fulfilled unless at least three aspects of a paradoxical nature are mentioned, whereby the complex relation between church continuity and modernity may become even more apparent:

1. The Danish versus the ecumenical

Grundtvig personally insisted upon the second part of the title *Song-Work for the Danish Church*. He was most conscious of the national character of his work, considering in particular his use of the Danish language. No less

---

1.   cf. Theodor Jørgensen's article, pp. 171-90 in this volume.

important for him was the national framework, in as far as it was based on his fundamental intention of giving his proclamation of the Gospel an expression formed within the context of national history and nature, thereby enabling the Danish congregations to connect that message with things familiar to them and existentially present.

In spite of this national note, however deeply rooted it may be, the *Song-Work* is eminently ecumenical. This is so, because Grundtvig adopts and reproduces hymns from almost all places and periods in Christian history. Just as fundamental as his address to his fellow countrymen and women is his constant eye for "Christianity". In this way Grundtvig deliberately expresses a notion of the Church as a spiritual institution that has existed from the first morning of creation ("the Church eternal") until this very day. He is aware of the tension between a popular and national ("folkelig") context and the ecumenical perspective in "universal history". Yet he never allows this tension to degenerate into a contradiction.

Any systematic consideration of Grundtvig has to come to terms with this dialectic between a specific framework and a universal approach.

2. Grundtvig's connection with the Oxford Movement

If we consider the time of its publication, it may at first sight appear a coincidence that the *Song-Work* was published exactly when the Tractarians were creating a turning point in the history of Anglicanism. A direct contact was established, but when, after several years of hesitation, it was just about to be realized, the conversation turned into a disastrous disagreement. The discrepancy, dramatically experienced on both sides, prevented the contestants from noticing the relevance of the subjects of their conversation. This negative outcome becomes even more apparent when another paradox is added: Obvious points of resemblance were never really observed, a fact which of course demands our attention if we are fully to apprehend the principal ideas.

To give only a preliminary account of some of these aspects of similarity, which were not observed at that time, the following points can be mentioned: It appears that Grundtvig never noticed John Keble's collection of hymns *The Christian Year* (1827). Nor did he take into account how far reaching was the agreement between his own evaluation of the sacraments and Edward Pusey's view. No less astonishing is the fact that John Henry Newman's notion of "ecclesial antiquity" never became a platform for a dialogue, in spite of its manifest agreement with Grundtvig's use of Irenaeus.

Thus, a merely historical description of the direct contacts of those years could only involve more or less secondary topics leading to the final disagreement of 1843. A systematic assessment, however, cannot stop there at the failure to establish a dialogue then, however deep the difference of opinion appeared. In the present situation it is accordingly an obligation on both sides to seek a generous interpretation of the texts and to observe points of resemblance as well as of difference. In other words, we must attempt the dialogue now, which failed to be established then, without ignoring historical matters of fact.

3. The sharpening of Grundtvig's polemics against Rationalism

Thus, in 1837 Grundtvig's criticism of radical theology was sharpened. His attack was no longer directed solely against rationalist theologians in Denmark, but with increasing vigour against leading representatives of that school in Germany. The specific occasion for his passionate protest was David F. Strauss' publication of his book *The Life of Jesus, critically examined* (first published in Germany 1835). In Germany, and in many neighbouring countries as well, this book caused excited debate sometimes indeed raising the question, whether radical views like those expressed by Strauss did not make it urgent to put limitations on the freedom of theological teaching.

Grundtvig for his part strongly dissociated himself from Strauss' method of critical textinterpretation, and even more from his philosophical recon struction of what he had previously dissected through his criticism of the biblical texts. In Grundtvig's view, however, Strauss should not be seen as an isolated radical. He had to be recognized as an exponent of a general tendency towards abstract philosophical rationalism. The fatal consequences of this way of thinking, according to Grundtvig's impression, could be observed easily in contemporary German universities. He regarded this tendency as just as dangerous and hostile to "education for life" as a Roman tradition of learning. Both were characterized by abstract thinking, carried on in an ivory tower; and both were at the same time controlled by judicial, hierarchial criteria of truth, which had no connection with popular thinking or common sense.

If we were to assess Grundtvig's theology exclusively from this uncompromising encounter, he would appear as a strict guardian of traditional orthodoxy. But such a characterisation taken on its own would be a fatal caricature. It is true that Grundtvig, in relation to Strauss, indicated his own position as traditionally orthodox ("gammelkirkelig") and that had been the case with even more emphasis in his polemic against professor H.N. Clausen.

Yet, this rootedness in a classical tradition of church teaching is only one side of his thinking. At the same time he was open to the historical interpretation of biblical texts, not to speak of his awareness of new theories of study in language and history. It would be no exaggeration to regard this coexistence of a tendency towards modern criticism on the one hand and a theology of liturgical praise on the other as the foundation of a consistent response to the challenge of modernity.

Having noticed this, it has to be admitted, however, that we are facing yet another paradox in Grundtvig's thinking: We are invited to look beyond his polemic against rationalist theology, in spite of the definite way in which he personally labelled his criticism. He wanted to liberate the Christian congregation from the trammels of a relativism, which results from dependence upon different schools of learning. Yet, this fact does not change the other fact, that Grundtvig paves the way for a theological approach which can confront the facts of modernity.

The task of subjecting Grundtvig to such an examination appears to be the touch-stone for a discussion of his importance as a teacher for church and theology in the present situation.

Grundtvig's Encounter with Rationalist Theology in the 1830's
David Friedrich Strauss' book *Life of Jesus, critically examined* caused a tidal wave of protest, because Strauss had used a historical-critical method and as a result characterized major parts of the Gospel-narratives as late additions with little reference to the historical core. Strauss claimed, however, that this critical dissection was not meant as a demolition of orthodox Christianity, although he came to acknowledge that such feelings dominated the reception of his book, even among liberal theologians. In an epilogue Strauss suggested a philosophical reconstruction of the Gospel, that was meant to replace the merely historical narratives in the Bible. This uplifting of the Gospel (the German word *Aufhebung* had acquired a double meaning since Hegel's philosophy of history) to an eternal truth, expressed by philosophical concepts, was seen by Strauss as the only way to meet the claims of modern philosophical criticism. Thus Strauss intended to pave a way which would lead from past patterns of belief (whether supernatural or rationalist) to a tenable, consistent theory of knowledge in the new era of modernity.[2]

Obviously Strauss' book showed many signs of immature emotion, but no less obvious was the opinionated bombast of many of his experienced colleagues, conservative and liberal alike in their replies. Strauss' many precise observations in his analysis of texts and in his considerations of

---

2.   D.F. Strauss, *Life of Jesus*, (concluding remarks). Concerning Strauss and the Strauss-debate cf. Horton Harris, *David F. Strauss and his Theology* (Cambridge, 1973); J. Pelikan, *Jesus through the Centuries* (New York, 1987), pp. 186ff.

philosophical method, which deserved a thorough reexamination, were left aside. The dramatic confrontations in the widespread public discussion drew the discussion away from the academic issues. Apologetic reactions came to dominate the scene of debate.

Grundtvig for his part joined the crowd of opponents of Strauss as early as the spring of 1836. The first hints are found in his sermons, but very soon Grundtvig expanded his first polemical remarks to a detailed attack. He saw Strauss as the most recent representative of a well-known German tradition of learning.

Thus Grundtvig's contribution to the Strauss-debate cannot be seen as a sign of real interest in the academic discussion taking place in the German universities. In this regard he was deeply suspicious, if not emotionally prejudiced. What had caused him to enter the scene of debate was probably the fact that H.N. Clausen had introduced *The Life of Jesus* in *The Journal of Foreign Theological Literature*, edited by Clausen and his colleague C.E. Scharling. Clausen's liberal presentation of Strauss contained a strong note of caution against the radical consequences which Strauss drew. Regardless of this, to Grundtvig's mind Clausen's review was yet another sign of the disastrous alienation between academics and servants of the church.

Critical theology within the horizon of modernity is in the first place marked by a consistent notion of the distance between Biblical and the modern time. This view had been expressed by the German theologian, philosopher and playwright G.E. Lessing. He had emphasized the "broad, insurmountable chasm" dividing the immediate witnesses to Jesus from modern man, who is unable to accept the truth of these accounts without receiving further proof "in spirit and power".

This notion of a historical gap was taken up by Grundtvig, when he made his counterattack against Strauss. According to Grundtvig, however, these 1800 years are not at all to be seen as a barrier for the modern mind. On the contrary, the long chain of tradition becomes for him a proof of the inscrutable, "wondrous" power behind the witness of the church.[3]

Because of this Grundtvig does not show the same signs of indignation, which had dominated reactions elsewhere. Whereas the most zealous conservative theologians had been scandalized by the radical restatement of traditional belief, Grundtvig in his response combines a furious attack with indulgent irony. He does not at all feel threatened in his general demand for tolerance and freedom of thought. Yet, this liberal indulgence to his opponent is only rightly understood, if it is comprehended as a result of his

---

3. N.F.S. Grundtvig, "Den Christne Kirke og den Tydske Theologi", (The Christian Church and the German Theology), in *US* VIII, pp. 161-169.

view of the church. What constitutes Christianity as a unique phenomenon in the history of mankind is not the book, which in itself contains nothing but "dead letters", but the Church as a living reality, based upon the Creeds and thus being "a recognizable community of believers".

Grundtvig does not feel threatened by Strauss, whom he sees as the most recent example of intellectual self-assurance, nor does he accept being forced into a forlorn defence, facing the challenge of modernity. On the contrary. He offers the modern critics full liberty to found a scientific school of their own, a "myth-christian" church, which would profit from full religious freedom. Only, he adds, this new religious society would have to be satisfied with more limited claims than those made by Strauss to constitute the logical fulfillment of all the previous stages in the history of ideas. According to Grundtvig, modern thinkers have a long road in front of them, before being able to prove the same viability that has been shown by the Christian church through 1800 years.

In this way Grundtvig turns the attack upon tradition and orthodoxy, as articulated by Lessing and Strauss, into a counterattack. He regards the 1800 years as a "historical evidence in power". He does not recognize any radical division between the era of Apostolic faith and modernity; instead the historical features of Christianity have been steadily enriched by the continuity of tradition.

In summoning up Grundtvig's polemic against Strauss, we have to concede, that his criticism of the German tradition of scholarship was more emotional and generalizing than fair and precise. Grundtvig's systematic insight, seen from our current perspective, does not depend on the details of this controversy. Rather more, his principal message should be assessed from the theological response, which is contained implicitly in his hymnody. Grundtvig's method of theology is connected with a balance between respect for the true character of the Church as a historical fact, recognizable by the confession of the creeds at baptism on the one side, and by freedom for rational debate within "the school" on the other. We shall return to these considerations in the conclusion.

Grundtvig and the Oxford Movement

During the years 1829-31 Grundtvig went to England to spend the summer period there. As a historian and poet he wanted to find material, first of all concerning Anglo-Saxon poetry.

Later in the 1830's he heard about the Oxford Movement, but at first no direct contact was established. It was only after several years of hesitation that he finally went to England for the fourth time, in 1843. This time his primary goal was to investigate the possibility of connections with the

Tractarians. This had been suggested many years earlier by the English chaplain at Elsinore, Nugent Wade, who had been persuaded of a basic similarity between the Oxford fathers and Grundtvig and had therefore advocated a direct dialogue with enthusiasm.[4] In the end, however, the encounter became a disaster. This may mainly be explained by the unhappy moment of Grundtvig's stay in Oxford, during the summer of 1843. John H. Newman's position as an Anglican was already fading, Edward Pusey was in a situation of deep personal sorrow and was forbidden from preaching in the University, and generally the atmosphere of the University was dense with inner crisis.

This is why the fundamental points of similarity of approach were not fully recognized by either side. As task of historical reconstruction and with the purpose of achieving clarification about central issues in today's situation we shall attempt to establish the dialogue now, which was unsuccessful then.

A. Grundtvig and Keble

The message of man created, fallen and reborn, is seen as the gospel preached on Sundays and festival days throughout the year in John Keble's collection of hymns *The Christian Year*. This central issue is also seen in terms of Life defeating Death, thus letting Easter Day throw the light of resurrection upon every day. This sacramental mystery is expressed by Keble in terms of poetic imagery, connecting existential experience with the universal renewals of nature and history. This comes strikingly close to Grundtvig's own antirational tone which dominates his kerygmatic Easter hymns after his "Greek awakening".

> Keble: Or, if she think, it is in scorn:
> The vernal light of Easter morn
> To her dark gaze no brighter seems
> Than Reason's or the Law's pale beams.[5]

> Grundtvig: Wise and valiant men of this world
> May well despise our hut
> Yet the greatest still will hold

4. P.G. Lindhardt, "Til belysning af Grundtvigs Englands-rejse 1843", in *Kirkehistoriske Samlinger* (1972), pp. 97ff.
5. John Keble, *The Christian Year*, 1827 (repr. 1977), Easter Day, pp. 72ff. Concerning Keble, cf. G. Rowell, *The Vision glorious. Themes and Personalities of the Catholic Revival in Anglicanism*, (1983), pp. 21ff.

Communion in the merest corner
Early he had curled up meekly
Happy as a child in his mother's lap
He who once lay in a manger
In the cottage will break bread.[6]

The way from Crucifixion to Resurrection, including also Easter Eve which had been known in the Early Church but forgotten by modern thought, is interpreted in a similar way by both poets, even if it is true that Keble does not give the same significance to Christ's descent into Hell as Grundtvig does. Still they converge in seeing the grave, closed by the great stone, as a basic feature. Keble gives life to the struggle between the powers of life and death and lets the "lifeless stone" and the "living grave" point to Christ's resurrection, proclaiming heavenly news to mourners anywhere at any time:

Yet e'en the lifeless stone is dear
For thoughts of Him who late lay here;
And the base world, now Christ hath died,
Ennobled is and glorified.

No more a charnel-house, to fence
The relics of lost innocence,
A vault of ruin and decay;
Th'imprisoning stone is roll'd away:

'tis now a cell, where angels use
To come and go with heavenly news,
And in the ears of mourners say,
"Come, see the place where Jesus lay.[7]"

Grundtvig (in verses translated from the Greek):

Come let us empty a cup once again
Not from the fount that flowed out from the blow of the staff,
But from the quickening spring from the grave

---

6.   *Danish Hymn Book* (DDS) no. 306, v.7. *Grundtvig's Song Work* (GSV), I, no. 13. Translation in *Tradition and Renewal*, p. 172 (here slightly improved by A.M. Allchin). About Grundtvig and the Oxford Fathers, cf. J.H. Schjørring, *Grundtvig og Påsken* (København, 1987), pp. 39ff.

7.   J. Keble, op.cit.

The Spring of salvation that bursts into life
Jesus, our life-force, who strengthens our hearts!

Everywhere light in abundance now dawns
Heaven and earth and hell are revealed
The whole world's foundation is quickly discovered
Easter to all His creation is given.
All is made strong through the Word's resurrection.[8]

B. Grundtvig and Pusey on sacramental presence

Of all the Tractarians Pusey had the closest connections with the Protestant theology in Germany. Thus he gained a detailed initiation from August Tholuck into the Strauss-debate. His reaction came at the same time as Grundtvig's, and had a similar accent.

Between Pusey and Grundtvig there was also a personal link in those years. A young Danish theologian, Frederik Hammerich, who supported Grundtvig's ideas, stayed in 1837-1838 in Pusey's house at Oxford. There he gave Pusey a detailed account of Grundtvig's view of the Church and the sacraments, with a special emphasis on Baptism. Pusey was enthusiastic and said in return: "exactly the line which our great Divines have taken against the Ultra-Protestants and the Puritans".[9] The relationship, however, did not mature, and the agreement was not fully understood during Grundtvig's visit in 1843. About their reaction to Strauss there was no direct dialogue.

As we have stated above Grundtvig saw Strauss' historical-critical method and his philosophical reconstruction as a consequence of the abstract tradition of scholarship characteristic of German universities. Pusey for his part turned his attention against the frequent neglect of sacramental presence, which can be observed in modern Protestant theology. He did not direct his polemics against Strauss specifically; rather more he saw modern puritan thinking as an individualist escape from church authority. Any such attempt, however, will instead prove to be in vain, according to Pusey. Other authorities claiming our assent will inevitably replace traditional church authority. In that case Pusey is persuaded that basic aspects of religious truth will be lost to view.

Thus his concern in the essay *Scriptural Views of Holy Baptism* is to convince the clergy of the necessity of seeking religious renewal through

8. *GSV* I, no. 220; *Tradition and Renewal*, pp. 180ff.
9. H. Toldberg, "Grundtvig og Puseys Oxfordbevægelse", *Kirkehistoriske Samlinger* (1948), pp. 272ff.

reconsideration of sacramental presence in the church. Baptismal regeneration is described by Pusey in a way which resembles Luther's theology of rebirth and faith.[10] Above all the essential similarity between Pusey and Grundtvig can be observed in the accentuation of baptism as an external sign and at the same time as bearer of "the living Word".

Likewise there is a close link between baptismal faith and justification, and between regeneration and incorporation into Christ. This harmony seems crucial, because Grundtvig points explicitly to Luther's theology of baptism as one of the greatest achievements of the reformation.[11]

Here again Grundtvig draws a line from the very beginnings of Christianity, through Irenaeus, Luther, coming finally to the present situation, in order to reconsider the witness of Scripture together with the confession of the Creeds in the community of the congregation. Only together can Scripture and the oral confession constitute the living Church.

The convergence between Pusey and Grundtvig about Baptism and regeneration can be illustrated from the following verse, where Grundtvig weaves the dynamic of recreation and forgiveness into the basic elements of the rite of Baptism:

> There Jesus forgives
> The whole guilt of my sin
> He bathes me in "God's Peace",
> and cures the hurts of death.
> He kills my life of sin
> Laying it in his grave,
> He renews the life of grace
> Which my creator first gave me.[12]

C. John Henry Newman and Grundtvig

Newman expanded his understanding of Anglican identity in his *Lectures on the prophetical Office of the Church viewed relatively to Romanism and popular Protestantism* (1837). This attempt to arrive at a balanced view between Roman and Protestant errors should not be regarded solely as the result of his determination to reach a compromise at any price in order to save the historically rooted picture of the Anglican church as a "via media". It is a

---

10. E.B. Pusey, "Scriptural Views of Holy Baptism as established by the Consent of the Early Church and contrasted with the Systems of modern Schools", *Tract for the Times*, 4th ed., Vol. II. Cf. *Pusey Rediscovered*, ed. P.Butler (1983).
11. "Kirkelige Oplysninger især for Lutherske Christne", in *US* VIII, p. 374f.
12. "O, hvor er Naade-Stolen" in *GSV*, V, I, no. 65. Cf. DHB no. 445. (Transl. by A.M. Allchin).

much fairer description to see Newman's position as the constructive result of an ecclesiology that in itself maintains the safeguarding criteria of true identity and authority in the church: the Essentials of the Gospel and Scripture.

In this context it is of primary concern to achieve a formulation of the Essentials of the Gospel. Only such an effort will allow us to make an answer which is neither the Romanist version of authority nor the subjectivity of Protestantism. The latter represent in Newman's view an abuse of private judgment and a groundless claim for the Scripture as being the exclusive and sufficient condition for a proper definition of Christian belief. Newman's answer is not derived from any single aspect of ecclesial authority, but rather contains a general view of episcopacy, ecclesiastical antiquity and the Essentials, comprising Scripture and the Creeds as well. "Scripture is the foundation of the Creed, but belief in Scripture is not the foundation of belief in the Creed".[13]

This view of Newman's comes very close to Grundtvig, when he makes his protest against rationalist neglect of any kind of church authority on the one hand, and on the other against a new version of papal authority resulting from an orthodox protestant understanding of the infallibility of the Bible. Such was the challenge that remained after his debate with Professor Clausen in *The Church's Retort*. In a series of lectures from the following years Grundtvig maintained that the Lutheran reformation must be continued, first of all towards a more comprehensive understanding of Scripture, the Creeds and ministry as a unity.[14] In this context his understanding of Irenaeus played a prominent role, in a way similar to what we have seen to be the case with Newman's view of ecclesiastical authority. Grundtvig for his part translated the fifth book of Irenaeus' book *Against the Heretics* (first published in 1826). In a preface he clearly indicated how important a fuller description of the criteria of the church was in the present situation. In order to refute the dangerous errors of the Gnostic heretics and their "self-invented, impious opinions" Irenaeus developed a theological method which is carried on by Grundtvig with satisfaction as follows:

13. J.H. Newman, "Lectures on the Prophetical Office of the Church, viewed relatively to Romanism and popular Protestantism", in *The Via Media of the Anglican Church*, 3rd ed. 1877, Lecture X, p. 244. Cf. John Coulson, *Newman and the Common Tradition. A Study in the Language of Church and Society* (1970); John Coulson, *Religion and Imagination "in aid of a grammar of assent"* (1980).
14. "Skal den lutherske Reformation virkelig fortsættes?" In *US* V, pp. 278ff.

it is the task to refute the heretics by means of sound judgment, based upon the evident truth and upon the manifest teaching of the Church as it was foretold by the Prophets, fulfilled by Christ, and proclaimed by the Apostles, which in the world is the only one who possesses the truth and passes it on to its children.[15]

What is remarkable here is not only Grundtvig's conviction of the coexistence of rational clarity and church authority, but also the coordination of oral proclamation of the Gospel, with Scripture, with the Creeds seen as *regula fidei* and with episcopal authority. This complex unity of criteria is seen as the necessary modern reformulation of the teaching of the early Christian congregations and of the Lutheran reformation. In Grundtvig's view there is an obvious link between the fact that radical thinkers in his own time have shown a constant tendency to neglect the Apostles' Creed as the rule of faith and their nullification of Irenaeus as a "fool and fanatic". Against all such modern inventions he takes pride in showing Irenaeus as a true witness of the Gospel, as a theologian who had passed on the teaching from the "Apostles" School and the Church eternal".

Faith – reason – heart
It was central for Newman to insist upon church continuity. This, however, should not be identified as the concern of a reactionary. He was very conscious of man's autonomy and of his dependence upon the results of scientific evidence and individual reason. Yet he was indignant at the constant criticism, expressed by the attack on his own rootedness in ecclesiastical antiquity, an attack which claimed that such a dependence meant a barrier to all modern thought. Newman responded that rational clarity and Christian belief do not exclude one another; on the contrary they are complementary. What is needed is therefore "a sound judgment, patient thought, a comprehensive mind, an abstinence from all private fancies and caprices and personal tastes, in a word, divine wisdom". This however, Newman goes on, does not contradict the fact, that basically faith and reason are contrasted as habits of mind. This is the title of a sermon, which Newman preached on Epiphany 1839. His primary interest here is the spiritual character of the faith; it is not something exclusively supernatural, but is manifest "to the illuminated mind", thus bridging the gulf between divine revelation and our senses and the heart. This for Newman is the true message of the incarnation.

15. N.F.S. Grundtvig, *Om Kiødets Opstandelse og det evige Liv*, p. 9. Cf. the modern English Translation in *The Anti-Nicene Fathers*, Vol. I.

Things external, local, and sensible being no longer objects to dwell upon their own account, but merely means of conveying onwards the divine gifts from the Giver to their proper home, the heart itself.[16]

This is not at all far from Grundtvig's accentuation of the heart as source of certainty. The gifts of the Spirit cannot be sensed by the rational mind, but must be accepted in joy by the heart:

The fiery tongues of the Spirit with the sign of the cross burn the name of Jesus into the heart. Thus the heart encounters the stamp which corresponds to the image of God in the depths of the heart. The sign of the cross as a promise, a heavenly letter about the operation of the new creation: faith, peace, hope and confidence, love and joy. It is basically a promise of Jesus' constant presence in the name which is on the heart, whence the Spirit can always lead us up to God in the word of faith.[17]

Church continuity

This similarity which has just been mentioned becomes even more striking when it is confronted with their understanding of the continuity of the church. In one of his most famous sermons, preached on the Purification 1843, Newman took his text from Luke 2,19, "But Mary kept all these things and pondered them in her heart".

Newman gives full expression to his understanding of Mary as "our pattern of faith". The historical course of Christianity may well be seen as changeable; yet it is in a much deeper sense constant. It is "the development of an idea", thus permitting us to see the church's tradition not as decline, but as a place of spiritual growth. What Newman calls "the certainty of advance" is closely linked with his accentuation of Mary as our pattern of life. "She does not think it enough to accept, she dwells upon it; not enough to assent, she develops it; not enough to submit the Reason, she reasons upon it".[18]

Grundtvig makes a similar point in his sermons on Annunciation Sunday.[19] But perhaps even more striking is his use of Irenaeus for developing a deeper understanding of Mary's role in universal history from creation to fulfillment. In the same context Adam and Christ are seen in

16. J.H. Newman, *University Sermons* (repr. 1970), pp. 170f.
17. Erik Krebs Jensen, "Hjertets gudbilledlighed", in *For sammenhængens skyld. Ord og motiver i Grundtvigs salmer og prædikener* (1977). Transl. by A.M. Allchin, in *The Kingdom of Love and Knowledge* (1979), p. 80.
18. J.H. Newman, *University Sermons*, p. 331. Cf. N. Lash, *Newman on Development. The Search for an Explanation in History*, 2nd. ed. (1979).
19. *N.F.S. Grundtvigs Prædikener*, ed. Chr. Thodberg, Vol. X, 1836-37 Copenhagen, 1985), pp. 151-156.

"cross reference"[20] to one another, just as Eve and Mary show us a fundamental pattern of human shortcoming as well as of life reborn through divine salvation:

for just as Eve let herself be led astray by the evil angel's word, so as to reject God and to transgress his Word, so also it happened that, through the angelic message to her about God's descent, a Word which she obeyed, the Virgin Mary let herself be persuaded to obey God, and thus excused the virgin Eve, who had let herself be deceived so as to reject God. So the simplicity of the Dove (that is of the dove which came down from heaven at Jesus" baptism) overcame the cleverness of the serpent.[21]

Thus Mary becomes a safeguard for the church's continuity, a symbol of "the historical evidence in power", which shows the real dynamic of the power of resurrection. Easter means much more than a single moment of particular divine presence on earth, it is the spiritual secret that gives each Sunday its true meaning, which is expressed in Christ's words to Mary Magdalen : "weep no more!" heard as a word addressed to the congregation today.

Two further quotations may show how close Newman and Grundtvig are to one another, even in terms of style. Newman often adopts a poetic style of proclamation, which is similar to the "prosepoems" marking the highlights in Grundtvig's sermons.[22] Newman:

When we read the Bible and religious books in private there is great comfort; but our minds are commonly more roused and encouraged in Church, when we see those great truths displayed and represented which Scripture speaks of. There we see "Jesus Christ, evidently set forth, crucified among us". The ordinances which we behold, force the unseen truth upon our senses. The very disposition of the building, the subdued light, the aisles, the Altar with its pious adornments, are figures of things unseen, and stimulate our fainting faith. We seem to see the heavenly courts, with Angels chanting, and Apostles and Prophets listening, as we read their writings in due course. And thus, attendance on a Sunday may, through God's mercy, avail even in the case of those who have not given themselves up to him – not to their salvation (for no one can be saved by one or two observances merely, or without a life of faith), but so far as to break in upon their dream of sin, and give them thoughts and notions which may be the germ of future good.[23]

20. J.L. Balling, *Poeterne som kirkelærere* (Copenhagen, 1983) pp. 108ff.
21. N.F.S. Grundtvig, *Om Kiødets Opstandelse* (note 14), ch. 19, cf. *The Ante Nicene Fathers*, p. 547.
22. Chr. Thodberg, "Grundtvig the Preacher", in *Tradition and Renewal* (1983) pp. 123ff.
23. J.H. Newman, *Parochial and Plain Sermons*, Vol. III, p. 251.

Grundtvig, preaching a sermon about one of his favourite texts, Christ's visitation to the widow and her son in Nain:

> Say not, where shall we find Him,
> for truly he is not far from any of us,
> He is as near to us as the word
> in our mouth and in our heart,
> the Word of Faith that we preach,
> and He has said:
> I dwell in the high and holy place,
> with him also that is of a contrite and humble spirit,
> to revive the spirit of the humble
> and to revive the heart of the contrite ones.
> Search for Him then in the Word alone,
> there you will find Him.[24]

Since the principal agreement has been emphasized in our previous considerations, perhaps it should be pointed out that here there appears a point of obvious disagreement, since Grundtvig develops a notion of the Word alone, which in the understanding of the Tractarians was considered to be specifically Lutheran or Puritan.

Conclusions

Before we can make some concluding statements about Grundtvig's theology as a response to the challenge of modernity, a few preliminary remarks have to made:

1. It would be misleading to regard a theological and philosophical position like that of Strauss as the only way of giving a definite answer to the questions asked within the horizon of "modernity". Such a premature identification of radical theology with the ability to respond to the challenge of modernity would create the impression that classical, orthodox belief always lies on the other side of the turning point that marks the beginning of the modern era. A radical historical criticism and a consequent philosophical reconstruction of traditional belief is not the only possible way of reformulating the Christian tradition in modern times.

What marks modernity in the present context is:

In terms of a negative demarcation, a full application of historical analysis to biblical texts and the recognition that pre-Kantian metaphysics

---

24. N.F.S. Grundtvig, 16th Sunday in Trinity, 1823, transl. in *Tradition and Renewal*, p. 152.

are untenable. Positively it is the willingness to regard the historical distance between the first witnesses and modern believers as a genuine problem, to admit a real change in conditions of understanding. Lessing, as mentioned above, described this experience as the "unacceptable, unbridge-able gap". In fact, Strauss' theology can only be taken seriously, if it is recognized as an attempt at a systematic consideration of this challenge. Furthermore, it has to be admitted that there is no easy way to the solution of this problem, either with regard to Grundtvig or with a view to the present situation.

2. In many ways Grundtvig's way of thinking is bound up with his own period. There is some justification in the characterization made by Regin Prenter that Grundtvig was first of all pre-modern and rooted in the old orthodoxy.[25] Consequently, any presentation of Grundtvig as a theological teacher for today has to be balanced. This means for instance that the world of poetic images – however much it may appear to many people now to be needed – has to be reconsidered within a general pattern and counter-balanced by philosophical criteria of consistency. Only when a juxtaposition of this kind is made possible between symbols in liturgy, poetry and art on the one hand and arguments distinguished by lucid rationality on the other, can Grundtvig's theology have an impact for us today.

However, when this reservation has been made it is justified to seek a response to the challenge of modernity in Grundtvig's work. The response will appear not in terms of one plain answer, but rather as a number of insights closely linked together:

a. Sacramental presence

Grundtvig often expresses a feeling of being cut off and in despair, separated from the voice of our Saviour by a huge wall. But even in such moments of scepticism and hopelessness, when the distance seems impene-trable, the miracle may happen, "the living Word" be heard anew, as powerful as ever. This proves possible on account of the presence which is the divine secret of the sacraments. This experience of God's presence is marked in Grundtvig's sermons and hymns by ecstatic proclamations on particular festival days. To give only one or two examples: Grundtvig regards the healing of the deaf-mute (Mk 7) as a text which relates to the wonder of baptism. The proclamation "Open thy ears!" is given to any person who is granted divine acceptance, even though deaf or helpless like

25. R. Prenter, "Grundtvig og Påsken", *Dansk teologisk Tidsskrift*, II, (1988), pp. 139ff.

a child.[26] Similarly, when Grundtvig interprets the Emmaus story on Easter Mondays: he sees this narrative as a pattern for church service ever since, centered around Holy Communion, the blessing and the greeting of peace.[27]

b. A method of existential interpretation

According to Grundtvig the persons in the Bible are not marked first of all by patterns of behaviour and thinking, which bind them to past centuries. On the contrary, in his eyes they serve as living examples of basic human characteristics. This is true for instance of the robber on Calvary who is a parable for everyone who is condemned and lost; in his guilt and under judgment he finds himself face to face with death. This very man, however, becomes for Grundtvig a fundamental part of the message of Good Friday, as he is the first person, in the midst of the darkness on that day, to receive forgiveness and to be led back to paradise reopened. Thus the first Adam, in his self-will, merges with the robber, who through the death of Jesus on the cross is reinstated in the restored creation.[28] In a parallel way the widow of Nain illustrates the grief of women's heart, thereby merging with Eve's guilt-laden remorse, but also with Mary, Christ's mother at the foot of the Cross and with Mary Magdalen, the first witness of the resurrection on Easter morning.[29]

c. Change of scenery

Grundtvig's interpretation of Holy Scripture contains ample recognition of man's connection with the nature and history of his own time and place. The specific scene of Palestine, too, is often made vividly present. At the same time, however, Grundtvig deliberately moves from the historical scene to a very national, modern one. His purpose is obviously to attempt over and over again to overcome the gap and to intensify the application of the message.[30]

---

26. N.F.S. Grundtvig, 12th Sunday after Trinity, for instance 1856, in *Regeneration. Grundtvigs prædikener i kirkeåret 1855-56*, ed. P.G. Lindhardt. Se also Chr. Thodberg, "En glemt dimension i Grundtvigs salmer", in *Syn og Sang. Poesi og teologi hos Grundtvig* (1989).
27. GSV II, no. 89. Cf. *N.F.S. Grundtvigs Prædikener*, Vol. IX, pp. 181ff.
28. "For den soleklare Gud", in *GSV* I, no. 215.
29. "Paaskemorgen Magdalene", in *GSV* II, no. 88.
30. "De to Disciplers Gang til Emaus", in *GSV* II, no. 89.

d. Historical continuity

Being both a professional historian and a theologian Grundtvig considered the essence of Christendom to be linked to the church as Church *in history*. In his works on the history of Christianity Grundtvig shows a deep understanding of the differences between the different periods in the history of the church. This does not change the basic feature of his ecclesiology, however, which is based upon his conviction that the essentials of the church are safeguards of what is *primordial, unchangeable and recognizable* in the church. Thus, neither obvious signs of decline in the life of the church, nor scepticism (whether his personal or that of other intellectuals) can threaten the divine power which lies behind the historical continuity of the church. This conviction is the real explanation for his use of ecclesiastical antiquity, not least Irenaeus, as an argument against modern radicals.

e. The distinction between faith and opinion, church and school

The distinction between faith as a conviction of the heart and opinion as an academic assertion was essential already in Grundtvig's early writings. And this theory never ceased to play a crucial role in his thinking. In this context it should be mentioned – with reference to our previous discussion of the *Song-Work* from 1837 – that he published some of his far-reaching works on education during the same years. This can hardly be explained as a matter of coincidence; it has to be seen as a direct result of his theory of the distinction between faith and opinion, church and school, *and* their juxtaposition.

Only when freedom of thought is respected in the school, including the school of theology, can its capacity as a place of intellectual training be safeguarded. This is what Grundtvig meant by calling the school a place where everything is necessarily in ferment, if it is not to degenerate into something obscurantist and useless. Whereas the church for its part is bound to rest upon its firm, unshakeable foundations.[31]

Thanks to such directions as these Grundtvig offers a response to the challenge of modernity. It is not of a response that can be literally reproduced 150 years after its first publication. Rather it offers an open invitation to new analysis and reflection which will have more bearing on our present situation than any simple conclusion could have done. Only if we take up the considerable, but doubtless fruitful task of rethinking his theology, can he serve as a teacher for us today.

31. "Kirken og Skolen" (The Church and the School), in *US* VIII, pp. 157ff.

N.F.S. Grundtvig's Position in Danish Nationalism

By Lorenz Rerup

For a better understanding of Grundtvig's position in Early Danish Nationalism I think it will be useful first to look at the background to his performance. This background was the very small – but still multinational – Danish empire as it existed from about 1800 to the 1830's. Then we have to examine the stages of Danish patriotism and nationalism. Finally I will try to say something about Grundtvig's spiritual and intellectual development.

The Danish Monarchy

In the period from 1780 to 1830 the Danish Monarchy – or as it is called in Danish: the *helstat* – was deeply changed.[1] Until 1814 its components were the kingdoms of Denmark and Norway, and the duchies Holstein and Slesvig, besides the North Atlantic islands, the Faroe Islands, Iceland, Greenland, and some minor colonies in Guinea and Tranquebar in India. The economy of this state was overwhelmingly agrarian; about 80% of the population lived outside the towns. Since the end of the Great Northern War in 1720 the Monarchy experienced peace. That meant low state expenditure and modest taxation. A slow, often interrupted economic growth went on both in the agrarian and in the urban sector of society, but Denmark remained a small agricultural country, poor in capital, poor in industry, and with very limited exports. In the frequent wars between the great powers in the 18th century the country remained neutral, and trade and shipping could benefit from this peace-policy in the course of many decades. In particular, from 1772 to 1807, Copenhagen had a flourishing trade with India and China. Most of this trade, however, was conducted under the Danish flag on Anglo-Indian business, and the Danish traders only drew a commission on it.[2] When Denmark joined an Armed Neu-

---

1. H. Arnold Barton, *Scandinavia in the Revolutionary Era, 1760-1815* (Minneapolis, 1986).
2. Ole Feldbæk, *India Trade under the Danish Flag 1772-1808. European Enterprise and Anglo-Indian Remittance and Trade* (Copenhagen, 1969), pp. 231-239.

trality Alliance of the North, including all the countries around the Baltic, the British Navy – the ships in battle under the leadership of Lord Nelson – bombarded Copenhagen and broke up the Alliance. This attack took place on April 2, 1801, and the dramatic event, of course, strongly impressed the inhabitants of the capital, the most immediate spectators of the cannonade. At the same time the action of the British Navy indicated that in the long run the Danish Monarchy might be involved in the universal contest between the Napoleonic Empire and Great Britain. Eventually this happened, in 1807 – a few weeks after the Peace of Tilsit – when a British expedition disembarked on Zealand, besieged Copenhagen for several weeks, bombarded the town, and seized the unrigged Danish Navy, in those days the last considerable navy on the continent and therefore a possible threat to Great Britain, if it fell into the hands of Napoleon. The following seven years of war destroyed the trade and the wealth of the monarchy. Most of the merchant navy was captured. The institutions of the state and the economy were in a poor condition when the war was over. The peace of 1814 brought with it the loss of Norway. Then followed a long period of economic depression. Stagnation succeeded the prewar reform policy of the government, and at the same time English capital reconstructed Hamburg – just outside the southern border of the monarchy – as a big credit and trade centre between Great Britain and Northern and Central Europe. It soon dominated the economy of the Duchies and of the southern parts of the kingdom.

Not till the 1830's, when trade and agriculture recovered their strength by the export of corn and cattle to England and to the German harbours, did the government take an important initiative in reforming the country. In the 1830's it began to construct a modern road system, to reform municipal and parochial councils, to modernize the army, to build the first railways, and – actuated by the French revolution of 1830 – it made the first steps towards a democratic political system: the consultive assemblies of the estates, two for the kingdom and two for the duchies. These estates were not identical to the old feudal groups: aristocrats, bourgeois, clergymen and peasants. But they were modern categories: big landowners, minor landowners (these were both peasants and tenants) and owners of property of a certain tax-value in the towns. There were no representatives of the aristocracy, and no intellectuals, but the king appointed a few members to represent the universities of Copenhagen and Kiel. In Copenhagen the intelligentsia sulked: 73 distillers got the franchise, but only 1 professor. This particular system reflects the tendency of the late Danish absolutism to level the feudal class differentiation and to abolish old privileges. The great agricultural reforms of the 1780's had been an enormous step-forward in this direction.[3] They created a very large middle class of freeholders and law-protected tenants in the country, owning almost 75 of the agricultural area. In Denmark-proper 4/5 of the population lived in the country. The existence of a large agricultural middle class – gradually becoming well established – was a decisive factor in Danish society.

This sketch is valid especially for the kingdom of Denmark, the core of the tiny empire. In the kingdom the native population only spoke Danish. It was governed in Danish and the education was in Danish. In the duchies – in particular in Holstein – a strong aristocracy existed, powerful enough to weaken the agrarian reforms and to counteract the levelling tendencies of the government. The population of the duchies – apart from the countryside in the Northern half of Slesvig – was German speaking, and the German language was dominant also in the towns of Northern Slesvig.[4] In Western Slesvig along the coast the population spoke several Frisian dialects, but German was the language of the church and the school. In Northern Slesvig the peasants spoke Danish dialects. Danish was also the language of the church and consequently of the school – the monarchy got a general school system in 1806 – but still the courts and the administration worked in German. This was changed into Danish 1840. The language issue, first raised in the Slesvig estates assembly in 1836, was originally a social question. The peasants – many of them at this time well-to-do people with a growing self-confidence – disliked having a need for interpreters in matters concerning the courts and the administration. Soon the language question initiated the political mass nationalism of the peasantry in North Slesvig, and of intellectual liberals in the kingdom. It became a movement against the Schleswig-Holstein movement's claim to the whole duchy, which together with Holstein should form a German Schleswig-Holstein inside the German Federation. Holstein (and the small duchy Lauenburg which was given to the Monarchy in 1815) belonged to the German Federation since its foundation in 1815. Slesvig did not, since it was a Danish duchy.

Danish patriotism and nationalism

The Danish reaction against the Schleswig-Holstein claims represents clearly one of the later stages of Danish nationalism. It had several

---

3. Jens Christensen, *Rural Denmark 1750-1980*, The Central Co-operative Committee of Denmark (Copenhagen, 1983), pp. 21-52.
4. W. Carr, *Schleswig-Holstein 1815-48. A Study in National Conflict* (Manchester, Manchester University Press, 1963), pp. 61-73.

forerunners. Firstly, a deep and old loyalty to the king, both among the peasantry of Denmark and among the German or Danish speaking peasantry of the duchies. The king was perceived as the guardian of justice and he could protect the peasants and common people against injustice committed by the nobility or by civil servants. A part of this conception may be a consequence of the agrarian reforms and of the government's anti-aristocratic policy, another much older part was caused by the church and its doctrine of obedience to the authorities.

Secondly, a patriotism of the Danish monarchy spread out in the well-to-do strata of the urban population, both in the kingdom and in the duchies. People were proud of belonging to a prosperous and progressive state, governed by a peace-loving king, protected by a considerable navy. They were proud of belonging to a wealthy society. Symbols of this ideology, often praised in enthusiastic poems and songs – some of them in German – were the old colours – the *Danebrog* – and the king and an institution like the Danish navy. This ideology had no preference for one language over the other but underlined that the languages might walk hand in hand like brothers. All subjects could praise the king or the state in their own language. This ideology was overtly nourished by the government – for instance in schoolbooks – but it corresponded very well to the feelings of upper strata in the towns of the realm.

There was also a growing awareness of a Danish identity.[5] The kingdom had been politically united since the time of the Vikings. The written language had been printed since the end of the Middle Ages and as long as that Denmark had a university of its own in Copenhagen. The church had a rich treasure of hymns, a Danish literature existed, the country had a "great history". All these important goals for a national movement were commonplace for Danes inside the kingdom. They did not have to fight for them – as in the case of many small oppressed nations in Europe – they had only to be aware of them.

This awareness grew stronger during the 18th century. In the 1740's a Royal Science Academy and a Royal Society for Danish History and Language were founded to systematize the exploring of the country's history and language. In the 1750's a Royal Academy of Art was founded too.

As prosperity continued and as overseas traders collected experience from all over the world, the upper class of the capital – and of the bigger towns in the provinces – as well as civil servants of a certain standing all developed a strong feeling of Danish identity which was in no way aimed

5.   Ole Feldbæk, Denmark, in: Otto Dann and John Dinwiddy, *Nationalism in the Age of the French Revolution* (London 1988), pp. 87-100.

at breaking up the multinational monarchy or at dominating the German-speaking parts of it in a nationalistic way. But the feeling of a special identity, consisting of language, culture and history, could react against a German-speaking aristocratic domination which existed in parts of the government and around the king's court. This happened several times in the 1770s, 1780s and 1790s. Also, the cultural domination of Germans in some of the fashionable salons of Copenhagen was strongly opposed.

However, this feeling of a Danish identity and patriotism did not include the enormous majority of the Danish population – the peasants – as compatriots. And yet they did think of them as compatriots, for in 1792, just outside the city-boundary, the Copenhageners erected a liberty obelisk to praise the king for the Great Agrarian Reforms. The obelisk had an inscription telling how the king ordered the reforms "so that the free peasant can become cheerful and enlightened, industrious and good, an honest citizen, happy." Clearly this was a vision, not yet an existing reality. The bearers of Danish identity had no political claims – except for a fair share in government. Much more interesting for them was the question whether the Nordic mythology was as good as the Greek/Roman for artists and poets, and whether it could underline Danish cultural characteristics. The distinction between the feeling of a Danish identity before 1800 and later political nationalism is clear: the ideology of identity had no concept of a politically active people. Danish identity had no specific programme for integrating the different ethnically identical parts of the population. Conscription, for instance, only fell on the peasantry. Danish identity was a feeling confined to small strata of the urban population in the capital and in the bigger towns.

After the loss of Norway in 1814 and until 1864, the multiethnic Danish United Monarchy consisted of Denmark and the duchies Slesvig, Holstein and Lauenburg besides the North Atlantic islands, the Faroe Islands, Iceland, Greenland, whereas the minor colonies in Guinea and Tranquebar in East India were sold in 1845 and 1850. In the first decades of the 19th century Danish patriotic poetry and literature represented a literary movement without political or national aims, and yet in a way it was similar to nationalism. Only after 1830 did Danish political nationalism develop, especially bound up with the national conflict in the Duchies and with the Liberal movement, which had no connection with Romanticism, but was rather a child of the Enlightenment. Like its forerunner, the strong patriotic ideology of the second half of the 18th century, Danish political nationalism was marked by anti-German sentiments. These feelings, however, were not important in the thinking of the younger Grundtvig and his contemporaries.

Unlike the earlier patriotism, the political nationalism of the 1830 s and

40 s claimed Danish administration and Danish courts for Danish peasants, argued for the reinstatement of the mother tongue, and insisted that Danish territory belongs to Denmark. In consequence of this and the corresponding German nationalism, the wars of 1848-50 and 1864 led to the dissolution of the Danish monarchy, and the remains of the patriotic feelings based on the monarchy disappeared very quickly, as did the strong German cultural influence on Denmark. In transport and economies Western Europe, especially Great Britain, played an important role in the last decades of the 19th century.

Grundtvig

In the interval between a growing and refining sense of Danish identity in the second half of the 18th century and the beginning of political mass nationalism in the 1830's, Grundtvig and other poets represent a literary movement without any political aims.[6] Nikolai Frederik Severin Grundtvig[7] was by far the most learned and original of these poets and writers, and from the viewpoint of posterity he had the convenient habit of constantly writing about his development in his diary and in his huge literary output. In a letter of 1824 to the Danish writer Bernhard Severin Ingemann about the poem *New Year's Morning* (1824)[8] Grundtvig fully realized that it would be difficult to understand his vision in the poem because people would not allow him to "use the only metaphor by means of which I can depict the vision in some brightness, namely myself."[9] Not until 1832 was Grundtvig's spiritual and mental universe fully unfolded, and only then did he develop the ideas which resulted in the Folk High School and were of immense importance for the emancipation of parts of the Danish peasantry. But in his formative years – he was born in 1783 – Grundtvig was strongly influenced by the German Romantic movement. This influence appears from his diaries as well from his output and from his vivid interest in Nordic mythology and in the great place occupied by the Scandinavian countries in history as a whole. This influence is evident

6. L. Rerup, Fra litterær til politisk nationalisme, in *Dansk identitetshistorie*, vol. II. (Copenhagen, 1991).
7. About Grundtvig in general, see Kaj Thaning, *N.F.S. Grundtvig* (Copenhagen, 1972), and the English Summary of Flemming Lundgreen-Nielsen, *Det handlende ord: N.F.S. Grundtvigs digtning, litteraturkritik og poetik 1798-1819* (Copenhagen, 1980), pp. 930-942.
8. *Nyaars-Morgen*, 1824.
9. Svend Grundtvig (ed.), *Grundtvig og Ingemann. Brevvexling 1821-1859*, p. 48. Flemming Lundgreen-Nielsen quotes another part of this letter, see his paper, pp. 15ff.

too from his linguistic development. His indignant *Masked Ball in Denmark* (1807)[10] was written in an enthusiastic and literary style. The first edition of his *Nordic Mythology* (1808)[11] had as subtitle: "View over the subjects of the Edda, written for educated men who are not mythologists themselves." About 1820 when he translated Saxo's *Gesta Danorum*, he rendered the elegant late classical Latin of the medieval monk into a prose influenced by the narrative skills of the peasants of South Zealand. His rediscovery of the peasant as the true guardian of ethnicity is clearly influenced by the younger Herder and romanticism. And in the poem *New Year's Morning*, Grundtvig pointed out, that the spirit must fly "but low above the ground" or "who will meet people must yelp, if people not are willing to bark."

Grundtvig is best known outside Denmark as the creator of the Folk High School. In Denmark he had a profound influence on various fields of cultural life. He studied theology and practiced as a clergyman at various periods of his life, but he was more important as a historian, a philosopher, a philologist and a poet. In old age he became something of a politician, too.

As a poet he wrote some 1.500 hymns. He had the marvelous gift to express complicated religious experiences in plain metaphors. He could revitalize old half-forgotten words or phrases that only lived in dialects – as he did in his translations, above all in Saxo's *Gesta Danorum*. Grundtvig therefore doubtless contributed to the development of the Danish language. He made it more Nordic, he enriched it, and – avoiding abstractions – he brought it nearer to the spoken language and reloaded it with reality. As his hymns were frequently used, their effects were repeated again and again. A Danish church service today would be unthinkable without him.

He produced secular poetry as well. The poem *Denmark's Solace* (1820)[12] described Danish identity in a positive way – in normative phrases, of course – including the famous verses:

> and then will we have achieved much wealth
> when few have too much, and fewer too little.

The beautiful poem about the mother tongue from his booklet about *The School for Life and the Academy in Sorø* (1838)[13] says:

---

10. *Maskeradeballet i Dannemark 1808. Et Syn*, 1808.
11. *Nordens Mytologi eller Udsigt over Eddalæren for dannede Mænd, der ei selv ere Mytologer*, 1808.
12. *Danmarks Trøst*, 1820.
13. *Skolen for Livet og Akademiet i Soer* (Copenhagen, 1838).

The mother tongue is a chain of roses
it entwines people great and small
only in it does the spirit of the ancestor live
only in it can the heart move freely.

His praise and love of the mother tongue had, of course, an effect on the people, who had been taught to admire educated persons who were able to speak foreign languages. It is a fact that Grundtvig and a few other poets created a Danish patriotic poetry inspired by Danish history and Old Norse literature. The earliest of this group was the very young poet Adam Oehlenschläger (1779-1850), who renewed Danish poetry after 1801. He also wrote a number of dramatic plays with topics taken from Old Norse history. Besides Grundtvig, the poet and novelist Bernhard Severin Ingemann (1789-1862) in particular had a lasting influence on the development of early Danish Nationalism. His novels about a medieval era of glory in Danish history – the era of the Valdemars (12th and 13th century) – were really the bestsellers of the time. These novels were read not only by the literary public but by ordinary people too. His novels depicted a glorious time of bravery, virtue and piety with the intention of a "historical rebirth" of the people. The ups and downs of our ancestors might teach us something about right conduct in our own time, especially what happened when piety abandoned the realm. These men – Oehlenschläger, Ingemann and Grundtvig – refused rationalism as superficial. They were influenced by German Idealism and Romanticism, though Grundtvig was influenced in a special way.

When Nelson attacked Copenhagen in 1801, Grundtvig and his fellow students took part in the defence of the city. The dramatic hours, however, did not release special nationalistic feelings in the young man. Neither did two series of lectures, delivered by his Norwegian/German cousin Henrik Steffens (1773-1845), although Grundtvig was present in the audience. Steffens was a messenger of the new Romanticism in Scandinavia. He helped Oehlenschläger to become a poet. Deep-rooted in biblical conceptions and in a widespread historical reading in childhood, Grundtvig resisted Steffens' message for several years. Only when an unhappy love affair opened his mind in 1805, did Grundtvig come closer to Romanticism. Now he read – or reread – Steffens, Fichte, Schiller, Goethe, the Schlegel brothers, Shakespeare (in German translation), Tieck, Novalis and Herder. For a time – about five years – Romanticism cast a spell over Grundtvig. Then he renounced it, especially the Romantic philosophy of nature. Romantic traits can be found in his later writings, above all in his interest in history, and in the belief that a nation's spirit is most clearly preserved by the peasants, a belief he shared with the younger Herder. Grundtvig's acquisition of Herder is of particular interest. It is original in that it avoids the normal idealistic interpretation of Herder by Fichte.[14] Eventually, Herder led Grundtvig back to Luther and an old-fashioned Christianity.

Grundtvig's impact on early Danish nationalism went further than his contributions to the idea of Danish identity mentioned above. The rule of the Danish king was not despotic, but political affairs could not be discussed and criticism of the king or his government was not allowed. Nationalism animates identity structures by politicizing them. This special animation could not happen in a quiet and contented society ruled by an absolute king. In addition, Grundtvig was an ardent admirer of kingship, and his way to democracy was thus a very long one. During the whole time when the constitution of Denmark was absolutist, Grundtvig supported it, even if later on – in the 1830s – he developed a model founded on a cooperation of the "king's hand" and the "people's voice". But in spite of the fact that Grundtvig neither could nor would move people politically, he could act on their morality and piety: without a renaissance of strong faith and piety the country never would be born again.

Spellbound by the ideas of Romanticism and shocked by the British siege and bombardment of Copenhagen in September 1807, Grundtvig wrote a little play *Masked Ball in Denmark* (1808). The piece was his contribution to a public discussion about the decency of arranging masked balls and other amusements when the country ought to be in mourning. He scourges his pleasure-seeking contemporaries and in his play a dying graybeard, personifying Denmark, calls the Danish men and women to awake, to remember their history, to pray in church and to revenge the British attack.

From a literary viewpoint this booklet is of no great value. However, Grundtvig's invocation of the people as the real actors in human history is an early sign that the patriotism which binds different regions to the king and other symbols of state is changing to a nationalism with its components, namely people/nation, language, common history and common culture. In the next decades much was added to such a tiny beginning. But his clerical background combined with his Romantic interest in the past and in folklore motivated Grundtvig in a most interesting direction. He was very concerned that the Lord's word had abandoned Denmark. He thought that that was because the people lived superficially. Therefore they had to be revived. When they were strong like their ancestors their faith would be strengthened.

14. William Michelsen, *Tilblivelsen af Grundtvigs historiesyn* (Copenhagen, 1954), pp. 311ss. English summary p. 361.

Like a real nationalist, he was concerned about *all* the people, the Danish people as a whole. He was not content with a small stratum of townsmen. Jesus Christ concerns everybody. His aim of reviving the strong faith of his ancestors and their great deeds gave his literary nationalism a missionary character, which had not been present in the older Danish forms of patriotism. Grundtvig had – like his contemporaries – by necessity to be unpolitical. The absolutist regime did not tolerate public criticism. But, of course, a missionary activity which was intended to strengthen the Christian faith was not unwelcome.

So Grundtvig seems to be a kind of missing link between the complacent patriotic ideology of the 18th century and the much later nationalism which was eager to propagate its sentiments and ideas in order to collect the masses around the national cause – whatever its contents may be. Of course Grundtvig's attempt failed. Denmark's inhabitants were still divided into two cultures, a "high"-culture in the upper strata of the urban population, and a "broad" culture among the peasants and common people. Some decades had to pass before the people who shared this "broad" culture felt the need of an ideology in order to be integrated into society, thus underlining their growing self-confidence. But Grundtvig's thinking had an importance, especially his ideas about a school which could help ordinary people to become active citizens. But that is another story, and it belongs to other thoughts, too.

Denmark, Slesvig-Holstein and Grundtvig in the 19th Century

By Vagn Wåhlin

Ideas and cultural influences come and go. The socio-economic and political structures determine the possibilities of cultural innovations as well as interacting with the ideological and cultural mainstream and, *vice versa*, ideological and cultural patterns and elements determine and interact with economic and political transformations. A genius like Grundtvig could not have had the success he had without the right economic, political and cultural preconditions and yet, at the same time he was an influential factor in transforming Danish social, political and cultural conditions and thus creating the future of Denmark. So to understand him and his influences we have to deal with the material, intellectual and historical conditions and transformations of the time in which he lived and in which he participated so vigorously.

I. The socio-economic structure

Land, people and agriculture
At the beginning of the 19th century Denmark proper – the Kingdom (without modern North Slesvig) – an area of some 35.000 km² was inhabited by a little less than a million people and was the heartland of quite a large State-system, *vide* map 1 (rear endpaper).

Many agricultural innovations interacted with the great land reforms of 1788-1814. In the agrarian sector the government, in co-operation with a solid fraction of the landowners, promoted and strengthened modernizations of ownership, the village system, enclosure, better schooling, etc., which had already been introduced. The European market for Danish agricultural products of the right sort expanded throughout the 18th century until 1807 (the English bombardment of Copenhagen) and again from the 1830's onwards. The internal demands for agricultural products also expanded as the Norwegian, Faroese and Icelandic parts of the realm could no longer feed their growing population.

Some 80% of the population in Denmark proper lived in the countryside in the 19th century, app. 10% lived in the smaller provincial towns and some 10 lived in the capital, Copenhagen. A slowly rising percentage lived in urban areas (1870: 25).

If we look at the distribution of *cultivated* land from the 17th century and up to around 1900 some 75% was in the hands of peasant-farmers, some 10 in the manors of the great land-owners (or the state) and some 10% with cottagers and some 5 belonged to others (parish ministers, towns, etc.).

Until the 1790's the overwhelming majority of the peasant-farms of app. 10-140 acres belonged to the landowners to whom the peasant-farmers paid rent in the form of money, agricultural products and labour with horses and agricultural implements. But the Danish tenant peasant-farmer never became a serf in the continental understanding of the word. Many of the legal rights and duties of the English yeomanry stayed with the Danish peasant-farmer, especially with the few freeholders.

The crown protected this distribution of land: *first*, for fiscal reasons (the direct manorial land paid no taxes); *secondly*, because already in the 18th century the central government realized that a pauperization of the peasantry would eventually result in uprisings and revolutions – and *finally*, because the leading circles in society influenced by the Enlightenment wanted to assure reasonable human conditions for the peasantry.

The good market prices in Europe for agricultural products at the time of the great land reforms (app. 1790-1807) allowed the peasant-farmers to buy their farms as freeholds from the landlords. In 1807 nearly 60% of the family farms were owned by the peasant-farmers themselves. Then came a stop until the 1830's in the taking over of freeholds. By 1870 less than 10% of the peasant-farms were still under feudal contracts. The explosive rise in population throughout the 19th century was to be found in the number of small-croppers (those with under 10 acres), cottagers and farmhands with no independent housing (owned or rented) at all.

An increasing part of the agrarian proletariat found a living in a combination of some special craft (mason, carpenter, weaver, etc.), with seasonal work as a farm hand on the manor or for the peasant-farmers or in the bogland and in road-building etc. The expansion of both specialization and total production in the agrarian sector was able to absorb the greater part of the population growth up to about 1870. From then on the growing industrialization in the urban world took over as the "attractive force" for surplus labour of both sexes. Compared to other European states emigration meant very little.

Another result of the modernization of the agrarian sector was the break up of the old collective village system. The farms had their formerly scattered pieces of land redistributed so that each farm had all its land situated in one place. Each peasant-farmer was now solely responsible for his own fortune and for the fate of his family. His ability as an agrarian entrepreneur and the invisible forces behind the actual market prices were now a determining factor in his daily life and future possibilities. Even though it took a long time (and some never made it), the peasant-farmer had either to conform to the logic of liberal capitalism or to find new collective solutions to the constant pressure for modernization and efficiency – which later from about 1890 and onwards he so successfully did in the co-operative movement. The village became the service centre. The price for this hundred year (1790-1890) period of modernization and general agrarian prosperity was paid by the hundred thousands of the agrarian proletariat – in 1905 the middle-sized family farms still had about 3/4 of all the cultivated land. The peasant-farmers were at the beginning of the 19th century *potentially* the dominating class and they slowly became the *leading* class.

In a class model it looks like this (Fig. 1):

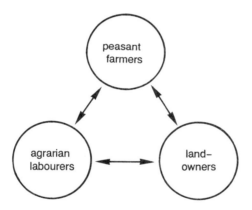

The urban world

The state-bankruptcy of 1813, the lack of Norwegian revenues after Norway's cession to Sweden in 1814 and the loss of the merchant marine in 1807-14 all combined to leave the economic life of Copenhagen from 1814-1840 in a rather deep depression. This again meant that there was no influential class of rich merchants and manufacturers (industrialists) to formulate a bourgeois capitalist political opinion. Liberal ideas came but they were put forward by academics, civil servants and – compared to the upper class of London, Paris and Hamburg – i.e., middle-class people. The academics as well as the lower middle-class of independent master-craftsmen and shopowners and other similar groups became more economically and politically influential in Copenhagen – which at that time constituted the urban world of Denmark – than one would otherwise expect. In the 1840's Copenhagen recovered but it was not until 1870 that a fully fledged capitalist class of bankers, industrialists and ship-owners really emerged in the capital at an international level and could counter the former middle middle-class domination. At the same time, from the 1870's and onwards, the unions and the socialist party (Social Democrats) effectively organized the new urban working class.

So, even though it is not the same sort of people in class terms who are placed at the top or the wings of the following model, that model is still valid for the urban sector from 1814 and throughout the 19th century and demonstrates how the urban class system within the capital was not bipolar but tri-polar (Fig 2.)

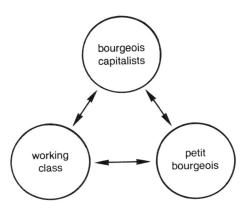

Economy, class and culture – city and countryside

Denmark in 1840 or 1864 had no iron and no coal, the two fundamentals of 19th century industrialization, and the valuable Norwegian timber resources were no longer part of the Danish export economy. Thus, to follow the modern way of economic prosperity Denmark needed to import a lot of raw materials and semifabrics. The only way to pay for that import was through the surplus of agrarian production sold on the market. And whoever dominated the area of agrarian exports dominated the whole economy of the country, i.e., the peasant-farmers, so:

– The *urban* world (Copenhagen) acquired (a) *economically*, one set of exchanges with the European market and the home market, (b) in *class terms*, its own set of socio-economically founded classes as well as (c) *culturally*, a very solid nationally based culture in spite of strong European influences (H.C. Andersen, S. Kierkegaard).

– The *agrarian* world got (a) *economically*, another set of contacts and a wider export market often through the provincial towns, (b) its own *class system* and especially from the 1860's, (c) its own *cultural system*, the folk-high schools, and for example, the culture of the meeting-house.

Denmark thus became divided between the *urban* and the *agrarian* world, as happened in many other countries. But it was in a special *Danish way* where the agrarian world had the upper hand in the national economy, and the lower middle-class of the peasant-farmers became the most influential class in society with its own cultural (folk high-schools) as well as economic system (the co-operatives). In the urban world the lower middle-class never found the same strength as the peasant-farmers although no party, whether conservative or labour, could ignore them.

When in the 1890's modern industrial capitalism really became powerful in Denmark, the peasant-farmers had had the time needed to build up effective cultural and economic organizations to withstand the growing pressure. The result was a complicated social and class model (Fig. 3):

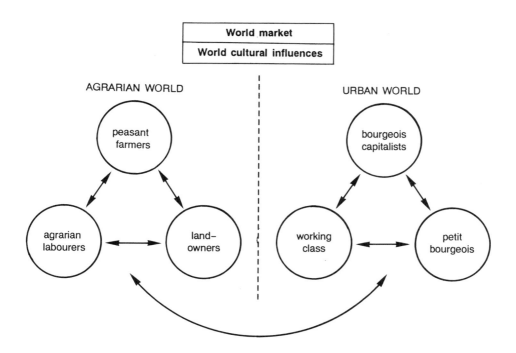

Constant conflicts and the constant need for party alliances were to result in a very complex Danish system where no single class and no affiliated political party could rule at the expense of the rest of the nation. This is still the case today. A social, political and cultural development of a "middle way", of co-operation, and of compromises, has therefore become characteristic of the Danish way to modern capitalism with a human face. The other possibility, total social paralysis, never occurred.

It is also understandable that a public figure, who was rooted in Christian faith, history, language and poetry – and who managed to place the peasant-farmer on his family farm together with the hard-working craftsman, at the centre of the social system, would have a great possibility of becoming a sort of national figure.

Grundtvig was the right man at the right time at the right place with the right ideas. But he was more than that. Parts of his work and thinking transcend the barriers of time and space – and that "more" is what intrigues and inspires us still today.

II. The political structure

King and government
The leaders of the central government in the 1830's had grown up and served their younger years in the absolutistic-bureaucratic multinational state of the Twin-Realm Denmark-Norway and the Duchies of Slesvig and Holstein.

Even the catastrophic results of the Danish involvement on the French side in the Napoleonic wars, the loss of Norway, could not really alter the widespread loyalty to the king although the central government strengthened its grip on power.

Public political debate had been allowed by the prime minister Struensee in 1772 but it was soon limited again. Yet in the many clubs and in printed periodicals a rather free debate existed in Denmark-Norway as long as it did not criticize the regime in principle but kept to practical matters such as adjustments of particular cases or the reform of local corruption.

A new local and efficient administration was introduced into the realm step by step from around 1800 with the parish parson as the central figure assisted by some well-respected peasant-farmers. Several laws for social modernization were introduced and in the years of 1837-1841 the whole system of local government was reorganized, introducing a democratically elected board at the parish level as well as on the county level and in the provincial towns. Even though the landowners and the more solid of the peasant-farmers and the better-off taxpayers gained some extra influence, the majority on the local boards from around 1840 consisted of persons elected by the voting rights of every male person with his own household and farm down to a size of about 10 to 12 acres – and the tenant-farmers were not excluded. Of adult males with their own families up to 25% got local political influence as voters. The democratic element in political institutions was strengthened throughout the 19th century and in 1915 women finally got voting rights along with men.

Consultative assemblies, representative democracy
At the national level, on May 28. 1831 the king issued a proclamation stating that democratically elected advisory assemblies (called estates) would be instituted and in 1834 the law appropriate followed. In 1835 the first meeting took place. There were 4 elected assemblies, one in Roskilde for the Danish islands, Iceland and the Faroes, one in Viborg for Jutland, one for Slesvig in the town of Slesvig and one for Holstein in Itzehoe. The little Duchy of Lauenburg, which was a compensation granted in 1814 and situated on the Eastern border of Holstein, kept its ancient representative body of the upper classes, the *Landtag*. In 1843 Iceland was granted its own advisory assembly under the age-old name of the *Althing*. Voting rights for the Danish assemblies and the possibility of being a candidate for election, required a somewhat higher social status but were very similar to those granting access to local government mentioned above: in principle the possession or tenancy of about 40 acres of land or the like in paid taxation was enough and this meant that about 5% of the population had political rights as electible in relation to the national assemblies. At the meetings the deputies dealt with proposals for laws presented to them by the govern-ment but could also take their own initiatives to make proposals or laws. Their recommendations were for the most part followed by the government and by the king who in the end kept the final decision to himself. In general the system functioned well on most practical matters and many needed modernizations found here a broadly acceptable solution.

The liberal opposition of Copenhagen was disappointed in their hope of further democratic reforms when the gifted king Christian VIII took over after the death of the old Frederik VI in 1839. The political power struggle between the liberals and the conservatives (even if they were not yet called that) was strengthened early in the 1840's. But soon the over-all problem became the *national question* between Danish and German in the old Danish Duchy of Slesvig.[1] This involved the whole future of the "Helstat", the *United State* of Denmark, Slesvig, Holstein, Lauenburg and Iceland as well

---

1.   See Rerup's contribution to this volume, pp. 233-42.

as the Faroe Islands. The liberals took up the national case and became *national liberals* from about 1841-42.

The voice of the common people, movements and organizations

The first outburst of local dissent came early in the 19th century and originated in small circles of religiously awakened common people of pietistic background. The "meeting movement" (i.e., religious lay meetings) was in strong opposition to the ruling Late-Enlightenment interpretation of the Bible and to the new hymn-book setout by the Lutheran state church. Because of Grundtvig's emphasising on freedom of choice in religious matters the "meeting" people got into contact with him; but it was the Grundtvigian, Lindberg, who really took the lead by supporting the meeting movement in his journal.

As long as the outer pressures of church, state and public opinion were strongly felt the meeting movement stood together. As soon as religious freedom was established by the Constitution of 1849 different parties appeared within the movement. The more pietistic organized themselves on a lay basis in 1854 but they first became influential from 1861 onwards after a reorganization under the leadership of some young priests taking the name of the *Indre Mission* (Home Mission).

Another group was soon known as the *Grundtvigians*, who already from the 1840's gathered around local *Danish Societies*, modelled on that established in Copenhagen from 1839/40. From the 1850's onwards some devotees flocked around early folk high-school principals such as Kristen Kold and around the Grundtvigian clergy. Several Grundtvigian folk high-schools were erected in the 1850's but the movement first really took off in the 1860's. Local private secondary schools of Grundtvigian conviction followed from 1856 onwards, when a new law made it more easy for a group of parents to establish their own school. In the 1860's the followers of Grundtvig had become so numerous that people from all over the country could meet in huge numbers at the *Vennemøderne* (the meetings of friends of Grundtvigian persuasion) but it was very clear at the same meetings that great internal differences existed among Grundtvig's followers. The Grundtvigians never wanted to organize too strongly for three major reasons: (1) the spiritual element in people's convictions could not be free if it was bound by organizational regulations or majority vote; (2) the danger of fossilization and misuse of any organized power was taken seriously; (3) the different factions were much too far from each other to allow any closer organization. The inner conflicts (as between the practical politicians and the more strict clergymen) would have been brought into the open – and as long as Grundtvig himself always denied he was a party man, who could be the practical leader? Yet, folk high-schools are effective organizations, and the parliamentary deputies had to organize their vote in order to get influence, and so semi-political associations of Grundtvigians were instituted and functioned as *The Church Society* from the 1860's. The various political journals such as Grundtvig's own *Danskeren* (The Dane) 1848-51 or the later *Dansk Folke-Tidende* (The Danish Folk News) from the 1860's edited by the Grundtvigian politician S. Høgsbro were more influential at least in organizing minds rather than bodies.

The first more solidly organized political grouping was *Bondevennerne* (The Friends of the Peasantry), 1846, headed by a group of liberal reformers and politicians and by a few leaders of more common origin. *The Friends of the Peasantry* managed to organize some 5,000 people and to dominate the elections to the consultative assemblies in 1847 and later to the *Rigsdag*, the parliament, so effectively that no one outside the cities could be elected if they were not their own candidates or at least candidates accepted by them.

III. The Slesvig-Holsteiners, the Slesvig wars of 1848-50 and 1864 and political Denmark 1848-70

In the 19th century national emotions and state controversies in the form of conflicts between *peoples* came to the centre of the stage of history all over Europe. Everybody who in the Danish realm took part in literature, culture and politics in those days had to take a stand on the national question between German and Danish because those problems influenced the whole of social and intellectual life. In Slesvig the national, linguistic and cultural problems were especially complicated and there were no simple solutions. As map 2 indicates there existed in Slesvig among the common people in the northern part a specific Danish dialect "sønderjysk" (southern Jutish) and to the south a special dialect of Low German; in between to the east ordinary people spoke a mixture of "sønderjysk" and Low German (but not a mixture of High German and King's Danish), to the west some 5,000 spoke the independent Frisian language and in some western areas people spoke a mixture of Frisian and "sønderjysk". Of the common people no one spoke King's Danish or High German, that is to say the language of the upper classes, the civil servants, the academics and some townspeople and the languages spoken in church and at court. So the linguistic lines of division ran between town and countryside, between social classes, between educated and uneducated people, between areas and landscapes and between different functions in daily and official life. For centuries this multi-lingual and multi-cultural reality had been accepted as normal by everybody in Denmark, Slesvig-Holstein and Germany; it was the *political* tensions between Denmark and the different lines of the dukes of Slesvig and Holstein and their foreign allies in Germany, Russia and Sweden that really mattered up to 1830-40.

A civil servant, Uwe Jens Lornsen, returning to Slesvig from service in the central government in 1830 started the public debate about the situation with a small pamphlet: *Ueber das Verfassungswerk in Schleswigholstein* (About the Constitution of Slesvig-Holstein) which came out in both Danish and German. The author argued, that the two Duchies ought to have one common constitution and become one state with the king as the only bond to Denmark. With an eye to the revolutions of 1830 in Europe the government took the challenge seriously. Lornsen was convicted and jailed for conspiracy against the state.

The significance of the Lornsen debate is twofold: *first*, the cause of Slesvig-Holstein was now no longer the exclusive affair of an aristocratic elite; and it became a case for the much *broader strata* of the intelligentsia, the civil service men, the middle-classes of the provincial towns and other groups in Slesvig and Holstein; *secondly, political* liberalism was now connected to the cause. Seen from abroad the national-liberals in Copenhagen and the bourgeois Slesvig-Holsteiners had much in common in their view of economic liberalism, in their taste for refined culture, in their social status and in their search for constitutional democracy. Often they knew each other personally.

There was never a question in the national-cultural and national-political fight of turning the common man of Holstein or Ditmarsken into Danes. It was the other way round for the Danish national groups. They were concerned to stop the *Germanification* of Slesvig and perhaps to regain some of the recently lost ground of Danish identification as well as to secure for the Danish speaking common man the possibility and right to stay Danish if he so wished.

The growing national tensions of the 1840's, the international rumours of political unrest following the scarcity of bread in the Winter of 1847-48 and the death of King Christian VIII in January 1848, all sharpened the internal tensions in Denmark and made clear the need for a more democratic constitution. The February Revolution in Paris sent shock waves through Europe. In Slesvig-Holstein this resulted in intense negotiations among the supporters of a more independent state consisting of Slesvig and Holstein in close contact with the German Confederation. A delegation of Slesvig-Holsteiners came to Copenhagen on March 20 1848, but could not achieve the acceptance of their claims and so left by ship for Slesvig. In the Duchies this meant a war of independence which the culturally and politically German orientated Slesvig-Holsteiners started by erecting a provisional government and seizing, without fighting, several of the great arsenals and fortresses in the Duchies. At the same moment the liberals in

Copenhagen demanded the resignation of the old government, a new constitution and a new liberal-dominated government. That government would
deal with immediate reforms and with a military mobilization of the
national resources to encounter the insurrection. The king and government
gave in and the new ministers were accepted. The time of the absolute
monarchy came to an end in the last few days of March 1848.

The new government had three immense tasks ahead of it: (1) to win the
war, (2) to carry through some much needed reforms, and (3) to promote
a new constitution.

The German states under Prussian leadership intervened in the civil war.
Thus it changed from a violent rebellion to a war of national survival for
the Danish state. The war lasted three years with several armistices. It was
costly and in the end the great powers pressed a non-solution on Denmark
which was like a ticking bomb which would explode sooner or later. The
Slesvig-Holsteiners did not achieve their common state. Denmark had to
accept that Slesvig could not be separated from Holstein and brought into
a nearer national and political contact with Denmark. A division of Slesvig
along linguistic-national lines (Grundtvig's suggestion, also promoted in
1838 by representatives in the Consultative Estates of Jutland) was
proposed in the negotiations but was unacceptable both to the Danes and
the Slesvig-Holsteiners.

Denmark won the war of 1848-50 but, with diplomatic "help" from the
great powers, lost the peace. The bitterness of the Slesvig-Holsteiners
supported by constant and massive anti-Danish propaganda in the German
press kept the tensions alive. The Holsteiners and many of the German-
oriented elite of Slesvig denounced and even sabotaged any steps towards
a real settlement. It became more and more obvious that a second round
was to come. In November 1863 the national-liberal government in
Copenhagen cut through the Gordian knot and introduced a new constitution whereby Slesvig came into direct union with Denmark while
Holstein and Lauenburg were left with looser ties to the dwindling Union-
State. It was a clear Danish breech both of the London Agreement and the
Peace Treaty of 1852/53 which stated clearly that Slesvig should not be
brought into a closer union with Denmark than Holstein. Prussia and
Austria issued an ultimatum but the Danish government did not yield. The
Second Slesvig War was a reality by February 1864.

Danish military resistance to Bismarck's well-trained Prussian army and
to the Austrian corps was bitter but fruitless. Denmark lost completely and
by the Peace Treaty in Prague 1864 had to cede Slesvig, with some minor
amendments, Holstein and Lauenburg to Prussia and Austria. Two years
later Bismarck took the whole after having defeated Austria in 1866.

As earlier, Russia, France and Great Britain did not want Prussia to command the Straits – the access to the Baltic – so Denmark was saved from total destruction by diplomatic intervention.

In exactly 50 years the whole kingdom of Norway and the richest provinces of the state, the Duchies with 2/5 of the inhabitants, had been lost. The losses of 1864 were a psychological shock to the nation as great as the catastrophes of 1807 and 1814. Yet, exactly as a result of these losses Denmark ended up as the most pure national state in Europe. Finally the people could concentrate their resources on internal development, finishing the modernization of society.

The Constitution of 1849 and the aftermath of the Second Slesvig War 1864
The democratically-elected Constitutional Assembly met in 1848 and already by June 5, 1849, by his signature the king confirmed the new democratic constitution. All the general elements of the rights and duties of the citizens of a modern democratic society were there: (a) free and open elections to a parliament with two chambers, (b) voting rights and rights to be elected for all males over 25 who did not receive or owe poor relief and who had their own household, (c) freedom of the press, (d) freedom of speech and public meeting, (e) freedom of religious faith, (f) open courts and a system of juries in major cases, *habeas corpus*, (g) military service extended to all classes of society.

The monarchy was preserved with a sort of veto accorded to the king since laws had to be signed both by the king and the minister responsible for the area of the law. The state church was renamed *The People's Church*. It was still a concern of the state and in practice was administered by the bishops and the provosts.

In 1856 by law it became more easy to erect private secondary schools, and soon particular families had the right to leave the parish congregation and join another parish if the priest there would accept them.

Liberalism in the economy was victorious over the old protectionism of the guilds and trades. Monopolies were lifted and around 1856 the royal monopoly on the Faroe Islands and the last monopoly on Iceland were removed. The century-old "Sundtold", i.e., customs on all traffic sailing through the Belts, was repealed. Some old feudal rights, for instance free hunting, were done away with. The internal traffic system expanded as new steamship routes were founded and the railway system developed – the Kingdom proper became a more unified state than ever before.

So liberalism flourished both politically and economically and the country soon overcame the losses of the First Slesvig War 1848-50.

The peace of 1864 left Denmark in a very difficult situation. The national-liberals bore the burden of a lost war, the conservatives saw their chance and made a quick move for the support of the lower middle-class peasant-farmers. Their sheer numbers in parliament made it short-sighted to try to govern without their consent. A somewhat more conservative constitutional reform followed the lost war of 1864 finally accepted after fierce political fights. An alliance of the "small and big farms" lasted for five years under the dominance of the great landowners. Much needed reform with less class nepotism than one might have expected was success-fully carried through. In 1870 the farmer-landlord alliance broke down. The parliamentary party of *Venstre* (the left, the liberals) was instituted as representative of the now leading lower and *middle* middle-class peasant-farmers and some new groups, such as the school teachers. Capitalists and landowners joined forces in the Conservative party ("Højre") in the 1880s.

The fierce political battle in parliament of the 1870's to 90's between the Conservatives and "Venstre" was mirrored at the local level; but in practice the solid hegemony of the peasant-farmers in local economic and cultural institutions was seldom seriously challenged.

Denmark was and is still today a *middle* middle-class society. The overwhelming majority wants a "middle-of-the-road" policy, a welfare state and a combination of public and private enterprise, so that most foreigners will have difficulties in finding any fundamental differences in the political practice and in the administration between Conservatives and Social Democrats when in power. A society where "few have too much and fewer too little" – as Grundtvig wrote in 1820 – is still the valid and broadly accepted aim of the Danes.

IV. The political Grundtvig on democracy, language and nationality in Denmark and Slesvig

To give the socio-economic background for Grundtvig's powers of penetrating into Denmark is difficult. To give a meaningful sketch of the immensely complicated conditions in Slesvig-Holstein is nearly impossible. But I have tried. Grundtvig lived with all this: the loss of Norway, the bankruptcy of the state, growing nationalism and liberalism, the rise of the peasant-farmer movement, the constitution and democracy, the two Slesvig wars, Denmark's reduction to a third rate small power. But he did more than live with it: he suffered it, took part in it, influencing and inspiring where ever he could.

A true citizen is a politician
If politics is about involvement in and power over the authoritative distribution and production of the material and immaterial wealth and

goods of society – as for instance land or freedom of the press – then Grundtvig was a politician from the first decennium of the 19th century onwards and throughout the rest of his life. Up to 1848 he worked as a writer and a scholar. From 1848 to 1865 he was at certain periods a parliamentary politician; as such he was too independent and unpredictable to be a party leader. Consequently, he did not have much direct influence compared to other leaders of his time. Apart from the paragraph in the constitution about the jury institution in the courts it is difficult to point to any *direct* political influence of Grundtvig. But *indirectly* he had already from the 1830's onwards influenced some younger men who soon became public figures. A growing group of members of parliament were known as Grundtvigians from the middle of the 1850's and were deeply influenced by his philosophy. In socio-political matters of daily life, more practical minds had to find out *how* to erect and run a folk high-school, a private secondary school or a political group in parliament – in short: how to transform Grundtvig's visions into practical actions and institutions.

For Grundtvig man lived in the temporal world and as a citizen he had to take part in worldly affairs. Christianity was to him a fundamental part of the conditions for a full human life. Both the earthly and the divine world were given; yet to many they seemed to be conflicting realities. The conflict did not seem to trouble Grundtvig too much. But it took him a long time to resolve the problem and he dealt with it partly through his famous dictum: "Menneske først Kristen saa" (Man first and then a Christian).

Poetry, obligations and true citizenship
Like many of his generation, Grundtvig was deeply moved by the fierce battle of Copenhagen in 1801, the English bombardment of Copenhagen and the taking of the battle-fleet in 1807, and the heroic naval battle of the last Danish man-of-war, *Christian*, against a fleet of five British ships of the Royal Navy in 1808, and finally by the loss of Norway in 1814.

One of his finest poems deals with the naval battle of 1808. The young lieutenant Willemoes is the central figure. At the time of its publication in 1810, the poem did not win much public attention. But in 1837 a beautiful melody was composed for it and it was sung by the listeners to the last of Grundtvig's famous public lectures of 1838, *Mands Minde* (Within Living Memory), the history of the last 50 years and of his own life-time. It is not a war song but rather a plea to follow the example of young Willemoes and to defend the fatherland in its deepest need.

Hundreds of songs with historical, political and national themes praising the landscape, the people, the past, the king, the Danish spirit and language came from his pen. In the sense defined above they were political, telling people to be aware of the dangers to society as well as of the good things and possibilities in daily life and in the national existence. Directly and indirectly they are telling people to take up their responsibilities as men and citizens and do something about it *themselves*.

History as a way to true citizenship

Grundtvig's immense work (a) on the periodical *Dannevirke*, vol's I-IV, 1816-19, as well as (b) his translations into modern Danish of the Old Norse historical texts: Snorre, *Heimskringla* (The history of the Norwegian kings) and (c) of the Latin *Gesta Danorum* (The Deeds of the Danes) by the Danish historian Saxo as well as (d) his three editions of *A world History* and his *Nordic Mythology* – all these were also political acts in a way parallel to that of the songs. Through history the reader should learn about himself, know where he came from, see that dark times have been overcome and thus get the courage to stand up and fight for a full life and for a better future. History and poetry expressed in the mother tongue both contributed to build up that understanding. Both the intellect and the feelings had to be involved.

The Danish "enlightened absolutism" of the early 19th century where the king was seen as the first servant of the country was in many ways acceptable to the younger Grundtvig as long as a reform policy was possible. Around 1830 he was influenced by his longer periods of studies in England. At the same time the example of the European revolution of 1830 of course influenced him like everyone else. As mentioned above the government decided to establish the democratically elected advisory assemblies in 1831. Modern Slesvig-Holsteinism found its first expression in Uwe Jens Lornsen's text of 1830 on a constitution.

The political Grundtvig 1831

Grundtvig combined those four influences: the English, the European, the constitutional-democratic and that of Slesvig-Holsteinism in a remarkable pamphlet published in 1831 in both Danish and German, *Politiske Betragtninger med Blik paa Danmark og Holsteen* (Political observations with an eye to Denmark and Holstein).

In the booklet he distinguished between nationally justified wars of independence (Greeks against Turks, Germans against the French under Napoleon) as contrasted with unjustified insurrections against a legitimate system like that of the French at the time of the revolution of 1830. The fundamental rights of man such as freedom of the press, freedom of speech, *habeas corpus*, combined with some degree of general welfare already existed in France 1830. The bourgeoisie in misusing the press allowed "Pøbel-Regimentet" (mob rule) to become all-powerful and uncontrolled. Democracy as such was limited for Grundtvig by the built-in danger that a great part of mankind instead of being mature and wise are such that: "vi ei kan kalde andet end Fæ" (we cannot label otherwise but beasts, p. 19). If people had clear insights into their obligations and the will-power to follow them only a few magistrates and laws chosen by them-selves would be necessary and then: "hverken Lov eller Øvrighed" (neither law nor government) would be needed. But alas, it was not so. Therefore: "behøves Orden og Forskiel" (order and difference (in authority) are needed).

Grundtvig made a comparison between a good monarchy and a demo-cracy as exemplified on the one side by an enlightened Danish estate con-trasted with an Anglo-American factory on the other. On the estate the lord ran its affairs for the common good of all involved, while the factory was run solely for the maximum profit of the shareholders: "mens Arbeiderne slides op og casseres med samme Ligegyldighed som Machinerne" (while the labour force is worn out and discarded with the same carelessness as is the machinery). In a democracy no organized sound sense could unite the conflicting interests of: "Kræmmer-Amerikansk" and "Pøbel-Parisisk" (profit-first-Americanism and mob-Parisianism, p. 20). It is here very clear that neither in politics – nor in economics – did he accept self-regulating "invisible hands". Chaos would be the result of lack of *outer* regulation.

Ethical strengths and moral values, *inner* forces, are to Grundtvig needed if external powers disappear. But what in a democracy can produce the needed virtues of: "sande Gudsfrygt, Ydmyghed, Nøisomhed, Beskedenhed, Føielighed og Menneske-Kierlighed" (true fear of God, humility, frugality, modesty, compliance, and love of mankind) – he had no direct answer.

Grundtvig found that the Danish peasant-farmers were no subdued band of slaves but, "et fribaarent Folk" (a freeborn people) who may, "uden Fare for Samfundet efterhaanden hæves til en langt friere Stilling, end de fleste andre Landes" (without danger be elevated to a much freer position than that of most other countries). He continued: "Forskiel maa der altid blive i en Stat, der netop som et Legeme maa have forskiellige Lemmer og forgaar, naar Haanden vil være Hoved, eller Øret være Øie" (there always has to be social difference in a state which like a human body has to have different limbs and will perish when the hand wants to be the head or the ear wants to be the eye).

Five theses on representative political assemblies

Where the elite and the government followed the ethical and moral com-mandments of enlightened rule an aristocratic-monarchical system was preferable, he argued. Consequently, parliaments in the continental versions of *Reichstage* were of no use. But governments like people were not always perfect. From the European debate of the day he extracted five major arguments for a democratic representative body, a parliament:

1. Royal government was not able to enforce large reforms for the general welfare as evidenced by France before 1789.
2. Only by a parliamentary system would the population become really conscious of the affairs of state and society.
3. The right to decide and control taxation and a state budget should rest with the parliament.
4. It is possible to elect deputies in such a way that the majority will be on the side of justice and wisdom.
5. A royal power of veto would be enough to secure the necessary continuity and authority of the regime.

Grundtvig countered the five theses point by point:

1. The Danish government (he is thinking of the great land reforms of 1788 and onwards) did act successfully for the general welfare, while the British society and parliament gave an example of dangerous class conflicts and opposing vested interests.
2. The love of fatherland in the hearts of all citizens and all men in public service could bring about more social responsibility and do more for the general welfare than any parliament.
3. Grundtvig himself was no expert on economics but most deputies knew even less than he did.[2] In practice this ignorance of economics meant either that the economic decision would be taken by a very few or that they would be poor decisions.
4. Elected deputies would tend to be greedy in relation to spiritual and cultural matters and would have no sense for the general development of society in all its dimensions to the benefit of the people. The majority would be led by money and eloquence, and not by wisdom.
5. A royal veto could prevent damage but it could not generate social progress.

Finally, with an eye to the rôle of the press in Paris in 1830 he wrote that Napoleon had perhaps had a point in restricting the freedom of the press.

---

2.   Wåhlin (1990), p. 248; the whole article demonstrates that Grundtvig had a rather elaborate economic insight.

To prevent misuse of the press Grundtvig argued that any print should be, not censured, but countersigned by somebody of good social standing and over the age of 40. If the author could not find even one such person the script might not be worth printing. At the end of his paper he returned to that point and stated the necessity of a public debate in print.

Class conflict and a responsible people

Let me summarize: In 1831 Grundtvig sees very clearly the power of class conflict between labour and bourgeoisie capital in modern urban-industrial societies. Mob regime to him is just as repulsive as the rotten parliamentarism of conflicting vested interests of his day. In Denmark the solid peasant-farmers are the class in which to vest the future of society under:
- an enlightened monarchy
- sustained by the stabilizing power of landed property and
- governed by moral obligations towards the general welfare and
- inspired by a national love of the fatherland.

Grundtvig is quite aware of the social dynamics of class conflicts for social changes (revolutions) but does not find them acceptable. He is also aware of the social dynamic of modern industrial capitalism but rejects it as the basis of a sound society. Landed property, small or large (peasant-farmers and landowners), is the material and stable basis for a sound society. But that is not sufficient: a society must have an *ethic* and *moral* "inner" foundation in its citizens and civil servants in order to promote social change and the general welfare, and that inner drive is found in love of the fatherland, in *national* feelings. It must be underlined that although heroism at times forms a part of national feeling, the true national feeling in Grundtvig's interpretation has nothing to do with French *grandeur* or the German nationalism of the expanding state. To Grundtvig national feeling means the *moral obligation* to do in daily life what is needed for the general welfare of the people. As he wrote in 1820 and later repeated in 1848 (*vide* Rerup): "It is a truly rich society where few have too much and fewer too little".

Grundtvig's economic and political understanding of the material and productive bases of modern class conflicts had evolved since 1808 and 1820. Typically for him he could live well with, on the one hand, denouncing too great differences in the distribution of wealth and, on the other hand, stating that differences in social influence and work must exist.

His solution lay in *education*; to educate the people not so much with academic knowledge as with insight in order to prepare them for full and responsible citizenship. Several programs and scripts from his hand deal with such an education in the 1830's and 1840"s.

Without saying so directly his booklet of 1831 is in fact a support to the government's intended proclamation of consultative assemblies for the realm.

Grundtvig on Slesvig-Holstein and nationalism

In chapter IV (p. 56ff.) of his little book Grundtvig dealt with the rising Slesvig-Holsteinism. He expressed understanding of the fear felt at the German-speaking university of Kiel of a policy of Danisation hidden in government decrees like the one which declared that all writs in the Duchies should be printed in parallel Danish and German, and of the idea that Holsteiners ought to learn Danish, and so forth. Since Grundtvig himself would not like to be made a German he understands the German claim for respect for their language and culture. Slesvig was, he remarked, *de facto* in matters of language and administration both Danish and German. But he respected those feelings in Holstein which wanted to have as little in common with Denmark as was practically possible; but he could not accept the claim on Slesvig which did not take into consideration the will of the people there.

In contrast to Dahlmann and Uwe Jens Lornsen he did not deal much with the historical and constitutional arguments for Slesvig-Holsteinism. What mattered to him were the sentiments, loyalty and national feelings of the present population of Slesvig. The school system of Slesvig was functioning well and literacy among the population was quite widespread. Consequently the population could follow a public debate and were able to express themselves. Every male citizen of Slesvig, to him, therefore had a right to be heard in a referendum about whether they wanted to have: "Lands-Fader tilfælles med os eller Konge-Hertug med Holsten" (Father-of-the-land (king) in common with us (the Danes) or king-duke with Holstein).

In 1848, on March 14th, when the Slesvig-Holsteiners were planning their insurrection Grundtvig repeated his views about the national fate of Slesvig in a lecture which was soon published under the title, *Frihed og Orden* (Freedom and Order),[3] where he stated that: "Freedom without order" was usually better than, "order without freedom". In this lecture he furthermore expressed the view that the kingdom of Denmark did not stretch farther than the northern borderline of Slesvig and that: "the Danish

---

3. *Danskeren*, vol. I, pp. 84-96; G. Christensen og Hal Koch (eds.), *N.F.S. Grundtvig, Værker i Udvalg*, vol. 5 (Copenhagen, 1942), pp. 260-61.

land only reached as far as Danish is spoken and basically not further [south, V.W.] than to a point where the people will go on speaking Danish ... to somewhere ... in the middle of the Duchy Slesvig"; but Danish, in his mind, must have the same rights as German in Slesvig and elsewhere. To accept the limitation of Danish was not to accept the dominance of German. He expressed fear of a coming civil war and stressed the point of a separation of Slesvig and Holstein. If the German states would not allow such a separation and interfered or if the Germans in Slesvig were to suppress the Danes a major war was inevitable. He repeated, as in 1831, that Denmark had no right to include Danish Slesvig in the Kingdom without the clearly expressed acceptance of the Slesvigers – i.e., respect of the right to national self-determination. After the war of 1848-50, at the London Conference, the proposal of a division of Slesvig along national lines was brought into the negotiations, but in vain.

The revolutions of 1830 spread new ideas; but it was quite remarkable in 1831 to suggest a line of division formed on the principle of self-determination and respect of the language, and to place the decision directly in the hands of the people by a referendum. The Holy Alliance of 1815 between the great European powers had, in the name of *legitimacy*, elevated the historical and inherited rights of the sovereigns above any ideas and feelings of the people. Around 1830 the Danish realm included several languages: Icelandic, Faroese, Frisian, Low German, High German and Danish. So to call for respect of linguistically based national identities was to ask for trouble in the multi-lingual Danish state. But this was exactly what Grundtvig did already before 1848. In 1845 he supported his son, Svend Grundtvig, when the younger Grundtvig warned the Danes against the Danish cultural suppression of the Faroese. In 1845 Faroese was not yet a written language, and therefore the new law about Faroese secondary schools had promoted Danish as the major language in the Faroese schools. The Grundtvigs then compared the Danish politics on the islands with that of the Germans in Slesvig who were suppressing the cultural and national rights of the Danish-speakers there.[4] This is an example of Grundtvig's transferring a Christian precept (do not do to others what you do not want done to yourself) into the world of practical politics. A true sense of national identity incorporates the moral principle of true respect for the rights of other people to preserve and develop their nationality.

As in many areas Grundtvig was far ahead of his time in these proposals from 1831 in respect for national self-determination and

---

4.   Thorsteinsson (1990), pp. 135-38.

referendum. Ninety years later and after two minor wars and a world war these principles were finally taken seriously by the World community and used in the determination of the state border between Denmark and Germany and in a few other places. I doubt whether President Wilson in 1918 had ever heard of Grundtvig when he introduced the idea of national self-determination as one of the leading moral principles in the war efforts of the Allied powers and at the peace conference after the First World War. The ideas had by then become common property.[5] Looking at the national problems in Eastern Europe in 1993 and elsewhere those ideas might still be worth considering.

The political Grundtvig in prose after 1831

Again and again in his songs and his writings Grundtvig places the peasant-farmers at the centre of society. He warned against the dangers of the merely superficial democracy of most parliamentary politics. Schooling was needed if in a representative political system the peasant-farmers and their compeers were not to be the victims of smart liberal orators. Grundtvig's text, presented earlier, dealt with the problems of its day: the erection of consultative representative assemblies as well as the problems of cultural and political nationalism in a multi-national state. In 1831 he did not deal with more economic questions of commerce, trade and production, about which he later expressed strong liberal viewpoints.

The introduction of local democracy in 1837-41 he welcomed from the heart. In 1848-49 he went directly into practical politics as a member of parliament and as editor of his own political journal, *Danskeren* (the Dane). In his political platform of 1848 the liberal economic parts are new to the 1831 paper, but they are in accordance with the ideas already mentioned in the *Mands Minde* lectures of 1838, the *Danske Samfund* lectures of the 1840"s, and the many prints advocating the ideas of schools for citizenship which inspired the folk high-schools to come, and many other of his writings.[6]

To Grundtvig a voice – as well as some practical activity – in the matters of society were integral parts of being a responsible citizen. To me, there is no doubt that in the above meaning he was a politician at least from 1831, even though he first stood for a seat in parliament in 1848. His placing of the peasant-farmer in the centre of the social system was a realistic, class based policy to avoid the dangers of modern industrial class wars (i.e.,

5.   Uffe Østergård (1992 A), p. 176 and Uffe Østergård (1992 B).
6.   Wåhlin (1990), pp. 293-94.

revolutions) between organized capital on the one side opposing organized, but desperate and dehumanized labour, on the other.

In 1838 he gave a lecture, *Mands Minde*, where he *first* expressed his admiration and fear of the mighty powers of industry and of the steam engines at the shipbuilding yard of Copenhagen as manifestations of the spiritual genius of the Nordic, Anglo-Saxon, mind and *later* rejected the *industrial system* as such because it:

... makes people in the thousands, tall and small alike, to be nothing but mere details, mere appendices to the machinery which is the main cause and fundamental power, so that even Englishmen – who never take the time to think of anything else but making everything they have into money – look with hidden terror on every new invention and colossal application of the mechanical basic powers which in time will expel all the former craftsmen and make them mere tools in the hands of the master-machinist, thoughtless slaves in the yard of the factory owner. ... (England makes a massive blunder) by sacrificing men in their hundred-thousands to machinery.[7]

In spite of such strong words Grundtvig was not against machinery as such. What he wanted was a re-direction of the immense potentiality of industry away from greedy exploitation, and towards the promotion of the general welfare.

Man as a social and Christian being

Grundtvig was a true Christian of the Lutheran confession. In Northern Europe and Denmark in particular the church and state had been closely related since the 16th century, in a state-church. In spite of this Grundtvig believed and openly argued that the state and the world of public politics should not intervene in spiritual matters of faith and, *vice versa*, that the church should not interfere with matters of the state.

On October, 10th, 1847, Grundtvig summarized his views on the question of state, people, church, and faith in an article much quoted later, *Folkelighed og Christendom* ("Folkelighed" and Christianity).[8] He denounced the widespread assumption that he was a party leader and declared that he knew nothing of a "Grundtvigian" party as such – therefore his following remarks were just his own. As the result of the preaching of the first missionaries of the 9th century, Ansgar and his followers, Christianity had

---

7.   Wåhlin (1990), p. 278.
8.   In *Dansk Kirketidende*, No. 107, 17/10 1847, cf. N.F.S. Grundtvig, *Værker i Udvalg*, vol. V, pp. 243-251.

been freely accepted by the Danes; and so it had been ever since in Denmark. No one was forced to be a Christian. Freedom in spiritual matters as well as "folkelighed" were essential for the right functioning of Christianity. Where they do not exist in any society Christianity must work for the establishment of those two essentials. For Grundtvig it was a matter of a deep personal choice to be a Christian and the choice could only be decided for, "when human nature and Christianity meet in a living way in a free inter-action". The "uprising of 'folkelighed'" has to come first before it is possible to speak to "the people (folket) about living Christianity", i.e.,: "a people (folk) has to be livingly aware of itself [as a people] just as a human being must be aware of himself [as human]" before it is of any use to talk about the "means of salvation" and "about what elevates man above beast" which is "the word by which the spiritual world is opened to us".

In Grundtvig's mind, Christianity could only be a part of real life when spoken in the language of the feelings and the heart, the mother-tongue. It was one of the finest achievements of the Reformation to bring the mother-tongue into the daily life of the church. Parallel to that, history has to be communicated in the mother-tongue where the "living conditions [i.e., not structural (dead), but genetic, live connections] of the past and today" are present in the heartfelt relationship between children and parents and where a "folkelig" word in the mother-tongue first has turned the hearts of the children to the fathers [both actual fathers and remote forefathers]".

In conclusion Grundtvig in this paper of 1847 argued for a *Folke-Skole* (a school for the people, the "folk") which was to be exclusively Danish, as opposed to the latinized grammar schools, because "first we have to be Danish – as all people have first to be truly alive – before it is of any use to talk to them either about temporal or eternal life".

People, objectively and subjectively – a true "Folk"
To understand Grundtvig's concept of politics and nationalism we have to deal with his concept of people, language, country (land), history, and culture. He operates with four *objective* or "outer" elements of a true people, a "Folk":

1) a common land – (so the Jews of his time were not a people)
2) a common language – (the mother-tongue, not a lingua franca)
3) a common history and forefathers – (these three then make: fatherland)
4) a common culture – (old ballads, folkdances, etc., close to "2").

In listing those four objective elements he had much in common with many of the cultural elite of Europe of his days who, like him, were influenced by Romanticism. What makes him different was his emphasis on the fact that the objective elements had to be supplemented with some, even more important, subjective or "inner" elements:

a) the person decides for himself to be part of that specific people or "folk";

b) the person should not just pay lip-service to the cause of his chosen people; he should act according to the general welfare of that people;

c) in so acting according to his choice, he should not be driven by fear or by hate of outsiders or strangers, but by love for his fellow men including everyone of that people as being equal in human value (but not necessarily equal in trade or in social influence): young and old, man and woman.

A true *nation* consists of a true *people* or "folk" in both the objective and subjective understanding of the words. So to be a "true people" in a Grundtvigian way involves such strong ethical and moral commandments that the words "people" and "popular" become too vague and merely descriptive. That is why we need to use the old Nordic and Anglo-Saxon word "folk" again, with the related terms "folkelig" and "folkelighed", seeing these as words with a strong positive and affirmative meaning. The words "commoner" and "people" in Grundtvig's days were looked down on by the elite – just as that elite looked down on the people they described as such. Grundtvig and his followers fought a long-lasting cultural battle to elevate the words, "folk", "folkelig", and "folkelighed", giving them strong positive connotations; and they were successful in that. Today in most Danish circles it is a compliment to be described as truly "folkelig" as opposed to being a demagogue or too intellectual.

The "true folk" in Grundtvig's understanding was made up of the peasant-farmer and the solid craftsman and everybody who in earnest joined in with their cause and worked for the general welfare of the people. The elite might become part of the "folk" by choice and by solid work for the general welfare – the de-humanized working men of the factories and in the countryside had to be raised by better living conditions and basic education to become true parts of the "folk".

The combined objective and subjective qualities of the "folk" were not just a categorization. They must be understood as implying a basic quality and commandment of social and national life. Love of the fatherland and of the mother-tongue was essential. The mother-tongue had two sides: it was the language of *the heart* by which the person at his deepest became truly human and, at the same time, it stood for the feminine side of human character – and by that doubleness the divine reached man. Therefore language for Grundtvig may be the dearest of all the objective categories.[9]

Christianity, for Grundtvig, was never forgotten. He had the conviction that a true people had to be or would become a Christian people by following the moral and ethical principles of being a "true folk".

True "folkelighed" and chauvinism

Grundtvig sometimes used the term nationalism; but most frequently he used instead some combinations of the word "folk", or "love of the fatherland", or "love of the mother tongue" to make it clear that the moral and ethical foundations of his nationalism meant that other nationalities (for instance the Germans) had the same fundamental claim to be respected in their similar rights. Again and again in writings and speeches he attacked, often violently, the Roman church and the German leadership and German intellectuals for what he saw as their hidden or open expansionism and their suppression of the rights of other peoples or nations to choose to be themselves, and not to be catholics or Germans.

From around 1840 and from then onwards patriotic sentiments mixed with linguistic and historical arguments were adopted by the policy makers of Prussia (as Pan-Germanism), Russia (as Pan-Slavism), and France (in cultural, economic and political expansion); and by speaking accordingly to the popular emotions of the people, the policy-makers of these states made those arguments a part of their foreign policy. Because of that European mixture of chauvinism and expansionism – which is still so obvious today – many both in Denmark and abroad misunderstood the basic ethical and moral foundations and implications of Grundtvig's nationalism and his deep conviction of the moral obligations involved in being part of a true "folk".

King and people – a social contract

In his *Mands Minde* lectures 1838 Grundtvig reminded his listeners that absolutism in 1660/61 was introduced into Denmark as a social contract between the king and the whole people and that it had worked in that way up to Grundtvig's time. The Danish kings never became tyrants (*Rex Tyrannus*), but proved to be responsible rulers with the general welfare of the people and just government as their main objectives (*Rex Justus*). The introduction of the advisory assemblies of the realm (called the *estates*)

---

9. *vide* Rerup: *"Mother-tongue is that string of roses ..."*

meant to Grundtvig that the voice of the people along with the king's hand (the action of government) came into focus in public matters. So to Grundtvig those advisory assemblies were just a prolongation of an ancient historical co-operation between king and people in Denmark.

The international and national turbulence of February-March 1848 created a new situation where parliamentary, representative democracy came into focus. As a citizen and politician Grundtvig at once accepted the new situation and the obligation to take part in this decisive social process and influence it however and wherever he could.

V. Final remarks

Parallel to *how* the congregation in worship become one voice and in some way one soul in the common singing of the hymns, so the individuals among the people could become united, express one public spirit, in the common singing of popular national songs *as long as* the texts were not just superficial or chauvinistic. Other poets and politicians of his day shared Grundtvig's conviction of the socially convincing power of popular songs; but no one in Denmark wrote so many popular national, historical and political songs of lasting value as he did. A great responsibility then lay on him in the task of writing good popular songs. Of course it took time for the Danish public to become a well singing unison choir at public meetings; but eventually common singing became widespread and popular. The folk high-schools and the army were especially active agents in that process, but soon the secondary schools followed and became perhaps the most influential institution in establishing a broadly accepted core of national songs well known for generations – at least up to about 1970. The songbook of the folk high-schools is now more than 100 years old. It is constantly re-edited and sold in 100,000's of copies.

Grundtvig's suggestion in 1831 of a division of Slesvig following linguistic lines and national borders, a division decided upon by all the people by a referendum was one of his most far-sighted suggestions. In a way in this early paper he included most of the essentials of his later philosophy of people, language, education, self-determination, respect for others, and love as a driving social force. In his writings from 1809 to 1830 he had already included the *objective* elements of the being of a true people, common history, land, language and culture as well as to a certain degree the *subjective* elements of *choice* of national identity, of proving this in *social actions* and of accepting *love* and not hate as the ruling social force in a sound and non-revolutionary society. Combined with his Christian understanding of man and his language as God's creations – where the spiritual and the earthly worlds meet – his ideas of *man, people* and *politics* are parts of a constantly clarifying process in which in his poetry and in his own social actions (even though in the latter he was often not successful) he is perhaps more clear, than in his prose.

To understand him we have to understand the time and the society in which he was a *citizen* and a Christian. To understand the engaged citizen Grundtvig we have to examine both his *social actions* and his *inner world* of thinking and emotions expressed in writings in *poetry* as well as in *prose*. If *politics* is about *influencing* the production and distribution of material wealth and of immaterial goods for society as a whole as well as about the *influence* of social and political thinking on the structures of society then Grundtvig was a *political being*, an active citizen, from 1809/10 and onwards with always widening fields of interest.

Bibliography

Bekker-Nielsen, T. (ed.), *Stykkevis og delt. 5 essays om Grundtvig og grundt-vigianisme* (Aarhus, 1986).

Baagø, K., "Grundtvig og den engelske liberalisme", in *Grundtvig-Studier* (Copenhagen, 1955), pp. 7-37.

Carr, W, *Schleswig-Holstein 1815-48. A Study in National Conflict* (Manchester, 1963).

Christensen, J., *Rural Denmark 1750-1980* (Copenhagen, 1983).

Grell, H., *Skaberånd og folkeånd. En undersøgelse af Grundtvigs tanker om folk og folkelighed og deres forhold til hans kristendomssyn.* (Aarhus, 1987).

Grundtvig, N.F.S., "Folkelighed og Christendom" in *Dansk Kirketidende*, no. 107, 17/10 1847, reprint in Grundtvig, N.F.S., *Værker i Udvalg*, vol. V, pp. 243-251.

Grundtvig, N.F.S., *Mands Minde 1788-1838*, Sv. Grundtvig (ed.) (Copenhagen, 1877

Grundtvig, N.F.S., *Politiske Betragtninger med Blik paa Danmark og Holsteen* (Copenhagen, 1831, parallel ed. in German).

Grundtvig, N.F.S., *Statsmæssig Oplysning - et Udkast om Samfund og Skole* (Copenhagen, 1983)

Grundtvig, N.F.S., "Tale i den Slesvigske Hjelpeforening 14/3. 1848", in *Danskeren*, I (Copenhagen, 1848), pp. 84-96; cf. Grundtvig, *Værker i Udvalg*, V, pp. 260ff.

Lornsen, U.J., *Ueber das Verfassungswerk in Schleswigholstein* (Kiel, 1830, parallel ed. in Danish).

Thorsteinsson, J., *Et Færø som Færø* (Aarhus, 1990).

Wåhlin, V., "Grundtvigs økonomiske tænkning", in *Grundtvig-studier*, (1989-90), pp. 246-303.

Wåhlin, V., "Religion, mentalitet og bevidsthedshistorie". in Wåhlin, V. (ed.), *Historien i kulturhistorien* (Aarhus, 1988, c), pp. 91-234.

Østergård, U., *Europas ansigter. Nationale stater og politiske kulturer i en ny, gammel verden* (Copenhagen, 1992 A).

Østergård, U., "What is national and ethnic identity?" in Zahle, J. (ed.) *Etnicity in Ptolemaic Egypt* (Aarhus, 1992 B); previous print: *Arbejdspapier, no. 72* (Aarhus, 1992).

The School for Life: The Basic Ideas of Grundtvig's Educational Thinking

By K.E. Bugge

Grundtvig probably never considered himself an educational thinker. It is typical that on the title page of his first major work on education he introduces himself as an "historian". It was on the basis of his historical insights that Grundtvig was convinced of his right and duty to participate in the debates of his time; nevertheless, it was as an educational thinker that he first gained international renown. All through his long life he was concerned with educational issues. The very first of his printed articles (from 1804) deals with the misery of a local country school and his last book, which was published only a few days before his death, was a selection of his educational writings.

The final clarification of Grundtvig's educational ideas takes place in the early 1830s. It is brought about by an interaction between a thorough critical review of his own thinking and external factors, such as travel impressions and current events. The radical change of outlook which Grundtvig experienced while working at his *Nordic Mythology* (1832) is important. The new elements which now entered into his educational thinking are a profound respect both for humanity and for the civic freedom which he had encountered in England. A third source of inspiration was an event in Danish political history: the first session of the Provincial Advisory Councils, which took place in 1835-36. Grundtvig was pleased with the way in which the spoken word was used in the discussions, and he described the event as "the secular resurrection of the word". In the spring of 1836 Grundtvig wrote his first major book on education: *Det Danske Fiir-Kløver* (*The Danish Four-leaved Clover*). The four leaves are king, people, country and language.

In the following years, he published a series of books on education: *Til Nordmænd om en Norsk Højskole* (*To Norsemen about a Norwegian High School*, 1837), *Skolen for Livet og Academiet i Soer* (*The School for Life and the Academy in Sorø* 1838), *Bøn og Begreb om en Dansk Højskole i Soer* (*Petition about and Concept of a Danish High School in Sorø*, 1840), and *Lykønskning til Danmark* (*Congratulations to Denmark*, 1847). Grundtvig also advocated his ideas through a number of songs, lectures and articles, the most important of which is probably the extensive treatise *Om Nordens Videnskabelige Forening*

(*On the Academic Union of Scandinavia*, 1839), where he envisages a new university jointly established by the Scandinavian countries.

The general content of Grundtvig's educational ideas are usually summarized under the following headings (1) emphasis on youth – as opposed to childhood – as the optimal period of schooling; (2) emphasis on oral teaching, in particular the inspiration to be derived from the stimulating, "spirited" lecture; (3) emphasis on the Danish-Norse cultural tradition as opposed to the classical-Latin as the best foundation for education, and finally (4) that these ideas are in some way linked to a Christian view of life. There is no denying that this characterization points to something of considerable importance. But in the light of recent Grundtvig-research we must make certain reservations concerning the fourth point.

According to Grundtvig it is important to understand that the relationship between a Christian view of life on the one side and education on the other is an open and indirect relationship. Grundtvig specifically rejects the inclusion of Christian concepts in determining the purpose of education. But that does not mean that the view that the Christian faith takes of life is completely set aside. The conviction of faith can only exist in an educational context as "an unspoken dimension". This open relationship between the work of the school and a Christian view of life is described by Grundtvig in various ways. The best-known formulation is to be found appropriately enough in the poem *Open Letter to My Children* (Aabent Brev til mine Børn) in 1839. Here he expresses the hope that the children's life here on earth may be "Well aware of the deep desires, only fulfilled by eternity's glory".

One might then ask the question of all the above four points: What is it that gathers these thoughts into a unity, into a distinctive world of ideas, which has its own specific character? What is the fundamental view that ultimately lies behind these ideas? An examination of the numerous unpublished drafts of Grundtvig's educational writings has revealed that the concept of "interaction" (vekselvirkning) plays a central role in his ideas about teaching and education. It seems appropriate therefore to direct our attention to this concept.

Of the adjectives that Grundtvig applies to "interaction", there are three that stand out: free, living and natural. Other adjectives could be mentioned, but let us dwell for a while on these, the most common. It would appear that Grundtvig applies these adjectives to two different subject-areas within the category of interaction: partly the function of interaction itself, and partly the conditions under which it functions; partly what actually happens, the actual life lived at the new school he envisages; and partly the conditions under which this can take place. Supreme importance is attached to the actual function, the actual life as it unfolds, not what all this might eventually lead to. He rarely expresses himself on this last point, and when he does so only in the vaguest of terms. For example, he can point out that it should serve "the common good".

With regard to the *freedom* of interaction, the lectures from 1838 – *Within Living Memory* (*Mands Minde*) are of particular interest. Here Grundtvig points out, for example, that it is a serious drawback of the lecture form that "no living interaction is reached between your thoughts and mine". He argues against a teaching method in which the teacher alone holds the floor:

I consider it to be cheating the service we do our audience so long as we alone speak and do not understand how to move on to a general participation and interaction through a lively conversation.

When he begins his lectures with the phrase (in Danish) "Mine Herrer", he emphasizes that he means this quite literally: "My masters". The teacher must in other words give up all his masterly ways and put on the form of a servant, as he says with an indirect reference to Phil 2:7. These ideas are later elaborated in his description of the great joint-Scandinavian high school "where everything that strongly attracts or awakes the spirit would be in the form of a constant brisk interaction in the well-regulated conversation".

So much for the function of interaction when it is characterized by freedom. With regard to freedom as a condition, it must be noted first and foremost that the freedom of interaction is conditioned by the freedom from an obligation to "the other life", i.e., life in the hereafter. It was precisely this "whim", according to Grundtvig, which over the centuries had led clergymen and teachers to try to make people pious against their will. And the inevitable consequence was that they tried to turn people into something created out of their own heads. Grundtvig on the other hand maintains that the world must be taken for what it is, and all worries must be set aside about the possible consequences of education for mankind's eternal salvation. Education must be worked out exclusively for this life. It must contribute to the "clarification of human life", i.e., the clarification of the meaning and aim of human life, in Danish: "Menneskelivets Forklaring". The "clarification" (*Forklaring*) takes place within temporal life in a historical process that is progressing towards the end of time. Not until time is no longer, will the final, everlasting "clarification" of the meaning of human life occur.

Another condition for interaction is freedom from "the Roman yoke". In Grundtvig's opinion the Latin-based education of his day rested on a mistaken assumption that mankind could be transformed. Thus the Latin education contained a strong dose of the "power-sickness" that precisely is what he wanted banned from the proper sort of school. He also believed that freedom for interaction – the free interactive relationship between teacher and pupil, is conditional on the freedom from obligation to sit examinations. This well-known idea of Grundtvig's thus takes up a natural place in the category of interaction.

True interaction – or genuine reciprocal teaching – is also characterized in Grundtvig's educational writings by *life*. Both pupils and teachers must be animated, he maintains. It is above all the use of living, oral communication that characterizes a living interaction. In the school for life, education begins with oral teaching by the experienced teacher and ends in a conversation between teacher and pupil, or among the pupils themselves. Here, as Grundtvig puts it, the purpose of education is manifested in a living interaction. What he is aiming for is a school

where the living word strives to recover its all-but-lost yet inalienable rights, and where everything is worked out in a living interaction, a genuine reciprocal education...

The life of this interaction finds expression in other ways, however. Grundtvig places great emphasis on appeal to the pupils' interest, and on conversation being diverted from the abstract to the here and now and the useful. And he often underlines the importance of "cheerfulness". Grundtvig emphasizes that "happy songs" are a sign of life at the school.

Among the conditions under which life can come to characterize the interaction, the factor that will define the new education is above all the removal of the book, the traditional basis of education. Books will of course be used, but they must be put in their proper place; they should be consulted "like good friends in reserve". We must fight the superstition that life springs out of books and that books can transform people. Living interaction presupposes that "when they talk to the people scholars can and will forget their books in order to concentrate on life".

Another important assumption for interaction is the close link with folk-culture in the past and the present. Education must be historical and poetical. With the aid of the poetry, mythology, and history of the nation, it must guide the young so that they can hear the voice of the past disclosing the basic conditions of life. In the myths, the poets employed poetic imagery to achieve the expression of this deep recognition. And history is not a chance accumulation of events, but at its deepest level it is an account of the gradual clarification of this recognition. History is "life-experience in its widest perspective". Education, however, also links up with folk-culture in the present. Education must desire "the welfare of the country and the general good". And so the following subjects should also be studied at the Folk High School: "folk-character, the Constitution, the fatherland in all respects ... in brief, what is living, common and general". A well-known expression of Grundtvig's efforts to put down the roots of education in the present life of the people is to be found in his idea that "the houses of clever and enterprising citizens could become schools that were far preferable to Latin schools". But he does not regard this home education as a goal in itself. It too has a further aim – towards the general good. Its main perspective is "Mankind in general and society in particular".

Lastly, interaction is characterized by *naturalness*. In Grundtvig's ideas for a "natural" education two lines of thought converge: partly the demand that education should "help" and develop the existing "character" or "nature" in a people and in individuals; partly the demand that education should respect a definite "order in nature".

Grundtvig's insistence that youth is the optimal period of schooling is closely bound up with his belief as to what is characteristic of the various stages in human development. The "nature" of youth, according to Grundtvig, is that the emotions are aroused. Within the framework of a natural interaction this awakening enters into a free relationship with the older, more experienced generation, whose "nature" is experience and reflection. Thus an interaction arises between "Light", in this context: experience and reflection, and "Life", which here designates the heart's emotions or the "bright heads and fiery, burning nature" of youth.

The two lines of thought that meet in Grundtvig's idea of natural education thus express both a respect for human life as it is lived and an awareness that human development is promoted in the confrontation with an external influence. What enables these two lines of thought to be fruitfully contained in one and the same concept is the fact that they are included in the category of interaction.

In the following section we shall consider the relevance of these ideas to current educational thinking.

The Threefold challenge

The word "relevance" raises some difficulties, which we will have to deal with. What does the word "relevance" mean? The answers may be reduced to two basic views:

The traditional view is that relevance means repetition. The idea is that words, sentences, theories and ideas from earlier times are relevant today, because they can and shall be repeated. The implication of this view is that such a repetition would have a beneficial, positive influence on current affairs.

The alternative view is that relevance means challenge. The basic idea is here that uncritical, literal repetition of words, sentences, theories and ideas from earlier times is not possible and not desirable. An additional deduction is that a transplantation of mutual basic concerns somehow is possible. This alternative view, according to which relevance is challenge, is the only way in which we can speak truthfully and realistically about the relevance of historical persons' ideas – including Grundtvig's own. It is as challenge that these ideas are relevant today.

A mere repetition of Grundtvig's words and ideas would be an easy and irresponsible way of dealing with the problems of our time. The responsibility of every new generation is to make a fresh beginning. There are no shortcuts. Our task cannot, however, be defined as a beginning out of a void, out of nothing, starting from zero. Our situation is much more complex. Our task is to make a fresh beginning in the face of three types of challenges: 1. The challenges from our fellowmen, who are there, whether we like it or not – and a great many of whom we shall never agree with on fundamental issues. 2. The challenges of the future, which are less manageable, less predictable and more dangerous than ever before. 3. The challenges arising from our historical heritage. We all have a history, a past, even though we might prefer to be totally independent individuals. We all have a history that is our own, and from which arises a number of challenges. It is in this context that it is possible to speak meaningfully about the relevance of Grundtvig for today.

Among the basic concerns in Grundtvig's writings, which in my opinion are relevant, i.e., challenging today, we shall concentrate on three:

A. Grundtvig's ideas of freedom and responsibility, in other words of emancipation and commitment.

B. Grundtvig's ideas of mutuality, that is his view of what he calls "living interaction" compared to dialogue and dialectics.

C. Grundtvig's ideas of cultural identity.

A. Freedom and Responsibility

Grundtvig grew up in a nation politically governed by an absolute monarchy. For a great many years Grundtvig was politically conservative and sympathized wholeheartedly with the paternalistic regime of the absolute monarch, King Frederik VI. Grundtvig's three visits to England in 1829-31 became, however, a turning point in his political views. Although through his extensive reading he had become acquainted with the then modern ideas of Adam Smith, before he went to England, he now saw these ideas put into practice. And what he saw filled him with admiration. "Liberty is the element of the Spirit", he wrote. From then on, Grundtvig steadfastly advocated freedom in all spheres of life, in church, in school and in society.

It is, however, characteristic of Grundtvig's independent way of thinking that he did not accept the tenets of liberalism uncritically. He remembered well the consequences which the idea of unfettered freedom had produced in France during and after the great revolution of 1789. As a positive alternative to the revolutionary French conception of freedom, and as an alternative to the British economic theory of liberalism, Grundtvig advocated what he called "a Nordic concept of freedom". Concerning this concept he writes:

I know from my own personal experience that it can be very difficult indeed ... to be satisfied with the amount of freedom that leaves some freedom also to my neighbour.

The liberty that Grundtvig advocated is therefore a liberty which is actively constrained by responsibility towards one's fellowman. Liberty is closely knit together with a commitment to care for the well-being of other people. Against the extreme liberal thesis: That free competition – cost it what it may – is in the long run beneficial to society, Grundtvig asserts that strife and competition are not in themselves a positive symptom of life. They are, on the contrary, a sign warning us that life is in danger! He who wishes to be free must therefore let his fellowman be free also. Otherwise freedom becomes a heavy yoke to carry.

From such ideas a challenge arises to the much debated idea of emancipation in our own days. We are challenged to rethink this concept over and over again. We are challenged to furnish emancipation with an ethical dimension. By so doing we could perhaps eliminate the harsh and inhuman consequences ensuing from situations where emancipation is forced upon people – for instance in the third world – who either do not want our freedom, or who have other ideas of its implications. Grundtvig's ideas on freedom thus contain a critical note well worth listening to.

B. Interaction in Education

As demonstrated above "interaction" is a key concept in Grundtvig's writings. Concerning the relevance of these ideas today, it would be easy to see that many of the details of Grundtvig's educational thinking challenge much of what is going on in Western educational practice today.

This challenge to details is of course important. But even more important is that we do not lose sight of the main structure. Therefore at this point we must outline the difference between Grundtvig's idea of interaction on the one hand, and dialogue and dialectics on the other hand. Grundtvig himself does not carry through such a comparison. However, I am convinced that if he were asked to do so, he would immediately point to the historical perspective of his thinking. His thoughts on educational interaction are embedded in an overall historical frame of reference. This needs some explanation.

Dialogue can very well be a static concept in so far as it does not entail any suggestion as to what goes before or what comes after the dialogue. The mutuality of the dialogue in itself is often considered to be of prime importance.

Dialectics, on the other hand, is a concept involving not only the present, but also past and future in a perspective of development. Dialectics, however, is essentially a logical concept. Applied to human life, every logic – and also dialectical logic – sometimes offers excellent interpretations, and sometimes it does not. And if not, then so much the worse for the facts of human life, which must then be shaped and reconstructed in order to fit the logic! In such instances, logic can easily turn out to be tyrannical with respect to life.

On the basis of his historical way of thinking, Grundtvig offers another, third, solution. Educational interaction is according to Grundtvig a way in which human beings gradually gain more and more insight into the meaning of life. In this connection he speaks about education contributing to "the clarification of human life". Grundtvig's concept of interaction, therefore, offers a challenge, a critical note, to our concepts of dialogue and dialectics. Being embedded in an overall historical perspective, which reaches from the beginning of time to the end of the world, Grundtvig's concept of educational interaction adds a development perspective to dialogue, and it adds a human perspective to the logic of dialectics. That being so, Grundtvig's ideas of interaction in education are very relevant to our educational debate today.

C. Cultural Identity

Apart from "interaction", two other concepts frequently occur in Grundtvig's educational writings. Those concepts are "folkelig" and "historical-poetical". We shall consider these terms in that order.

As many translators of Grundtvig's writings have experienced, the translation of the word "folkelig" is very difficult – if not impossible! It is an adjective referring to the noun "folk", which means a people, understood in its totality. It is a term including all the inhabitants of a nation and the togetherness of this nation in history and in the present situation. The adjective "folkelig" therefore means: pertaining to that people, and even more: expressing the identity of that people. Such expressions of identity are to be found in the totality of its culture, but are concentrated in its history, its myths and its lasting values.

"Folkelig" therefore does not mean: popular, in the sense of what the people like, or what appeals to their tastes. Understood in that way, the term would become selective. It would divide the people according to individual tastes and wants. The words "folk" and "folkelig" contain, on the contrary, a strong element of fate. The terms point to historical facts, which are there, whether people like it or not. In that sense all men and women are born into a people, are born into an existing tradition. This is not a matter of choice.

According to Grundtvig, education should be "folkelig" in order to be true to life. Above, when we dealt with educational interaction, we already met a series of suggestions from Grundtvig concerning the way in which such a new type of education could function, and concerning the preconditions necessary. Among these suggestions we have several times met a reference to the history of the people. We shall now see how this reference is combined with a reference to the ancient myths of the people.

The new education Grundtvig has in mind, he not only calls "folkelig". He also calls it "historical-poetical". This means that what is characteristic of a people reveals itself in the long and winding history of that particular people, in the decisions made, and in the way in which it responded to challenges; the identity of a people also expresses itself in the myths of that people. In these myths the people have expressed their fundamental ideas concerning the meaning of human life, in short all their fundamental values. In order to be "folkelig", in order to be truly pertaining to the people, in order to be in accordance with its particular identity, education must also therefore be mythological. It is no coincidence that the ancient Nordic myths have for generations been a favourite educational theme at the Danish Folk High Schools.

Concerning the relevance of these ideas, I can do no better in conclusion than quote some passages of a speech held at the UNESCO conference in Belgrade (1980). The speech was given by Mr. M'Bow, who according to the conference report said:

Cultural identity is universally present today ... A culture makes itself seen, heard and understood through the intermediary of all the works which express it ... in particular (in) its myths. (One must) identify its customs, become acquainted with its plastic arts and literature, study its philosophers, contemplate its monuments and listen to its music. The sum total of the ways in which a culture thus expresses itself to the rest of the world, each of them keys to unlock its mystery, may be grouped together under the heading of the cultural heritage ... In the face of the constraints or pressures bearing on a community from the outside, culture is more and more frequently proving to be the mainspring of its truthfulness to itself. Inside the community it sets against the centrifugal forces of economics or politics its basic integrating power; and to the great variety of trends towards technical specialization and the compartmentalization of individual activities, it opposes a feeling for the fullness of the meanings of life ... The irreducible uniqueness of a people's cultural identity is ... the hallmark of the unique contribution by that people to the universal cultural heritage.

In his stand against all alienating forces of culture, and in his positive assertion of the importance of concentration on cultural identity – especially in education – Mr. M'Bow very much agrees with Grundtvig, of whom he may perhaps never have heard. And this congeniality between the two is the best proof of the relevance of Grundtvig's educational ideas in our time, both in the Western World and in the Third World.

Bibliography

Borish, S.M., *The Land of the Living. The Danish Folk High Schools and Denmark's Non-violent Path to Modernization* (Grass Valley, California, 1991).

Bugge, K.E., (ed.), *Grundtvigs skoleverden i tekster og udkast*, I-II, (Copenhagen, 1968).

Bugge, K.E., *Skolen for livet. Studier over N.F.S. Grundtvigs pædagogiske tanker* (Copenhagen, 1965).

Bugge, K.E., "Grundtvig, Nicolaj Frederik Severin 1783-1872", in *International Biography of Adult Education*, eds. Thomas, J.E., and Elsey, B. (Nottingham, 1985).

Davies, N., *Education for Life. A Danish Pioneer* (London, 1931).

Grundtvig, N.F.S., *Statsmæssig Oplysning*, edited by Bugge, K.E. and Nielsen, V. (Copenhagen, 1983).

Grundtvig, N.F.S., *To Dialoger om Højskolen*, edited by Christensen, D. (Copenhagen, 1983).

Grundtvig, S.,(ed.), Mands Minde 1788-1838. Foredrag over det sidste halve Aarhundredes Historie, holdte 1838 af Grundtvig, N.F.S. (Copenhagen, 1877).

Koch, H., *Grundtvig* (Yellow Springs, Ohio, 1952).

Lindhardt, P.G., *Grundtvig. An Introduction* (London, 1951).

Rørdam, T.,*The Danish Folk High Schools* (Copenhagen, 1980).

Stewart, D.W., *Adult Learning in America* (Malabar, Florida, 1978), pp. 115-130.

Thaning, K., *N.F.S. Grundtvig* (Copenhagen, 1980).

The Danish Folk High School

By Hans Henningsen

The Folk High Schools in Denmark began to spring up in different places throughout the country from the middle of the 1840s, and especially after the 1864 war with Germany. But none of the schools were simply the implementation of Grundtvig's thoughts. According to him only one *big* institution was needed. This should have been situated at Sorø, a town in the middle of Zealand. Grundtvig, therefore, talks about "The School at Soer". This school was in fact never realized. But this does not mean, that the Folk High School movement in Denmark was not "grundtvigian". Quite the contrary is true, but the relation between Grundtvig's thinking and the practical impact of his ideas on Danish society is a complicated one.

First of all a distinction must be made between the concept of a Folk High School institution, as it is to be found in Grundtvig's writings from the 1830s onward, and on the other hand his ideas of man and history, which developed much earlier. These ideas became fundamental to the grundtvigian concept of "life's enlightenment", which unlike Grundtvig's idea of the institution itself were widely adopted by the Folk High School movement. Furthermore, this influence was not limited to the Folk High Schools, but spread all over the society.[1] The way of thinking both in Danish education and politics is quite unintelligible without a knowledge of Grundtvig. Even today no one can fully understand what is happening in Denmark without some reference to Grundtvig.[2]

Few if any have had such a radical and wide-ranging influence on an entire society. The Danish language is also deeply influenced by Grundtvig. Thus in Danish the concept of enlightenment goes far beyond the views normally held in the European tradition. According to Grundtvig enlightenment means first and foremost enlightenment for life.

Enlightenment for Life

Behind Grundtvig's ideas for the setting up of the school at Sorø there lay first and foremost considerations determined by current political develop-

1. Chr. Thodberg & A. Pontoppidan Thyssen (eds.), *N.F.S. Grundtvig, Tradition and Renewal* (Copenhagen, 1983), esp. chapter III.
2. Kaj Thaning, *N.F.S. Grundtvig* (Copenhagen, 1972), p. 160.

ments. But at the same time the school at Sorø was envisaged as more than just a school for political education. Another assumption was Grundtvig's idea of a common education for life, based on his views of man and reality which he had fully developed long before that time, primarily in the so called "Danne-Virke period", about 1816-19.[3]

Through his clash with Romantic and Idealistic philosophy Grundtvig came to an understanding of language – or "the word" as he preferred to call it – which in reality became the foundation for his entire view of society and culture. He perceived that language is not just an outer clothing in which a world of higher concepts is carried, a world of reason or ideas existing before the word or behind the word in the Idealistic sense. For him, the world of the spirit is identical with the world of language. Word and thought are one. The word, not the abstract thought or the pure reason, but the speech of man makes him what he is. Man is a "word-user". "The word" is the hallmark of people, differentiating them from animals as well as from stones. And "the word" always means the spoken word, which is the only "living word".

With this in mind it was possible for Grundtvig to take up the cudgels against, what he calls, the "cold" and "self-willed" reason of the Rationalists – "those transparently enlightened people" who would "divide light from life". Cold intellectualism and individualism had characterised the ideas of the French revolution far too much, and in this Grundtvig saw the deeper cause of its tragic course. But he also found the same features in the political currents that reached Denmark from the south throughout the 1830s and 1840s. For him, this necessitated an enlightenment and an education that was all the more comprehensive and penetrating. True enlightenment brings not only light but also warmth. With such formulations Grundtvig distanced himself from the rationalism of the time, though this does not automatically make him an "irrationalist". But on three crucial issues he disagreed with the rationalists.

First, Grundtvig maintained that there are contradictions and opposing forces in life that cannot be resolved by any rational thought-system. They can only find expression in poetry – in myth, which unlike ideology demands the freedom of contradiction and thus allows for a deeper understanding. If we wish to understand life and history, we cannot be satisfied with building on reason or science; we must take as our starting-point the word in its broadest sense.

Secondly, he realised that the autonomous subject of reason or science is a hugely problematic starting-point in the case of politics and popular

---

3. *Danne-Virke* was a periodical written and published by Grundtvig.

education, because he maintained it inevitably leads to egoism and individualism, traits which in his opinion were abundantly in evidence in his
time. Grundtvig himself was incapable of thinking individualistically.
Reality everywhere consists of relations. Freedom must therefore always
rest on reciprocity, he believed. Whoever would be free must also grant his
neighbour freedom. Neither individuals nor social classes can liberate
themselves at the expense of others without freedom being lost in the end.

Thirdly, Grundtvig had a far more comprehensive idea of what is
possible and meaningful to include in a conversation. Normally reason and
feeling are regarded as phenomena that must be kept apart from one
another in regard to education. Grundtvig maintained the opposite. All
living knowledge or knowledge about life is nothing other than a feeling
within us that comes to light and thus itself becomes clear, as he says in
The School for Life and the Academy at Soer.[4] At the deepest level, the old
proverb that love is blind is untrue. On the contrary, love brings sight: "It
becomes the kingdom of light where it streams in", he wrote in a poem that
also contains the famous lines: "And the man has never lived who has
understood anything without first loving it". All true enlightenment is
gentle and soft so that it pleases our heart.

The fact that Grundtvig dared in this way to acknowledge feeling, even
after his break with Romanticism, is bound up with his understanding of
language. For there are clear and unmistakable words for feeling, the
"words of the heart", that is, the words for all that we as humans are
linked to in our heart. To call forth feeling in order to reflect on it is the
purpose of the "historical-poetic" education at the Folk High School, an
education that could take the form of conversation, story-telling, poetry or
song.

Thus it was not just because ordinary people could only speak Danish
and not Latin or some other language that everything should take place in
the mother-tongue at the Folk High School. There was also a deeper reason.
For true education for life can only take place in the mother-tongue, since
"only within it does the heart move freely". Only in the language of the
heart can history be told, if it is to be more than just a recitation of dead
facts. Only through the power of the mother-tongue can a living link exist
between generations.

When Grundtvig ventures to call the mother-tongue a "word of
power",[5] it is precisely because the native language alone offers access to

4.   *A Grundtvig Anthology* (1984), pp. 66-82.
5.   "Skolen for Livet og Academiet i Soer", in K.E. Bugge, *Grundtvigs skoleverden i
     tekster og udkast* (Copenhagen, 1968).

some of the sources of life that makes it stronger than all other forms of
language or conceptual devices. There is therefore a double reason why
conversation at the Folk High School should not merely be a general
discussion but a conversation in the mother-tongue. This is partly because
the mother-tongue – the language of the people – is the only language that
unites feeling and reason, and partly because it contains a knowledge of
life. The language of the people has grown out of life, and it has absorbed
into itself both the history and the nature of the country and the people.

This view is reflected in Grundtvig's vision of the Folk High School at
Sorø. The subjects there were to be not only politics, constitutional questions and commercial matters, but also – above all – history, literature and
poetry, and Danish folk songs.

The trips to England

Grundtvig's visits to England between 1829 and 1831 proved to be of crucial importance for his later development and for his educational thinking.[6]

In England Grundtvig experienced a society that in nearly every respect
differed from the stagnant, agrarian Denmark under its absolute monarch
which he already knew. In England he saw the modern "machine system"
at work, an experience that both fascinated and frightened him. Grundtvig
did not close his eyes to the social side effects of industrialisation, describing them in terms that yield nothing to other writers like Marx or Dickens.
But in England he also felt the presence of a living "public spirit" that
could not fail to impress him. He was convinced that as long as a people
possesses such a power, it will also know how to recognise and correct its
own faults.

In England Grundtvig made one of his most important discoveries,
namely the discovery of the present. Admittedly, he still insisted that
history is above all the source for the enlightenment of man, but his
attention to history now turned to the present, as well as to the future – to
the possibilities and tasks that lay ahead. Grundtvig had become conscious
of himself as a modern man. From now on, this took the form of a living
concern for what was happening in the present. He rejected his old love of
the past and openly declared that recent history is the most important.[7]

In England Grundtvig also discovered "that the world exists outside our
mind", as he put it. He had become a realist once and for all, and had
learned with the English "to take life as it is". Life is worthwhile in itself,

6.   "Within Living Memory", in *A Grundtvig Anthology*, pp. 104-21.
7.   See e.g. ibid., p. 95.

irrespective of what one thinks of it or about it. Life is meaningful before any religious or philosophical interpretation is made. All such interpretations are interpretations of what already means something.

Grundtvig now realised that unless there is a universally available enlightenment of life that is given with life itself, then no further enlightenment will be possible, Christian or otherwise. The preconditions for understanding will be lacking. Any talk of love will pass by the person who does not know beforehand what love is. The same could be said of truth.

But both love and truth are universal phenomena in the everyday life of man and not narrowly linked to particular religions or philosophies of life.

On this basis, Grundtvig was able to formulate the often-quoted expression: "First a Man, then a Christian", which from now on became the leitmotif of all that he thought and wrote. This involved among other things a change in his view of the Church, a new understanding of the relationship between culture and Christianity, and a shift in his attitude towards history. Grundtvig had by now become the direct opposite of the Bible-based Christian zealot he had been some years previously.[8]

The England experiences released in Grundtvig an enormous productivity in various fields, including a rewriting of his *World History* and a new *Norse Mythology* (1832), which was a completely new work rather than a revision of the 1808 edition. In the introduction, we find newly-won insights and the resultant view of popular education and science. Over the next 15 years, work after work on these subjects poured out from Grundtvig's study. He used every available opportunity to advocate the establishment of his High School for the people.

The Folk High School at Sorø

In 1831 the King had ordered the introduction of consultative assemblies of the Estates of the Realm, and four years later the first of these began its work. Grundtvig thought that the ordinary people should be equipped as soon as possible, to be able to work on an equal footing with the upper classes and the civil service. It was not enough merely to proclaim the opportunity for the people to make their influence felt; was the proclamation practicable? To make it so, there was a desperate need for a school of higher learning for a people's education, social and political, in particular for intelligent young people from all social levels. This breadth would serve to promote a "living interaction" ("levende vekselvirkning") among teachers and students. The best definition of "people's education" was to

8. See especially Thaning, cf. note 2.

ask what members of such a people's state council would need in order to fulfill their duties in a mature and responsible way. They must be "of the people", i.e., know the people, its nature and its thought, its history and its language – not least its poetry. For all that is new makes its presence felt first in poetry. They must be strengthened in their mothertongue, be able to express themselves orally with vigour and ease. They must be well-informed on the country's situation, have a feeling for something beyond their own advantage, and know what best serves the welfare of society.

Not only the members of the people's council but also the civil servants would benefit from such a Folk High School, where they could come into a living interaction with a large number of their contemporaries who only spoke ordinary Danish and had no Latin, the language of the professional. In this way they would learn far more about their country than they could find in books. There were enough educational institutions already, said Grundtvig, and adding to them would only increase, not reduce, the need for a people's High School, for, as Grundtvig puts it, the great stumbling-block on the school-path to understanding life is that pursuing the single entity we forget the whole, and pursuing the separate entity we forget the common good. Increasingly, he maintained, light is being cut off from life, and thus all living bonds are being dissolved, the mother-tongue is being warped, and a childish self-conceit is being cultivated, i.e., a cold, merely intellectual, reason.

The same education that was demanded of a politician or a civil servant must also be available to others. On this Grundtvig had no doubts. Once the education of the people had begun, it would spread in ever-widening circles. Then we would meet it even in the cottages on the moors, and the High School would be in the very centre as the great focus in which all the rays are gathered, only to return with renewed strength to enlighten life and clarify sight in every corner of the land.

Grundtvig did not want any examinations at the people's High School. What is learned for an exam or to earn one's daily bread is soon forgotten he maintained. But what is learned for pleasure is never forgotten, and one tries to pass it on.

The national and the international

The word folkelig ("of the people") appears often in Grundtvig. He prefers for example "people's education" to "popular education". Grundtvig did not always expressed himself succinctly and unambiguously on the subject of "folkelig", but in the context of his ideas as a whole there can be no doubt that the central content is to be found in the words "interaction", "conversation", "mother-tongue", and "enlightenment for life".

In the wake of Romanticism, a stream of German literature reached Denmark on "Volksthümlichkeit" and "Volksthum", terms which Grundtvig had been interested in but not uncritical of. He accepted in particular the ideas championed first and foremost by Herder about language as the central expression of the spirit in a people and of interaction between the peoples. On the other hand, he was unsure what the Germans meant by their use of the word "spirit", when they talked about the "spirit of the people", "Volksgeist". This can clearly be seen both in the *World Chronicle* of 1817 and in articles in the periodical *Danne-Virke*. If "spirit" was only to be understood as an expression of the character of a people – its distinctive feature or its cultural stamp – then Grundtvig had to reject it. For him spirit was always synonymous with a greater endeavour than the mere cultivation of national, ethnic or cultural character.

For Grundtvig was anything but a nationalist, however often he was misunderstood on this point. He was a universalist. Three times he wrote the history of mankind, but never the history of Denmark alone. He thought in terms of universal history. Admittedly the Folk High School was to be Danish, but not in contrast to anything else.

Grundtvig recognised nationality, even after having rejected Romanticism, because, according to his view, mankind only exists in the form of specific peoples, and language only as different languages. Only through the people's language, which unites reason and feeling, is education for life possible. But the national and the international were for Grundtvig two sides of the same coin:

The more strongly and boldly any people protects its freedom and independence, its mother country and its mother-tongue, the more fruitfully human life develops in every direction, and the more favourable, the more happy and the more fertile is the interaction between the peoples of the Earth and the truer and clearer is the enlightenment of the whole of human life. Just as it is true for individuals – the more freely they can follow their inclinations in the service of the life of the people without upsetting one another, tread their own path and use their strengths and abilities to the full, the more the life of the people will blossom in its orbit for the common good.[9]

Statements such as these are not the result of a liberal influence picked up in England. They are rather, a rejection of rationalism's false belief in the existence of a universal, supra-historical, reason, and in the possibility of a supra-historical language. To Grundtvig all reason and enlightenment are linked to the word. That is, to the languages of the peoples in all their diversity.

9. *US*, vol. X, pp. 53f.

However, Grundtvig did not draw the conclusion that there is therefore
no universal human history or common human experiences. On the contrary, he assumed the existence of such experiences, with the path to them
passing through the language of the peoples, their poetry and their
literature, as they are found in the various languages. He likewise took for
granted the possibility of a fruitful interaction between peoples. A people's
common humanity and its specific characteristics are woven together in the
people's nature, and the two are difficult to separate from one another. The
element of common humanity will always take on a specific cultural form.

Grundtvig presented his understanding of these matters as a liberation;
for in this world, he says, considering how little one beech leaf resembles
another and considering how much one spoils two horses of different tem-
peraments by treating them the same way, it is the wisdom of the mad-
house to want to make every person, society or culture alike.[10]

People's education and science

In the 1830s Grundtvig conceived the idea of a Nordic Scientific Society. He
imagined the establishment of a joint-Nordic university in Gothenburg – to
replace the four "Latin" universities in Copenhagen, Oslo, Lund and Upp-
sala. There were not enough forces for more than one proper university in
the North, but then there was also only one spirit in the North, and one
indeed that could add an important element to the scientific consideration
of human life, namely the historical perspective. The university at Gothenburg would be the framework for a new, historical, universal science,
encompassing the whole of human life.

Thus the aim was in no way to create something exclusively Nordic. On
the contrary, Grundtvig spoke of the joint-Nordic university as a "purely
human High School" – in contrast to the Danish High School at Sorø and
corresponding schools in other Nordic countries.

There ought to be a place where, independent of the practical demands
of the moment, one could dedicate oneself to pure science and the free
scientific life in an open "interaction" between scientists, both in history
and in the natural sciences, and between the scholars themselves. On the
other hand, there should also be a place in each country where everything
was in the mother-tongue and was concerned with the mother country, its
current welfare and prospects. What was needed was put into words in *On
the Nordic Scientific Society* (1839). It was nothing less than what Grundtvig
called a "divorce" between pure science and people's science. In fact,

---

10. ibid., p. 53.

Grundtvig had realised the need for this immediately after his trips to England, as is clear from the introduction to his new *Nordic Mythology* (1832). There were two giant strides which had now to be taken, he wrote. The one was a stride that could transform science from a national scourge into a national blessing. That was the stride from the grave to the living. The other was the creation of a genuine people's education.[11]

Grundtvig's ideas were revolutionary in breaking completely with the contemporary view of popular education, which had its roots in the age of enlightenment and was defined as the spreading of the results of science in popularised form. Science had become the authority, as the Church had once been. What Grundtvig wanted, however, was to bring things into the light in the context of the living interaction in society. The education of the people could no longer define itself as the herald of science but must also be regarded as an evaluating instance, out of regard for what "serves the interests of life", as Grundtvig put it. This expression must not be understood in a narrowly pragmatic sense but should be seen in the context of Grundtvig's far wider concept of education for life.

Between the two instances, science and the people's education, there should be a steady interaction, for the people's education will soon develop into a superficial polish unless scholarship keeps it in the spirit. Science likewise can easily lose its way when it is not confronted by a people's education that forces it to take the present life and moment into consideration.[12] There is an interesting vision – contained in a later manuscript – of the Folk High School as the place where new discoveries "are put through purgatory", that is, become the object of general debate and evaluation among professionals and laymen alike.

However, things turned out quite differently from Grundtvig's dream. At any rate as far as science is concerned, the unity that he presupposed has been lost to sight and few could care less. He did not really know research in the modern technical sense of the term. It is a completely different kind of science that popular education must interact with these days, something considerably closer to technology. But this, as the example shows, is in a way what is anticipated by Grundtvig himself.

The High School Movement

Grundtvig's dream of a large Folk High School in the historic town of Sorø was never fulfilled, even though he canvassed it widely in speeches and

11. *A Grundtvig Anthology*, pp. 46-48.
12. ibid., pp. 48f.

writings, for over a decade. King Christian VIII and Queen Caroline Amalie were strongly attracted to the idea. In 1847, a royal decree was issued for a so-called "realschool" (a commercially and practically orientated secondary school) in Sorø. The list of subjects reflected Grundtvig's ideas, and he himself interpreted the ordinance with the best intentions. But shortly afterwards the King died, the war broke out, and the National Liberals came to power with a quite different view of education. The "School at Soer" remained a utopia.

Instead, a variety of smaller Folk High Schools began to spring up here and there, established not by the King – as Grundtvig had imagined, but by groups of private people. The first was *Rødding Folk High School*, founded 1844 in North Slesvig. Here, in the border area, national motives played an important role and the establishment of a Folk High School was for once even supported by the National Liberals in Copenhagen. Often however it was people from the revival movements who stood behind a High School. Grundtvig had a somewhat ambivalent relationship with these movements, for although in other matters happy to take the side of the peasants and the common people, he saw tendencies in these assemblies towards sectarianism and social fragmentation, which he felt was inconsistent with his Folk High School idea and with popular enlightenment. The essence of popular enlightenment was "the living interaction", which should embrace the whole people, not only certain groups and social classes. The Folk High School should not be an instrument in the hands of only one group in society.

But the exact opposite is what happened. The Folk High Schools became associated with a particular social class – the peasantry. The almost revolutionary development of Danish agriculture during the latter half of the last century has, perhaps rightly, been attributed to the social effects of the Folk High School. And the Folk High School movement, just like the cooperative movement, is generally considered to be an important factor in the political emancipation of the peasantry. It has been said that the Folk High School movement in both respects performed miracles in Danish society in the last century.

But true as this may be, it was not as a result of any particular agricultural teaching or social criticism carried out in these schools – and this was perhaps the greatest miracle. In the Folk High Schools they always talked more about human life than social life, more about the admirable than the reprehensible, more about happiness than indignation, and at times a lot about faith and personal life.

The Folk High Schools did not really flourish until towards the end of the last century. After the disastrous loss of Slesvig and Holstein to Germany in 1864, a national revival spread throughout the land, and agriculture underwent a comprehensive renewal. Everywhere, the life of the people flourished, not just in folklore, but as a modern, consciously national life. Village halls were built, where typical Folk High School activities took place on a smaller scale. A wealth of societies and clubs were founded, and the co-operative movement arose in its various forms.

The Folk High School of today

This picture of the historical Folk High School became normative for the Folk High School concept down till today. As time went by it was generally accepted, even by those social groups which traditionally had been in direct opposition to the Folk High School. The Danish Folk High School became a national treasure, which also attracted considerable attention from abroad.

It is of course a good thing to have such a wellacknowledged tradition, but it can also be dangerous, especially if the concept of enlightenment itself becomes too tightly linked with ideas which are more ephemeral then of universal nature. Perhaps it could be said with some justification that the latest chapter in the Danish Folk High School's history shows an inclination to bask in the light of a glorious past at the expense of undertaking the necessary discussion of the Folk High School idea in present society.

The Folk High School and popular enlightenment are, for example, in more recent years often simply identified with "what comes from the grass-roots", from the people itself. This happened so uncritically, that soon any whim, as long as it was new, could be accepted as popular enlightenment, while the care for enlightenment, understood in terms of living interaction, the most important concept in Grundtvig's vision, was consequently pushed into the background. According to Grundtvig's view, the place of the Folk High School is in the middle, and what comes from the bottom and what comes from the top must both stand the test of mutual interaction and dialogue.

In about 1970, a number of marxist-socialist Folk High Schools were founded, inspired by the desire once again to place the Folk High School in the conventionally-conceived class struggle. An attempt to transform the basis of the High School's meaning for the emancipation of the peasantry in the nineteenth century, in the hope that something similar could be created in our own time. But where in the present society is that social class, which could form the basis of such a renewal? The answer to that question is that you will *not* be able to find such a basis. For a long time there has not existed a single social group, which can represent the people in the way the farmers did in a previous century, and the working class more recently. Both classes have long ago sought and attained political influence and their share in society's advantages. A completely new type of "revival" was imminent, that is the awakening of a consciousness about the environment, and this in time came to characterise both these new political schools and most of the others.

The development in the 1970's and 1980's led to a growth in the number of schools – roughly from about 70 to 100 – while the number of students remained nearly unchanged. The period was characterised by an increasing pluralism more than by a renewal of the Folk High School concept. It became more and more common to regard the Folk High Schools as means of promoting certain specific ideas, rather than something meaningful in themselves.[13]

There has been one matter, however, on which the very different kinds of Folk High Schools have been in wide agreement: the Folk High Schools are not tied to the official education and examination system. If they are supposed to be useful in a society, then that society must in return understand that the Folk High School exists as a *free* school. The Folk High School has something to give which one cannot get just as well anywhere else.

In the past few years, there have been many examples of fruitful cooperation between Folk High Schools and Trade Unions, and also with industry. The more recent extension of adult education has included the Folk High Schools to a certain degree. But a comprehensive adult education reform with real possibilities for sabbatical and *paid* leisure-time to be used for education is something that has yet to become a reality.

The need for living interaction in contemporary society

So much for the external side of the matter. What about the idea itself? As already mentioned, the growing awareness of environmental issues in the 1970s came to set its mark on the Folk High Schools. This also reflects a change of paradigm. The era of the original Folk High School and the class society with its own thought forms and educational theory has given way to a new picture of reality.

This organic movement is still going on in society. Many of the political parties have difficulty in keeping up with the process. They are like the agricultural movements and the workers movements – products of another age, when it was still possible to think almost exclusively in the categories of production, growth and distribution of goods, and when the political

---

13. On the situation today see: Steven M. Borish, *The Land of the Living. The Danish Folk High Schools and Denmark's Non-violent Path to Modernization* (Grass Valley, California, 1991).

debate had not been forced to be essentially ethical in the same degree as it is now.

But this development is irreversible. Less and less are individual countries free to impose energy policies on themselves or on their neighbours or to consider only the needs of the external environment without considering society itself and democracy as a true part of that environment. Today there arises question after question of a deeply serious nature which science alone cannot answer. One thing is sure: there will be more of these kinds of questions in the future. The Danish parliament, for example, has appointed a so-called "ethical council", to advise parliament itself on questions concerning medical technology, but above all to stimulate public attention and debate. No single science, no political party, no philosophy or religion can cope with these things alone. They must be dealt with by means of what Grundtvig called "living interaction". This is even more evident today than at the time of Grundtvig. Things must be brought out into the light, where they can be seen by everyone, within the common sphere of life, where other dimensions, such as poetry and history, are present too.

A frequent catch-phrase of our time is "value-crises". People ask: "Where should our values come from?" Or: "Are there any values at all that we can agree upon in a yet more pluralistic society?" This leads directly to the germ of Grundtvig's formulation of the problem in the Folk High School manuscripts from the 1830s. Some seem to think that the sources for values are to be found in theories, whether of a philosophical or religious nature. According to Grundtvig, however, values come from life itself – in a totally elementary meaning. And that is Human existence within a framework of meaning which is not primarily produced by language as such but is only reflected in language.

Where meaning exists, people usually know when someone has failed, and also therefore, what one should do about it. Most people are still familiar with this, for example, from their family, from their circle of friends, and perhaps also from their workplace. But it can be difficult for many people in present day society to see the connection between the universe of meaning close at hand and the world where all things have only a function. We simply cannot forget that in some parts of today's society circumstances are created in which it is difficult to find any meaning whatever. But where nothing has meaning, there can be no responsibility either.

What has meaning is known by language, the common language. And this is Grundtvig's point. The mother tongue, not any theoretical or technical language, is the source of values and ethics. The values disappear in technical languages. In our ordinary language, they are maintained with the help of poetry, literature and history, to which one must also add art. A general education without poetry was unthinkable for Grundtvig. Of art, however, he showed less understanding.

Nonetheless, Grundtvig was far ahead of his time in his ideas. Today they have to be rediscovered. This is to a large extent, what is happening in other parts of the world, and it is hardly a coincidence that today's society witnesses a growing interest in Grundtvig and the Folk High School movement. This is happening abroad, and also in those very parts of the Danish society which were once traditionally outside the Folk High School community.

Educational thought is one thing, the institutional form is something else. Is there any chance that Grundtvig's educational concepts could be better able in our own time to play a part outside the traditional milieu of the Folk High School?

The Folk High School on its own does not suffice. Grundtvig's ideas go much further. That much is sure. But conversely, the Folk High School holds out possibilities which one day will be inconceivable in other parts of our society, which are far from existing within the orbit of the educational system. People with completely different backgrounds, both social and political are meeting at the Folk High School. They also differ as to educational training, to say nothing of profession, age, opinion and faith.

In the Folk High Schools we find the conditions for real interaction and serious working together for weeks and months at a time. Here one can find the ideal conditions for general education in an increasingly specialised society. According to Grundtvig, general education is not merely a supplement to professional education. The basis of true general education is personal interaction.

In the Folk High School one has the opportunity to meet and communicate with people who belong to quite different groups and professions in society. One has, therefore, to transcend the barriers of professional language, so that instead only the common language is used, and that is the basis of democracy and ethics.

Today, the Folk High School's expanded contact with the Danish population is larger than in any earlier period in its history, thanks largely to the increased number of short courses. Moreover, the Folk High School has put down its roots in the cities. But the Folk High School can hardly be said to have entered modern Danish society today with the same strength as it did the agricultural society of one hundred years ago.[14]

The Folk High School of today constantly finds itself in danger of being

14. cf. note 10.

swallowed up by an aggressively pluralist society. It must, therefore, find a way of confronting that society in a living and effective manner. Where it *does* manage to do this, it embodies a vital dimension for today's world – the possibility of interaction which we need now more than ever.

Grundtvig and the Third World: The Transfer of Grundtvig's Ideas to Other Peoples and Cultures

By Holger Bernt Hansen

At a first glance a title like "Grundtvig and the Third World" appears to be a contradiction in terms. "The Third World" as a concept was certainly not invented in the era of Grundtvig. It belongs to the postwar period when the unequal distribution of the world's goods began to feature on the international agenda and introduced more global perspectives in the relations between peoples and cultures. Even as late as Grundtvig's own 19th century the idea of a non-European or extra-European world as an entity had not yet emerged. The concept of the world was still bound to Europe as the absolute centre from which all activity originated and to which the rest of the world was subjected.

Nonetheless, since the 1950s it has often been suggested that it makes sense to link Grundtvig and the Third World. First of all, because Grundtvig's ideas and his importance for developments in Denmark over the last century, not least in adult education and more specifically the Folk High School movement, have presented answers and solutions which have been considered very appropriate to the challenges now facing Third World countries.

But connections between Grundtvig and the Third World have also been made at a more analytical and theoretical level. It has been argued, not least by the leading French researcher on Grundtvig, Erica Simon, that Grundtvig's ideas of nation and people, of national identity or *Folkelighed*, of the need for an awakening from below against imposed foreign values, offered a very adequate ready-made framework for the understanding and interpretation of the present circumstances of the Third World in the aftermath of colonialism, and in view of the need for a cultural revolution against the foreign yoke.[1]

---

1. See in particular Torben Lundbæk (ed.), *African Humanism – Scandinavian Culture: a dialogue* (Copenhagen, 1970), being a report from a DANIDA-supported seminar held in 1967 and organized by Erica Simon. See also Vilhelm Nielsen, "Den tredje Verden og Grundtvig", in Jørgen I. Jensen & Erik A. Nielsen (eds.), *Efterklange – et Grundtvig Seminar* (Copenhagen, 1983), pp. 143ff.; and Erica Simon: *"-og solen står*

An important part of this argument has been that in Grundtvig's thinking there was a universal element going beyond the particular people and nation in which he lived. Erica Simon demonstrated the universality in Grundtvig's thinking by employing a term suggested by the Senegalese president and poet Leopold Senghor, *l'humanisme de l'universel*, a humanism comprising all cultures. It is significant that Leopold Senghor is quoted, since he used to be one of the leading figures in the *Négritude* movement in French-speaking Africa. Erica Simon deliberately draws a parallel between Grundtvig and *Négritude* as both of them emphasized an awakening based on people's own identity and traditional values. On this basis Grundtvig's message could be an important one for the process of enlightenment and for that of raising consciousness of human life in its totality which is so desirable in many Third World countries.[2]

Following these leads, in this chapter we will first discuss whatever perception of the non-European world we can find or infer from Grundtvig's own writings, especially from his ideas on Christian mission, and then move on to a more detailed examination of some recent attempts to transfer Grundtvig's ideas to Third World countries.

Grundtvig and the non-European world

In the 19th century there were two main lines of connection between Europe and the outside world. The first was a result of missionary activity in the so-called heathen parts of the world. During the 19th century, with Britain as the centre, this assumed proportions unprecedented in history, and by the end of the century had led to the optimistic slogan "the evangelization of the world in this generation".

The second line of connection was the drive for political domination and political control on a global scale. At the beginning of the century in the British context there were colonies which became the dominions, covering those regions where emigrants had settled. The process escalated during the century – first to what might be called an informal empire, and then during the last decades to a formal empire following the growth of colonialism, and the consequent emergence of what Hobson called imperialism.

In the Danish context, these two lines of connection with the non-European world could be seen in combination during some of Grundtvig's most active years. In 1845 the two Danish possessions in India, Tranquebar

---

med bonden op –". *De nordiske folkehøjskolers idehistorie* (Vojens, 1989), pp. 150ff. For a more critical opinion see Holger Bernt Hansen: "Møde mellem Afrika og Grundtvigs Norden", *Den Ny Verden* 4:5 (1968), pp. 3ff.
2. Erica Simon, op.cit., p. 150.

and Serampore – both significant from a missionary point of view – were handed over to British rule; and five years later the only Danish colony in Africa, the Gold Coast, was sold to Britain.[3] In the Danish period these overseas possessions served primarily commercial purposes, but as an element in Company rule there were also Danish chaplains who did some missionary work among the local Company employees and neighbouring peoples. It was in this connection that the young Grundtvig had a chance to learn something of Danish overseas activities, since in the first few years of the century his two elder brothers served as chaplains to the Company in the Gold Coast, where both of them died after very short periods of service. But this early, more personal experience of the non-European world does not seem to have had much influence on Grundtvig's later opinion of missionary work and relations with other people and cultures.[4]

Around 1830, while visiting England at a more mature age, Grundtvig had another opportunity to acquaint himself with activities directed towards non-European areas. While it had not been widely known that a group of Baptist missionaries with the well-known William Carey as their head had found a sanctuary for their missionary work in the Danish colony of Serampore for the preceding thirty years, their activity in fact formed part of the strong Evangelical revival which was then sweeping the Church of England and exerting great influence abroad. The Evangelicals' engagement in missionary work especially influenced the founding of the *Danish Missionary Society* in 1821, and before this there was also a strong Evangelical influence on the establishment of the *Danish Bible Society* in 1814. One special feature at about the time of Grundtvig's visits to England was the missionary movement's commitment to the abolition of slavery and the slave trade, a cause which became a mainstay of the missionary endeavour. And the slavery problem had also been a topical issue in the Gold Coast around the turn of the century, when Grundtvig's two brothers had their brief tours of service.

Grundtvig's visits thus took place during one of the strongest expressions of a revivalist movement ever seen in England, one which was significant for its missionary zeal and its anti-slavery commitment and was closely associated with humanitarian groups and personalities like William Wilberforce and Thomas Fowell Buxton. But in spite of his family background and some parallels to the Danish situation, this particular part of the life of church and society is hardly reflected in Grundtvig's writings,

---

3.   For a recent work on the former Danish colonies see Ole Feldbæk and Ole Justesen: *Kolonierne i Asien og Afrika* (Politikens Danmarks Historie, Copenhagen, 1980).
4.   For a contemporary account of the Grundtvig brothers in the Gold Coast see H.C. Monrad, *Bidrag til en Skildring af Guineakysten og dens Indbyggere* (Copenhagen, 1822).

the main reason presumably being that Grundtvig had come to England for different purposes.

We may add to this interpretation of Grundtvig's position by introducing the concept of history which he developed in the contemporary *Handbook on World History*, the first volume of which was published shortly after his last visit to England (1833). This is basically a political history, dealing mainly with states. The organizing principle linking the major events is that history is concerned with the development of "major peoples" in terms of their attitude to *human life*. Other peoples are only included as far as they are important for such a development.

World history has nothing to do really with those countries where human life does not visibly stir itself or express itself.[5]

It follows that the non-European areas now called the Third World are not taken into consideration. But it is important to remember that for Grundtvig the dividing line was not between Europe and the rest of the world. A number of European countries did not fulfill the requirement of awareness of the totality of human life, nor was Europe important as such – only the individual peoples. Hence Grundtvig's concept of Europe appears to be different from the one that prevailed in missionary circles, where Europe was seen as the centre of Christianity and civilization. Furthermore, this concept of history raises some questions about missionary activity in general, since for Grundtvig Christianity should never be imposed on people in a way which will undermine the national character.

In order to develop these latter points further, it will be useful to take a closer look at Grundtvig's concept of, and attitude to, Christian missionary activity. A mission has something to do with the transfer of ideas to other people and other cultures – it is a translation process – and this may help us towards some categories and a conceptual framework that we can employ when we later turn to the modern process of transferring Grundtvig's ideas to the Third World. The intention is not to go into detail in this somewhat controversial area of Grundtvig's thinking – only to point

5. About Grundtvig's *Handbook on World History* see Sigurd Aage Aarnes, "Grundtvig the Historian" in Christian Thodberg and Anders Pontoppidan Thyssen (eds.): *N.F.S. Grundtvig. Tradition and Renewal*, (Copenhagen, 1983), (quotation p. 68). J.L. Balling's lecture "Grundtvig's Concept of Church History", Aarhus University 24 April 1992, has been very helpful for this part of the analysis. Regarding Grundtvig's concept of Europe see Holger Bernt Hansen, "Grundtvig, Europe and the Third World", in *Grundtvigs-studier*, 1993.

out the three kinds of paradox or dichotomy found in Grundtvig's thinking
on missionary issues. In a broader Grundtvigian context, they may be
explicable or even soluble, but for our present purposes they can be
illustrative and helpful in an assessment of whether some of Grundtvig's
ideas can be transferred to Third World countries.[6]

The first paradox appears in Grundtvig's own writings, where in many
places we encounter a strong missionary dimension. He takes the missionary command in Matt. 28 very seriously, and many of his hymns are
strongly influenced by the obligation to extend the Gospel to non-
Christians, not least the hymns on the Holy Spirit and the Pentecost hymns.
On the other hand, Grundtvig is adamant that the era of mission has not
yet arrived. In spite of his concept of history, which brought him close to
an eschatological interpretation of the present stage of the world, and in
spite of his concept of the history of salvation – which for him meant the
extension of the Gospel to all corners of the world – he denounced efforts
to send out missionaries because he thought such a strategy premature. The
time was not yet ripe; the conditions both for going out to preach the
Gospel and for receiving the Gospel had not yet been established. One
needed only to look at the damage that missionary activity had in most
cases inflicted so far on the people concerned.

This leads to a second paradox. Grundtvig stood aloof from precisely the
group of people who were his natural allies, and who looked to him for
guidance and leadership. This was the diverse mixture of people who first
joined the revival movement. They, or at least their leaders, were inspired
by the Moravian missionary tradition and later by the Evangelical
movement in Britain with its strong missionary engagement. In Denmark,
as mentioned above, the example of England led to the formation of the
Danish Bible Society in 1814, and seven years later to the foundation of the
Danish Missionary Society. Grundtvig took a negative view of both ventures.
It was wrong to send Bibles to non-Christian countries; it would lead to a
theology of scripture and prevent them from receiving the "living word",
particularly in the form it took when Baptism was performed in the mother
tongue, not in a foreign language. Similarly, any attempt to send out
missionaries under the present conditions in the Danish Church, where

6.   Regarding Grundtvig's attitude to missionary activity see Torben Christensen,
     "Missionstankens vækst og udvikling i Danmark fra 1821 til ca. 1920", *Dansk
     Teologisk Tidsskrift* 45 (1982), pp. 126-44; Johannes Aagaard, "Grundtvigs og
     grundtvigsk missionsforståelse og missionspraksis, kritisk forstået", *Nordisk
     Missionstidsskrift* 94:4 (1983), pp. 142-82; Hans Iversen, "Grundtvig som inspiration
     til mission" in *NMT* 94: 3 (1983), pp. 94-120. Cf. also articles by Edvard Wulff
     Pedersen and Elna Vinther in *NMT* 94: 3 (1983).

awareness of the "living word" had *not* yet won the day, would turn out just as disastrously as earlier cases of what Grundtvig called "mission by the sword", which meant luring people into the universal church by force, or at least by improper means, instead of by using their mother tongue.

This situation was paradoxical for Grundtvig's followers. It created uncertainty, even confusion, and led later in the century to some more or less misguided missionary enterprises. This was not least due to a third paradox or dichotomy in Grundtvig's thinking on the concept of mission. If the time was not yet ripe, and preparations not yet complete, the onus fell on what could be done to reach a level from which one could envisage the start of such work and thus fulfill the missionary obligation expressed by Jesus at the end of Matt. 28. According to Grundtvig, the real and only preparation lies in the building up of awareness, and of *belonging*, in the sense that man exists as part of a community of people, a nation or "folk" community, with its special history, myths, language and cultural traits. Every man should be conscious of belonging to and existing within a living community in which the living word should then be preached and observed in life.

In this conception of Christian mission the preparatory, pedagogical and educational element assumes great importance. It is education for life, not training in skills. But this raises the question of how closely such education is related to the church. Is the educational aspect an end in itself inde-pendent of the church and its mission? Such a question needs to be asked, not least among the people at the receiving end, because educational work has its own legitimate purpose – to awaken them, and to make them aware of what it means to be a human being at a special point in history, with their own identity as expressed in myths, language and cultural traditions, and with the ability to utilize their resources and take their destiny in their own hands.

This dual function of education for life, in the interpretation given here, has certain consequences for the transfer and functioning of Grundtvig's ideas in the wider world. First of all, we are concerned here with Grundt-vig's paramount theme in the missionary context: "First a Man – Then a Christian". The recipients must thus feel themselves to be a community, and be awakened as a *Folk* with all the connotations of the word. The living word must be spoken in the context of the people as a whole, not of indi-viduals, as earlier missionaries, especially the more Evangelical ones, had done. But the risk is clearly that the effort to discover and develop a people, a *Folk* rooted in its history and traditions, becomes the ultimate goal, an independent goal which can stand on its own, without the addition of "the living word". Education, more specifically adult education, becomes the essence of the missionary task, and in the wider perspective the essence of the transfer of Grundtvig's ideas.

This is one consequence which we need to keep in mind when discussing modern attempts to transfer Grundtvig's ideas to the Third World. It has in fact been aptly illustrated by one of the first attempts to conduct a mission according to Grundtvig's ideas. In 1872, the year Grundtvig died, Eduard Løventhal, supported by a small group of like-minded people, went to India convinced that it was now time for a mission and that the Hindus constituted a nation ready to receive the Gospel along with other Asian nations and peoples. He failed, because he found that the Hindus did not constitute a "nation", not even a community.[7] His successor, Anne Marie Petersen, assessed the situation differently immediately after the First World War. She confined herself to what was *folkeligt*, to man in his natural surroundings, and did not go on to start a congregation as the first step towards founding a church. She concentrated on schooling, and the church took second place. In her view it was not yet time for missionary work, only for preparation, which meant concentrating on the "First a Man" element. She was greatly influenced by her meeting with Indian nationalism, not least by her personal contact with Mahatma Gandhi. In her educational work, she was an interesting combination of Grundtvig's and Gandhi's ideas, as she strove to awaken people and to make them conscious of their situation and the great possibilities before them. This was the start of the *Porto Novo Mission*, which still exists as the most Grundtvigian of the Danish Missions, and which still concentrates on education, mainly of girls.[8]

The example illustrates the distinction between Folk and Church and the independent function of education in realizing the "First a Man" tenet. But it brings us to another crucial issue: the relationship between *Folkelighed* and Christianity in Grundtvig's thinking. It is a necessary precondition of any missionary undertaking that the right balance between the two is established. For the receivers of the Gospel, this also means according to Grundtvig that Christianity must not work against or be hostile to existing traditions and values – in short the *folkelige* community in which man lives.

7. cf. Torben Christensen, "Danish Missions in India", in Torben Christensen and William R. Hutchison (eds.), *Missionary Ideologies in the Imperialist Era: 1880-1920* (Aarhus, 1982), pp. 121ff. See also Henriette Bugge, "Mission and Tamil Society. Sixty Years of Interaction, 1840-1900" (Ph.D. thesis, Department of History, University of Copenhagen, 1991) pp. 67ff.
8. cf. Bent Smidt Hansen, *Afhængighed og Identitet. Kulturmødeproblemer i forbindelse med dansk mission i Sydindien mellem de to verdenskrige* (Aarhus, 1992).

Man is created in God's image, and there are values inherent in his culture
to which the living word can speak.

It follows that in this respect Grundtvig differs substantially from most
of his contemporaries. Although he often used the rhetoric of his time to
characterize people abroad in negative terms, he basically took a positive
and optimistic view of their cultures and their community. In this respect
he stood out from the prevailing view of people in the non-Christian world
– that in such cultures people lived under deplorable conditions, entirely
given over to sin and the influence of the Devil. Missionaries starting out
with such assumptions would first have to remove these obstacles before
they could start evangelizing and preaching the Gospel. For Grundtvig on
the other hand it was essential to start with the community as it was, with
the inherent values and cultural identity expressed in its "Folk spirit".
Otherwise the mission would involve *alienation* – and here in fact we have
the essence of Grundtvig's opposition to "mission by the sword". And in
using the concept of alienation we have also indicated that Grundtvig was
in this respect far ahead of his time, because he was pointing to missionary
ideas which were not to prevail for another hundred years. Or, as K.E.
Bugge has put it, "Grundtvig's thinking is far removed from imperialistic
tendencies". To put it in even more contemporary language, cultural
imperialism is for him no part of the essence of Christianity.[9]

We come here to a crucial point in any discussion of Grundtvig's relevance
to the Third World, not just in terms of Christianity and the Church, but
also of his educational ideas. This can be made even clearer by drawing a
somewhat untraditional parallel to one of Grundtvig's contemporaries – of
whom he may have known but with whom he was certainly not well
acquainted: the explorer and missionary David Livingstone.

Livingstone too argued that missionaries should not go out and preach
the Gospel, and try to "plant" a church without first preparing the people
properly. The new converts had no chance of living a Christian life under
the conditions prevailing in their society. Livingstone therefore advocated
that before any missionary enterprise, some kind of "civilizing" should take
place. Societies should be changed through civilizing measures like trade
and agriculture. Livingstone's ideas were later summarized as the "three
Cs": Civilization, Commerce and Christianity. These three elements had to
go together – and this suggests the need for an indirect method in
missionary work.

9.   K.E. Bugge, "Grundtvig and India", *Bangalore Theological Forum* 17:2, p. 58. Cf. Elna
     Vinther, op. cit., p. 138.

This approach exerted considerable influence on missionary practice. In the 1840s the *Church Missionary Society* sent a ship loaded with the best of western civilization – agricultural experts, doctors, tools and equipment, almost a Noah's ark – up the Niger River in West Africa. And in the 1860s the Universities' Mission to Central Africa sent Bishop Mackenzie up the Zambezi River, equipped in the same manner, and with the explicit purpose of ensuring that civilizing measures should go hand in hand with evangelization. In his *Mackenzie's Grave* (1959) Owen Chadwick has vividly recorded how that mission utterly failed.[10]

The differences from Grundtvig are significant. For Livingstone it was not a question of making people aware of their own identity and possibilities in their own setting and within their own way of life, of putting man at the centre in his historical, national and religious context. On the contrary, it was about replacing all that with the best of European civilization. Grundtvig warned against such a process of alienation. On the one hand it involved a negative, pessimistic view of the naturally given conditions and the heritage of the past; and conversely it took a positive, very optimistic view of European civilization and its universal value. This belief escalated during the 19th century. It turned the latter part of the century and the early part of the 20th century into the period in the history of Christian mission when European self-confidence and Eurocentric thinking were at their most extreme, and tolerance and understanding of other peoples and other cultures were least developed.

But the Livingstone approach stresses another factor. It is not only a question of the relationship between *Folkelighed* and Christianity, but also of the difference between *Folkelighed* and civilization. In the first place, *Folkelighed* has nothing to do with the alien European kind of civilization that Livingstone advocated, but is an awareness of man's roots in his whole context. In the second place, *Folkelighed* and the corresponding process of awareness are not identical to the concept of development involved in Livingstone's civilizing process. Development, in the sense of the changing of structures and conditions in society, was not Grundtvig's concern. His concern was with what it means to be man at a given time and place, and the growth of such an awareness was his goal.

Having outlined the relationship between Christianity, *Folkelighed* and civilization in Grundtvig's thinking on mission, we can now identify two sets of problems which are important for the following discussion of the

10. W.O. Chadwick, *Mackenzie's Grave* (London, 1959), discusses also Livingstone's missionary methods. Cf. Roland Oliver, *The Missionary factor in East Africa* (London, 1952), chapter 1.

prospects for transferring Grundtvig's ideas to the Third World. In the first place, how is it possible in these societies to identify the natural units that are based on a common feeling of identity? We do not have nations in the European sense with a long unitary history behind them; but we have, for example, castes and tribes whose boundaries are difficult to define. *The Danish Santal Mission*, of all the Danish missions the most Grundtvigian in influence, has struggled with this problem over the years. But the problem is also relevant for people who work with "education for life".

Secondly, and in relation to education for life, is it possible in societies with hardly any tradition of education to separate "education for life" from formal education, or even to make the concept of "education for life" understandable in such an environment? Furthermore, is it possible to separate education from "civilizing measures" (in the Livingstonian sense), and from development, in societies and nations which in the post-colonial period have "development" as the keynote of their entire political approach?

These are questions which arise from the analysis of Grundtvig's attitude to missionary activity, and by implication also from his attitude to foreign cultures and what is now called the Third World. It is essential to consider them when focusing on the relevance of Grundtvig's ideas to Third World countries and the potential for transferring them to such countries.

The transfer of the Folk High School idea: first phase
Historically the process of exporting – and correspondingly importing – Grundtvigian ideas may be ascribed to two main factors, both peculiar to the postwar situation. First of all, with the new embryonic world order in which anti-colonialism and the drive for independence were main elements, the destiny and the future of the non-European world loomed larger on the Danish and Scandinavian horizon. The people who first became aware of the changes, apart from missionaries and the business community, were primarily groups related to the Folk High School movement. Naturally, it was people associated with the *International People's College* in Helsingør, among whom were Danish Quakers, who played a leading role. But *Mellemfolkeligt Samvirke*, the Danish Association for International Cooperation, was also very active and had close relations with the Folk High School movement.[11]

11. Oral information, and Holger Bernt Hansen, "Mission og u-landshjælp" in Steffen Johannessen and Torben Krogh, *Livsoplysning. Festskrift til K.E. Bugge* (Frederikshavn 1988), pp. 183ff. See also Klaus Jørgensen, *Hjælp fra Danmark. En studie i dansk u-*

These groups of people led the way in creating in the population a steadily growing body of opinion supporting Danish involvement in the underdeveloped or developing countries (as they were called in those early days). Looking back at the scene in the 1950s, the Chairman of the *Danish Association for International Cooperation* has remarked that the situation could best be compared with the 19th century's Revival movements and the Folk High School movement.[12]

This interesting comparison brings us to the second main motivation at this stage for "exporting" Grundtvig's ideas, especially his educational ideas, to the Third World. The commitment of the Danish Folk High Schools has been called an "original spiritual export product".[13] *The International People's College* published a book with a preface by Jawaharlal Nehru and with the significant title *Rural Development and the Changing Countries of the World. A Study of Danish Rural Conditions and the Folk High School with its Relevance for the Developing Countries.*[14] The relevance of this book is the very firm conviction – one could even say philosophy – that the experience of "development" in 19th century Denmark could be transferred to the "developing" world.

The major force behind this process of change was said to be Grundtvig's ideas as manifested first and foremost in the Folk High School movement with its "enlightening and enlisting" approach, but also in adult education in general. This whole approach had worked as a leaven in society, mapping out new directions for "development" in Denmark.

Striking parallels with the developing countries were seen. They too had to liberate themselves mentally and culturally from the colonial yoke, and they too faced tremendous social changes, first of all in the agrarian sector and in the rural areas in general, but also in areas affected by growing urbanization and industrialization. In Danish circles there was little doubt that the Folk High Schools would work as an instrument of change. When established in the local setting, they would become "counter-cultural" schools, marked by self-awareness and participation. They would therefore generate a development towards democracy and social justice on the Danish or Scandinavian model.

This was why the Folk High School idea was a valuable "spiritual export product". It was "a school for life", aiming at the creation of awareness and the development of personal identity within the context of

landspolitik 1960-71 (Odense, 1977), pp. 9ff., 59ff.
12. Klaus Jørgensen, op. cit., pp. 62-3.
13. *Lederbladet*, December 1963, pp. 158-59, cf. Klaus Jørgensen, op.cit., p. 295.
14. Edited by Peter Manniche et al., Oxford, 1969.

the community or nation, its history and culture. The aim was not "to mould the masses into predefined shapes, but challenge and assist people to grasp their own identity" and utilize their potential and skills in the best possible way. The method was to be indirect: the development of agriculture and other occupational sectors through the improvement of historical and cultural awareness. If the student really knows who he is and has confidence in himself he is certain to make innovations and improvements in his daily work and life. In this way, school and life would be closely knit together and would give meaning to the teaching of practical skills which had to be part of the curriculum in a developing country.

Based on these ideas, and modelled on the Folk High School, a number of institutions were established in the developing world during the 1950s and 1960s, some of them with support from the Danish government's new assistance programme. A start was often made via contacts established when Third World people had attended courses at Danish schools, mainly the agricultural colleges, where they studied rural development and the cooperative movement. A special institution, the Rural Development College, was even started to meet the needs of Third World people more systematically in these two areas.[15]

There are thus two directions or dimensions for the transfer of ideas: the import dimension with its focal point in the Third World, and the export dimension with its focal point in Denmark. They are naturally interrelated and interdependent. And that of course raises a special feature of the problem: on whose terms is the transfer of Grundtvig's ideas taking place? Is it entirely a Danish initiative or is it a response to Third World requests? The success of the export/import venture could easily depend on the answer to these questions.

A key phase of this whole activity began at a workshop in 1980, a year which may also be taken to mark the end of the first phase of "the possible use of the Nordic Folk High School Idea in Developing Countries" – to quote the subtitle of the workshop.[16] Apart from the Nordic participants, there were "representatives from developing countries which, over a number of years, had used the FHS model in their efforts to mobilize rural leadership and development..." (p. 1). The most important schools were in India and Ghana – probably no accident, since these two countries as we have already seen had historical connections with Denmark. In addition,

---

15. It operated from 1964 to 1973, cf. Klaus Jørgensen, op. cit., pp. 62-3.
16. *Workshop on Economic and Social Development. The Possible Use of the Nordic Folk High School Idea in the Developing Countries*, (DANIDAs Dokumentationscentral, Copenhagen, 1980).

there were reports from adult education movements and schools in Tanzania and Zambia.

Only three of the movements will be considered in this analysis on the basis of criteria developed above: to what extent does their pattern of work follow the Folk High School idea, and can they really be based on the heritage of Grundtvig?

The Morogoro Folk Development College in Tanzania, established in 1976, was originally part of a programme of Folk Development Colleges which were defined as

rural training institutions which provide adult learning for effective development...in order to raise the general level of economic activity (p. 4).

Contacts with and visits to Sweden impressed on the Tanzanians that some of their institutions should be developed along the lines of the Swedish Folk High Schools, in view of the role this whole idea has played in the development of Swedish society. The Folk High School idea was clearly reflected in the first declared objective of the Folk Development Colleges:

They aim at the development of the whole personality, the ability to think, participate in the economic, cultural, political and social life of the community. They aim at producing self-actualizing human beings who can be able to identify their problems and act upon them in an intelligent way (p. 4).

Following on from this, it is made clear that the Folk Development Colleges have a political, an economic, a social and a cultural function. This still falls within the overall Folk High School idea, but when it comes to a more detailed clarification of aims and objectives, the aims become more questionable. A major objective is "to help all people understand the country's policy of socialism and self-reliance", not least in relation to the then recently-introduced cooperative system of Ujamaa villages. In order to realize this policy, the colleges aim to improve "the knowledge and skills of adults in such fields as agriculture, handicrafts, domestic science, health and water supply".

Three features of this system of adult education stand out, and lead us to the conclusion that, although the Folk High School idea may have influenced some of the overall objectives, the schools are in fact based on a different complex of ideas and were established for quite different purposes. First, the main emphasis is clearly on practical skills, almost vocational training, and the students' performance is judged by the appropriate criteria.

Secondly, the programme of Folk Development Colleges is closely linked to the political ideology and philosophy of the country, as expressed by the then President Julius Nyerere in the Arusha Declaration of 1967. Accordingly, political education is first on the list of courses offered, and the schools are financed and managed by the government through the Ministry of National Education. They are not part of an alternative system of education which is a normal feature of the Folk High Schools.

Thirdly, the programme is closely linked to the idea of development. It is changes in the structures of society – its development – which take priority, and the role of man is viewed in that context. The aim is not "Enlightenment about Life", nor is it to help people to come to terms with the basic realities of life *via* the historical experience and knowledge of present conditions of life.[17]

In general, the Tanzanian experience leads to a rather negative conclusion when we are assessing the transfer of Grundtvigian ideas to the Third World. Not all kinds of adult education are necessarily Grundtvigian and synonymous with the Folk High School idea.

In *Ghana* a much earlier start was made. In 1950 the *Awudome Residential College* was established as a local initiative in order to cater for young people who failed to enter secondary school. Soon afterwards it became part of a country-wide system of colleges affiliated to the Institute of Adult Education as part of the University's extramural programme. The aim was now changed to providing adult education for the rural population of the area. In the late 1950's contact was established with the Danish Association for International Cooperation which, with support from the Danish government, sent out a family to act as Folk High School tutors.

Since then, the College has had the intention of working along the lines of a Danish Folk High School. It describes itself as a centre for continuing education in a rural setting with three main objectives. The first one is to encourage studies in rural development, aimed especially at community development in its widest sense. The second objective is leadership training, especially through courses for the local chiefs. And the third objective is to

raise the consciousness of the local people to become more aware of the rich potential which they possess as individuals and communities...

The impact of the programme has, however, been hampered by financial constraints, so that only short courses of one or two weeks' duration have been available; and this has in turn meant that interaction between staff and students and among the students themselves has not been achieved.

17. cf. K.E. Bugge, op. cit., p. 54.

Unlike the Tanzanian case, the Ghanaian college is not part of the formal educational system. There are no examinations, and it is independent of the government both in its finances and management. There is little doubt that it has been greatly influenced by the Folk High School idea, and that it tries to realize elements of it, especially the important objective of consciousness raising. But financial and other constraints have limited its impact, and it is wholly geared to a rather practical kind of rural development in a purely local setting. There does not seem to be any scope or any resources for opening up the wider horizons inherent in the "education for life" concept.

This last issue is deliberately addressed in the example from *India.* In the state of Karnataka (formerly Mysore), an adult education movement was formed around the time of India's independence in 1947. Its activity included the building of a number of so called *Vidyapeeths*, which means "people's schools" or "folk schools", for the education of young farmers. In the early 1950s, contact was established with the Danish Association for International Cooperation, and the inspiration and guidance of the Folk High School movement changed the overall goal:

The new institution was to have the appearance of an Ashram (traditional educational institution) and the principles and philosophy of the Folk High Schools (p. 3).

To implement this at once traditional and new concept, the Karnataka State Adult Education Council – a kind of a parastatal organization – received support from Denmark, thus initiating the first Danish development project in India. The initiative was soon followed by the posting of Danish personnel, often people with experience of Danish Folk High Schools.[18]

The target group became young men and women who had not had sufficient schooling in their younger days.

Once again, adult education was linked to the process of development, and its value was recognized by the local government, which paid all the expenses of the courses at the Vidyapeeths. Although the schools were not part of the formal educational system, diplomas, officially recognized by the government, were granted after the ten-month courses.

Again, the inspiration from the Folk High School movement is strong and was deliberately sought – the main hall of the leading Vidyapeeth bears the name "Grundtvig Hall". Despite this, it is difficult to assess the

---

18. An evaluation of the first phase of the Danish Mysore Project was presented in Steen Folke, Ib Jørgensen, and Jakob Kjær, *An Evaluation of the Danish Mysore Project* (Copenhagen, 1969). The report does not really discuss the use of the Folk High School idea, but mentions it in chapters 1, 5 and 6.7.

extent to which Grundtvig's ideas were integrated in the adult education programme. A kind of answer appears, however, in a case study by two Indians presented at the 1980 workshop, where they commented both on Grundtvig's ideas as such and on the process of transferring them to India. Of the Folk High School scheme they say frankly that

it did best to promote a sense of respect for human dignity and courage and national integration in Denmark, when the country suffered externally from political wars, internally from economic depression...

[The writers go on to elaborate on the effects:] The Folk High School ideas tend to enlarge the mental horizon and ennoble the spirit. They develop a right perspective in outlook on life and are capable of counteracting the deadening effects of the formal system practised through schools and universities (p. 11).

But what works at a certain time and place in history may not necessarily be suitable for export to a different setting like the Indian one.

Now in the scheme, with the march of time, many changes so as to suit the requirement of society will have to be made. A more realistic and practical approach to the problems of the soil should be made...[and this new approach is made quite specific:] The pedagogy of learning should include all aspects of learning, engineering, mechanics, arts and crafts useful to daily life.

In many ways we are here faced with a rejection of parts of the Grundt-vigian Folk High School idea, at least when it is transferred to modern India. We also get a comment on the shortcomings pointed out in the two earlier cases, for it is clear that Grundtvig's ideas have to be updated and translated with careful reverence for the soil to which they are transplanted and in which they are supposed to grow at a particular time. We even have suggestions for one part of the process of transfer. It is evident that the emphasis has moved from consciousness-raising, the crucial factor in "education for life", to the development aspect. The consciousness-forming element is scaled down and focused on such changes in society as are really necessary. Consequently, more space is given to the skills needed in a society in transformation – first of all to vocational training.

So when we ask whether it is possible to separate education from civiliz-ing measures, and from the development aspect, in societies where deve-lopment is the main, and almost the only, item on the agenda, we cannot answer in the affirmative. In emphasizing the socio-economic process of change, we are in fact closer to the Livingstone model than to Grundtvig's ideas of nation, people and common identity. Yet if we consider how the Folk High School idea has worked in practice in the Danish context, the deviation from the original idea may not be as great as it seems. After all, in their earliest period the Folk High Schools were closely geared to the agrarian society of the day, with manual skills in the curriculum, for example. And the movement was not very old before it experienced its own divisions, as some schools either turned into, or were even started as, primarily agricultural colleges. They certainly felt rooted in the original tradition and kept it alive, but inevitably they had to give priority to vocational training and specialized education to meet the need for skilled people in a predominantly agricultural society.[19]

In view of the diminishing importance of consciousness-raising, we have heard little or nothing about what constitutes the units upon which a common identity and a common sense of history and destiny are based. Nor have we heard anything about the nation as a separate cultural entity, or that essential factor, the use of a common language.[20]

This is of course a most difficult area for the post-colonial states with their "unhistorical" boundaries, but it means that there are different foundations for *Folkelighed* or national identity from those on which the normal Grundtvig-inspired way of thinking is based. It leaves open the question whether there is any basis for the emergence of *Folkelighed*, and whether it is compatible with the modern nation-state.

From this assessment of the first phase of the use of the Folk High School idea in developing countries up to 1980, we have to conclude that the process of transfer and the translation of the whole idea met with a number of difficulties. The initiative and the interpretation have mainly come from Danes who brought with them their own historical experience, while so far there have been few Third World voices who have commented on the suitability of Grundtvig's ideas for the challenges they face. Only the two Indians quoted above pointed out that an updating and a more practical approach were necessary at the expense of the consciousness-raising measures. The impetus should come from the need for development, not so much from the need to liberate the human being.

19. cf. Roar Skovmand, "Grundtvig and the Folk High School Movement" in Christian Thodberg & Anders Pontoppidan Thyssen, op.cit., pp. 321-43. The oldest agricultural college, Lyngby Landbrugsskole, which celebrated its 125th anniversary in 1992, represents an interesting example of the "dialectic" between the original Folk High School idea and the more professional training in agriculture, see *Annual Report* for 1991.
20. cf. K.E. Bugge, op. cit., p. 58.

The transfer of the Folk High School idea: second phase

It is remarkable that, in spite of these uncertainties, the whole idea of using the Folk High School concept in the Third World has continued into a second phase throughout the 1980s and up to the present day. There have been some changes in the actors involved. The Danish Folk High School Association, as the Non-Government Organization (NGO) which administers government support for the activity, has become much more involved. More important, the initiative and the planning of the transfer of the Folk High School idea are now more in the hands of Third World people themselves than before. The projects are now much more responses to local initiatives, and they are implemented with greater local involvement, not least in order to make them self-sustaining in the long run.

This may be one factor behind the continued official support for the various schemes. Yet it is remarkable that the Folk High School idea still plays a role in Danish relations with the developing countries, not just among grass-root movements and committed pressure groups, but also among decision-makers, be they politicians or bureaucrats who provide state support for the enterprise. It is not just the general idea of adult education and the importance of vocational training that generate the support. It is a belief in the Folk High School idea itself – that it is a valuable instrument in a process of change and that it can become a mobilizing force in the developing countries. One motive may be uncertainty in the face of the complexity of the Third World's problems, but it does also illustrate how deeply ingrained the Folk High School idea has become in the Danish value system.

The activities of recent years will be illustrated by three Folk High School projects in Bangladesh, Ghana and Nigeria. Since 1981 the Danish Development Agency (Danida) has supported a private organization, the *Bangladesh Association of Community Education* in establishing four so-called *Gonobidyalayas*, which means adult education centres which cater for the poorer segments of the rural population with special attention to school drop-outs. From the beginning, the Gonobidyalayas have drawn inspiration from the Danish Folk High School traditions, which emphasize the use of participatory methods to achieve integration between general subjects and practical work, without holding formal exams.[21]

While in some ways these Gonobidyalayas have come close to realizing

---

21. Material about the Gonobidyalaya Project is limited and not generally available. A main source is the Appraisal Report from July 1990.

the basic ideas of the Folk High School movement especially by granting "consciousness-raising" a dominant position over "skills-training", experience has shown, that it is sometimes difficult for the local people to understand and accept the Gonobidyalaya concept, with its non-formal type of education. But the donor agency *Danida* is willing to run the risk that in five years' time when the grant of 16.5 million Danish kroner has been spent, the schools will not be self-sustaining, in spite of income-generating activities, and that if external support stops the schools will almost certainly have to close. This gives some perspective to the belief in the benefits of the Folk High School system in the Bengali setting, even if it only manages to educate 1900 students over the five-year period.

In the case of *Ghana*, a Danish voluntary organization called the *Ghana Friendship Groups* has been establishing close contacts with four villages in a poor part of northern Ghana since the early 1980s. They have especially supported rural development activities, and in 1987 work was started to create a so-called Centre for General Learning based on the Folk High School concept.[22] The local population has been closely involved in the planning, and the school is very much a grass-roots activity, with agriculture taking up half of the available time. In general, the teaching is practically oriented, as most of the students cannot read and write. In many ways the whole set-up is reminiscent of the pioneer Christen Kold's first implementation of the Folk High School idea.[23]

In this rather backward area, where people feel very much that they are in a minority position, a special aim of the school is to strengthen the participants' self-awareness. This is done by a strong emphasis on the language, history and culture of the area, by linking up with the traditions of the old kingdom of Dagomba which used to cover the whole area, and by including local traditions like storytelling, singing and dancing.

Compared to the examples discussed earlier, we have here a situation where the basis of the people's historical and cultural identity has been clearly defined, and where language and myth are used in a truly Grundtvigian way. There is little doubt as to what constitutes the *Folk* and *Folkelighed*, and the boundaries with other traditions can easily be drawn. But the fellowship of the community has been established on a purely tribal or ethnic basis, which tends to cut off the links with the wider unit, the nation-state Ghana, and emphasize its heterogeneous character. It is acknowledged that problems arise in relation to the history of Ghana and

22. Reports and other documents kindly supplied by Mr. Leif Frandsen, a founding member of the Ghana Friendship Groups.
23. cf. Roar Skovmand, op. cit., pp. 327ff.; Erica Simon, op. cit., pp. 31ff.

not least in relation to English, which is the official national language. But the limited local focus is so valuable in terms of the overall intention that, in spite of obvious shortcomings, it has to take priority.

The Ghanian example brings out a fundamental problem in Africa, but it does not point to any kind of ultimate solution. We have to turn to neighbouring *Nigeria* to find virtually the only Third World figure who has tried so far to address and tackle the basic paradox inherent in the transfer of Grundtvig's ideas to the Third World in general and to Africa in particular.

The person in question is the founder and leader of *the Grundtvig Institute*, Dr. Kachi Ozumba. His school lies in the Igbo area which was formerly called Biafra. The new buildings which *Danida* has agreed to support with a grant of 31.5 million Danish kroner approved in 1991 will be based on the concept of an Igbo village. The school itself, which has been functioning since 1984, is based on the Danish Folk High School model, but Ozumba has developed his own approach to Grundtvig's ideas and has translated his "school for life" into a Nigerian context.[24] The school is designed to cater for 400 students, primarily young women who are drop-outs from school with no chance of further training. The school has a vocational curriculum as well as a socalled awareness curriculum. The special feature of *the Grundtvig Institute* is the way it attempts to combine the need for basic skills (core curriculum) with an awareness of oneself, one's community and one's nation. This is based on Kachi Ozumba's profound understanding of the Grundtvig slogan "Education for Life" and the translation of the idea into the Nigerian context.

Ozumba's own life story illustrates the whole process. He was once a secondary school master, then a university lecturer, until around 1980, when he became a top official on the West African Examination Board. In the latter position he became more and more desperate as he witnessed the high rate of failure, which in practice meant failure in life as a whole with no hope of a decent job and no hope of self-respect. He became more and more agitated as he discovered that what he regarded as the irrelevant elitist school system was a general African phenomenon.

24. Most material about the Grundtvig Institute has been compiled in the voluminous report *"Education for Life". Proposal for a Cooperation between the Grundtvig Institute Movement, Nigeria, and the Danish Folk High School Association, Denmark,* (Copenhagen, 1990). References and quotations in the text are all from this report. Cf. also Poul Kjær, *Gæstelærer på Grundtvig-Institutet i Nigeria,* (Helsingør, 1987) (report from a teaching period at the Grundtvig Institute in November 1987), and the useful research report *Grundtvig i Nigeria. Et projekt om bevidstgørelse,* by 7 students at Roskilde University Centre, May 1991.

Then he came across the above-mentioned report from the 1980 work-shop on the application of Grundtvig's ideas in developing countries. He read about the concept of a school for life, and became convinced that this was *the* solution for his country. He tried to get "a school for life" started, and when he finally succeeded he took the bold step of resigning from his job in 1983. He still felt unfulfilled and needed, as he says, "to experience Grundtvig". In 1985 he visited Denmark and established a number of con-tacts, especially with people from *the International People's College*. Soon afterwards, a return visit to Nigeria by a few Danish colleagues had the effect of convincing himself and his staff members that they could "see themselves as part of the Grundtvigian movement". This is clearly echoed in the constitution of *the Grundtvig Institute*, which states about its principles and ideology:

The Movement is inspired by Bishop N.F.S. Grundtvig, the great Danish thinker, it is guided by the humanitarian and democratic principles developed and propagated in the concept "Education for Life" by Bishop Grundtvig. And Education for Life means education that equips students with attributes to live lives useful to themselves, to their communities and to the nation.

While Ozumba can say without any hesitation, "Grundtvigianism is for all times and places", he is fully aware that carbon copies of the Grundtvigian ideas and the Folk High School idea will never work. While he can say that "Grundtvigian ideals can provide answers to most of our problems of deve-lopment", he immediately adds that "while remaining faithful to the ideals, it is our right to see, feel and live them as Nigerians".

We can see this adaptive approach when Ozumba makes use of Grundt-vig to interpret the situation in Nigeria. Just as Grundtvig fought "the Latin school" and the alienating "Roman yoke", Ozumba has designated what he calls "the school for death" as the enemy. The school for death with its elitist system was forced upon Nigeria and Africa as part of colonialism with all its alienating influences. The school for life must replace the school for death, and must include the use of the living word, history, folklore and traditional arts. It is into these peculiar cultural conditions that the spirit of Grundtvigianism should be translated, as his hymns should be translated into Igbo and set to Igbo music.

When it comes to the actual implementation of Grundtvig's ideas in the Nigerian setting, things become more difficult. Ozumba has identified three major issues which he and his colleagues have encountered.

The first and most fundamental problem concerns the awareness curri-culum, a problem brought on by the ambivalence of the whole culture. When we talk about rediscovery of self and community, what kind of self and community are we referring to? In what sense, if any, can we speak of a Nigerian *Folkelighed*? There is the indigenous tradition from the old days, and there are the self and the community from the recent past "bastardized" by colonialism and so-called western civilization.

This question becomes even more pressing when we come to a second problem: the language situation. At *the Grundtvig Institute*, English is the medium of instruction. But is it possible to generate *Folkelighed* in a language which is foreign to the people concerned? According to Grundtvig's standards a foreign language can hardly be the carrier of a common system of values, or favour a community spirit.

A third area, religion, presents another picture of diversity. Ozumba claims that *the Grundtvig Institute* is based on the Christian ethic, and that "Education for Life" leads to "life for Christ" (thus reflecting the idea of "First a Man, then a Christian"). Nonetheless, services have to be held by representatives of other faiths, so that religion cannot be a strong factor in strengthening common identity and fellowship.

It is therefore clear that some of the usual vehicles for realizing Grundtvig's ideals cannot be used in the Nigerian situation. Ozumba consoles himself by saying that if only the spirit of Grundtvigianism is not violated, then ways and means can be kept flexible. And he adds that

in *the Grundtvig Institute* we are exploring the potentials of Grundtvigian ideals in the Igbo community. This will demonstrate its possibilities in other Nigerian communities.

Concluding remarks

Since the 1950s several attempts have been made to transfer the Grundtvig-inspired Folk High School institution to a number of Third World countries. Apart from the Danish initiatives and strong Danish support two forces in particular seem to have been at work. First, the Folk High School concept has been used as an alternative to the existing educational system with its elitist bias inherited from the colonial period and as a chance to cater for the otherwise neglected groups: the school drop-outs, the poor, the women etc. The Folk High School has functioned as a kind of adult education based on new pedagogical methods; but in the process essential elements of the Folk High School idea have often been dropped.

This is confirmed by the second force which is at work. Under the circumstances prevailing in Third World countries, the Folk High School concept has often been linked to the concept of development, and thus geared to current ideas of societal change, which in turns means a strong emphasis on vocational skills and training at the expense of what has been called the awareness curriculum or consciousness-raising which addresses human development as a precondition of any kind of change.

The cases from the second phase indicate a change in the trend even if it is too early to reach a firm conclusion. Changing conditions in the Third World, and not least the lack of progress over two decades, have left more room for the human dimension and reduced the importance assigned to the developmental and socio-economic dimensions. And this has opened up avenues for a better match between the Grundtvig-inspired Folk High School concept and the needs and challenges of the Third World.

Of even greater importance is the active involvement of people from the Third World itself. This has been the case at the grass-roots level in Bangladesh and Ghana, and at the more theoretical level we have encountered representatives of Third World countries who have studied the whole idea behind the Folk High School movement, the most outstanding so far being Kachi Ozumba. It is quite clear that Ozumba's reading of Grundtvig and his knowledge of Grundtvig's own ideas have enabled him to make the necessary translation of the Folk High School idea into another culture and another society. It has also enabled him to warn against carbon copying and to look instead for the spirit of Grundtvigianism. He speaks of a meaningful synthesis between Grundtvig's ideals and the local traditions and culture, but in view of the diversity that exists, he ends up questioning whether it will ever be realistic to talk about a Nigerian *Folkelighed*.

This last point raises some more issues of principle related to the transfer of Grundtvig's ideas to the Third World. Ozumba's last question implies that he has given up on the necessary relationship between language, culture and nation – an essential element in Grundtvig's thinking. It leaves us with the question whether Grundtvig's thinking and ideas are so rooted in a Danish – or Scandinavian – context, in small nations with a common language and a homogenous culture, that they are not amenable to export. Some of the shortcomings the Folk High School idea has experienced so far in Third World countries seem to confirm that impression.

Ozumba's doubts also lead us to the suggestion that Grundtvig's categories and conceptual framework may not be fully adequate to the analysis of the Third World's present and future position. We have already seen that while Ozumba employs Grundtvig's framework in explaining Nigeria's situation after colonialism he does not go as far as Erica Simon's grand scheme, which as stated at the beginning of this chapter conceives of the Third World in terms of alternative, confrontational categories and emphasizes revolt and cultural revolution against alienation and foreign dominance as the driving forces. This kind of radicalism and cultural revolution, extracted from Grundtvig's concept of history and clearly modelled on the precepts of the academics in the *Négritude* movement, presupposes a universalism and homogeneity which are absent from a continent where the nation hardly exists and in any case is not coextensive with one culture and one language.[25] It is exactly this diversity that Ozumba is struggling with in his attempt to apply Grundtvig's ideas to the African realities, and one reason for his difficulties could well be that he is too dependent on Grundtvig's own familiar categories of nation, language, mythology etc.

This raises a last issue which has a general bearing on much of the discussion in this chapter. We have dealt at length with the prospects of transferring the Folk High School idea to Third World countries and discussed its ability to function in the prevailing circumstances. The main criterion in judging the outcome has been how far it has functioned according to the original idea and the basic principles associated with the Folk High Schools and first outlined by Grundtvig himself.

We should now ask whether it is the right approach first to link the Folk High School concept so closely with a specific historical situation, and secondly to identify it so intimately with the whole complex of Grundtvig's ideas and visions, in short the "Grundtvigian superstructure". While the idea is not viable without Grundtvig's prescription and inspiration, we may need to develop a different set of criteria not only when we plan activities for Folk High Schools in the Third World, but also when we assess their performance and longer-term sustainability.

25. This argument has been developed at greater length in an earlier article, Holger Bernt Hansen 1968 (see note 1).

List of Authors

Canon, Professor Dr. Arthur Macdonald Allchin
Oxford

Professor, dr.theol. Jakob L. Balling
Faculty of Theology
Aarhus University

Professor, Dr. S.A.J. Bradley
Department of English and Related Literature
University of York

Professor, dr.theol. K.E. Bugge
The Royal Danish School of Educational Studies
Copenhagen

Professor, dr.phil. Holger Bernt Hansen
Faculty of Theology
University of Copenhagen

Former principal of Askov High School, cand.theol. Hans Henningsen
Askov, Denmark

Professor, Dr. David Jasper
Centre for the Study of Religion and Literature
University of Glasgow

Professor, dr.theol. Theodor Jørgensen
Faculty of Theology
University of Copenhagen

Associate professor, dr.phil. Flemming Lundgreen-Nielsen
Department of Nordic Literature
University of Copenhagen

Professor, dr.theol. Bent Noack
Løgumkloster, Denmark

Professor, dr.theol. Anders Pontoppidan Thyssen
Aarhus University

Associate professor, dr.theol. Jens Holger Schjørring
Faculty of Theology
Aarhus University

The Rev. Rector, Dr. Kenneth Stevenson
Guildford

Professor, dr.phil. Christian Thodberg
Faculty of Theology
Aarhus University

Professor, Dr. Geoffrey Wainwright
Divinity School
Duke University
Durham, N.C.

Professor, Dr. J.R. Watson
School of English
University of Durham

Associate professor, mag.art. Vagn Wåhlin
Department of History
Aarhus University

Index

Wulfstan *64*
Wyatt, A.J. *36*
Wåhlin, Vagn *15, 259, 263-4, 270*

Yates, A.S. *201*

Zahle, J. *270*

Østergård, Uffe *263, 270*
Aagaard, Johannes *303*
Aarnes, Sigurd Aage *57, 302*